15 Practice Sets

RRB

Assistant Loco Pilot (ALP) & Technicians Stage - 2 (Part-A)

- **Corporate Office :** 45, 2nd Floor, Maharishi Dayanand Marg, Corner Market,
Malviya Nagar, New Delhi-110017
Tel. : 011-49842349 / 49842350

Typeset by Disha DTP Team

Printed at Repro Knowledgecast Limited, Thane

DISHA PUBLICATION

ALL RIGHTS RESERVED

For further information about books from DISHA,

Log on to **www.dishapublication.com** or email to **info@dishapublication.com**

CONTENTS

1. Practice Set-1 with solutions — 1-12

2. Practice Set-2 with solutions — 13-24

3. Practice Set-3 with solutions — 25-36

4. Practice Set-4 with solutions — 37-48

5. Practice Set-5 with solutions — 49-60

6. Practice Set-6 with solutions — 61-72

7. Practice Set-7 with solutions — 73-84

8. Practice Set-8 with solutions — 85-96

9. Practice Set-9 with solutions — 97-108

10. Practice Set-10 with solutions — 109-120

11. Practice Set-11 with solutions — 121-132

12. Practice Set-12 with solutions — 133-144

13. Practice Set-13 with Solutions — 145-156

14. Practice Set-14 with Solutions — 157-168

15. Practice Set-15 with Solutions — 169-180

PRACTICE SET 1

Time: 90 minutes **Max. Marks: 100**

MATHEMATICS

1. When the price of a radio was reduced by 20%, its sale increased by 80%. What was the net effect on the sale?
   - (a) 44% increase
   - (b) 44% decrease
   - (c) 66% increase
   - (d) 75% increase

2. How much water must be added to 48 ml of alcohol to make a solution that contains 25% alcohol ?
   - (a) 24 ml
   - (b) 72 ml
   - (c) 144 ml
   - (d) 196 ml

3. Ravi's salary is 150% of Amit's salary. Amit's salary is 80% of Ram's salary. What is the ratio of Ram's salary to Ravi's salary ?
   - (a) 1 to 2
   - (b) 2 to 3
   - (c) 5 to 6
   - (d) 6 to 5

4. A sum of money invested at compound interest amounts in 3 years to ₹ 2,400 and in 4 years to ₹ 2,520. The interest rate per annum is :
   - (a) 6%
   - (b) 5%
   - (c) 10%
   - (d) 12%

5. A man goes to a place on bicycle at speed of 16 km/hr and comes back at lower speed . If the average speed is 6.4 km/hr in total , then the return speed (in km/hr) is
   - (a) 10
   - (b) 8
   - (c) 6
   - (d) 4

6. At what percentage above the cost price must an article be marked so as to gain 33% after allowing the customer a discount of 5% ?
   - (a) 48%
   - (b) 43%
   - (c) 40%
   - (d) 38%

7. The batting average of 40 innings of a cricket player is 50 runs. His highest score exceeds his lowest score by 172 runs. If these two innings are excluded, the average of the remaining 38 innings is 48. His highest score was :
   - (a) 172
   - (b) 173
   - (c) 174
   - (d) 176

8. The lengths of three sides of a triangle are known. In which of the cases given below, it is impossible to get a triangle ?
   - (a) 15 cm, 12 cm, 10 cm
   - (b) 3.6 cm, 4.3 cm, 5.7 cm
   - (c) 17 cm, 12 cm, 6 cm
   - (d) 2.3 cm 4.4 cm, 6.8 cm

9. The perimeters of two similar triangles ABC and PQR are 36 cm, and 24 cm, respectively. If PQ = 10 cm, then the length of AB is :
   - (a) 16 cm
   - (b) 12 cm
   - (c) 14 cm
   - (d) 15 cm

10. Two isosceles triangles have equal vertical angles and their areas are in the ratio 9 : 16. The ratio of their corresponding heights is :
    - (a) 3 : 4
    - (b) 4 : 3
    - (c) 2 : 1
    - (d) 1 : 2

11. A cricket player after playing 10 tests scored 100 runs in the 11th test. As a result, the average of his runs is increased by 5. The present average of runs is
    - (a) 45
    - (b) 40
    - (c) 50
    - (d) 55

12. A circle road runs around a circular garden. If the difference between the circumference of the outer circle and the inner circle is 44 m, the width of the road is
    - (a) 4 m
    - (b) 7 m
    - (c) 3.5 m
    - (d) 7.5 m

13. The sixth term of the sequence 2, 6, 11, 17, ... is
    - (a) 24
    - (b) 30
    - (c) 32
    - (d) 36

14. The average of 18 observations is recorded as 124. Later it was found that two observations with values 64 and 28 were entered wrongly as

46 and 82. Find the correct average of the 18 observations.

(a) $111\dfrac{7}{9}$ (b) 122

(c) 123   (d) $137\dfrac{3}{7}$

15. If there is a profit of 20% on the cost price of an article, the percentage of profit calculated on its selling price will be

(a) 24   (b) $16\dfrac{2}{3}$

(c) $8\dfrac{1}{3}$ (d) 20

16. The number of seats in an auditorium is increased by 25%. The price of a ticket is also increased by 12%. Then the increase in revenue collection will be

(a) 40%   (b) 35%
(c) 45%   (d) 48%

17. A certain amount of money earns ₹ 540 as Simple Interest in 3 years. If it earns a Compound Interest of ₹ 376.20 at the same rate of interest in 2 years, find the amount. (in rupees)

(a) 2100   (b) 1600
(c) 1800   (d) 2000

18. A boatman rows 1 km in 5 minutes, along the stream and 6 km in 1 hour against the stream. The speed of the stream is

(a) 3 kmph   (b) 6 kmph
(c) 10 kmph   (d) 12 kmph

19. The ratio of income and expenditure of a person is 11 : 10. If he saves ₹ 9,000 per annum, his monthly income is

(a) ₹ 8,000   (b) ₹ 8,800
(c) ₹ 8,500   (d) ₹ 8,250

20. 465 coins consists of 1 rupee, 50 paise and 25 paise coins. Their values are in the ratio 5 : 6 : 4. The number of each type of coins respectively is

(a) 155, 186, 124   (b) 154, 187, 124
(c) 154, 185, 126   (d) 150, 140, 175

21. The ratio of the radii of two wheels is 3 : 4. The ratio of their circumferences is

(a) 4 : 3   (b) 3 : 4
(c) 2 : 3   (d) 3 : 2

22. A 4–digit number is formed by repeating a 2–digit number such as 1515, 3737, etc. Any number of this form is exactly divisible by

(a) 7   (b) 11
(c) 13   (d) 101

23. $(1^2 + 2^2 + 3^2 + \ldots\ldots + 10^2)$ is equal to
(a) 380   (b) 385
(c) 390   (d) 392

24. The average age of four boys, five years ago was 9 years. On including a new boy, the present average age of all the five is 15 years. The present age of the new boy is

(a) 14 years   (b) 6 years
(c) 15 years   (d) 19 years

25. If the cost price of 15 books is equal to the selling price of 20 books, the loss percent is

(a) 16   (b) 20
(c) 24   (d) 25

GENERAL INTELLIGENCE AND REASONING

DIRECTIONS (Qs. 26-28) : In questions, select the related word/letters/number from given alternatives.

26. Crime : Court : : Disease : ?

(a) Doctor   (b) Medicine
(c) Hospital   (d) Treatment

27. ADGJ : BEHK : : DGJM : ?

(a) KPUB   (b) GJMP
(c) KNQT   (d) PSVY

28. 7 : 56 : : 5 : ?

(a) 25   (b) 26
(c) 30   (d) 35

29. In a class of 45 students, a boy is ranked 20th. When two boys joined, his rank was dropped by one. What is his new rank from the end ?

(a) 25th   (b) 26th
(c) 27th   (d) 28th

30. Introducing a girl, Ram said to his son-in-law. "Her brother is the only son of my brother-in-law." Who is the girl of Ram?

(a) Sister-in-law   (b) Niece
(c) Daughter   (d) Sister

31. If BLACKSMITH is coded as CNBELUNKUJ, then CHILDREN will be coded as ?

(a) DIJMESFO   (b) DJJNETFP
(c) DJINETEP   (d) DJJNETEP

32. Which figure represents the relation among Computer, Internet and Information Communication Technology?

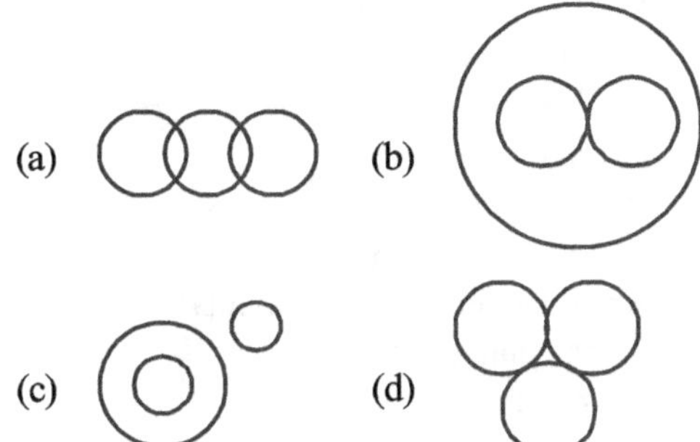

(a)   (b)

(c)   (d)

33. Choose the correct alternative.

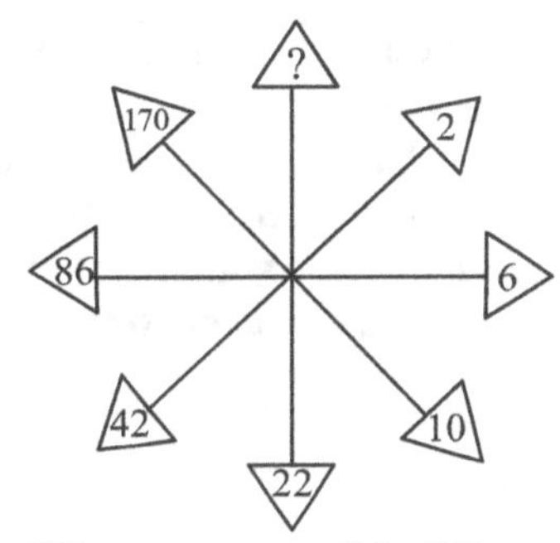

(a)   422   (b)   374
(c)   256   (d)   342

34. Find the answer of the following:

$7 + 3 = 421$

$11 + 7 = 477$

$9 + 5 = 445$

$6 + 2 = ?$

(a)   444   (b)   412   (c)   475   (d)   487

35. Ashok's mother was 3 times as old as Ashok 5 years ago. After 5 years she will be twice as old as Ashok. How old is Ashok today?

(a)   10 years   (b)   15 years
(c)   20 years   (d)   25 years

36. If a mirror is placed on the line MN, then which of the answer figures is the correct image of the question figure?

Question figure:

Answer figures :

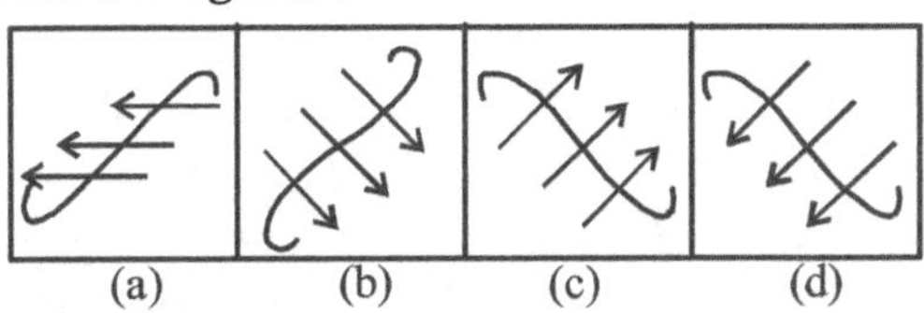

(a)   (b)   (c)   (d)

37. How many triangles are there in the following figure ?

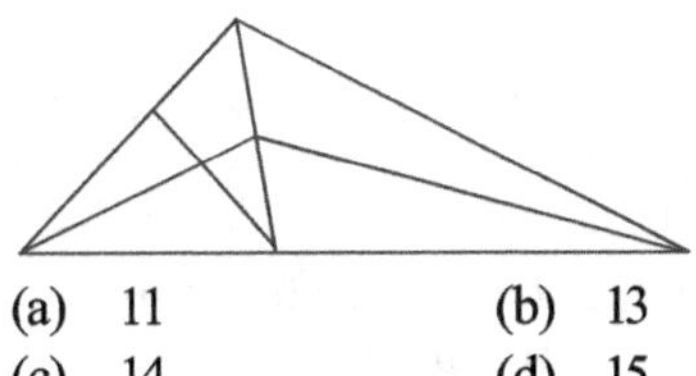

(a)   11   (b)   13
(c)   14   (d)   15

DIRECTION (Q. 38) : In question, which answer figure will complete the pattern in the question figure?

---

38. **Question figure:**

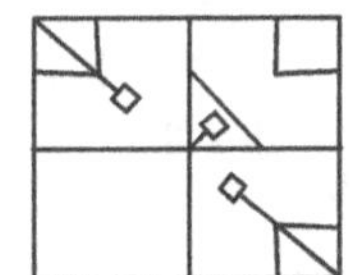

Answer Figures :

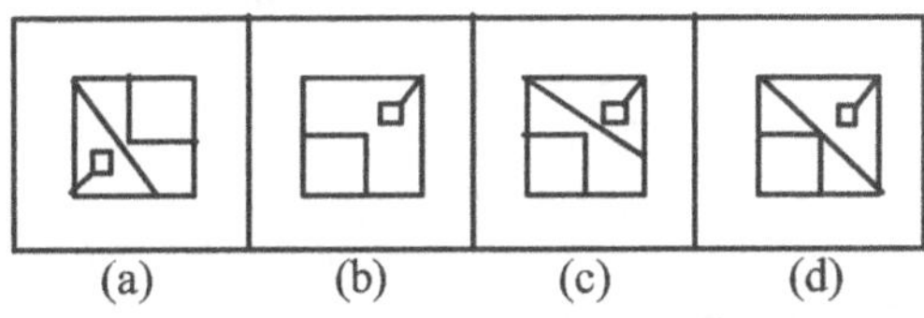

(a)   (b)   (c)   (d)

DIRECTIONS (Qs. 39-40) : In each of the following questions, a series is given with one term missing. Choose the correct alternative from the given ones that will complete the series.

---

39. 3, 4, 7, 11, 18, 29, ?
    (a)   31   (b)   39
    (c)   43   (d)   47

40. 975, 864, 753, 642, ?
    (a)   431   (b)   314
    (c)   531   (d)   532

41. If HOSPITAL is written as 32574618 in a certain code, how would POSTAL be written in that code?
    (a)   752618   (b)   725618
    (c)   725168   (d)   725681

42. If SPARK is coded as TQBSL, what will be the code for FLAME ?
    (a) GMBNF   (b) GNBNF
    (c) GMCND   (d) GMBMF

43. M is the son of P. Q is the grand daughter of O who is the husband of P. How is M related to O?
    (a) Son   (b) Daughter
    (c) Mother   (d) Father

44. After interchanging ÷ and +, 12 and 18, which one of the following equations becomes correct?
    (a) $(90 \times 18) + 18 = 60$ (b) $(18 + 6) \div 12 = 2$
    (c) $(72 \div 18) \times 18 = 72$ (d) $(12 + 6) \times 18 = 36$

45. Which number space indicated Indian teachers who are also advocates?

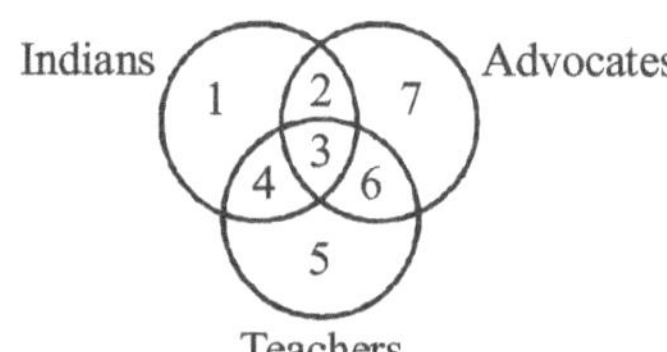

    (a) 2   (b) 3   (c) 4   (d) 6

46. If the number indicates the number of persons, then how many youth graduates are there ?

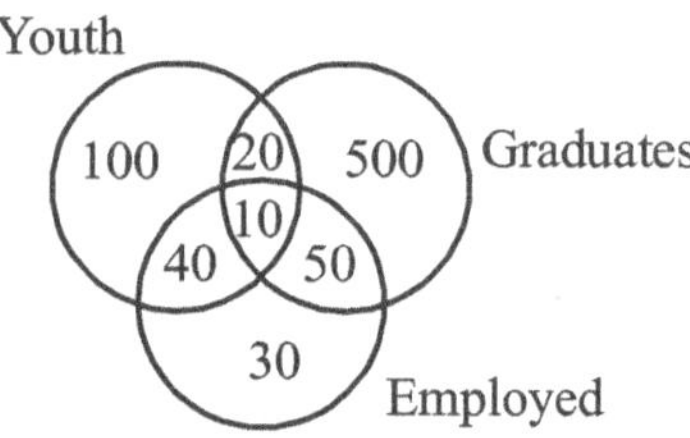

    (a) 20   (b) 30
    (c) 40   (d) 50

DIRECTIONS (Qs. 47-48): In each of the questions below are three statements followed by two conclusions numbered I and II. You have to take the three statements to be true even if they seem to be at variance from commonly known facts and then decide which of the given conclusions logically follows from the three statements disregarding commonly known facts.

Give answer (a) if **only** conclusion **I** follows.
Give answer (b) if **only** conclusion **II** follows.
Give answer (c) if **neither** conclusion **I** and conclusion **II** follow.
Give answer (d) if **both** conclusion **I** and conclusion **II** follow.

47. **Statements:**
    All plants are bottles.
    All bottles are caps.
    All caps are crowns.
    Conclusions:
    I.   Atleast some crowns are bottles.
    II.   All plants are caps.

48. **Statements:**
    Some shoes are hankerchiefs.
    Some hankerchiefs are calculators.
    All calculators are paper.
    Conclusions:
    I.   No calculator is a shoe.
    II.   No shoe is a paper.

DIRECTIONS (Qs. 49-50): In each question below is given a statement followed by two conclusions numbered I and II. You have to assume everything in the statement to be true, then consider the two conclusions together and decide which of them logically follows beyond a reasonable doubt from the information given in the statement.

49. Statements: The old order changed yielding place to new.
    Conclusions:
    I.   Change is the law of nature.
    II.   Discard old ideas because they are old.
    (a) Only conclusion I follows
    (b) Only conclusion II follows
    (c) Either I or II follows
    (d) Neither I nor II follows

50. **Statements:** The manager humiliated Sachin in the presence of his colleagues.
    Conclusions:
    I.   The manager did not like Sachin.
    II.   Sachin was not popular with his colleagues.
    (a) Only conclusion I follows
    (b) Only conclusion II follows
    (c) Either I or II follows
    (d) Neither I nor II follows

BASIC SCIENCE AND ENGINEERING

51. A circle will appear on an isometric drawing as a(n) __________ .
    (a) ellipse   (b) cycloid
    (c) circle   (d) parabola

52. Unit of magnetic moment is
    (a) ampere–metre^2
    (b) ampere–metre
    (c) weber–metre^2
    (d) weber/metre
53. Specific weight of mercury is
    (a) $13.6 kg/m^3$ (b) $13600 kg/m^3$
    (c) $136 kg/m^3$ (d) all the above
54. If the v-t graph is a straight line inclined to the time axis, then
    (a) $a = 0$
    (b) $a \neq 0$
    (c) $a = \text{constant} \neq 0$
    (d) $a \neq \text{constant} \neq 0$
55. Capacity of a body to do work is called
    (a) energy
    (b) work load
    (c) kinetic energy
    (d) potential energy
56. Which of the following is a poor conductor of heat ?
    (a) Copper   (b) Concrete
    (c) Mercury   (d) Air
57. Which of the following is an active component?
    (a) Inductor   (b) Capacitor
    (c) Resistor   (d) Diode
58. What type of simple machine is an inclined plane wrapped around a pole?
    (a) Lever   (b) Wheel and Axle
    (c) Pulley and Wedge   (d) Screw
59. The responsibility for maintenance of employee health and safety is with
    (a) employees
    (b) employers
    (c) government
    (d) All of the above
60. Which atmospheric layer is closest to the Earth's surface?
    (a) Troposphere   (b) Thermosphere
    (c) Stratosphere   (d) Mesosphere
61. The physical components of a computer system.
    (a) Software   (b) Hardware
    (c) ALU   (d) Control Unit
62. ELA is related to:
    (a) Environmental Impact Assessment
    (b) Environmental and Industrial Activities
    (c) Environmental Internal Activities
    (d) Environmental Impact Activities
63. Which of the following is not a pictorial drawing?
    (a) isometric   (b) multiview
    (c) perspective   (d) axonometric
64. A measuring tape can measure length more than a/an
    (a) meter
    (b) inch but less than a foot
    (c) foot but less than a meter
    (d) centimeter
65. Density of a substance is defined as
    (a) its mass per unit volume
    (b) its mass per unit area
    (c) its volume per unit mass
    (d) its weight per unit volume
66. A velocity-time graph can give you
    (a) Velocity of the moving object
    (b) Acceleration of the moving object
    (c) Displacement of the moving object
    (d) All of the above.
67. In order to do work, energy is
    (a) transferred or converted
    (b) used up
    (c) lost
    (d) lost or transferred
68. If a substance is hot, its particles will
    (a) move fast than the cooler object
    (b) move slow than the cooler object
    (c) move as the cooler object
    (d) may move fast or slow than the cooler object
69. Property of an electric circuit that dissipates electric energy:
    (a) Reactance
    (b) Impedance
    (c) Resistance
    (d) Conductance
70. Class 3 levers have
    (a) Effort between the load and the fulcrum
    (b) Fulcrum placed between the effort and load
    (c) Load in-between the effort and the fulcrum
    (d) None
71. Workplace related injuries, illnesses and deaths impose costs upon?
    (a) Employers
    (b) Employees
    (c) The community
    (d) All of these.

72. Organic farming is
    (a) enhancing biodiversity
    (b) promoting soil biological activity
    (c) farming without using pesticides and chemical fertilizers
    (d) all the above
73. Environmental pollution can be controlled by:
    (a) Checking atomic blasts
    (b) Manufacturing electric vehicles
    (c) Sewage treatment
    (d) All of the above
74. _________ is the process of dividing the disk into tracks and sectors
    (a) Tracking   (b) Formatting
    (c) Crashing   (d) Allotting
75 Which of the following is not a source of the law on health and safety at work?
    (a) Common law.
    (b) Recent case law.
    (c) Guidance notes
    (d) Regulations.

GENERAL AWARENESS AND CURRENT AFFAIR

76. Which of the following symbiotic associations forms a lichen?
    (a) An algae and a fungus
    (b) An algae and a bryophyte
    (c) A bacterium and a fungus
    (d) A bacterium and a gymnosperm
77. Which Amendment Act is referred as mini constitution?
    (a) 7th Constitutional Amendment Act, 1956
    (b) 24th Constitutional Amendment Act, 1971
    (c) 42nd Constitutional Amendment Act, 1976
    (d) 44th Consitutional Amendment Act, 1978
78. Inflation is caused by
    (a) decrease in production
    (b) increase in money supply and decrease in production
    (c) increase in money supply
    (d) increase in production
79. Denatured alcohol
    (a) is a form of alcohol
    (b) is unfit for drinking as it contains poisonous substances
    (c) contains coloured impurities
    (d) is sweet to taste
80. The antiseptic compound present in dettol is
    (a) Iodine   (b) Enloroxylenol
    (c) Biothional   (d) Cresol
81. Chromosomes are made up of
    (a) DNA   (b) Protein
    (c) DNA and Protein (d) RNA
82. While the computer executes a program, the program is held in
    (a) RAM   (b) ROM
    (c) Hard Disk   (d) Floppy Disk
83. Presidential form of government consists of the following?
    (a) Popular election of the President
    (b) No overlap in membership between the executive and the legislature
    (c) Fixed term of office
    (d) All of the above
84. Who was the author of "India of My Dreams" ?
    (a) J.B. Kripalani   (b) M.K. Gandhi
    (c) G.K. Gokhale   (d) Jawaharlal Nehru
85. How many players are there in a Polo team ?
    (a) 4   (b) 7
    (c) 8   (d) 6
86. Hemophilia is –
    (a) caused by bacteria
    (b) caused by virus
    (c) caused by pollutants
    (d) a hereditary defect
87. In human body, vitamin A is stored in the –
    (a) liver   (b) skin
    (c) lung   (d) kidney
88. Ondometer is a –
    (a) Measuring instrument for distance covered by motor wheels
    (b) Measuring instrument for frequency of electromagnetic waves
    (c) Device for measuring sound intensity
    (d) Measuring instrument for electric power
89. Which acid is used in rubber, textile, leather and electroplating industries ?
    (a) Ethanoic acid
    (b) Methanoic acid

(c) Malanic acid

(d) Butairic acid

90. Name the North-eastern state, which will host the 2022 National Games coinciding with its 50 years of statehood.

(a) Assam   (b) Manipur

(c) Meghalaya   (d) Mizoram

91. Who represented India at the G20 Digital Economy Ministerial Meeting 2018?

(a) Ravi Shankar Prasad

(b) Piyush Goyal

(c) Sushma Swaraj

(d) Sushma Swaraj

92. Which sportsperson has clinched India's first men's triple jump gold in 48 years at the 18th Asian Games 2018?

(a) Shivpal Singh

(b) Rakesh Babu A V

(c) Sreeshankar

(d) Arpinder Singh

93. Which method is used for the purification of Bauxite ore?

(a) Magnetic separation

(b) Electrolysis

(c) Leaching

(d) Levitation

94. Cement does not contain

(a) iron   (b) aluminium

(c) calcium   (d) sulphur

95. Gold dissolves in aqua regia to produce

(a) $AuCl_4$ (b) $HAuCl_4$

(c) $HAuCl_3$ (d) $[Au(CN)_2]$

96. The process in which water is split during photosynthesis is

(a) Photolysis

(b) Hydrolysis

(c) Plasmolysis

(d) Hemolysis

97. Hormone helping in cell division

(a) IAA

(b) NAA

(c) Cytokinin/Zeatin

(d) Gibberellin

98. Gene are made up of

(a) DNA

(b) RNA

(c) DNA & RNA

(d) Protein

99. Who is the father of Genetics?

(a) Darwin

(b) Mendel

(c) Bridge

(d) Wiseman

100. The pH value of milk is

(a) 2.4   (b) 3.8

(c) 6.6   (d) 8.0

HINTS & EXPLANATIONS

1. (a) Let the original price be x and sale be of y units.

   Then, the revenue collected initially $= x \times y$

   Now, new price $= 0.8x$, new sale $= 1.8\,y$

   Then, new revenue collected $= 1.44xy$

   % increase in revenue $= \dfrac{0.44xy}{xy} \times 100 = 44\%$

2. (c) Let quantity of water to be added be x ml.

   Then, $(x + 48) \times \dfrac{25}{100} = 48$ or $x = 144$ ml.

3. (c) Let the salary of Ram be ₹ 100.

   Then, salary of Amit $= ₹ 80$

   and salary of Ravi $= 150\%$ of $80 = ₹ 120$

   Ratio of Ram's salary to Ravi's salary $= 100 : 120 = 5 : 6$

4. (b) Let the rate of interest be r %.

   Therefore, $\dfrac{2520}{2400} = \dfrac{\left(1 + \dfrac{r}{100}\right)^4}{\left(1 + \dfrac{r}{100}\right)^3}$

   $\Rightarrow 1 + \dfrac{r}{100} = \dfrac{21}{20}$ or $r = 5\%$

5. (d) Average speed when speed x and y are given $= \dfrac{2xy}{x + y}$

   $\dfrac{2 \times 16 \times x}{x + 16} = 6.4$

   $32x = 6.4(x + 16)$

   $x = 0.2(x + 16)$

   $0.8x = 3.2$

   $x = 4$

6. (c) Let the cost price be ₹ 100.

   Gain of $33\% = ₹ 33$

   $\Rightarrow$ SP $= ₹ 133$

   Let the marked price be ₹ x. The SP of ₹ 133 has been arrived after giving a discount of 5% on marked price.

   i.e. $x \times 0.95 = ₹ 133$

   $\Rightarrow x = \dfrac{133}{0.95} = ₹.140$

   Required increase $= ₹ 140 - ₹ 100 = ₹ 40$

   Hence required percentage $= 40\%$.

7. (c) Total score of 40 innings $= 40 \times 50 = 2000$

   Total score of 38 innings $= 38 \times 48 = 1824$

   Let the highest score be x and the lowest score be y.

   Sum of the highest and the lowest score

   $= x + y = 2000 - 1824$

   $\Rightarrow \quad x + y = 176 \qquad \text{...(i)}$

   and by question, $x - y = 172 \qquad \text{...(ii)}$

   Solving (i) and (ii), we get $x = 174$

8. (d) To construct a triangle, it is necessary that the sum of any two sides is greater than the third side. Checking with options, we find that it is not possible for the measurements given in (d) as $2.3 + 4.4 < 6.8$.

9. (d)

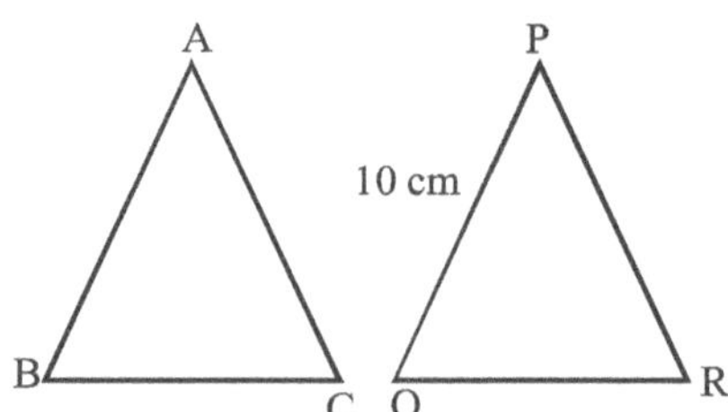

   $\triangle ABC$ and $\triangle PQR$ are similar.

   $\dfrac{AB}{PQ} = \dfrac{\text{Perimeter of } \triangle ABC}{\text{Perimeter of } \triangle PQR} \Rightarrow \dfrac{AB}{PQ} = \dfrac{36}{24}$

   or $AB = \dfrac{36}{24} \times 10 = 15$

10. (a) For the two similar triangles, we have

   $\dfrac{h_1^2}{h_2^2} = \dfrac{\text{Area of 1st } \Delta}{\text{Area of IInd } \Delta} = \dfrac{9}{16}$

   $\Rightarrow h_1 : h_2 = 3 : 4$

11. (c) If the average in 10 tests be x, then,

$$\frac{x \times 10 + 100}{11} = x + 5$$

$$x \times 10 + 100 = (x + 5) \times 11$$

$$\Rightarrow 11x - 10x = 100 - 55$$

$$\Rightarrow x = 45$$

∴ Required average = 50

12. (b) Let R be the radius of circular road

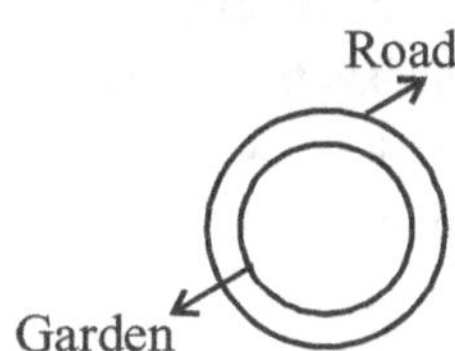

i.e., R = radius of outer circle.

Let r be the radius of inner circle(garden).

circumference of the road = $2\pi R$

circumference of the garden = $2\pi r$

Given : $2\pi R - 2\pi r = 44\,m$

$\Rightarrow \quad 2\pi(R-r) = 44 \Rightarrow R - r = 7m$

Hence, the width of the road = $R - r = 7m$

13. (c) $2 + 4 = 6$

$6 + 5 = 11$

$11 + 6 = 17$

$17 + 7 = 24$

$24 + 8 = \boxed{32}$

14. (b) Difference in observations

$= 64 + 28 - 46 - 82 = -36$

∴ Correct average

$= 124 - \dfrac{36}{18} = 122$

15. (b) If the CP = ₹100, then SP = ₹120 and gain = ₹20

$$\text{Gain }\% = \frac{20}{120} \times 100 = \frac{50}{3} = 16\frac{2}{3}\%$$

16. (a) Required increase

$$= \left(25 + 12 + \frac{25 \times 12}{100}\right)\% = 40\%$$

17. (d) S.I of 3 years = ₹540

$$\text{S.I. of 1 year} = \frac{540}{3} = ₹180$$

S.I. of 2 years = $2 \times 180 = ₹360$

CI of 2 years = ₹376.20

Difference between CI and SI

$= 376.20 - 360 = ₹16.20$

If we take P = ₹180 R = R% and Time = 1 year

$$\frac{180 \times R \times 1}{100} = 16.20$$

$$R = \frac{1620}{180} = 9\%$$

So S.I. $= 540 = P \times 9 \times \dfrac{3}{100}$

$$P = \frac{540 \times 100}{9 \times 3} = ₹2000$$

18. (a) Speed of current

$= \dfrac{1}{2}$ (Rate downstream – Rate upstream)

$= \dfrac{1}{2}(12 - 6)\,kmph$ [Rate downstream]

$= 3\,kmph$

19. (d) Let the income of man be Rs. = 11x and his expenditure be ₹ 10x.

∴ Savings x = ₹ 9000

∴ Monthly income of man $= \dfrac{11 \times 9000}{12}$

$= ₹ 8250$

20 (a) The ratio of number of coins = 5 : 6 : 4

∴ The number of one rupee coins

$$= \frac{465}{5 + 6 + 4} \times 5 = 155$$

The number of 50 paise coins

$$= \frac{465}{5 + 6 + 4} \times 6 = 186$$

The number of 25 paise coins

$$\frac{465}{5 + 6 + 4} \times 4 = 124$$

21. (b) Ratio of the circumferences

= Ratio of radii = 3 : 4

$$\frac{R_1}{R_2} = \frac{3}{4}$$

$$\frac{C_1}{C_2} = \frac{2\pi r_1}{2\pi r_2} = \frac{r_1}{r_2} = \frac{3}{4}$$

22. (d) $xyxy = xy \times 100 + xy$
$= xy(100+1) = 101 \times xy$
Hence, the number is exactly divisible by 101.

23. (b) $1^2 + 2^2 + 3^2 + \dots + n^2 = \dfrac{n(n+1)((2n+1)}{6}$

$\therefore 1^2 + 2^2 + 3^2 + \dots + 10^2$

$= \dfrac{10(10+1)(20+1)}{6} = 385$

24. (d)   Sum of the present ages of four boys
$= 9 \times 4 + 20 = 56$ years
Sum of the present ages of five boys
$= 15 \times 5 = 75$ years
$\therefore$ Present age of new boy
$= 75 - 56 = 19$ years

25. (d)   If the CP of each book be ₹1, then
SP of 20 books = ₹15
CP of 20 books = ₹20

$\therefore \text{L\%} = \dfrac{20-15}{20} \times 100 = 25\%$

26. (c)   "Court" is the place where the judge gives his decision on crime. Similarly, Hospital is the place where the doctor diagnoses the disease of the patient.

27. (b)   As,

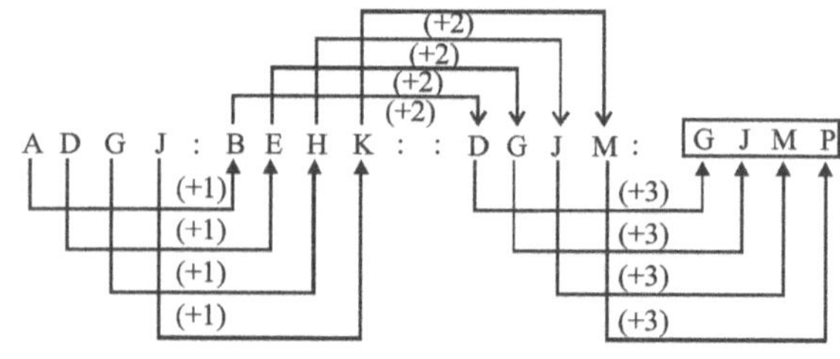

So, GJMP is the correct answer.

28. (c)   As,

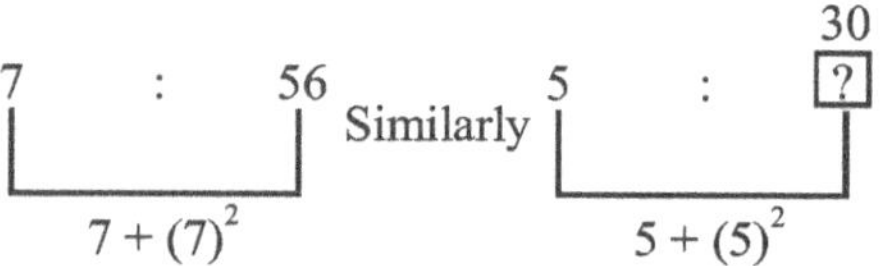

29. (c)   After 2 boys joined, total strength of class $= 45 + 2 = 47$
As, rank was dropped by one from 20th rank, new rank is 21st.
Rank of the boy from the begining $= 21$
No. of students below his rank $= 47 - 21 = 26$
Rank from the end $= (47 - 21) + 1 \Rightarrow 27$.

30. (b)

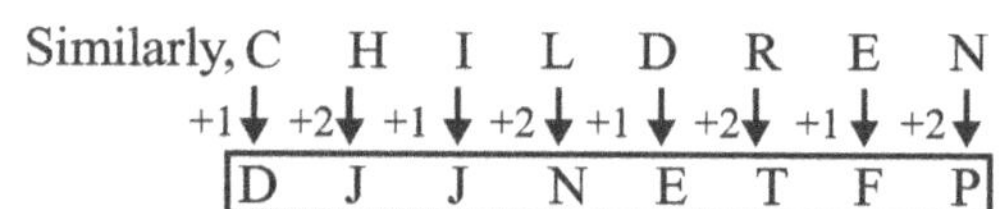

Hence, girl is the niece of Ram.

31. (b)   As,

```
B  L  A  C  K  S  M  I  T  H
C  N  B  E  L  U  N  K  U  J
```

Similarly,
```
C  H  I  L  D  R  E  N
D  J  J  N  E  T  F  P
```

32. (b)

33. (d)

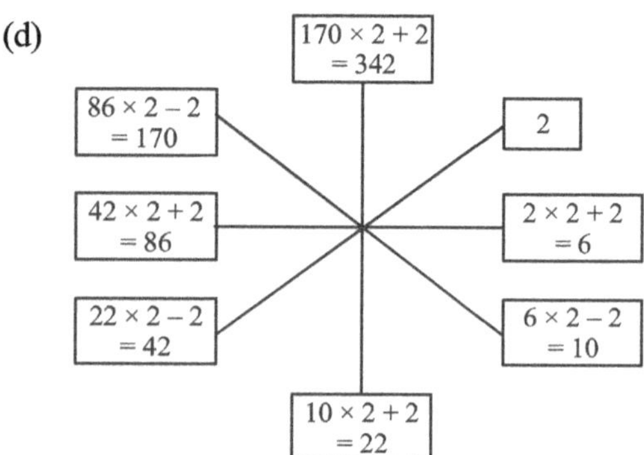

34. (b)   As, $7 + 3 = 421 = (7-3)(7 \times 3)$
$11 + 7 = 477 = (11-7)(11 \times 7)$

$9+5=445=(9-5)(9\times5)$

$6+2=(6-2)(6\times2)=412$

35. (b) Suppose the present age of Ashok is x years and that of his mother is y years.

5 years ago,

$3(x-5)=(y-5)$

$3x-15=y-5$

$3x-y=10$ ...(i)

5 years hence,

$2(x+5)=(y+5)$

$2x+10=y+5$

$2x-y=-5$ ...(ii)

From equations (i) and (ii)

$x=15$ years

36. (d) 37. (b) 38. (c)

39. (d) $3+1=4;$ $3+4=7;$

$4+7=11;$ $7+11=18$

$11+18=29;$ $18+29=\boxed{47}$

40. (c)

975   864   753   642 $\boxed{531}$

-111 -111 -111 -111

41. (b) As, H O S P I T A L

↓ ↓ ↓ ↓ ↓ ↓ ↓ ↓

3 2 5 7 4 6 1 8

Therefore,

P O S T A L

↓ ↓ ↓ ↓ ↓ ↓

$\boxed{7\ 2\ 5\ 6\ 1\ 8}$

42. (a)

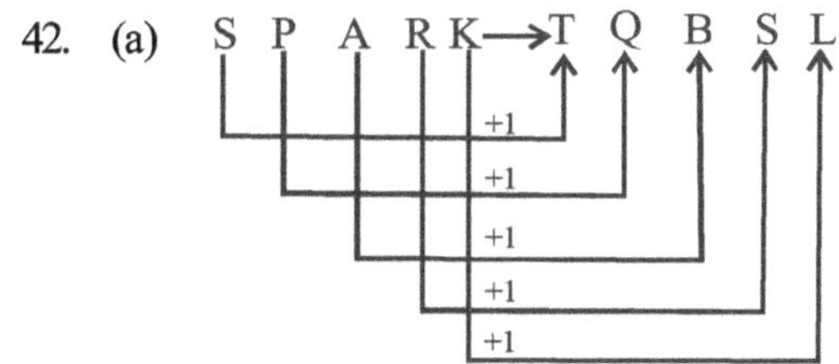

Similarly,

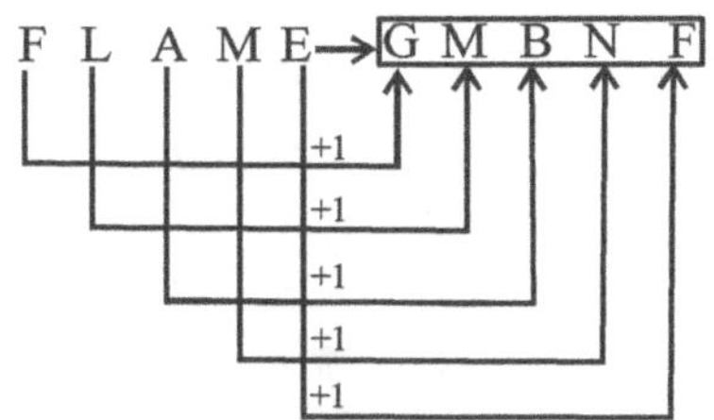

43. (a) O is the husband of P. M is the son of P. Therefore, M is the son of O.

44. (d) $(12+6)\times18=36 \Rightarrow (18\div6)\times12=36$

$\Rightarrow 3\times12=\boxed{36}$

45. (b) The number '3' space represents Indian teachers who are also advocates as this number is common to given condition.

46. (a)

47. (d)

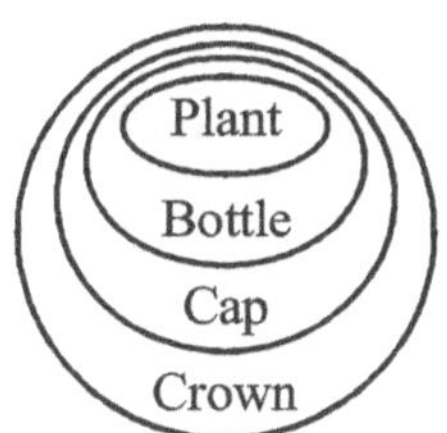

So, Both I and II follow.

48. (c)

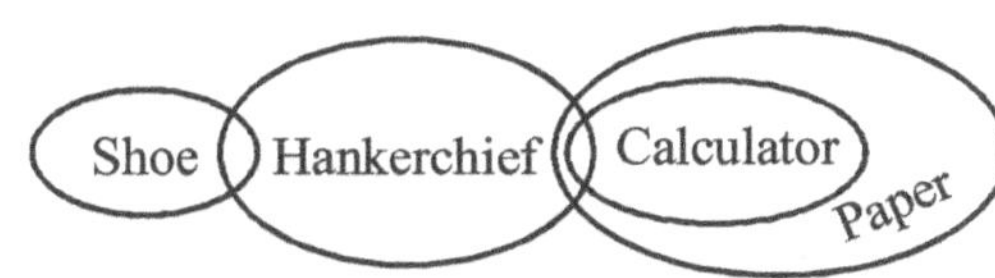

So, Neither I nor II follows.

49. (a) Clearly, I directly follows from the given statement. Also, it is mentioned that old ideas are replaced by new ones, as thinking changes with the progressing time. So, II does not follow.

50. (d) The manager might have humiliated Sachin not because of his dislike but on account of certain negligence or mistake on his part. So, I does not follow. Also, nothing about Sachin's rapport with his colleagues can be deduced from the statement. So, II also does not follow.

51. (a)	52. (a)	53. (b)	54. (c)	79. (b)	80. (b)	81. (c)	82. (a)
55. (a)	56. (d)	57. (d)	58. (d)	83. (d)	84. (b)	85. (a)	86. (d)
59. (d)	60. (a)	61. (b)	62. (a)	87. (a)	88. (b)	89. (b)	90. (c)
63. (b)	64. (a)	65. (a)	66. (d)	91. (a)	92. (d)	93. (b)	94. (d)
67. (a)	68. (a)	69. (c)	70. (a)	95. (b)	96. (a)	97. (c)	98. (a)
71. (d)	72. (d)	73. (d)	74. (b)	99. (b)	100. (c)		
75. (b)	76. (a)	77. (c)	78. (b)				

Time: 90 minutes   **Max. Marks: 100**

MATHEMATICS

1. A bag contains Rs 216 in the form of one rupee, 50 paise and 25 paise coins in the ratio of 2 : 3 : 4. The number of 50 paise coins is :

   (a) 96   (b) 144

   (c) 114   (d) 141

2. In a mixture of 45 litres, the ratio of milk and water is 4 : 1. How much water must be added to make the mixture ratio 3 : 2 ?

   (a) 72 litres   (b) 24 litres

   (c) 15 litres   (d) 1.5 litres

3. Out of 10 teachers of a school, one teacher retires and in his place, a new teacher of age 25 years joins. As a result, average age of teachers is reduced by 3 years. The age (in years) of the retired teacher is :

   (a) 50   (b) 58

   (c) 60   (d) 55

4. A cistern has two taps (which fill it in 12 min and 15 min, respectively) and an exhaust tap. When all three taps are opened together, it takes 20 min to fill the empty cistern. How long will the exhaust tap take to empty it ?

   (a) 20 min   (b) 16 min

   (c) 12 min   (d) 10 min

5. 12 men complete a work in 18 days. Six days after they had started working, 4 men joined them. How many days will all of them take to complete the remaining work ?

   (a) 10 days   (b) 12 days

   (c) 15 days   (d) 9 days

6. A motor boat whose speed is 15 km/h in still water goes 30 km downstream and comes back in four and a half hours. The speed of the stream is :

   (a) 46 km/h   (b) 6 km/h

   (c) 7 km/h   (d) 5 km/h

7. A reduction of 20% in the price of sugar enables me to purchase 5 kg more for ₹ 600. Find the price of sugar per kg before reduction of price.

   (a) ₹ 24   (b) ₹ 30

   (c) ₹ 32   (d) ₹ 36

8. A sum of ₹ x was put at simple interest at a certain rate for 2 years. Had it been put at 3% higher rate, it would have fetched ₹ 300 more. The value of $4x$ is

   (a) ₹ 16, 000   (b) ₹ 20,000

   (c) ₹ 36, 000   (d) ₹ 24,000

9. a, b, c and d are four consecutive numbers. If the sum of a and d is 103, what is the product of b and c ?

   (a) 2652   (b) 2562
   (c) 2970   (d) 2550

10. The wheel of a motor car makes 1000 revolutions in moving 440 m. The diameter (in metre) of the wheel is

    (a) 0.44   (b) 0.14

    (c) 0.24   (d) 0.34

11. Semi-circular lawns are attached to all the edges of a rectangular field measuring 42 m × 35 m. The area of the total field is :

    (a) 3818.5 m^2 (b) 8318 m^2
    (c) 5813 m^2 (d) 1358 m^2

12. A steel wire has been bent in the form of a square of area 121 cm². If the same wire is bent in the form of a circle, then the area of the circle will be :

   (a) 130 cm²   (b) 136 cm²
   (c) 145 cm²   (d) None of these

13. If the cost price of 30 books is equal to the selling price of 40 books, the loss percent is

   (a) 16   (b) 20
   (c) 24   (d) 25

14. When the price of sugar decreases by 10%, a man could buy 1 kg more for ₹ 270. Then the original price of sugar per kg is

   (a) ₹ 25   (b) ₹ 30
   (c) ₹ 27   (d) ₹ 32

15. The compound interest on ₹ 12000 for 9 months at 20% per annum, interest being compounded quarterly is :

   (a) ₹ 1750   (b) ₹ 1891.10
   (c) ₹ 2136.40   (d) ₹ 2089.70

16. A man can row 6 km/h in still water. If the speed of the current is 2 km/h, it takes 3 hours more in upstream than in the down–stream for the same distance. The distance is

   (a) 30 km   (b) 24 km
   (c) 20 km   (d) 32 km

17. A can do a work in 12 days. When he had worked for 3 days, B joined him. If they complete the work in 3 more days, in how many days can B alone finish the work?

   (a) 6 days   (b) 12 days
   (c) 4 days   (d) 8 days

18. If $W_1 : W_2 = 2 : 3$ and $W_1 : W_3 = 1 : 2$ then $W_2 : W_3$ is

   (a) 3 : 4   (b) 4 : 3
   (c) 2 : 3   (d) 4 : 5

19. The present ages of two persons are 36 and 50 years respectively, if after n years the ratio of their ages will be 3 : 4, then the value of n is

   (a) 3   (b) 4
   (c) 7   (d) 6

20. If the length of a rectangle is increased by 10% and its breadth is decreased by 10%, the change in its area will be

   (a) 1% increase   (b) 1% decrease
   (c) 10% increase   (d) No change

21. If $a^3 - b^3 = 56$ and $a - b = 2$, then the value of $(a^2 + b^2)$ is:

   (a) – 10   (b) – 12
   (c) 20   (d) 18

22. A number, when divided by 136, leaves remainder 36. If the same number is divided by 17, the remainder will be

   (a) 9   (b) 7
   (c) 3   (d) 2

23. If the average of 39, 48, 51, 63, 75, 83, x and 69 is 60, then the value of x is

   (a) 52   (b) 53
   (c) 50   (d) 51

24. If an article is sold at 200% profit, then the ratio of its cost price to its selling price will be

   (a) 1 : 2   (b) 2 : 1
   (c) 1 : 3   (d) 3 : 1

25. The salary of an employee increases every year in the month of July by 10%. If his salary in May 2000 was ₹ 15,000, his salary in October 2001 was

   (a) ₹ 16,500   (b) ₹ 18,000
   (c) ₹ 18,150   (d) ₹ 19,965

GENERAL INTELLIGENCE AND REASONING

DIRECTIONS (Qs. 26-28): In questions, select the related word/letters/number from given alternatives.

26. Uttarakhand : Dehradun : : Mizoram : ?
   (a) Aizawl   (b) Kohima
   (c) Shillong   (d) Darjeeling

27. YQXP : JBIA : : OVNU : ?

(a) FAGZ   (b) HRIS

(c) DKCJ   (d) DNEO

28. 1 : 1 : : 10 : ?

(a) 12   (b) 110

(c) 210   (d) 1000

DIRECTIONS (Qs. 29-30): In questions, a series is given, with one term missing. Choose the correct alternative from the given ones that will complete the series.

---

29. CEG, JLN, QSU, __?__ .

(a) QOS   (b) TVY

(c) HJL   (d) UVW

30. 285, 253, 221, 189, ?

(a) 150   (b) 182

(c) 157   (d) 156

31. In a certain code language PRESENTATION is written as ENESTATIPRON. How would INTELLIGENCE be written in that code language?

(a) TETGLLTNENCE

(b) LLKKTGTEEBTB

(c) LLENLLTNTETG

(d) LLTEIGENINCE

32. Rakesh ranks 15th from the top and 45th from the bottom in a class. How many students are there in the class?

(a) 64   (b) 59

(c) 54   (d) None of these

33. Moni is daughter of Sheela. Sheela is the wife of my wife's brother. How is Moni related to my wife?

(a) Cousin   (b) Niece

(c) Sister   (d) Sister-in-law

34. Ram moves from a point X to 20 metres towards North. Then he moves 40 metres towards West. Then he moves 20 metres North. Then he moves 40 metres towards East and then 10 metres towards right and he reaches to a point Y. Find the distance and direction of Y from X ?

(a) 30 metres, North   (b) 30 metres, South

(c) 40 metres, North   (d) 40 metres, South

35. Which figure represents the relation among Currency, Rupee and Dollar ?

(a) 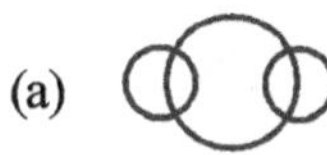   (b) 

(c)    (d) 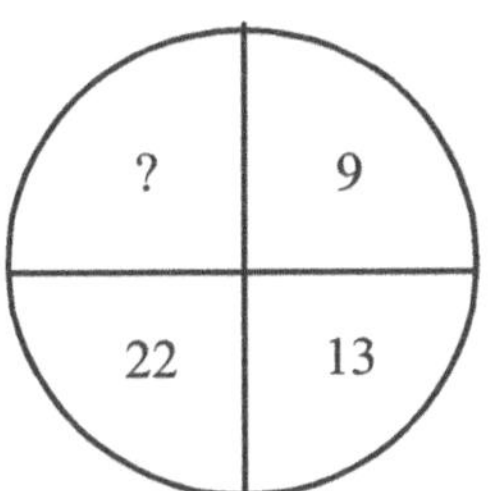

36. Find the missing number from the given responses.

?	9
22	13

(a) 40   (b) 38

(c) 39   (d) 44

37. Nitin's age was equal to square of some number last year and the following year it would be cube of a number. If again Nitin's age has to be equal to the cube of some number, then for how long he will have to wait?

(a) 10 years   (b) 38 years

(c) 39 years   (d) 64 years

38. After interchanging ÷ and +, 12 and 18, which one of the following equations becomes correct?

(a) (90 × 18) + 18 = 60   (b) (18 + 6) ÷ 12 = 2

(c) (72 ÷ 18) × 18 = 72   (d) (12 + 6) × 18 = 36

39. Which answer figure will complete the pattern in the question figure?

Question Figure :

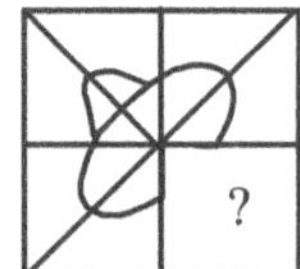

Answer Figures :

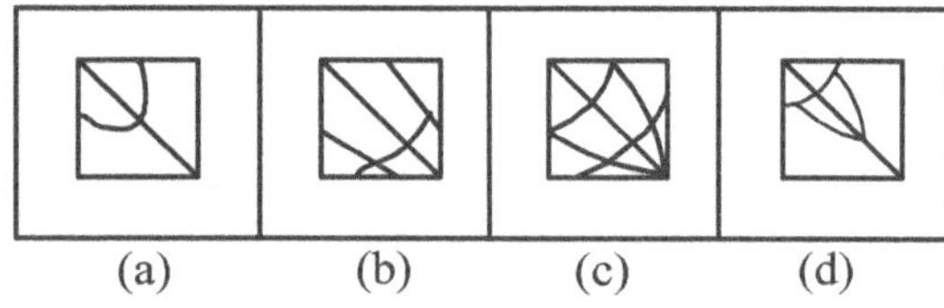

(a)   (b)   (c)   (d)

40. Select the answer figure in which the question figure is hidden/embedded.

Question Figure:

Answer Figures:

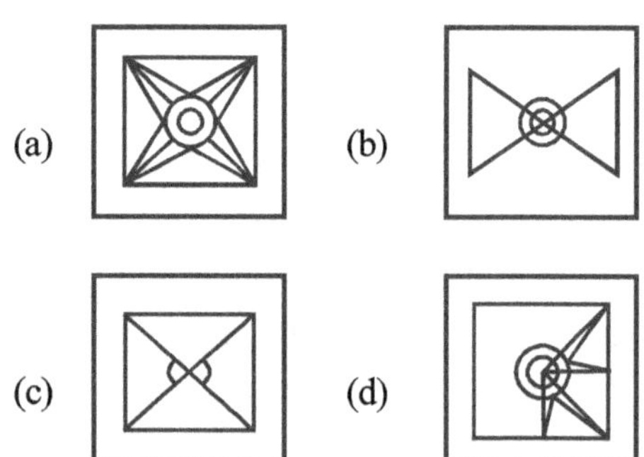

(a)   (b)

(c)   (d)

41. How many triangles are there in the following figure?

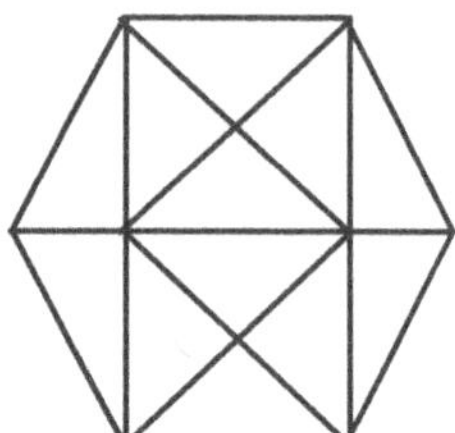

(a) 20   (b) 24
(c) 28   (d) 32

42. Which answer figure is the exact mirror image of the given question figure when the mirror is held from the right at PQ?

Question Figure:

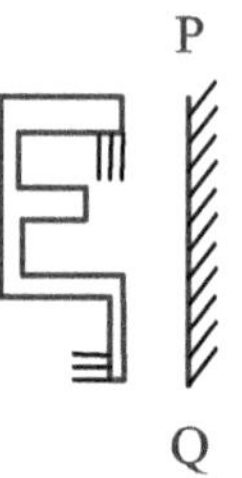

Answer Figures:

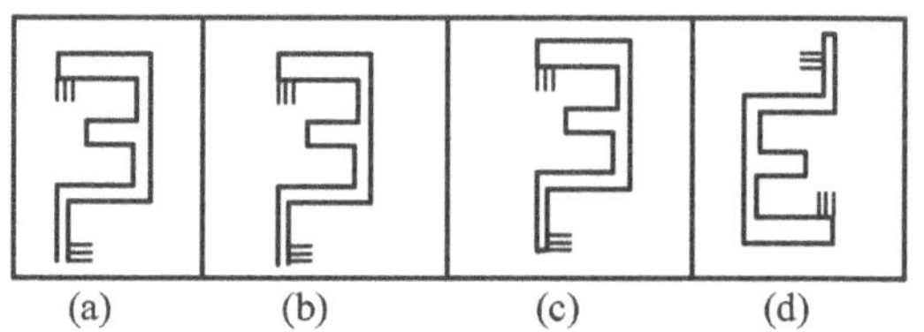

(a)   (b)   (c)   (d)

43. If HONESTY is written as 5132468 and POVERTY as 7192068, how is HORSE written in a certain code?
(a) 50124   (b) 51042
(c) 51024   (d) 52014

44. After interchanging ÷ and =, 2 and 3 which one of the following statements becomes correct ?
(a) $15 = 2 \div 3$ (b) $5 \div 15 = 2$
(c) $2 = 15 \div 3$ (d) $3 = 2 \div 15$

45. In the following figure, how many educated people are employed ?

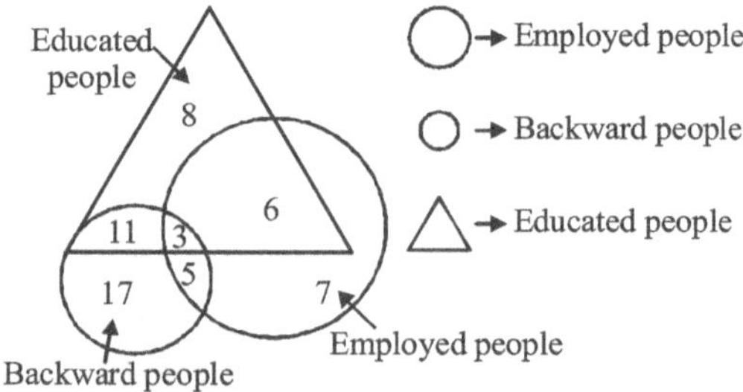

(a) 18   (b) 20
(c) 15   (d) 9

46. The information collected through a survey conducted among the public is represented in the Venn diagram given below. Study the diagram and answer the question.

Which of the following represents Govt. Servents who are tax payers, but are neither females nor graduates?

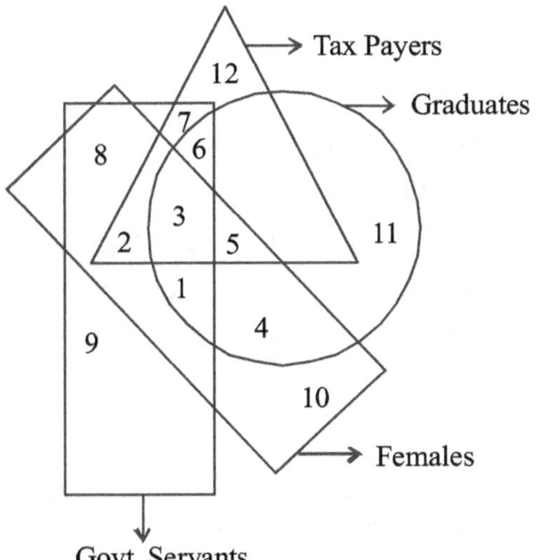

(a) 5

(b) 7

(c) 12

(d) 6

DIRECTIONS (Qs. 47-48): In each of the questions below are three statements followed by two conclusions numbered I and II. You have to take the three statements to be true even if they seem to be at variance from commonly known facts and then decide which of the given conclusions logically follows from the three statements disregarding commonly known facts.

Give answer (a) if **only** conclusion **I** follows.

Give answer (b) if **only** conclusion **II** follows.

Give answer (c) if **either** conclusion **I** or conclusion **II** follows.

Give answer (d) if **both** conclusion **I** and conclusion **II** follow.

47. **Statements:**
    All zebra are cows.
    All camels are cows.
    All tigers are zebra.
    Conclusions:
    I. All tigers are cows.
    II. All camels being tigers is a possibility.

48. **Statements:**
    Some pencils are mobiles.
    All mobiles are grass.
    All grass is green.
    Conclusions:
    I. All grass being pencils is a possibility.
    II. No Green is mobile.

DIRECTIONS (Qs. 49-50): In each question below is given a statement followed by two conclusions numbered I and II. You have to assume everything in the statement to be true, then consider the two conclusions together and decide which of them logically follows beyond a reasonable doubt from the information given in the statement.

49. **Statements:** Nation X faced growing international opposition for its decision to explode eight nuclear weapons at its test site.

    Conclusions:

    I. The citizens of the nation favoured the decision.

    II. Some powerful countries do not want other nations to become as powerful as they are.

    (a) Only conclusion I follows

    (b) Only conclusion II follows

    (c) Either I or II follows

    (d) Neither I nor II follows

50. **Statements:** National Aluminium Company has moved India from a position of shortage to self-sufficiency in the metal.

    Conclusions:

    I. Previously, India had to import aluminium.

    II. With this speed, it can soon become a foreign exchange earner.

    (a) Only conclusion I follows

    (b) Only conclusion II follows

    (c) Either I or II follows

    (d) Both I and II follow

BASIC SCIENCE AND ENGINEERING

51. The following is not included in title block of drawing sheet.

    (a) Sheet No

    (b) Scale

    (c) Method of Projection

    (d) Size of sheet

52. The S.I. unit of universal gas constant is

    (a) Watt K–1mol–1

    (b) N K–1mol–1

    (c) JK–1mol–1

    (d) erg K–1mol–1

53. Kepler's second law is based on
    (a) Newton's first law
    (b) Newton's second law
    (c) Special theory of relativity
    (d) Conservation of angular momentum

54. Free fall of an object (in vacuum) is a case of motion with
    (a) uniform velocity
    (b) uniform acceleration
    (c) variable acceleration
    (d) constant momentum

55. In case of negative work, the angle between the force & displacement is:
    (a) 0°   (b) 45°
    (c) 90°   (d) 180°

56. Choose the correct equation for interconversion of temperature scales.
    (a) $\dfrac{T_C - 0}{100} = \dfrac{T_F - 32}{180}$

    (b) $\dfrac{T_F - 32}{180} = \dfrac{T_K + 273.15}{100}$

    (c) $\dfrac{T_F - 32}{180} = \dfrac{T_K - 273.15}{180}$

    (d) $\dfrac{T_C - 0}{180} = \dfrac{T_F - 32}{100}$

57. Electric current is a quantity of
    (a) scalar
    (b) vector
    (c) Both (a) and (b)
    (d) None of these

58. What are the two families of simple machines?
    (a) First class and second class
    (b) pulley and screw
    (c) inclined plane and lever
    (d) wedge and compound.

59. Ensuring the safety, health and welfare of the employees is the primary purpose of the
    (a) Factories Act, 1948
    (b) Payment of Wages Act, 1936
    (c) Equal Remuneration Act, 1976
    (d) Industrial Disputes Act, 1947

60. The radiations absorbed by ozone layer are
    (a) Ultra-violet   (b) Infra-red
    (c) Gamma rays   (d) Visible

61. Ctrl, shift and alt are called __________ keys.
    (a) adjustment   (b) function
    (c) modifier   (d) alphanumeric

62. Protection of organizational facilities and employees is called
    (a) adverse situation   (b) security
    (c) safety   (d) health

63. Which of the following is the responsibility of the production manager?
    (a) People
    (b) plants
    (c) processes
    (d) all of the above

64. In a third angle projection method, right hand side view of an object is drawn front view.
    (a) Left side of
    (b) Right side of
    (c) Rear side of
    (d) None of above

65. One watt-hour is equivalent to
    (a) 6.3×10^3 J
    (b) 6.3×10^{-7} J
    (c) 3.6×10^3 J
    (d) 3.6×10^{-3} J

66. Mass of an electron is about
    (a) 10^{-3} kg
    (b) 10^{-6} kg
    (c) 10^{-30} kg
    (d) None of the above

67. A train covers a distance of 5 km in 5 minutes; its average speed is equal to

    (a) 1 km / h

    (b) 25 km / h

    (c) 60 km / h

    (d) None of the above

68. A ball is dropped from a height of 10 m.

    (a) Its potential energy increases and kinetic energy decreases during the falls

    (b) Its potential energy is equal to the kinetic energy during the fall.

    (c) The potential energy decreases and the kinetic energy increases during the fall.

    (d) The potential energy is increases and kinetic energy minimum while it is falling.

69. The form of energy that produces feeling of hotness is called as:

    (a) work

    (b) Heat

    (c) Energy

    (d) None of the above

70. Two resistors are said to be connected in series when
    (a) some current passes in turn through both
    (b) both carry the same value of current
    (c) total current equals the sum of branch currents
    (d) sum of IR drops equals the applied e.m.f.

71. Which simple machine makes up a pencil sharpener (The one mounted on the wall)?
    (a) Lawn tractor
    (b) pulley
    (c) inclined plane
    (d) wheel and axle

72. Under the OSH (occupational safety and health) Act, employers are responsible for providing a ______.
    (a) Safe workplace
    (b) Land
    (c) Insurance
    (d) Estimation

73. An ecosystem consists of
    (a) Population
    (b) A biotic community
    (c) A population and its non-living elements
    (d) A biotic community and its non-living elements

74. Greater population can be supported on the earth only if we eat more
    (a) eggs
    (b) mutton
    (c) beef
    (d) plant products

75. A .... is approximately one billion bytes
    (a) Megabyte
    (b) Gigabyte
    (c) Terabyte
    (d) None of these

GENERAL AWARENESS AND CURRENT AFFAIR

76. Which Article of the Indian Constitution guarantees rights to arrested persons ?
    (a) Article 22   (b) Article 35
    (c) Article 20   (d) Article 42

77. Cryogenic is a science deals with
    (a) High Temperatures (b) Low Pressure
    (c) High Pressure   (d) Low Temperature

78. One Carat of diamond is equal to ....
    (a) 200m   (b) 100m
    (c) 150m   (d) 300m

79. Wood Spirit is which of the following ?
    (a) Ethyl Alcohol   (b) Propanol
    (c) Methyl Alcohol   (d) Butanol

80. Which of the following is chief source of Napthalene ?
    (a) Moth balls   (b) Mothflakes
    (c) Tar Camphor   (d) Coal tar

81. Study of crop production is ....
    (a) Entology   (b) Ecology
    (c) Botany   (d) Agronomy

82. Who was the last guru of the Sikhs ?
    (a) Guru Granth Sahib
    (b) Guru Gobind Singh
    (c) Guru Angad
    (d) Guru Amar Das

83. What is the Normal Blood Volume in human adult?
    (a) One litre   (b) Three litres
    (c) Five litres   (d) Seven litres

84. 2018 FIFA World Cup to be held in ....
    (a) China   (b) Russia
    (c) India   (d) Brazil

85. The book titled 'The Life and Death of Adolf Hitler' is penned by
    (a) Z.A. Bhutto
    (b) James Cross Giblin
    (c) J.M. Barrie
    (d) Gunnar Myrdal

86. .... is the Kuchipudi dancer
    (a) Anupama Mohan
    (b) Bimbavati Devi
    (c) Arush Mudgal
    (d) Swapnasundari

87. Which hill station is called as the 'Queen of the Satpuras'
    (a) Pachmarhi   (b) Nilgiri
    (c) Mahenderagiri   (d) Cardamom

88. Which Indian Naval Ship is participating in the multilateral regional maritime engagement exercise "KAKADU 2018"?
    (a) INS Vikramaditya
    (b) INS Satpura
    (c) INS Sahyadri
    (d) INS Viraat

89. The Union Cabinet has recently approved umbrella scheme "O-SMART" of Ministry of Earth Sciences. What does "O" stands here?
    (a) Opacity
    (b) Orach
    (c) Oilcloth
    (d) Ocean

90. Who was officially sworn-in as the new President of Zimbabwe?
    (a) Robert Mugabe
    (b) Emmerson Mnangagwa
    (c) Canaan Banana
    (d) Constantino Chiwenga

91. Who has been appointed new chairman of the Defence Research and Development Organisation (DRDO)?
    (a) G Satheesh Reddy
    (b) Sanjay Mitra
    (c) S Christopher
    (d) Mrinal S Das

92. Metal with maximum density here is
    (a) Fe   (b) Mo
    (c) Hg   (d) Os

93. Which gas is formed on lightning?
    (a) N_2O (b) NO
    (c) NO_2 (d) N_2O_5

94. Which has the maximum protein?
    (a) Groundnut
    (b) Cow-milk
    (c) Egg
    (d) Wheat

95. The temperature of the sun is measured with
    (a) Platinum thermometer
    (b) Pyrometer
    (c) Gas thermometer
    (d) Vapour pressure thermometer

96. Which one of the following is not an enzyme?
    (a) Ptyalin   (b) Pepsin
    (c) Trypsin   (d) Oxytocin

97. Who composed the Gayatri Mantra?
    (a) Vishwamitra   (b) Vashistha
    (c) Indra   (d) Parikshit

98. Largest River of Peninsular India is
    (a) Narmada   (b) Godavari
    (c) Krishna   (d) Kaveri

99. Inflation is caused by
    (a) Increase in supply of goods
    (b) Increase in cash with the Government
    (c) Decrease in money supply
    (d) Increase in money supply

100. The Item education belongs to
    (a) Union List
    (b) State List
    (c) Concurrent List
    (d) Residuary Objects

HINTS & EXPLANATIONS

1. **(b)** Let the no. of one rupee, 50 paise and 25 paise coins be 2x, 3x and 4x respectively. According to question,

$$₹\left(2x+\frac{3x}{2}+\frac{4x}{4}\right)=₹\,216$$

$$\Rightarrow \frac{8x+6x+4x}{4}=216$$

$$\therefore\ x=48$$

$\therefore$ Number of 50 paise coins $= 48\times3 = 144$

2. **(c)** Quantity of milk $= 45\times\dfrac{4}{5}=36$ litres

Quantity of water $= 45\times\dfrac{1}{5}=9$ litres

Let x litres of water be added to make the ratio $3:2$

Then, $\dfrac{36}{9+x}=\dfrac{3}{2}$

$\Rightarrow\ 72=27+3x \Rightarrow\ x=15$ litres

3. **(d)** Age of retired teacher $= 25+3\times10=55$ years

4. **(d)** Let the exhaust tap empties the tank in x minutes.

Then, $\dfrac{1}{12}+\dfrac{1}{15}-\dfrac{1}{x}=\dfrac{1}{20}$ or

$$\frac{1}{x}=\frac{1}{12}+\frac{1}{15}-\frac{1}{20}$$

or $\dfrac{1}{x}=\dfrac{5+4-3}{60}=\dfrac{6}{60}=\dfrac{1}{10}$ or $x=10$ min

5. **(d)** In 1 day, work done by 12 men $=\dfrac{1}{18}$

In 6 days, work done by 12 men $=\dfrac{6}{18}=\dfrac{1}{3}$

Remaining work $=\dfrac{2}{3}$

Now, $m_1\times d_1\times w_2 = m_2\times d_2\times w_1$

or $12\times18\times\dfrac{2}{3}=16\times d_2\times1$

or $d_2=\dfrac{4\times18\times2}{16}=9$ days

6. **(d)** Let the speed of the stream be x km/h. Then, upstream speed $=(15-x)$ km/h. and downstream speed $=(15+x)$ km/h.

Now, $\dfrac{30}{(15+x)}+\dfrac{30}{(15-x)}=4.5$

Solving these equations, we get x = 5 km/h.

7. **(b)** Let CP = x, Total ₹ = 600, Sugar bought

$$=\frac{600}{x}$$

$$\text{ATQ}\ \frac{80x}{100}\left[\frac{600}{x}+5\right]=600$$

$$480+4x=600$$

$$4x=120$$

$$x=30$$

8. **(b)** Let the sum be ₹x & original rate R%, then,

$$\left(\frac{x\times(R+3)\times2}{100}\right)-\left(\frac{x\times R\times2}{100}\right)=300$$

$$6x=300\times100 \Rightarrow x=5000$$

The value of $4x = 4\times5000 = 20000$

9. **(a)** Here $d = a+3$

$$a+a+3=103$$

$$2a=100$$

$$a=50$$

So, numbers are 50, 51, 52 and 53

$\therefore\ b\times c=51\times52=2652$

10. **(b)** Distance covered by wheel in one revolution

$= $ Circumference of wheel

$\therefore\ \pi\times$ diameter $=\dfrac{440}{1000}$

$\Rightarrow\ \dfrac{22}{7}\times$ diameter $=\dfrac{440}{1000}$

$\Rightarrow$ Diameter $=\dfrac{440}{1000}\times\dfrac{7}{22}$

$=0.14$ cm

11. **(a)** Area of the field = Area of rectangle + Area of circle with diameter 35 m + Area of circle with diameter 42 m.

$$= 42 \times 35 + 2 \times \frac{1}{2} \times \frac{22}{7} \times (21)^2 + 2 \times \frac{1}{2} \times \frac{22}{7} \times (17.5)^2$$

$$= 1470 + 1386 + 962.5 = 3818.5 \ m^2$$

12. (d)　Perimeter of the square = circumference of the circle

We have, $4 \times 11 = 2\pi r \Rightarrow r = \frac{4 \times 11}{2 \times \pi}$

Area of the circle $= \pi r^2$

$$= \pi \times \left(\frac{4 \times 11}{2 \times \pi}\right)^2 = 49\pi$$

$$= 154 \ cm^2$$

13. (d)　If the CP of each book be ₹1, then
SP of 40 books = ₹30
CP of 40 books = ₹40

$$\therefore L\% = \frac{40 - 30}{40} \times 100 = 25\%$$

14. (b)　Let the original price of sugar be ₹ x/kg.

$$\therefore \text{New price} = ₹\ \frac{9x}{10} \ /kg$$

$$\therefore \frac{270}{\frac{9x}{10}} - \frac{270}{x} = 1$$

$$\Rightarrow \frac{300}{x} - \frac{270}{x} = 1 \Rightarrow \frac{30}{x} = 1$$

$$\Rightarrow x = ₹\ 30/kg$$

15. (b)　$P = ₹\ 12000;$
$R = 20\%$ per annum = 5% per quarter
$T = 9$ months $= 3$ years (quarterly)

So, $A = 12000 \left(1 + \frac{5}{100}\right)^3 = 12000 \times 1.05 \times 1.05 \times 1.05$

$$= ₹\ 13891.1$$

So, CI $= 13891.10 - 12000 = ₹\ 1891.10$

16. (b)　Let the required distance be x km.

$$\therefore \frac{x}{6 - 2} - \frac{x}{6 + 2} = 3$$

$$\Rightarrow \frac{x}{4} - \frac{x}{8} = 3$$

$$\Rightarrow \frac{2x - x}{8} = 3$$

$$\Rightarrow x = 3 \times 8 = 24 \ km.$$

17. (a)　ATQ

$$\frac{3}{A} + \frac{3}{A} + \frac{3}{B} = 1, \quad \frac{6}{12} + \frac{3}{B} = 1$$

$$\frac{3}{B} = \frac{1}{2}$$

$$B = 6 \ days$$

18. (a)　$\dfrac{W_1}{W_2} = \dfrac{2}{3}$

$$\Rightarrow \frac{W_2}{W_1} = \frac{3}{2} \ \text{and} \ \frac{W_1}{W_3} = \frac{1}{2}$$

$$\therefore \frac{W_2}{W_1} \times \frac{W_1}{W_3} = \frac{W_2}{W_3} = \frac{3}{2} \times \frac{1}{2} = \frac{3}{4}$$

19. (d)　According to question,

$$\frac{36 + n}{50 + n} = \frac{3}{4}$$

$$36 \times 4 + 4n = 50 \times 3 + 3n$$

$$4n - 3n = 150 - 144$$

$$n = 6$$

20. (b)　Required change in area

$$\boxed{= \frac{-10 \times 10}{100} = -1\% \quad \text{trick} = \frac{-x^2}{100}}$$

Negative sign shows a decrease.
Net change

$$10 - 10 - \frac{10 \times 10}{100}$$

$$= -1\%$$

or 1% decreasing.

21. (c)　$(a - b)^3 = a^3 - b^3 - 3ab \ (a - b)$
$\Rightarrow 8 = 56 - 3ab \ (2)$
$\Rightarrow 6ab = 56 - 8 = 48$
$\Rightarrow 2ab = 16$ 　　　　　　...(i)
$\therefore a^2 + b^2 = (a - b)^2 + 2ab$
$= 4 + 16 = 20$

22. (d)　If the first divisor be a multiple of the second divisor, then required remainder = remainder obtained by dividing the first remainder (36) by the second divisor (17) = 2
$\because$ 17 is a factor of 136
$\therefore$ Remainder when 36 is divided by $17 = 2$

23. (a)　$39 + 48 + 51 + 63 + 75 + 83 + x + 69 = 60 \times 8$
$\Rightarrow 428 + x = 480$
$\Rightarrow x = 480 - 428 = 52$

24. (c)　Let CP = 100
P = 200
SP = CP + P = 300

$$\frac{CP}{SP} = \frac{100}{300} = \frac{1}{3}$$

25. (c) Salary in May 2000 = ₹ 15000
Salary in July 2000 ⇒ 15000 + 10% of 15000
= ₹16500
Salary in October 2001 = 16500 + 10% of
16500 = ₹18150

26. (a) Dehradun is capital of Uttarakhand.
Similarly, Aizawl is capital of Mizoram.

27. (c) 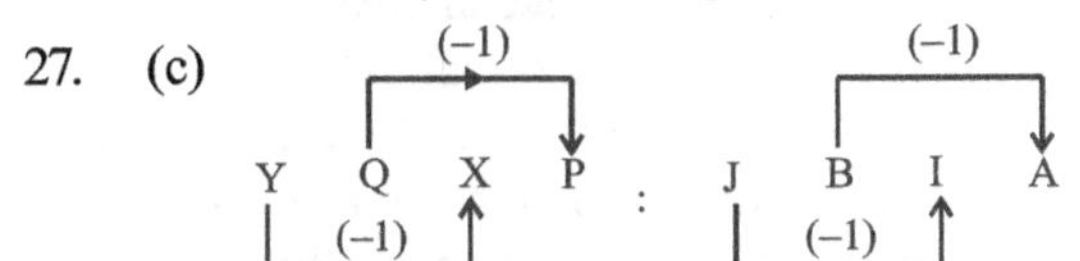

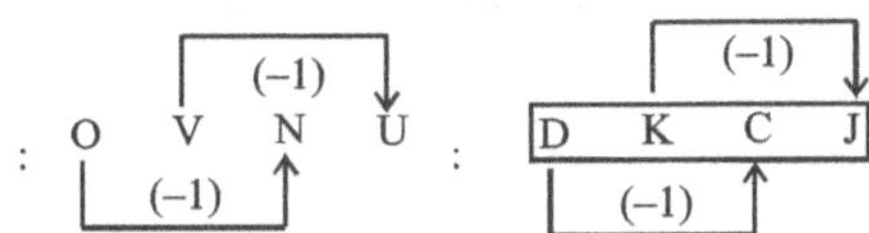

28. (d) As, $(1)^3 : 1$
Similarly,
$(10)^3 : 1000$

29. (c) $C \xrightarrow{+2} E \xrightarrow{+2} G \quad J \xrightarrow{+2} L \xrightarrow{+2} N \quad Q \xrightarrow{+2} S \xrightarrow{+2} U$

Similarly, $H \xrightarrow{+2} J \xrightarrow{+2} L$

30. (c) $285 \xleftarrow{-32} 253 \xleftarrow{-32} 221 \xleftarrow{-32} 189 \xleftarrow{-32} \mathbf{157}$

31. (d)

PR	ES	EN	TA	TI	ON		EN	ES	TA	TI	PR	ON
1	2	3	4	5	6	→	3	2	4	5	1	6

Similarly,

IN	TE	LL	IG	EN	CE		**LL**	**TE**	**IG**	**EN**	**IN**	**CE**
1	2	3	4	5	6	→	**3**	**2**	**4**	**5**	**1**	**6**

32. (b) Clearly, no. of students in the class = 14+1
+44 ⇒ 59.

33. (b)

34. (a)

Required distance = XY = AX + AY
= 20 + 10
= 30 m, North

35. (b) Dollar — O O — Rupee
Currency

36. (b)

37. (b) Clearly, we have to first find two numbers
whose difference is 2 and of which the
smaller one is a perfect square and the big-
ger one a perfect cube.
Such numbers are 25 and 27.
Thus, Nitin is now 26 years old. Since the
next perfect cube after 27 is 64,
So required time period = (64 – 26) years =
38 years.

38. (d) $(12 + 6) \times 18 = 36 \Rightarrow (18 \div 6) \times 12 = 36$
$\Rightarrow 3 \times 12 \boxed{36}$

39. (d) 40. (a)

41. (c) 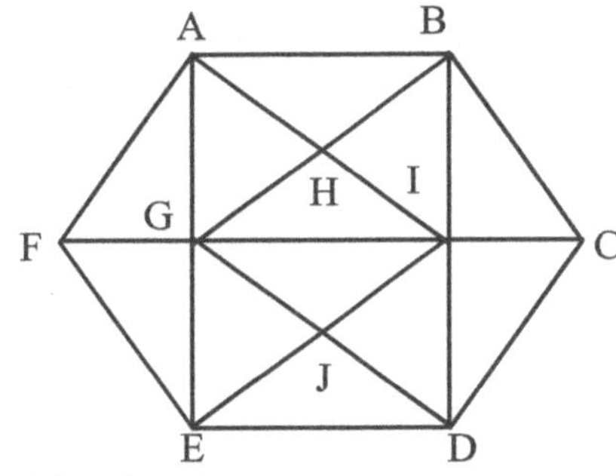

The triangles are:
ΔFEA ; ΔCBD ; ΔFAG ; ΔFEG :
ΔBCI ; ΔCDI ; ΔAFI ; ΔEFI ;
ΔBGC; ΔDCG; ΔAGI ; ΔBIH :
ΔAGB; ΔABI; ΔHAB; ΔHBI:
ΔHGI; ΔHAG; ΔGEI; ΔGED:
ΔIDE; ΔIDG; ΔJGI; ΔJDI:
ΔJGE; ΔJDE; ΔAIE; ΔBGD:
Thus, there are 28 triangles.

42. (c)

43. (b) As, H O N E S T Y
↓ ↓ ↓ ↓ ↓ ↓ ↓
5 1 3 2 4 6 8

and, P   O   V   E   R   T   Y
↓   ↓   ↓   ↓   ↓   ↓   ↓
7   1   9   2   0   6   8

Therefore,

H   O   R   S   E
↓   ↓   ↓   ↓   ↓
5   1   0   4   2

44. (b) $5 = 15 \div 3$
45. (d) $3 + 6 = 9$
46. (b) '7' represents Govt. servants who are tax payers, but are neither females nor graduates.

47. (d)

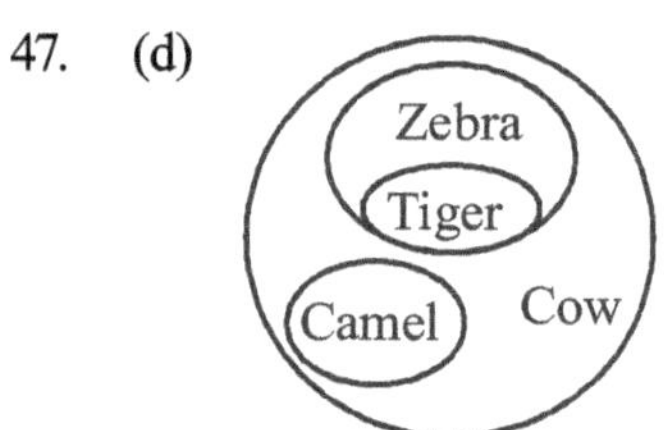

So, Both I and II follow.

48. (a)

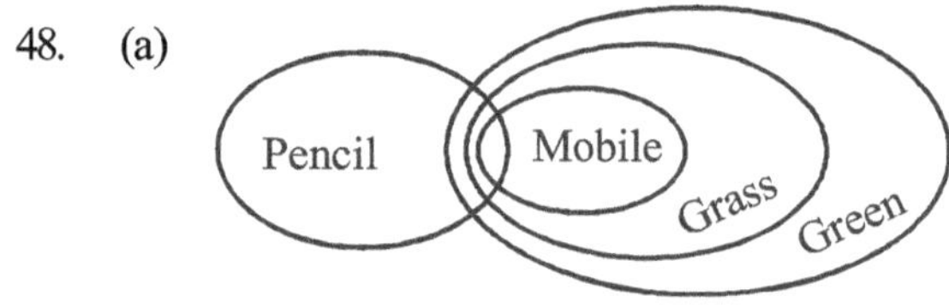

So, Only I follows.

49. (d) Neither the citizens response to the decision nor the reason for opposition by other nations can be deduced from the statement. So, neither I nor II follows.

50. (d) According to the statement, National Aluminium Company has moved India from a position of shortage in the past to self-sufficiency in the present. This means that previously, India had to import aluminium. So, I follows. Also, it can be deduced that if production increases at the same rate, India can export it in future. So, II also follows.

51. (d)	52. (c)	53. (d)	54. (b)	55. (d)
56. (a)	57. (a)	58. (c)	59. (a)	60. (a)
61. (c)	62. (b)	63. (d)	64. (a)	65. (c)
66. (c)	67. (c)	68. (c)	69. (b)	70. (a)
71. (d)	72. (a)	73. (d)	74. (a)	75. (b)
76. (a)	77. (d)	78. (a)	79. (c)	80. (d)
81. (d)	82. (b)	83. (c)	84. (b)	85. (b)
86. (a)	87. (a)	88. (c)	89. (d)	90. (b)
91. (a)	92. (c)	93. (b)	94. (a)	95. (b)
96. (d)	97. (a)	98. (b)	99. (d)	100. (c)

PRACTICE SET 3

MATHEMATICS

1. The least number which when divided by 6, 9, 12, 15, 18 leaves the same remainder 2 in each case is:
   (a) 178   (b) 182   (c) 176   (d) 180

2. A sum of money is divided among A, B, C and D in the ratio 3 : 5 : 8 : 9 respectively. If the share of D is ₹ 1,872 more than the share of A, then what is the total amount of money of B & C together?
   (a) ₹ 4,156   (b) ₹ 4,165
   (c) ₹ 4,056   (d) ₹ 4,068

3. What approximate compound interest can be obtained on an amount of ₹ 3,980 after 2 years at 8 p.c.p.a. ?
   (a) ₹ 650   (b) ₹ 680
   (c) ₹ 600   (d) ₹ 662

4. A man walks at the speed of 5 km/hr and runs at the speed of 10 km/hr. How much time will the man require to cover the distance of 28 km, if he covers half (first 14 km) of his journey walking and half of his journey running ?
   (a) 8.4 hrs   (b) 6 hrs
   (c) 5 hrs   (d) 4.2 hrs

5. In a 30 litres mixture of water and milk, 50% is milk. How much pure milk need to be added to this mixture to make mixture 30% water?
   (a) 10 litres   (b) 18 litres
   (c) 15 litres   (d) 20 litres

6. A bag contains 5 green and 7 red balls. Two balls are drawn. The probability that one is green and the other is red is
   (a) $\dfrac{5}{132}$ (b) $\dfrac{7}{132}$ (c) $\dfrac{35}{66}$ (d) $\dfrac{31}{66}$

7. By selling 8 dozen pencils, a shopkeeper gains the selling price of 1 dozen pencils. What is the gain?
   (a) $12\dfrac{1}{2}\%$ (b) $13\dfrac{1}{7}\%$
   (c) $14\dfrac{2}{7}\%$ (d) $87\dfrac{1}{2}\%$

8. The average of 50 numbers is 38. If two numbers namely 45 and 55 are discarded, the average of the remaining numbers is :
   (a) 36   (b) 35
   (c) 32.5   (d) 37.5

9. The difference between a discount of 40% on ₹500 and two successive discounts of 36%, 4% on the same amount is
   (a) ₹ 0   (b) ₹ 2
   (c) ₹ 1.93   (d) ₹ 7.20

10. X and Y can do a piece of work in 30 days. They work together for 6 days and then X quits and Y finishes the work in 32 more days. In how many days can Y do the piece of work alone?
    (a) 30 days   (b) 32 days
    (c) 34 days   (d) 40 days

11. If $\left(x+\dfrac{1}{x}\right)=4$, then the value of $x^4+\dfrac{1}{x^4}$ is :
    (a) 124   (b) 64
    (c) 194   (d) 81

12. If the number p is 5 more than q and the sum of the squares of p and q is 55, then the product of p and q is
    (a) 10   (b) -10
    (c) 15   (d) -15

13. The income of a company increases 20% per annum. If its income is ₹ 26,64,000 in the year 2012, then its income in the year 2010 was :
    (a) ₹ 28,20,000   (b) ₹ 28,55,,000
    (c) ₹ 18,50,000   (d) ₹ 21,20,000

14. A student goes to school at the rate of $2\dfrac{1}{2}$ km/h and reaches 6 minutes late. If he travels at the speed of 3 km/h. he is 10 minutes early. The distance (in km) between the school and his house is
    (a) 5   (b) 4
    (c) 3   (d) 1

15. A and B can complete a piece of work in 8 days, B and C can do it in 12 days, C and A can do it in 8 days. A, B and C together can complete it in
    (a) 4 days
    (b) 5 days
    (c) 6 days
    (d) 7 days

16. A bicycle wheel makes 5000 revolutions in moving 11 km. Then thme radius of the wheel (in cm) is

    (Take $\pi = \dfrac{22}{7}$)

    (a) 70
    (b) 35
    (c) 17.5
    (d) 140

17. A copper wire is bent in the shape of a square of area 81 cm^2. If the same wire is bent form of a semicircle, the radius (in cm) of the semicircle is

    (Take $\pi = \dfrac{22}{7}$)

    (a) 16
    (b) 14
    (c) 10
    (d) 7

18. The H.C.F. and L.C.M. of two numbers are 12 and 336 respectively. If one of the numbers is 84, the other is
    (a) 36
    (b) 48
    (c) 72
    (d) 96

19. The least among the fractions $\dfrac{15}{16}, \dfrac{19}{20}, \dfrac{24}{35}, \dfrac{34}{35}$ is

    (a) $\dfrac{34}{35}$
    (b) $\dfrac{15}{16}$
    (c) $\dfrac{19}{20}$
    (d) $\dfrac{24}{25}$

20. The average temperature of Monday, Tuesday and Wednesday was 30°C and that of Tuesday, Wednesday and Thursday was 33°C. If the temperature on Monday was 32°C, then the temperature on Thursday was:
    (a) 33°C
    (b) 30°C
    (c) 41°C
    (d) 32°C

21. If on a marked price, the difference of selling prices with a discount of 30% and two successive discounts of 20% and 10% is ₹ 72, then the marked price (in rupees) is
    (a) 3,600
    (b) 3,000
    (c) 2,500
    (d) 2,400

22. If the price of sugar is raised by 25%, find by how much percent a householder must reduce his consumption of sugar so as not to increase his expenditure?
    (a) 10
    (b) 20
    (c) 18
    (d) 25

23. The population of a town increases by 5% every year. If the present population is 9261, the population 3 years ago was
    (a) 5700
    (b) 6000
    (c) 7500
    (d) 8000

24. Walking at $\dfrac{6\text{th}}{7}$ of his usual speed a man is 25 minutes too late. His usual time to cover this distance is
    (a) 2 hours 30 minutes
    (b) 2 hours 15 minutes
    (c) 2 hours 25 minutes
    (d) 2 hours 10 minutes

25. X is 3 times as fast as Y and is able to complete the work in 40 days less than Y. Then the time in which they can complete the work together is
    (a) 15 days
    (b) 10 days
    (c) $7\dfrac{1}{2}$ days
    (d) 5 days

GENERAL INTELLIGENCE AND REASONING

DIRECTIONS (Qs. 26-28): In questions, select the related word/letters/number from given alternatives.

26. ACE : FHJ : : OQS : ?
    (a) TVX
    (b) UWY
    (c) PRT
    (d) RTU

27. Saint : Meditation : : Scientist : ?
    (a) Research
    (b) Knowledge
    (c) Spiritual
    (d) Rational

28. 18 : 5 :: 12 : ?
    (a) 4
    (b) 10
    (c) 3
    (d) 6

DIRECTIONS (Qs. 29 & 30): In questions below, a series is given with one term missing. Choose the correct alternative from the given ones that will complete the series.

29. FAG, GAF, HAI, IAH, ________
    (a) JAK
    (b) HAK
    (c) JAI
    (d) HAL

30. 3, 6, 9, 15, 24, 39, 63, ?
    (a) 100
    (b) 87
    (c) 102
    (d) 99

31. Govind is 48 years old. He is twice as old as his son Prem is now. How old was Prem seven years before?
    (a) 16 years   (b) 17 years
    (c) 13 years   (d) 18 years

32. Pointing to a man, a lady said "His mother is the only daughter of my mother". How is the lady related to the man?
    (a) Mother   (b) Daughter
    (c) Sister   (d) Aunt

33. After walking 10 m, Shankar turned left and covered a distance of 6 m, then turned right and covered a distance of 20 m. In the end, he was moving towards the south. From which direction did Shankar start his journey?
    (a) West   (b) North
    (c) South   (d) East

34. If '−' stands for '+', '+' stands for '×', '×' stands for '−' then which one of the following is not correct ?
    (a) $22 + 7 - 3 \times 9 = 148$
    (b) $33 \times 5 - 10 + 20 = 228$
    (c) $7 + 28 - 3 \times 52 = 127$
    (d) $44 - 9 + 6 \times 11 = 87$

35. Find the missing number-

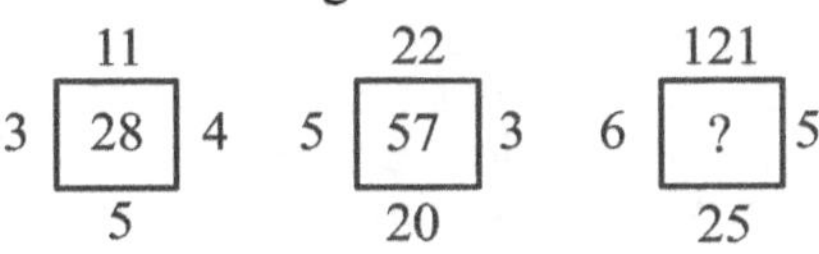

    (a) 176   (b) 115
    (c) 157   (d) 131

36. A man is 3 years older than his wife and four times as old as his son. If the son becomes 15 years old after 3 years, what is the present age of the wife ?
    (a) 60 years   (b) 51 years
    (c) 48 years   (d) 45 years

37. If HOSPITAL is written as 32574618 in a certain code, how would POSTAL be written in that code?
    (a) 752618   (b) 725618
    (c) 725168   (d) 725681

38. **Statement :** Songs always have singers to sing them.
    Conclusions:
    I. Singers make a song.
    II. There is no un-sung song.
    (a) Only conclusion II follows
    (b) Both conclusions I and II follow
    (c) Neither conclusion I nor II follows
    (d) Only conclusion I follows

39. Which of the following states the relationship between Sociology, Psychology and Humanities ?

(a) 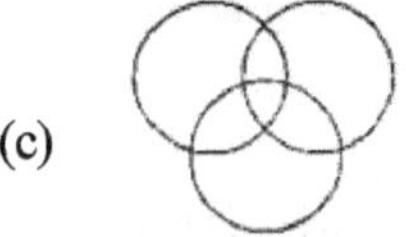   (b) 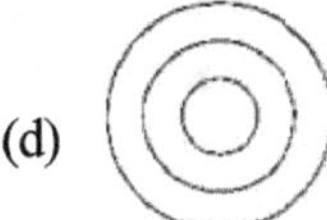

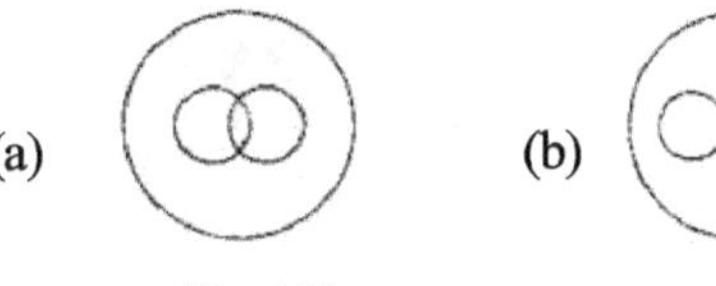

(c) 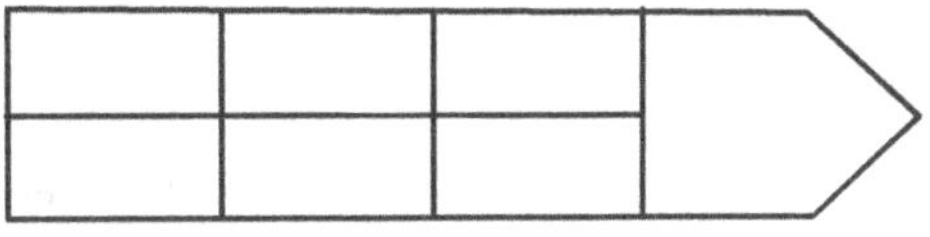   (d)

40. How many rectangles are there in the given diagram?

    (a) 4   (b) 7
    (c) 9   (d) 18

41. In the following question, select the answer figure in which the question figure is hidden / embedded.
    Question Figure:

    Answer Figures:

(a) 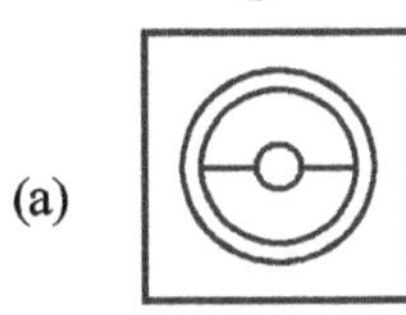   (b) 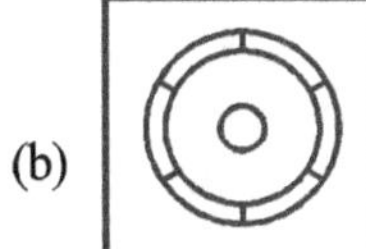

(c)    (d) 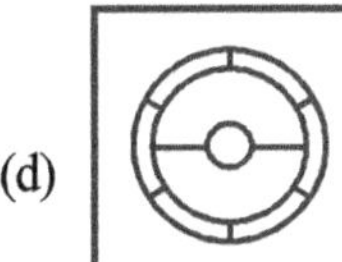

42. Which answer figure completes the form in question figure ?
    Question Figure :

Answer figures :

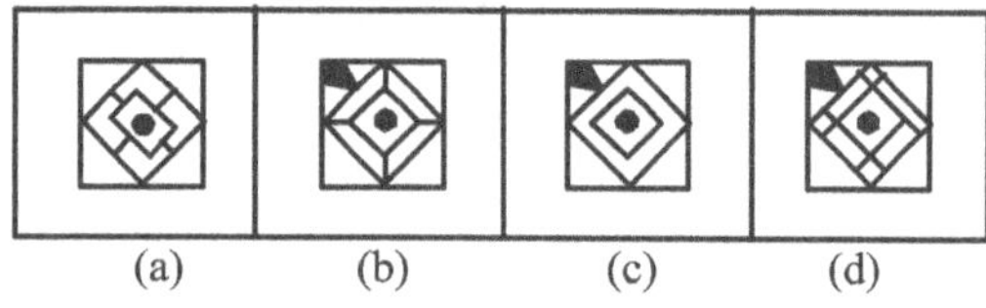

| (a) | (b) | (c) | (d) |

43. If DELHI is coded as 73541 and CALCUTTA as 82589662, then how can CALICUT be coded?

(a) 5279431   (b) 5978013

(c) 8251896   (d) 8543691

44. X and Y are brothers. R is the father of Y. S is the brother of T and maternal uncle of X. What is T to R?

(a) Mother   (b) Wife

(c) Sister   (d) Brother

45. If a man on a moped starts from a point and rides 4 km South, then turns left and rides 2 km to turn again to the right to ride 4 km more, towards which direction is he moving?

(a) North   (b) West

(c) East   (d) South

46. 25 * 2 * 6 = 4 * 11 * 0

Which set of symbols can replace * ?

(a) ×, −, ×, +   (b) +, −, ×, +

(c) ×, +, ×, −   (d) ×, +, +, ×

47. In the given diagram, Circle represents strong men, Square represents short men and Triangle represents military officers. Which region represents military officers who are short but not strong?

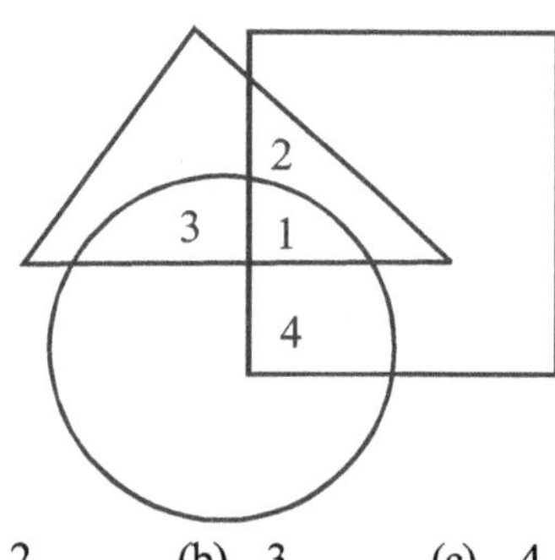

(a) 2   (b) 3   (c) 4   (d) 1

48. Triangle represents school teachers. Square represents married persons. Circles represents persons living in joint families. Married persons living in Joint families but not working as school teachers are represented by

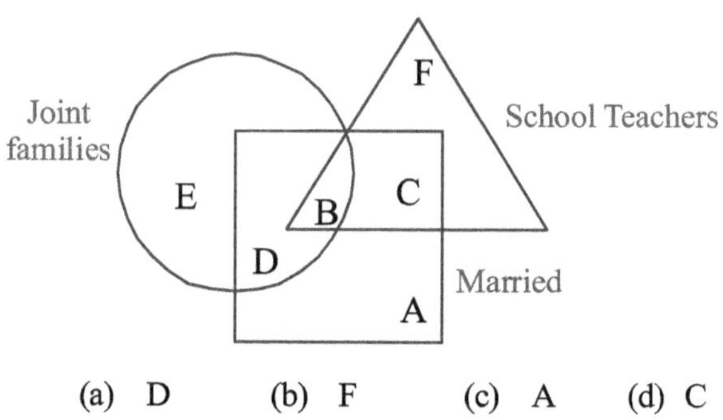

(a) D   (b) F   (c) A   (d) C

DIRECTIONS (Qs. 49 & 50): In each question below are given two/three statements followed by two conclusions numbered I and II. You have to take the given statements to be true even if they seem to be at variance with commonly known facts. Read all the conclusions and then decide which of the given conclusions logically follows from the given statements, disregarding commonly known facts. Give answer

(a) if only conclusion I follows.
(b) if only conclusion II follows.
(c) if either conclusion I or conclusion II follows.
(d) if neither conclusion I nor conclusion II follows.

49. **Statements**   : All rings are circles.
                         All squares are rings.
                         No ellipse is a circle.

   Conclusions : I. Some rings being ellipses is a possibility.
                   : **II.** At least some circles are squares.

50. **Statements** : No house is an apartment.
                       Some bungalows are apartments.

   Conclusions : I. No house is a bungalow.
                     II. All bungalows are houses.

BASIC SCIENCE AND ENGINEERING

51. The internal angle of regular hexagon is ___ degree.
(a) 72   (b) 108
(c) 120   (d) 150

52. The dimensions of k in the equation $W = \dfrac{1}{2}kx^2$ is
(a) $[ML^0T^{-2}]$ (b) $[M^0LT^{-1}]$
(c) $[MLT^{-2}]$ (d) $[ML^0T^{-1}]$

53. Newton is unit of
    (a) Weight (b) Mass
    (c) Energy (d) Power
54. Stopping distance of a moving vehicle is directly proportional to
    (a) square of the initial velocity
    (b) square of the initial acceleration
    (c) the initial velocity
    (d) the initial acceleration
55. When a body vibrates, it produces
    (a) sound (b) water
    (c) heat (d) electricity
56. Stainless steel pans are usually provided with copper bottoms. The reason for this could that.
    (a) copper bottom makes the pan more durable
    (b) such pans appear colorful
    (c) copper is a better conductor of heat than the stainless steel
    (d) none of the above
57. The safe current for the fuse wire of radius r is I, then
    (a) $I \alpha r^{1/2}$ (b) $I \alpha r$
    (c) $I \alpha r^{3/2}$ (d) $I \alpha r^2$
58. Ramps, a wedge, and a screw are all examples of
    (a) Levers (b) Pulleys
    (c) Wheels and axles (d) Inclined plane
59. The person or organization responsible for rehabilitation is:
    (a) an employee's doctor
    (b) the insurance company
    (c) the employer
    (d) the employee, when better
60. Word "Environment" is derived from:
    (a) Italy (b) French
    (c) German (d) English
61. An error is also known as
    (a) bug (b) debug
    (c) cursor (d) icon
62. The example of non-ohmic resistance is
    (a) diode
    (b) copper wire
    (c) filament lamp
    (d) carbon resistor
63. Which type of line is particular to section drawings?
    (a) break lines (b) phantom lines
    (c) extension lines (d) cutting plane lines
64. SI unit' stands for
    (a) Symbolically Integrated Unit
    (b) Standard Integrated Unit
    (c) Scientific International Unit
    (d) Standard International Unit
65. One oscillation completes when bob moves from
    (a) A to B
    (b) A to B and then again
    (c) A to B and then back to A
    (d) A to B and then in center
66. Quantity that varies due to gravitational pull variations is
    (a) Mass (b) Time
    (c) Weight (d) acceleration
67. Speed of light in vacuum is
    (a) 0.3×107 m s-1 (b) 3×107 m s-1
    (c) 30×107 m s-1 (d) None of the above
68. We can say that one watt is defined as
    (a) rate of work done or energy conversion of one joule per second
    (b) rate of time of one second per joule
    (c) rate of distance of one meter per joule
    (d) rate of work done or energy conversion of one joule per meter
69. The amount of heat required to raise temperature of a substance by 1°C is called as:
    (a) work capacity (b) heat capacity
    (c) energy capacity (d) none of the above
70. Ohm's law is not applicable to
    (a) vacuum tubes
    (b) carbon resistors
    (c) high voltage circuits\
    (d) circuits with low current densities
71. Which simple machine does a flagpole make use of?
    (a) Lever (b) screw
    (c) pulley (d) inclined plane
72. What are the most common injuries in the hospitality industry?
    (a) Sprains and strains
    (b) Being hit by falling objects
    (c) Falls
    (d) All of these.

73. The environment includes
    (a) Abiotic factors
    (b) Biotic factors
    (c) Oxygen and Nitrogen
    (d) Abiotic and Biotic factors
74. The smallest unit in a digital system is a.........
    (a) Bit   (b) Byte
    (c) Character   (d) Kilobyte
75. A ______ is a push or a pull.
    (a) Force   (b) friction
    (c) simple machine   (d) pulley

GENERAL AWARENESS AND CURRENT AFFAIR

76. Who among the following was the first Governor General of India?
    (a) Wollen Hastings
    (b) Lord William Bentinck
    (c) Sir Charles Metcalfe
    (d) Robert Clive
77. Which one of the following is not a constituent of biogas?
    (a) Methane   (b) Carbon dioxide
    (c) Hydrogen   (d) Nitrogen dioxide
78. Bar is a unit of which one of the following?
    (a) Force   (b) Energy
    (c) Pressure   (d) Frequency
79. Which of the following metals are present in haemoglobin and chlorophyll, respectively?
    (a) Fe and Mg   (b) Fe and Zn
    (c) Mg and Zn   (d) Zn and Mg
80. A mother of blood group O has a group O child. What could be the blood group of father of the child?
    (a) Only O   (b) A or B or O
    (c) A or B   (d) Only AB
81. Who among the following was the founder of the Muslim League?
    (a) Muhammad Ali Jinnah
    (b) Shaukat Ali
    (c) Nawab Salimullah
    (d) Aga Khan
82. Which one of the following causes the chikungunia disease?
    (a) Bacteria   (b) Helminthic worm
    (c) Protozoan   (d) Virus
83. Which one of the following vitamins helps in clotting of blood?
    (a) Vitamin-A   (b) Vitamin-B_6
    (c) Vitamin-D   (d) Vitamin-K
84. The 'Thomas Cup is associated with
    (a) Table Tennis   (b) Lawn Tennis
    (c) Badminton   (d) Billiards
85. What is the purpose of adding baking soda to dough?
    (a) To generate moisture
    (b) To give a good flavour
    (c) To give good colour
    (d) To generate carbon dioxide
86. Which one of the following glands in the human body stores iodine?
    (a) Parathyroid   (b) Thyroid
    (c) Pituitary   (d) Adrenal
87. The device used for measuring the wavelength of X-rays is
    (a) Bragg Spectrometer
    (b) Mass Spectrometer
    (c) G. M. Counter
    (d) Cyclotron
88. Tejinder Pal Singh Toor, who clinched Gold in men's Shot-Put event at the 2018 Jakarta Asian Games, has set new Asiad record of how much meters?
    (a) 20.55m   (b) 20.75m
    (c) 20.85m   (d) 20.65m
89. What is the India's GDP forecast for 2018, as per Moody's Investors Service report "Global Macro Outlook for 2018-19"?
    (a) 7.8%   (b) 7.5%
    (c) 7.6%   (d) 7.7%
90. Who heads the steering committee which recently submitted 'Making India 5G Ready' report to government?
    (a) Aruna Sundararajan
    (b) Vinod Tawde
    (c) Waqar Ali
    (d) AJ Paulraj

91. Which of the following substance does not have a melting point
    (a) Bromine (b) Sodium Chloride
    (c) Mercury (d) Glass

92. The pH scale had been given by
    (a) Arrhenius (b) Bronsted
    (c) Sornsen (d) Lewis

93. Which has maximum calorific value?
    (a) Protein (b) Carbohydrates
    (c) Fats (d) Amino Acids

94. Which one of the following has the highest fuel value?
    (a) Hydrogen (b) Charcoal
    (c) Natural Gas (d) Gasoline

95. Which one of the following is used to remove ink and rust stains on cloths?
    (a) Oxalic acid (b) Alcohol
    (c) Ether (d) Kerosene oil

96. Flowering plants are grouped under
    (a) Cryptogames (b) Phanerogames
    (c) Bryophytes (d) Pteridophytes

97. How many Fundamental Rights are now guaranteed under the constitution of India?
    (a) Eight (b) Seven
    (c) Nine (d) Six

98. All the executive power in Indian Constitution are vested with
    (a) President of India
    (b) Prime Minister of India
    (c) Parliament
    (d) Council of Minister

99. The famous woman ruler of the Gupta period was:
    (a) Kuberanga (b) Kumardevi
    (c) Prabhabati (d) Rajyashree

100. The book 'Sahibs Who Loved India' has been written by :
    (a) Khushwant Singh
    (b) Pankaj Mishra
    (c) Usha Bhagat
    (d) Mulk Raj Anand

HINTS & EXPLANATIONS

1. (b) LCM of 6, 9, 12, 15 and 18

$$
\begin{array}{c|l}
2 & 6,9,12,15,18 \\
\hline
3 & 3,9,6,15,9 \\
\hline
3 & 1,3,2,5,3 \\
\hline
& 1,1,2,5,1
\end{array}
$$

LCM $= 2 \times 3 \times 3 \times 2 \times 5 = 180$

Least number $= 180 + 2 = 182$

2. (c) Share of B + C $= \dfrac{1872}{9-3} \times (5+8) = ₹\,4056$

3. (d) Equivalent % interest for compound rate of interest of 8% for 2 years

$$
= 8 + 8 + \frac{8 \times 8}{100} = 16.64\%
$$

So, interest $= 16.64\%$ of $3980 \approx ₹\,662$

4. (d) Total time required $= \dfrac{14}{5} + \dfrac{14}{10}$

$$
= \frac{28 + 14}{10} = 4.2 \text{ hrs}
$$

5. (d) 30 litres mixture contains 15 litres of water. When milk added to this, quantity of water will same in the solution (*i.e.* 15 ℓ).

Let x ℓ of pure milk to be added, then 30% of $(30 + x) = 15$

solve, $x = 20$ litres.

6. (c) There are $5 + 7 = 12$ balls in the bag and out of these two balls can be drawn in $^{12}C_2$ ways. There are 5 green balls, therefore, one green ball can be drawn in $^5C_1$ ways; similarly, one red ball can be drawn in $^7C_1$ ways so that the number of ways in which we can draw one green ball and the other red is $^5C_1 \times {}^7C_1$. Hence, P (one green and the other red)

$$
= \frac{{}^5C_1 \times {}^7C_1}{{}^{12}C_2} = \frac{5}{1} \times \frac{7}{1} \times \frac{1 \times 2}{12 \times 11} = \frac{35}{66}
$$

7. (c) Let the cost price of one dozen pencil $= ₹\,x$

Profit $= ₹\,x$

Cost price of 8 dozen pencil $= ₹\,7x$

Gain per cent $= \dfrac{x}{7x} \times 100$

$$
= \frac{100}{7} = 14\frac{2}{7}\%
$$

8. (d) New averag

$$
= \frac{38 \times 50 - 45 - 55}{48}
$$

$$
= \frac{1800}{48} = 37.5
$$

9. (d) Single equivalent discount for 36% and 4%

$$
= \left(36 + 4 - \frac{36 \times 4}{100} \right) = (40 - 1.44)\%
$$

$$
= 38.56\%
$$

∴ Required difference $= 1.44\%$ of 500

$$
= \frac{500 \times 1.44}{100} = ₹7.20
$$

10. (d) $(x+y)$'s 6 days' work $= \left(\dfrac{1}{30} \times 6 \right) = \dfrac{1}{5}$.

Remaining work $= \left(1 - \dfrac{1}{5} \right) = \dfrac{4}{5}$

Now, $\dfrac{4}{5}$ work is done by y in 32 days.

Whole work will be done by y in $\left(32 \times \dfrac{5}{4} \right) = 40$ days.

11. (c) $\left(x + \dfrac{1}{x} \right) = 4$

On squaring both sides

$$
x^2 + \frac{1}{x^2} + 2 = 16
$$

$$\Rightarrow x^2 + \frac{1}{x^2} = 14$$

On squaring again

$$x^4 + \frac{1}{x^4} + 2 = 196$$

$$\Rightarrow x^4 + \frac{1}{x^4} = 194$$

12. (c) $p = q + 5$
$$\Rightarrow p - q = 5$$
$$p^2 + q^2 = 55$$
$$\therefore (p - q)^2 + 2pq = 55$$
$$\Rightarrow 25 + 2pq = 55$$
$$\Rightarrow 2pq = 30$$
$$\Rightarrow pq = 15$$

13. (c) Income in 2012 = ₹26,64,000
Every year % of increase in income = 20%
So, income of company in 2012 = 26,64,000
$$\times \frac{100}{120} \times \frac{100}{120} = ₹18,50,000$$

14. (b) Let the required distance be x km.
$$\frac{x}{\frac{5}{2}} - \frac{x}{3} = \frac{16}{60}$$

$$\Rightarrow \frac{2x}{5} - \frac{x}{3} = \frac{4}{15}$$

$$\Rightarrow \frac{6x - 5x}{15} = \frac{4}{15} \Rightarrow x = 4 \,\text{km}.$$

15. (c) $(A + B)$'s 1 day's work $= \dfrac{1}{8}$

$(B + C)$'s 1 day's work $= \dfrac{1}{12}$

$(C + A)$'s 1 day's work $= \dfrac{1}{8}$

On adding,
$2(A + B + C)$'s 1 day's work

$$= \frac{1}{8} + \frac{1}{12} + \frac{1}{8} = \frac{3 + 2 + 3}{24} = \frac{8}{24} = \frac{1}{3}$$

$$\therefore (A + B + C)\text{'s 1 day's work} = \frac{1}{6}$$

Hence, the work will be completed in 6 days.

16. (b) Distance covered by wheel in one revolution
= Circumference of wheel

$$= \frac{11000}{5000} = \frac{11}{5} \,\text{m}$$

$$= \frac{11}{5} \times 100 \,\text{cm} = 220 \,\text{cm}$$

$$\therefore 2\pi r = 220$$

$$\Rightarrow 2 \times \frac{22}{7} \times r = 220$$

$$\Rightarrow r = \frac{220 \times 7}{2 \times 22} = 35 \,\text{cm}$$

17. (d) Side of a square $= \sqrt{81} = 9$ cm
$\therefore$ Length of the wire
$= 4 \times 9 = 36$ cm.
$\therefore$ Perimeter of semi-circle $= (\pi + 2)r$
where r = radius

$$\Rightarrow \left(\frac{22}{7} + 2 \right) r = 36$$

$$\Rightarrow \frac{36}{7} r = 36$$

$$\Rightarrow r = \frac{36 \times 7}{36} = 7 \,\text{cm}.$$

18. (b) First number × second number
= HCF × LCM
$\Rightarrow 84 \times$ second number $= 12 \times 336$
$\therefore$ Second number

$$= \frac{12 \times 336}{84} = 48$$

$$p \times q = \text{HCF} \times \text{LCM}$$

$$q = \frac{12 \times 336}{84} = 48$$

19. (b) $\dfrac{15}{16} = 0.94; \quad \dfrac{19}{20} = 0.95$

$\dfrac{24}{25} = 0.96; \quad \dfrac{34}{35} = 0.97$

20. (c) $M + T + W = 90°$ ...(i)

$T + W + Th = 99°$ ...(ii)

By equation (ii) − (i)

$Th − M = 9° \Rightarrow Th − 32 = 9$

$\Rightarrow Th = 9° + 32 = 41° C.$

21. (a) Let the marked price be ₹ x.

$\therefore$ In case I, SP $= ₹ \dfrac{70x}{100}$

Single discount equivalent to successive discounts of 20% and 10%.

$= \left(20 + 10 − \dfrac{20 \times 10}{100}\right)\% = 28\%$

$\therefore$ S.P. in this case $= ₹ \dfrac{72x}{100}$

$\therefore \dfrac{72x}{100} − \dfrac{70x}{100} = ₹ 72$

$\Rightarrow \dfrac{2x}{100} = 72$

$\therefore x = \dfrac{72 \times 100}{2} = ₹ 3600$

22. (b) Percentage decrease $= \dfrac{25}{125} \times 100 = 20$

23. (d) Population 3 years ago $= \dfrac{9261}{\left(1 + \dfrac{5}{100}\right)^3}$

$= \dfrac{9261 \times 20 \times 20 \times 20}{21 \times 21 \times 21} = 8000$

24. (a) $\dfrac{S_2}{S_1} = \dfrac{6}{7}$ $\dfrac{T_2}{T_1} = \dfrac{7}{6}$

$\therefore 7x − 6x = 25$

$x = 25 \min$

$T_1 = 6x = 6 \times \dfrac{25}{60}$ hr

$= 2 hr \, 30 \min$

25. (a) If X completes a work in x days, Y will do the same in 3x days.

$\therefore 3x − x = 40 \Rightarrow x = 20$

$\therefore$ Y will finish the work in 60 days.

$\therefore$ (X + Y)'s 1 days work

$= \dfrac{1}{20} + \dfrac{1}{60} = \dfrac{3+1}{60} = \dfrac{1}{15}$

$\therefore$ Both together will complete the work in 15 days.

26. (a)
$$
\begin{array}{ccc}
A & C & E \\
+5\downarrow & +5\downarrow & +5\downarrow \\
F & H & J
\end{array}
$$

Similarly,
$$
\begin{array}{ccc}
O & Q & S \\
+5\downarrow & +5\downarrow & +5\downarrow \\
\boxed{T} & V & X
\end{array}
$$

27. (a) As, a saint practices meditation. Similarly, a scientist does research.

28. (c) $18/3 − 1 = 5$

$12/3 − 1 = \boxed{3}$

29. (a)

30. (c) $3 + 3 = 6$

$6 + 3 = 9$

$9 + 6 = 15$

$15 + 9 = 24$

$24 + 15 = 39$

$39 + 24 = 63$

$63 + 39 = 102$

31. (b) Govind's age = 48 years

According to question

Prem's age = 48/2 = 24 years

Prem's age seven years before = 24 − 7

                          = 17 years.

32. (a)
$$
\begin{array}{l}
\text{Mother} \\
\downarrow (-) \\
\text{Mother} = \text{Lady} \\
\downarrow (-) \\
\text{Man} \\
(+)
\end{array}
$$

man

(His) mother is the only daughter of (my) mother.   lady

33. (b) 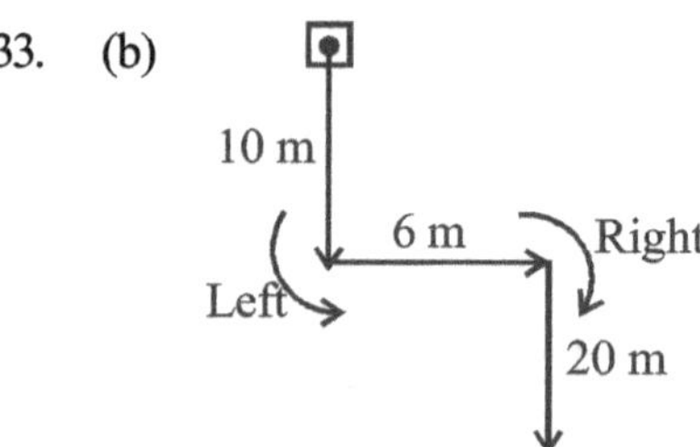

From the diagram, it is clear that Shankar started his journey from North to South.

34. (c) $7 \times 28 + 3 - 52 = 127$
$196 + 3 - 52$
$199 - 52 = 127$ (Incorrect)

35. (a)

11	22	121
3 | $11 + 5 + 4 \times 3$ $=16 + 12 = 28$ | 4	5 | $22 + 20 + 5 \times 3$ $= 42 + 15 = 57$ | 3	6 | $121 + 25 + 6 \times 5$ $=146 + 30 = 176$ | 5
5	20	25

36. (d) Suppose the present age of son is x years. Therefore, present age of the father = 4x years
According to question,
$x + 3 = 15$
$\therefore x = 15 - 3 = 12$ years
The present age of father
$= 4x = 4 \times 12 = 48$ years
$\therefore$ The present age of man's wife
$= 48 - 3 = 45$ years

37. (b) As, H O S P I T A L
↓ ↓ ↓ ↓ ↓ ↓ ↓ ↓
3 2 5 7 4 6 1 8

Therefore,

P O S T A L
↓ ↓ ↓ ↓ ↓ ↓
7 2 5 6 1 8

38. (d) Any written piece is recognised as song when it is sung by a singer. Therefore, only Conclusion I follows.

39. (a)

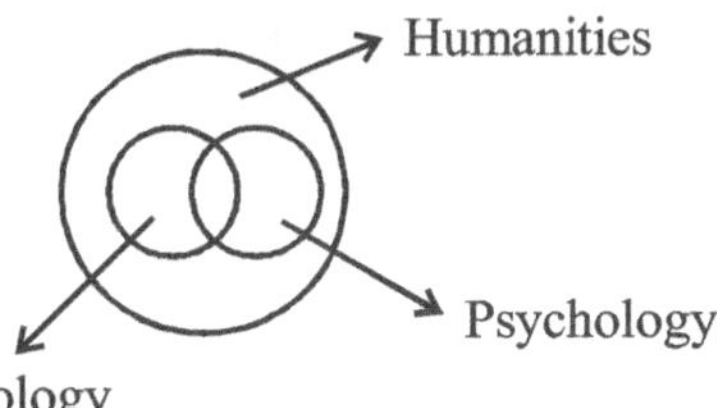

40. (d)
41. (d)
42. (b)

43. (c) As, D E L H I
↓ ↓ ↓ ↓ ↓
7 3 5 4 1

and C A L C U T T A
↓ ↓ ↓ ↓ ↓ ↓ ↓ ↓
8 2 5 8 9 6 6 2

Therefore,

C A L I C U T
↓ ↓ ↓ ↓ ↓ ↓ ↓
8 2 5 1 8 9 6

44. (b) R is father of X and Y.
S is maternal uncle of X and Y Considering the given options, it may be assumed that T is wife of R.

45. (d) The direction diagram is as follows:
Starting point

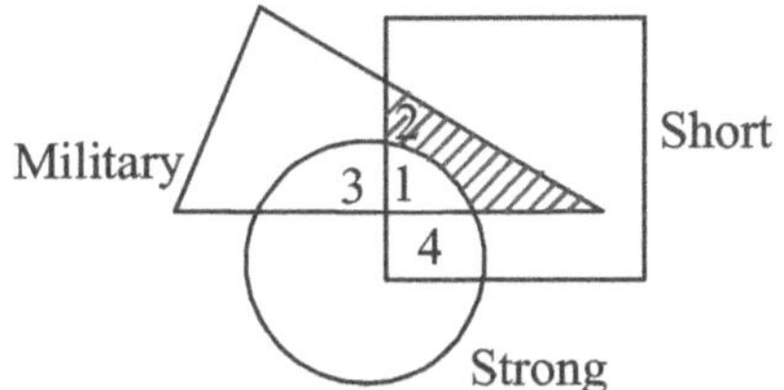

It is clearly shown that he is moving south direction.

46. (a) $25 \times 2 - 6 = 4 \times 11 + 0$
$\Rightarrow 50 - 6 = 44 + 0 , \Rightarrow 44 = 44$

47. (a)

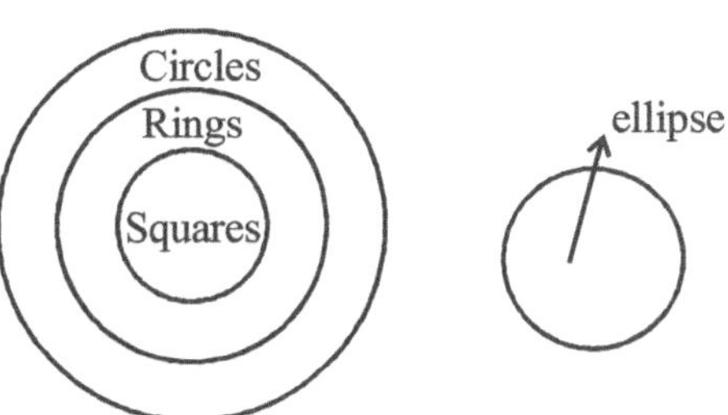

Hence, darken portion in above diagram represents that there are 2 military officers who are short but not strong.

48. (a) Married persons living in joint families but not working as school teachers are represented by 'D'.

49. (b)

Conclusion I : False
Conclusion II : True

50. (d)

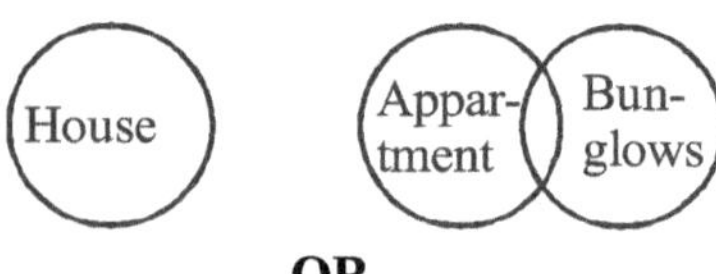

OR

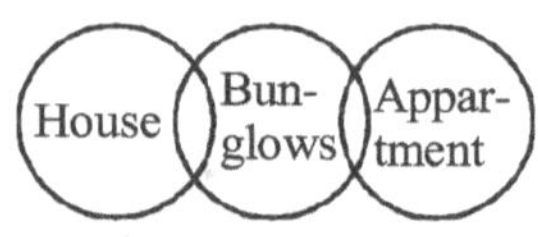

Conclusion I : False
Conclusion II : False

51. (a)	52. (a)	53. (a)	54. (a)	55. (a)
56. (c)	57. (c)	58. (d)	59. (c)	60. (b)
61. (a)	62. (a)	63. (d)	64. (d)	65. (c)
66. (c)	67. (c)	68. (a)	69. (b)	70. (a)
71. (c)	72. (b)	73. (d)	74. (a)	75. (a)
76. (a)	77. (d)	78. (c)	79. (a)	80. (b)
81. (c)	82. (d)	83. (d)	84. (c)	85. (d)
86. (b)	87. (a)	88. (b)	89. (b)	90. (d)
91. (d)	92. (c)	93. (c)	94. (a)	95. (a)
96. (b)	97. (d)	98. (a)	99. (c)	100. (a)

PRACTICE SET   4

Time: 90 minutes   **Max. Marks: 100**

MATHEMATICS

1. A man walks a certain distance and rides back taking a total time of 37 minutes. He could walk both ways in 55 minutes. How long would he take to ride both ways?
   - (a) 9.5 minutes
   - (b) 18 minutes
   - (c) 19 minutes
   - (d) 20 minutes

2. A bag contains 5 white and 7 black balls and a man draws 4 balls at random. The odds against these being all black is :
   - (a) 7 : 92
   - (b) 92 : 7
   - (c) 92 : 99
   - (d) 99 : 92

3. A trader marked a watch 40% above the cost price and then gave a discount of 10%. He made a net profit of ₹ 468 after paying a tax of 10% on the gross profit. What is the cost price of the watch?
   - (a) ₹ 1200
   - (b) ₹ 1800
   - (c) ₹ 2000
   - (d) ₹ 2340

4. 42 men take 25 days to dig a pond. If the pond would have to be dug in 14 days, then what is the number of men to be employed?
   - (a) 67
   - (b) 75
   - (c) 81
   - (d) 84

5. If the diameter of a wire is decreased by 10%, by how much per cent (approximately) will the length be increased to keep the volume constant?
   - (a) 5%
   - (b) 17%
   - (c) 20%
   - (d) 23%

6. From a series of 50 observations, an observation with value 45 is dropped but the mean remains the same. What was the mean of 50 observations?
   - (a) 50
   - (b) 49
   - (c) 45
   - (d) 40

7. Mr Duggal invested ₹20,000 with rate of interest @ 20 pcpa. The interest was compounded half-yearly for the first one year and in the next year it was compounded yearly. What will be the total interest earned at the end of two years?
   - (a) ₹ 8,800
   - (b) ₹ 9,040
   - (c) `8,040
   - (d) ₹ 9,800

8. If the area of a circle, inscribed in an equilateral triangle is 4π cm², then what is the area of the triangle?
   - (a) $12\sqrt{3}$ cm²
   - (b) $9\sqrt{3}$ cm²
   - (c) $8\sqrt{3}$ cm²
   - (d) 18 cm²

9. The prize money of ₹ 1,800 is divided among 3 students A, B and C in such a way that 4 times the share of A is equal to 6 times the share of B, which is equal to 3 times the share of C. Then A's share is
   - (a) ₹ 400
   - (b) ₹ 600
   - (c) ₹ 700
   - (d) ₹ 800

10. The ratio of the length and the breadth of a rectangle is 4 : 3 and the area of the rectangle is 1728 sq cm. What is the ratio of the breadth and the area of the rectangle ?
    - (a) 1 : 38
    - (b) 1 : 24
    - (c) 1 : 42
    - (d) 1 : 48

11. A person has four iron bars whose lengths are 24 m, 36 m, 48 m and 72 m respectively. This person wants to cut pieces of same length from each of four bars. What is the least number of total pieces if he is to cut without any wastage?
    - (a) 10
    - (b) 15
    - (c) 20
    - (d) 25

12. What number should be added to or subtracted from each term of the ratio 17 : 24 so that it becomes equal to 1 : 2?

(a) 5 is subtracted   (b) 10 is added
(c) 7 is added   (d) 10 is subtracted

13. The ratio of age of two boys is 5 : 6. After two years the ratio will be 7 : 8. The ratio of their ages after 12 years will be
(a) 11/12   (b) 22/24
(c) 15/16   (d) 17/18

14. The volume (in m^3) of rain water that can be collected from 1.5 hectares of ground in a rainfall of 5 cm is
(a) 75   (b) 750
(c) 7500   (d) 75000

15. If $\dfrac{3x+5}{5x-2} = \dfrac{2}{3}$, then the value of x is :
(a) 11   (b) 19
(c) 23   (d) 7

16. If 'n' be any natural number, then by which largest number $(n^3 - n)$ is always divisible ?
(a) 3   (b) 6
(c) 12   (d) 18

17. The mean of 19 observation is 24. If the mean of the first 10 observations is 17 and that of the last 10 observations is 24, find the 10th observation.
(a) 65   (b) 37
(c) −46   (d) 53

18. Successive discounts of 10%, 20% and 30% is equivalent to a single discount of
(a) 60%   (b) 49.6%
(c) 40.5%   (d) 36%

19. 72% of the students of a certain class took Biology and 44% took Mathematics. If each student took Biology or Mathematics and 40 took both, the total number of students in the class was
(a) 200   (b) 230
(c) 250   (d) 320

20. In certain years a sum of money is doubled itself at $6\dfrac{1}{4}\%$ simple interest per annum, then the required time will be
(a) $12\dfrac{1}{2}$ years   (b) 8 years
(c) $10\dfrac{2}{3}$ years   (d) 16 years

21. Walking at 5 km/hr a student reaches his school from his house 15 minutes early and walking at 3 km/hr he is late by 9 minutes. What is the distance between his school and his house?
(a) 5 km   (b) 8 km
(c) 3 km   (d) 2 km

22. 'x' number of men can finish a piece of work in 30 days. If there were 6 men more, the work could be finished in 10 days less. The original number of men is
(a) 6   (b) 10
(c) 12   (d) 15

23. The ratio of weekly incomes of A and B is 9 : 7 and the ratio of their expenditures is 4 : 3. If each saves ₹ 200 per week, then the sum of their weekly incomes is
(a) ₹ 3,200   (b) ₹ 4,200
(c) ₹ 4,800   (d) ₹ 5,600

24. A invests ₹ 64,000 in a business. After few months B joined him with ₹ 48,000. At the end of year, the total profit was divided between them in the ratio 2 : 1. After how many months did B join ?
(a) 7   (b) 8
(c) 4   (d) 6

25. The length of the two sides forming the right angle of a right-angled triangle are 6 cm and 8 cm. The length of its circum-radius is :
(a) 5 cm   (b) 7 cm
(c) 6 cm   (d) 10 cm

GENERAL INTELLIGENCE AND REASONING

DIRECTIONS (Qs. 26-28) : In questions, select the related word/letters/number from given alternatives.

26. ACE : BDF : : GIK : ?
(a) HJL   (b) AXP
(c) CFG   (d) GFC

27. hive : bee :: eyrie : ?
(a) Pigeon   (b) Sparrow
(c) Parrot   (d) Eagle

28. 5 : 27 :: 9 : ?
(a) 83   (b) 81
(c) 36   (d) 18

DIRECTIONS (Qs. 29-30) : In questions below, a series is given with one term missing. Choose the correct alternative from the given ones that will complete the series.

29. 24, 35, 20, 31, 16, 27, __ , __
    (a) 9, 9   (b) 5, 30
    (c) 8, 25   (d) 12, 23
30. AGMSY, CIOUA, EKQWC, ? IOUAG, KQWCI
    (a) GMSYE   (b) FMSYE
    (c) GNSYD   (d) FMYES
31. A is in the east of B which is in the North of C. If D is in the South of C, then in which direction of A, is D.
    (a) North – West   (b) South
    (c) East – East   (d) South–West
32. Introducing a boy, a girl said, "He is the son of the daughter of the father of my uncle." How is the boy related to the girl?
    (a) Brother   (b) Nephew
    (c) Uncle   (d) Son-in-law
33. Some equations are solved on the basis of a certain system. Find the correct answer for the unsolved equation on that basis.
    $5 * 6 = 35, 8 * 4 = 28, 6 * 8 = ?$
    (a) 46   (b) 34
    (c) 23   (d) 38

DIRECTION (Q. 34) : In the following question, select the missing number from the given responses.

34.

12	15	16
03	04	05
04	06	04
40	66	?

    (a) 104   (b) 320
    (c) 25   (d) 84

DIRECTION (Q. 35) : In the following question, two statements are given followed by four conclusions I, II, III and IV. You have to consider the statements to be true even if they seem to be at variance from commonly known facts. You have to decide which of the given conclusions, if any follow from the given statements.

---

35. **Statements :**
    I. Some cats are dogs.
    II. No dog is a toy.

    Conclusions :
    I. Some dogs are cats.
    II. Some toys are cats.
    III. Some cats are not toys.
    IV. All toys are cats.

(a) Only Conclusions I and either II or III.
(b) Only Conclusions II and III follow
(c) Only Conclusions I and II follow
(d) Only Conclusion I follows

36. At present, the ratio between the ages of Arun and Deepak is 4 : 3. After 6 years, Arun's age will be 26 years. What is the age of Deepak at present?
    (a) 15 years   (b) 19 years
    (c) 24 years   (d) 12 years

DIRECTION (Q. 37): In Question which one of the following diagrams represents the correct relationship among

---

37. Lion, Fox and Carnivorous

(a)    (b) 

(c)    (d) 

38. Which answer figure complete the form in question figure?

Question Figure

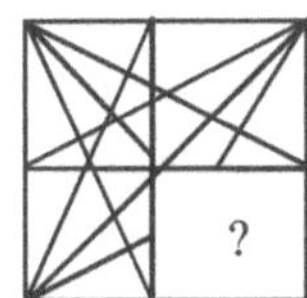

Answer Figures

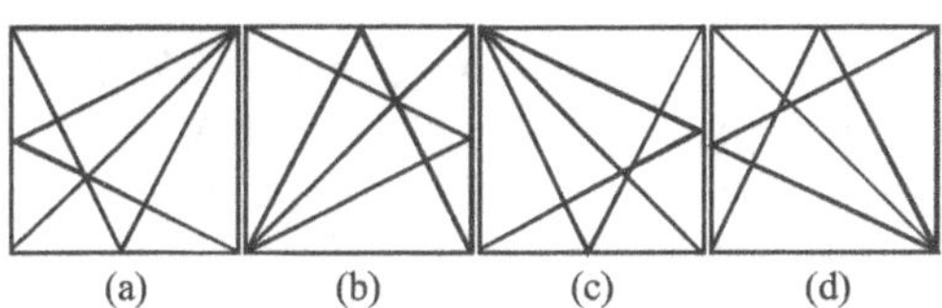

  (a)   (b)   (c)   (d)

DIRECTION (Q. 39) : In the following questions, if a mirror is placed on the line AB, then which of the answer figures is the right image of the given figure?

---

39. **Question Figure:**

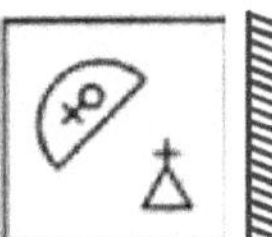

Answer Figures:

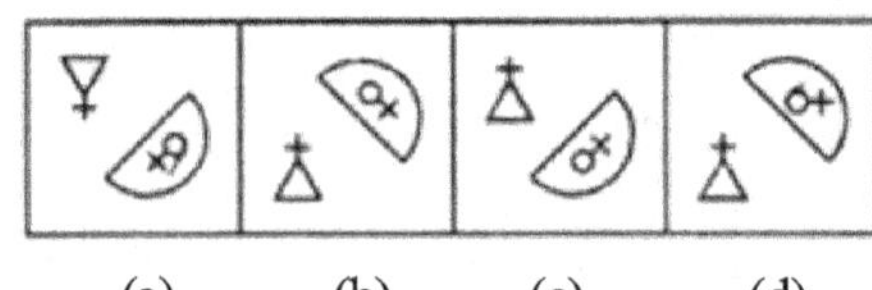

    (a)   (b)   (c)   (d)

40. How many triangles are there in the following square ?

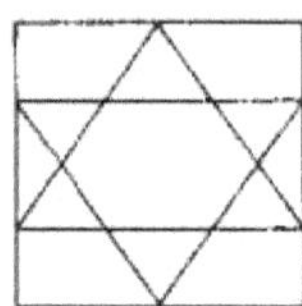

(a) 7   (b) 12   (c) 6   (d) 9

41. If in a certain code, RAMAYANA is written as PYKYWYLY, then how MAHABHARATA can be written in that code?
    (a) NBIBCIBSBUB   (b) LZGZAGZQZSZ
    (c) MCJCDJCTCVC   (d) KYFYZFYPYRY

42. Vinod introduces, Vishal as the son of the only brother of his father's wife. How is Vinod related to Vishal?
    (a) Cousin   (b) Brother
    (c) Son   (d) Uncle

43. If '−' stands for '÷' '+' stands for '×', '÷' for '−' and '×' for '+', which one of the following equations in correct?
    (a) $30 - 6 + 5 \times 4 \div 2 = 27$
    (b) $30 + 6 - 5 \div 4 \times 2 = 30$
    (c) $30 \times 6 \div 5 - 4 + 2 = 32$
    (d) $30 \div 6 \times 5 + 4 - 2 = 40$

44. If L denotes × M denotes ÷ ; P denotes + ; Q denotes − then $16\,P\,24\,M\,8\,Q\,6\,M\,2\,L\,3 = ?$
    (a) 10   (b) 9
    (c) 12   (d) 11

45.

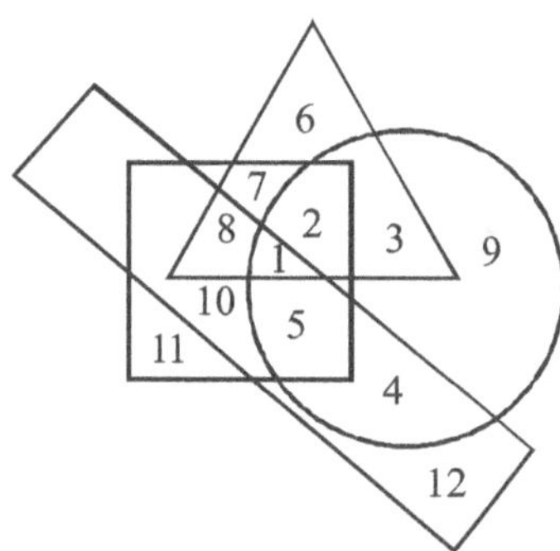

In the above figure, the circle stands for employed, the square stands for social worker, the triangle stands for illiterate and the rectangle stands for truthful. Employed, truthful and illiterate social workers are indicated by which region?

(a) 5   (b) 4   (c) 2   (d) 1

46. In the given figure, how many pens are blue?

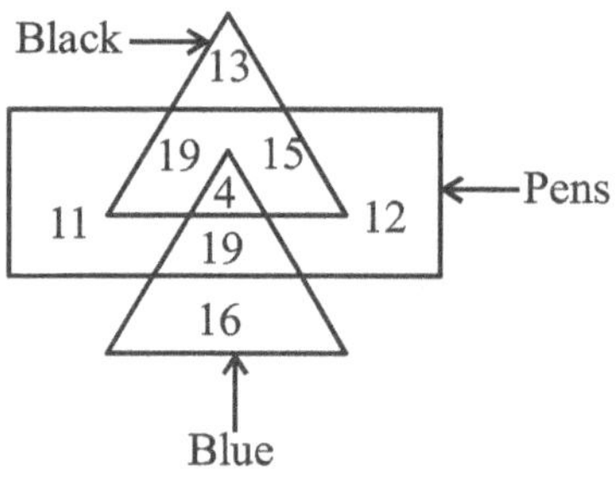

(a) 23   (b) 19   (c) 12   (d) 15

DIRECTIONS (Qs. 47-48): In each question below are given two/three statements followed by two conclusions numbered I and II. You have to take the given statements to be true even if they seem to be at variance with commonly known facts. Read all the conclusions and then decide which of the given conclusions logically follows from the given statements, disregarding commonly known facts. Give answer

(a) if only conclusion I follows.
(b) if only conclusion II follows.
(c) if either conclusion I or conclusion II follows.
(d) if neither conclusion I nor conclusion II follows.

47. **Statements** : Some gases are liquids.
    All liquids are water.
    Conclusions :
    I. All gases being water is a possibility.
    II. All such gases which are not water can never be liquids.

48. **Statements:** All minutes are seconds.
    All seconds are hours.
    No second is a day.
    Conclusions:
    I. No day is an hour.
    II. At least some hours are minutes.

DIRECTIONS (Qs. 49-50): In each question below is given a statement followed by two conclusions numbered I and II. You have to assume everything in the statement to be true, then consider the two conclusions together and decide which of them logically follows beyond a reasonable doubt from the information given in the statement.

49. **Statements:** All those political prisoners were released on bail who had gone to jail for reasons other than political dharnas. Bail was not granted to persons involved in murders.
    Conclusions:
    I. No political - prisoner had committed murder.
    II. Some politicians were not arrested.
    (a) Only conclusion I follows
    (b) Only conclusion II follows
    (c) Either I or II follows
    (d) Neither I nor II follows

50. **Statements:** Modern man influences his destiny by the choice he makes unlike in the past.
    Conclusions:
    I. Earlier there were fewer options available to man.
    II. There was no desire in the past to influence the destiny.
    (a) Only conclusion I follows
    (b) Only conclusion II follows
    (c) Either I or II follows
    (d) Neither I nor II follows

BASIC SCIENCE AND ENGINEERING

51. Which line type is thin and light?
    (a) Visible lines
    (b) center lines
    (c) construction lines
    (d) all of the above

52. The unit of absolute permittivity is
    (a) Fm (farad-metre)
    (b) Fm^{-1} (farad/metre)
    (c) Fm^{-2} (farad/metre^2)
    (d) F (farad)

53. Mass is property of a body that cannot be changed by its
    (a) location   (b) speed
    (c) shape   (d) all of above

54. Which of the following is the correct definition for Average speed?

(a) Average speed $= \dfrac{\text{total displacement}}{\text{total time}}$

(b) Average speed $= \dfrac{\text{total path length}}{\text{total time}}$

(c) Average speed $= \dfrac{\text{change in speed}}{\text{total time}}$

(d) Average speed $= \dfrac{\text{sum of all the speeds}}{\text{total time}}$

55. If a bulb uses energy of 100 J and remains on for 25 s, power consumed by bulb will be
    (a) 125 W   (b) 4 W
    (c) 2500 W   (c) 75 W

56. Expansion during heating
    (a) occurs only in solids
    (b) increases the weight of a material
    (c) generally decreases the density of a material
    (d) occurs at the same rate for all liquids and solids

57. The element in an electric stove is made of
    (a) copper   (b) nichrome
    (c) platinum   (d) tungsten

58. A wire cutter is an example of:
    (a) Lever of first order
    (b) Lever of second order
    (c) Lever of third order
    (d) None of these

59. Check list for Job Safety Analysis (JSA) consists of
    (a) Work area, material, machine, tools
    (b) Men, machine, material, tools
    (c) Men, machine, work area, tools
    (d) Men, work area Material, tools

60. Which of the following is a major environmental issue in mining activities?
    (a) Water pollution
    (b) Soil Degradation
    (c) Air pollution and dust
    (d) All of these

61. Sending an e-mail is similar to
    (a) picturing an event (b) narrating a story
    (c) writing a letter   (d) creating a drawing

62. Heat applied to a piece of metal will cause
    (a) increase in its mass

(b) increase in its volume
(c) increase in its density
(d) increase in its internal energy

63. Which set of lead grades has a grade out of sequence?
(a) H, HB, B, 3B   (b) 7B, H, F, 3H
(c) 6B, B, H, 4H   (d) 9H, HB, B, 2B

64. in first angle projection method, object is assumed to be placed in
(a) First quadrant
(b) Second quadrant
(c) Third Quadrant
(d) Fourth quadrant

65. Error due to manually stopping a stopwatch is termed as
(a) climax error
(b) human reaction error
(c) human reaction time
(d) ratability error

66. Gradient of a displacement-time graph gives
(a) Velocity of the moving object
(b) Distance travelled by the object
(c) Acceleration of the moving object
(d) None of the above

67. Making a body or machine to move to achieve a purpose is known as
(a) Power   (b) Work
(c) Energy   (d) Efficiency

68. At night a current of air blows from the colder land to the warmer sea is called as:
(a) Air Breezes
(b) Sea Breezes
(c) Land of the above
(d) none of the above

69. For which of the following 'ampere second' could be the unit?
(a) Reluctance   (b) Charge
(c) Power   (d) Energy

70. Ohm's law is not applicable to
(a) semi-conductors
(b) D. C. circuits
(c) small resistors
(d) high currents

71. OSHA (occupational safety and health act) assignment is to set standards and conduct ______
(a) Inspections   (b) Tests
(c) Analysis   (d) Estimation

72. Acceptable "Noise Pollution Level" in India range between:
(a) 16-35 dec   (b) 40-45 dec
(c) 70-100 dec   (d) 10-15 dec

73. Junk e-mail is also called______
(a) Spam   (b) Spoof
(c) Sniffer script   (d) Spool

74. The box that contains the central electronic components of the computer is the ______
(a) Motherboard   (b) System Unit
(c) Peripheral   (d) RAM

75. When should be the OSHA Form 300A posted?
(a) January   (b) February
(c) March   (d) April

GENERAL AWARENESS AND CURRENT AFFAIR

76. Who among the following is the author of the book. 'The Namesake'?
(a) Arundhati Roy   (b) Amitava Ghosh
(c) Jhumpa Lahiri   (d) Kiran Desai

77. Who among the following was not a member of the Constituent Assembly?
(a) Sardar Vallabhbhai Patel
(b) Acharya JB Kriplani
(c) Lok Nayak Jayprakash
(d) K M Munshi

78. Carbon dioxide is called a greenhouse gas because
(a) its concentration remains always higher than other gases
(b) it is used in photosynthesis
(c) it absorbs infrared radiation .
(d) it emits visible radiation

79. Laser is a device to produce
(a) a beam of white light
(b) coherent light
(c) microwaves
(d) X-rays

80. In the human body, Cowper's glands form a part of which one of the following system?
(a) Digestive system
(b) Endocrine system
(c) Reproductive system
(d) Nervous system

81. Fiscal Policy in India is formulated by
    (a) the Reserve Bank of India
    (b) the Planning Commission
    (c) the Finance Ministry
    (d) the Securities and Exchange Board of India
82. Malaria in the human body is caused by which one of the following organisms?
    (a) Bacteria (b) Virus
    (c) Mosquito (d) Protozoan
83. The focal length of convex lens is
    (a) the same for all colours
    (b) shorter for blue light than for red
    (c) shorter for red light than for blue
    (d) maximum for yellow light
84. Which one of the following endocrine gland is situated in the neck?
    (a) Pancreas (b) Thyroid
    (c) Pituitary (d) Adrenals
85. Soil erosion can be prevented by
    (a) Increasing bird population
    (b) Afforestation
    (c) Removal of vegetation
    (d) Overgrazing
86. Earth received heat from the sun is known as:
    (a) Insolation (b) Infrared heat
    (c) Solar radiation (d) Thermal radiation
87. Who is the founder of quantum theory of radiation?
    (a) Einstein (b) Bohr
    (c) Plank (d) S.N. Bose
88. The Copernicus project, under which wind-sensing satellite "Aeolus" has been launched recently, is a joint project of __:
    (a) European Union and European Space Agency
    (b) ISRO and JAXA
    (c) NASA and ISRO
    (d) Roscosmos and ISRO
89. The International Council on Monuments and Sites (ICOMOS) has launched an initiative to save cultural heritage in flood-devastated Kerala. Where is the headquarters of ICOMOS?
    (a) Geneva
    (b) Paris
    (c) London
    (d) New York
90. Which Indian woman cricketer has recently announced her retirement from International T20 cricket?
    (a) Mansi Joshi
    (b) Puja Vastrakar
    (c) Shikha Pandey
    (d) Jhulan Goswami
91. The pigment involved photosynthetic activity is
    (a) anthocyanin (b) fucoxanthin
    (c) carotenoid (d) chlorophyII
92. The study of visceral organs is
    (a) Angiology (b) Arthrology
    (c) Anthrology (d) Splanchnology
93. What part of the eye gets inflamed and becomes pink when dusts gets into?
    (a) Cornea (b) Choroid
    (c) Conjunctiva (d) Sclerotic
94. In Ms-Word, Replace option comes under the …. Menu.
    (a) View (b) file
    (c) insert (d) edit
95. When did India join the United Nations?
    (a) 1945 (b) 1947
    (c) 1950 (d) 1954
96. World Heritage day observed on ?
    (a) 17 April (b) 18 April
    (c) 19 April (d) 20 April
97. Seaweeds are important source of _____
    (a) Fluorine (b) Chlorine
    (c) Bromine (d) Iodine
98. Which one of the following pairs is correctly matched?
    (a) Tetanus – BCG
    (b) Tuberculosis – ATS
    (c) Malaria – Chloroquin
    (d) Scurvy – Thiamin
99. Tear gas used by the police to disperse the mob contains _____
    (a) Carbon dioxide
    (b) Chlorine
    (c) Ammonia
    (d) Hydrogen Sulphide
100. 'Subroto Cup' is associated with which games/sports?
    (a) Hockey (b) Foot ball
    (c) Tennis (d) Badminton

HINTS & EXPLANATIONS

1. (c) To walk both ways, duration = 55 minutes

$\therefore$ To walk one way, duration = $\dfrac{55}{2}$ minutes

To walk one way + To ride one way = 37 minutes

$\therefore$ To ride both ways = $2 \times \dfrac{19}{2} = 19$ minutes

2. (b) There are $7 + 5 = 12$ balls in the bag and the number of ways in which 4 balls can be drawn is $^{12}C_4$ and the number of ways of drawing 4 black balls (out of seven) is $^{7}C_4$. Hence, P (4 black balls)

$$= \dfrac{^{7}C_4}{^{12}C_4} = \dfrac{7.6.5.4}{1.2.3.4} \times \dfrac{1.2.3.4}{12.11.10.9} = \dfrac{7}{99}$$

Thus the odds against the event 'all black balls' are

$$(1 - \dfrac{7}{99}) : \dfrac{7}{99} \; i.e., \; \dfrac{92}{99} : \dfrac{7}{99} \text{ or } 92 : 7$$

3. (c) Let the cost price of the watch = ₹x
After 40% marked price and 10% discount

$$= x \times \dfrac{90}{100} \times \dfrac{140}{100} = \dfrac{126x}{100}$$

$$\text{Profit} = \dfrac{126x}{100} - x = \dfrac{26x}{100}$$

According to question,
Pay 10% tax on profit

$$= \dfrac{26x}{100} \times \dfrac{90}{100} = 468$$

$$x = \dfrac{468 \times 100 \times 100}{26 \times 90} = ₹2000$$

4. (b) Let the number of men be n

Men	Days
42 $\downarrow$	25 $\uparrow$
n	14

$$\therefore \quad \dfrac{n}{42} = \dfrac{25}{14} \Rightarrow n = 75$$

5. (d) Volume of wire = $\pi r^2 h$

New radius of the wire = $\dfrac{r \times 90}{100} = \dfrac{9r}{10}$

Let new length of the wire be L.

$\therefore$ Volume of new wire

$$= \pi \left(\dfrac{9r}{10}\right)^2 \times L = \dfrac{81}{100} \pi r^2 L$$

According to question,

$$\pi r^2 h = \dfrac{81}{100} \pi r^2 L \Rightarrow L = \dfrac{100}{81} h$$

$$\text{Increase in length} = \dfrac{100}{81} h - h = \dfrac{19}{81} h$$

$$\text{Percent increase} = \dfrac{19/81 h}{h} \times 100\% = 23.46\%$$

$$= 23\% \text{ (approx)}$$

6. (c) Let the observation mean = x
$\therefore$ Sum of 50 observations = 50x
According to question,

$$\therefore \quad \dfrac{50x - 45}{49} = x$$

$$\Rightarrow \quad 50x - 45 = 49x$$

$$\therefore \quad x = 45$$

7. (b) Interest earned in 1st half of a year

$$= 20{,}000 \times \dfrac{1}{2} \times \dfrac{20}{100} = 2000$$

Similarly, During second half, interest earned = 2200

During second year, interest earned = 4840 (Note : Interest is calculated as compound)

Total interest earned at the end of two years = $2000 + 2200 + 4840 = ₹9040$.

8. (a) Since, area of circle = 4π cm² (given)

$$\Rightarrow \quad \pi r^2 = 4\pi \Rightarrow r = 2 \text{ cm}$$

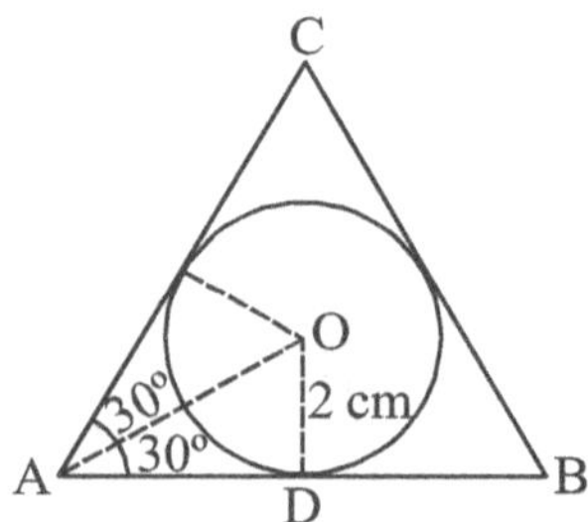

In $\triangle OAD$, $\tan 30° = \dfrac{OD}{AD} \Rightarrow AD = 2\sqrt{3}$ cm

Now, AB = 2 AD = $4\sqrt{3}$ cm

$\therefore$ Area of equilateral ΔABC

$$= \frac{\sqrt{3}}{4}(AB)^2 = \frac{\sqrt{3}}{4}(4\sqrt{3})^2 = 12\sqrt{3} \text{ cm}^2$$

9. (b) $4A = 6B \Rightarrow 2A = 3B \Rightarrow A:B = 3:2$
    $6B = 3C \Rightarrow 2B = C \Rightarrow B:C = 1:2$

$$A : B : C$$
$$3 : 2 \searrow 2$$
$$\searrow 1 : 2$$
$$\overline{3 : 2 : 4}$$

A's share

$$= \frac{3}{(3+2+4)} \times 1800 = \frac{3}{9} \times 1800 = 600$$

10. (d) $(4x)(3x) = 1728$
    $\Rightarrow x^2 = 144 \therefore x = 12$
    $\Rightarrow$ length $= 48$; breadth $= 36$

$$\therefore \text{ Required ratio} = \frac{36}{36 \times 48} = 1:48$$

11. (b) $24 = 12 \times 2,$
    $36 = 12 \times 3,$
    $48 = 12 \times 4,$
    and $72 = 12 \times 6$
    $\therefore$ HCF $(24, 36, 48, 72) = 12$
    Total pieces $= 2 + 3 + 4 + 6 = 15$

12. (d) Let the number x be added

$$\therefore \frac{17+x}{24+x} = \frac{1}{2}$$
$$\Rightarrow 34 + 2x = 24 + x$$
$$\Rightarrow 2x - x = 24 - 34$$
$$\Rightarrow x = -10$$

Hence, 10 should be subtracted.

13. (d) $\dfrac{A}{B} = \dfrac{5}{6} \Rightarrow B = \dfrac{6}{5}A$ ...(1)

$$\frac{A+2}{B+2} = \frac{7}{8} \Rightarrow 8A + 16 = 7B + 14 \Rightarrow 7B -$$
$8A = 2$ ...(2)
From (1) and (2), $A = 5, B = 6$

$$\frac{5+12}{6+12} = \frac{17}{18}$$

14. (b) 1 hectare $= 10000$ sq. metre
    $\therefore$ Area of the ground $= 15000$ sq. metre

$$\therefore \text{ Required volume} = 15000 \times \frac{5}{100} = 750 \text{ m}^3$$

15. (b) $\dfrac{3x+5}{5x-2} = \dfrac{2}{3}$
    $\Rightarrow$ $9x + 15 = 10x - 4$
    $\Rightarrow$ $15 + 4 = 10x - 9x$
    $\Rightarrow$ $x = 19$

16. (b) $n^3 - n = n(n^2 - 1)$
    $\Rightarrow n(n+1)(n-1)$
    For $n = 2$, $n^3 - n = 6$
    $2^3 - 2 = 6$
    i.e. $n^3 - n$ is always divisible by 6.

17. (c) 10th observation
    $= 24 \times 10 + 17 \times 10 - 19 \times 24$
    $= 240 + 170 - 456 = -46$

18. (b) Single equivalent discount for successive
    discounts of 10% and 20%.

$$= \left(10 + 20 - \frac{20 \times 10}{100}\right)\% = 28\%$$

Single equivalent discount for 28% and 30%

$$= \left(28 + 30 - \frac{28 \times 30}{100}\right)\% = 49.6\%$$

19. (c) Let the total number of students in the class be x.

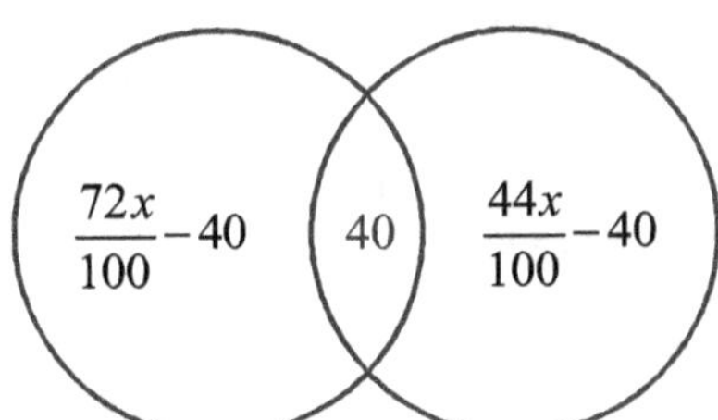

$$\because \frac{72x}{100} - 40 + 40 + \frac{44x}{100} - 40 = x$$

$$\Rightarrow \frac{72x}{100} + \frac{44x}{100} - x = 40$$

$$\Rightarrow \frac{16x}{100} = 40 \Rightarrow x = \frac{40 \times 100}{16}$$

$$\Rightarrow x = 250$$

20. (d) Let x be the principal amount
    'y' be the time to double the money.
    Then interest will also be 'x'.

$$\therefore \quad x = \frac{x \times 25 \times y}{4 \times 100}$$

$400 = 25y$ $\therefore y = 16$ years

21. (c) Let the required distance be x km.

$$\therefore \ \frac{x}{3} - \frac{x}{5} = \frac{24}{60}$$

$$\Rightarrow \frac{5x - 3x}{15} = \frac{2}{5} \Rightarrow \frac{2x}{3} = 2$$

$$\Rightarrow 2x = 2 \times 3 \Rightarrow x = 3 \text{ km}$$

22. (c) $m_1 d_1 = m_2 d_2$
$x(30) = (x+6)\,20$
$\Rightarrow 2x + 12 = 3x$
$\Rightarrow 3x - 2x = 12$
$\Rightarrow x = 12$ men

23. (a) Let weekly income of A and B be 9x and 7x
Expenditure = Income – Saving
ATQ

$$\frac{9x - 200}{7x - 200} = \frac{4}{3}$$

$27x - 600 = 28x - 800$
$x = 200$
Sum $= 200 \times 16 = 3200$

24. (c) Suppose, B Joined after x month
Then B's money was invested for $(12 - x)$ months
$\therefore$ According to question

$$\frac{64000 \times 12}{48000 \times (12 - x)} = \frac{2}{1}$$

$$\frac{16}{12 - x} = \frac{2}{1} \Rightarrow 16 = 24 - 2x$$

$2x = 24 - 16 \Rightarrow x = 4$
Hence, B joined after 4 months

25. (a) In a right angled Δ, the length of circumradius is half the length of hypotenuse.
$\therefore \quad H^2 = 6^2 + 8^2$
$H^2 = 36 + 64 \Rightarrow 100$
$H = 10$ cm
Circumradius $= 5$ cm

26. (a)

27. (d) A hive is a shelter for bees. Whereas, A eyrie is a large nest of an eagle.

28. (a) As, $5 \times 5 + 2 = 27$
Similarly, $9 \times 9 + 2 = \boxed{83}$

29. (d) There are two numbers series:

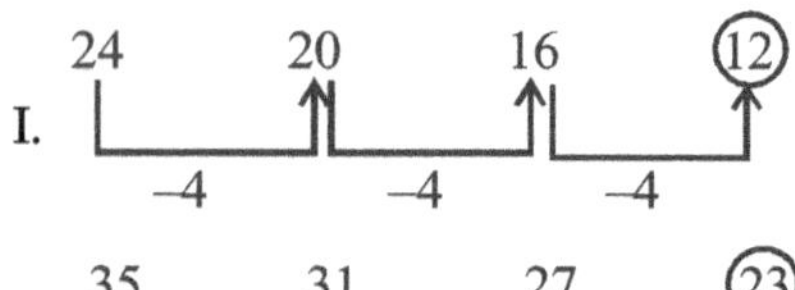

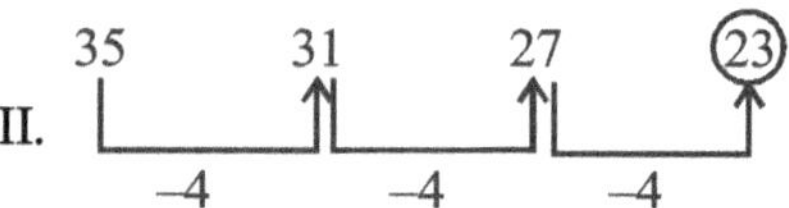

30. (a)   **31.** (d)

32. (a) The father of the boy's uncle $\rightarrow$ the grandfather of the boy and daughter of the grandfather $\rightarrow$ sister of father.

33. (a)

5   *   6/2   3 5
8   *   4/2   2 8
6   *   8/2   4 6

34. (d) First Column
$12 \times 3 + 4 = 40$
Second Column
$15 \times 4 + 6 = 66$
Third Column
$16 \times 5 + 4 = \boxed{84}$

35. (a)

Cats ( ) Dogs   Toy

OR
Conclusion I : True
II : Complementary Pair
III : Complementary Pair
IV : False
So, only conclusion I and either II or III.

36. (a) Suppose the present age of Arun is $4x$ years and that of Deepak is $3x$ years.
6 years hence,
Arun's age $= 4x + 6 = 26$
$\Rightarrow 4x = 26 - 6$

$$x = \frac{20}{4} = 5$$

$\therefore$ Present age of Deepak $= 3x = 15$ years

37. (c)   **38.** (d)   **39.** (b)   **40.** (b)

41. (d) As,

R	A	M	A	Y	A	N	A
−2↓	−2↓	−2↓	−2↓	−2↓	−2↓	−2↓	−2↓
P	Y	K	Y	W	Y	L	Y

Similarly,

M	A	H	A	B	H	A	R	A	T	A
−2↓	−2↓	−2↓	−2↓	−2↓	−2↓	−2↓	−2↓	−2↓	−2↓	−2↓
K	Y	F	Y	Z	F	Y	P	Y	R	Y

42. (a) Wife of Vinod's father means the mother of Vinod.

Only brother of Vinod's mother means maternal uncle of Vinod.

Therefore, Vinod is cousin of Vishal.

43. (a) $30 - 6 + 5 \times 4 \div 2 = 27$

$\Rightarrow 30 \div 6 \times 5 + 4 - 2 = 27$

$\Rightarrow 25 + 4 - 2 \Rightarrow 27 = 27$, option (a) is correct

$30 + 6 - 5 \div 4 \times 2 = 30$

$\Rightarrow 30 \times 6 \div 5 - 4 + 2 = 30$

$\Rightarrow 36 - 4 + 2 \neq 30$, option (b) is wrong

$30 \times 6 \div 5 - 4 + 2 = 32$

$\Rightarrow 30 + 6 - 5 \div 4 \times 2 \neq 32$, option (c) is wrong

$\Rightarrow 30 \div 6 \times 5 + 4 - 2 = 40$

$\Rightarrow 30 - 6 + 5 \times 4 \div 2 \neq 40$

option (d) is wrong.

44. (a)

L ⇒ ×	M ⇒ ÷
P ⇒ +	Q ⇒ −

$16 \, P \, 24 \, M \, 8 \, Q \, 6 \, M \, 2 \, L \, 3 = ?$

$\Rightarrow ? = 16 + 24 \div 8 - 6 \div 2 \times 3$

$\Rightarrow ? = 16 + 3 - 3 \times 3$

$\Rightarrow ? = 16 + 3 - 9 = \boxed{10}$

45. (d) Employed, truthful and illiterate social workers would be indicated by the region common to all the four geometrical figures. Such region is marked '1'.

46. (a) Total number of pens are blue = $19 + 4 = 23$.

47. (a)

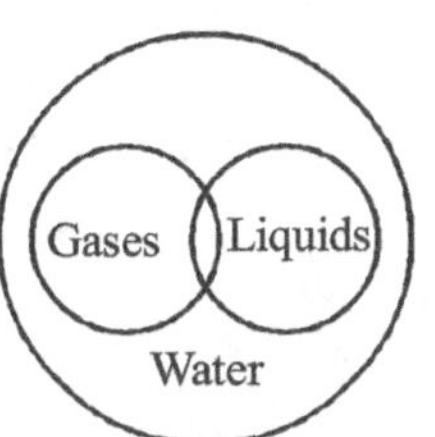

OR

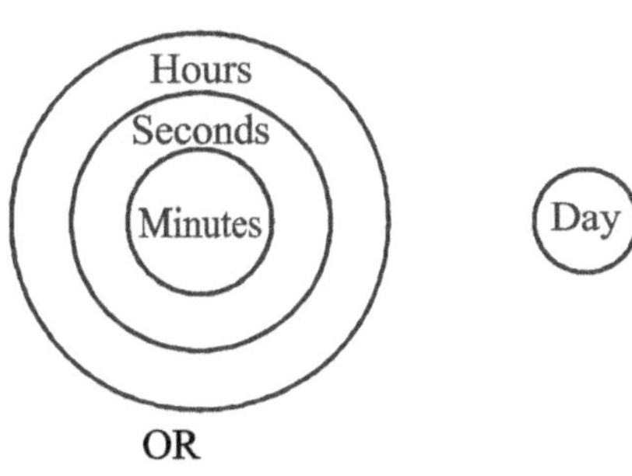

Conclusion I : True
Conclusion II : False

48. (b)

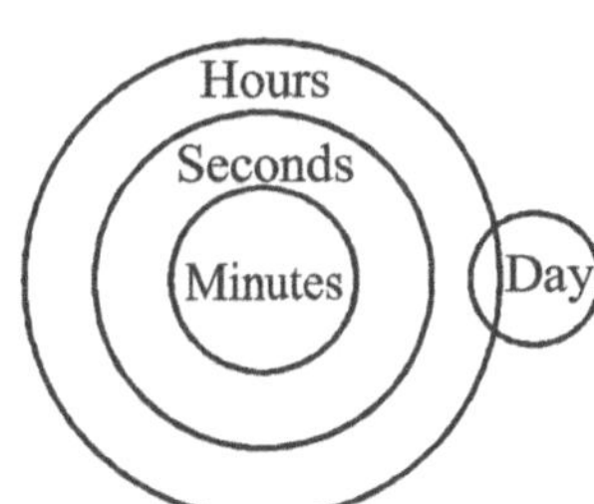

OR

Conclusion I : False
Conclusion II : True

49. (a) According to the statement, the political prisoners can be divided into two groups - those who were released and those who were put in jail for political dharnas. However, no person involved in murder was released. This means that no political prisoner had committed murder. So, I follows. Clearly, II is not directly related to the statement and does not follow.

50. (a) Clearly, I directly follows from the statement while II cannot be deduced from it.
51. (c) 52. (b) 53. (a) 54. (b)
55. (b) 56. (c) 57. (b) 58 (a)
59. (a) 60. (d) 61. (c) 62. (d)
63. (b) 64. (a) 65. (a) 66. (a)
67. (b) 68. (c) 69. (b) 70. (a)
71. (a) 72. (b) 73. (a) 74. (b)
75. (b) 76. (c) 77. (c) 78. (c)
79. (b) 80. (c) 81. (c) 82. (d)
83. (b) 84. (b) 85. (a) 86. (a)
87. (c) 88. (a) 89. (b) 90. (d)
91. (d) 92. (d) 93. (c) 94. (d)
95. (a) 96. (b) 97. (d) 98. (c)
99. (b) 100. (b)

PRACTICE SET 5

Time: 90 minutes   **Max. Marks - 100**

MATHEMATICS

1. What is the sum of the digits of the least number which when divided by 52, leaves 33 as remainder, when divided by 78 leaves 59 and when divided by 117, leaves 98 as remainder?
   (a) 17 (b) 18
   (c) 19 (d) 21

2. If the cost price of 15 articles is equal to the selling price of 12 articles, find gain %
   (a) 20% (b) 25%
   (c) 18% (d) 21%

3. 38L of milk was poured into a tub and the tub was found to be 5% empty. To completely fill the tub, what amount of additional milk must be poured?
   (a) $1L$ (b) $2L$
   (c) $3L$ (d) $4L$

4. Prakash, Sunil and Anil started a business jointly investing ₹11 lakhs, ₹16.5 lakhs and ₹8.25 lakhs respectively. The profit earned by them in the business at the end of three years was ₹19.5 lakhs. What will be the 50% of Anil's share in the profit?
   (a) ₹4.5 lakhs (b) ₹2.25 lakhs
   (c) ₹2.5 lakhs (d) ₹3.75 lakhs

5. A man borrowed some money from a private organisation at 5% simple interest per annum. He lended 50% of this money to another person at 10% compound interest per annum and thereby the man made a profit of ₹3205 in 4 years. The man borrowed
   (a) ₹80,000 (b) ₹1,00,000
   (c) ₹1,20,000 (d) ₹1,50,000

6. If ₹8400 is divided among A, B and C in the ratio $\dfrac{1}{5} : \dfrac{1}{6} : \dfrac{1}{10}$, what is the share of A?
   (a) ₹3200 (b) ₹3400
   (c) ₹3600 (d) ₹3800

7. There are 45 male and 15 female employees in an office. If the mean salary of the 60 employees is ₹4800 and the mean salary of the male employees is ₹5000, then the mean salary of the female employees is
   (a) ₹4200 (b) ₹4500
   (c) ₹5600 (d) ₹6000

8. Which one of the following relations for the numbers 10, 7, 8, 5, 6, 8, 5, 8 and 6 is correct?
   (a) Mean = Median (b) Mean = Mode
   (c) Mean > Median (d) Mean > Mode

9. By selling an artcile for ₹21,000, a man gains 5%. To get a profit of 15%, he has to sell it for
   (a) ₹19,800 (b) ₹20,700
   (c) ₹23,000 (d) ₹25,000

10. If 10 men or 18 boys can do a work in 15 days, then the number of days required by 15 men and 33 boys to do twice the work is
    (a) $4\dfrac{1}{2}$ days (b) 8 days
    (c) 9 days (d) 36 days

11. By decreasing 15° of each angle of a triangle, the ratios of their angles are 2 : 3 : 5. The radian measure of greatest angle is:
    (a) $11\pi/24$ (b) $\pi/12$
    (c) $\pi/24$ (d) $5\pi/24$

12. A river 3 m deep and 40 m wide is flowing at the rate of 2 km per hour. How much water (in litres) will fall into the sea in a minute?
    (a) 4,00,000 (b) 40,00,000
    (c) 40,000 (d) 4,000

13. If the difference of two numbers is 3 and the difference of their squares is 39; then the larger number is :
    (a) 9 (b) 12
    (c) 13 (d) 8

14. The H.C.F. and L.C.M. of two numebrs are 8 and 48 respectively. If one of the numbers is 24, then the other number is
    (a) 48 (b) 36
    (c) 24 (d) 16

15. The value of $\dfrac{2\frac{1}{3} - 1\frac{2}{11}}{3 + \cfrac{1}{3 + \cfrac{1}{3 + \cfrac{1}{3}}}}$ is

(a) $\dfrac{38}{109}$ (b) $\dfrac{109}{38}$

(c) 1 (d) $\dfrac{116}{109}$

16. The average age of a jury of 5 is 40. If a member aged 35 resigns and a man aged 25 becomes a member, then the average age of the new jury is
(a) 30 years   (b) 38 years
(c) 40 years   (d) 42 years

17. The price of an article was first increased by 10% and then again by 20%. If the last increased price be ₹ 33, the original price was
(a) ₹ 30   (b) ₹ 27.50
(c) ₹ 26.50   (d) ₹ 25

18. If the price of sugar is raised by 25%, find by how much percent a householder must reduce his consumption of sugar so as not to increase his expenditure?
(a) 10   (b) 20
(c) 18   (d) 25

19. A certain sum will amount to ₹ 12,100 in 2 years at 10% per annum of compound interest, interest being compounded annually. The sum is:
(a) ₹ 12000   (b) ₹ 6000
(c) ₹ 8000   (d) ₹ 10000

20. A work can be completed by P and Q in 12 days, Q and R in 15 days, R and P in 20 days. In how many days P alone can finish the work?
(a) 10 days   (b) 20 days
(c) 30 days   (d) 60 days

21. Among three numbers, the first is twice the second and thrice the third. If the average of the three numbers is 49.5, then the difference between the first and the third number is
(a) 54   (b) 28
(c) 39.5   (d) 41.5

22. Three numbers are in the ratio 1 : 2 : 3. By adding 5 to each of them, the new numbers are in the ratio 2 : 3 : 4. The numbers are :
(a) 5, 10, 15   (b) 10, 20, 30
(c) 15, 30, 45   (d) 1, 2, 3

23. The length of radius of a circumcircle of a triangle having sides 3 cm, 4 cm and 5 cm is:
(a) 2 cm   (b) 2.5 cm
(c) 3 cm   (d) 1.5 cm

24. If $5a + \dfrac{1}{3a} = 5$, then the value of $9a^2 + \dfrac{1}{25a^2}$ is
(a) $\dfrac{51}{5}$ (b) $\dfrac{29}{5}$
(c) $\dfrac{52}{5}$ (d) $\dfrac{39}{5}$

25. A man buys 3 cows and 8 goats in ₹ 47,200. Instead if he would have bought 8 cows and 3 goats, he had to pay ₹ 53,000 mroe. Cost of one cow is :
(a) ₹ 10,000   (b) ₹ 11,000
(c) ₹ 12,000   (d) ₹ 13,000

GENERAL INTELLIGENCE & REASONING

DIRECTIONS (Qs. 26-28) : In questions below, select the related word/letters/number from the given alternatives.

26. 9 : 24 :: ? : 6
(a) 3   (b) 2
(c) 1   (d) 5

27. STAR : SBUT :: WARD : ?
(a) XBAW   (b) ESBX
(c) FAME   (d) DRAW

28. Sty : Pig : : Byre : ?
(a) Eagle   (b) Cow
(c) Tiger   (d) Hem

29. If GOODNESS is coded as HNPCODTR, how can GREATNESS be written in that code?
(a) HQFZSMFRT   (b) HQFZUFRTM
(c) HQFZUODTR   (d) HQFZUMFRT

30. Seema walks 30 m North. Then she turns right and walks 30 m then she turns right and walks 55 m. Then she turns left and walks 20 m. Then she again turns left and walks 25m. How many metres away is she from her Original position?
(a) 45 m   (b) 50 m
(c) 66 m   (d) 55 m

31. Find out the correct answer for the unsolved equation on the basis of the given equation

    If $6 * 5 = 91$
    $8 * 7 = 169$
    $10 * 7 = 211$
    then $11 * 10 = ?$
    (a) 331   (b) 993
    (c) 678   (d) 845

32. Which of the following states the relationship between Manager, Labour Union and Worker?

    (a)  (b)

    (c)   (d)

33. 12 year old Rahul is three times as old as his brother Paras. How old will Rahul be when be is twice as old as Paras?
    (a) 14 years   (b) 20 years
    (c) 16 years   (d) 18 years

34. In the following question, select the missing number from the given responses.

    | 5 | 4 | 7 | 8 |
    | 6 | 9 | 5 | ? |
    | 3 | 7 | 2 | 6 |

    (a) 6   (b) 4
    (c) 10   (d) 8

35. There are five houses P, Q, R, S and T. P is right of Q and T is left of R and right of P. Q is right of S. Which house is in the middle?
    (a) P   (b) Q
    (c) T   (d) R

36. How many triangles are there in the given figure?

    (a) 5   (b) 12
    (c) 9   (d) 10

37. From the given answer figures, select the one in which the question figure is hidden/embedded in the same direction.

Question Figure:

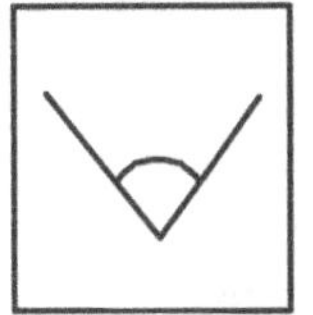

Answer Figures:

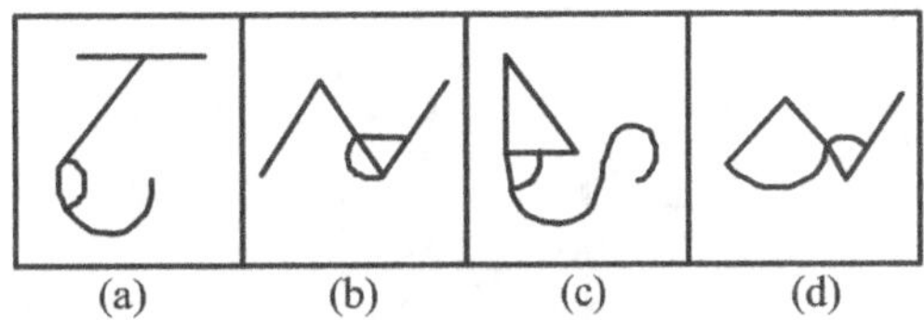

(a)   (b)   (c)   (d)

38. Which is the correct image if the picture is held in front of a mirror?

Question figure:

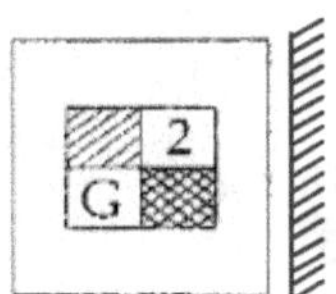

Answer figures:

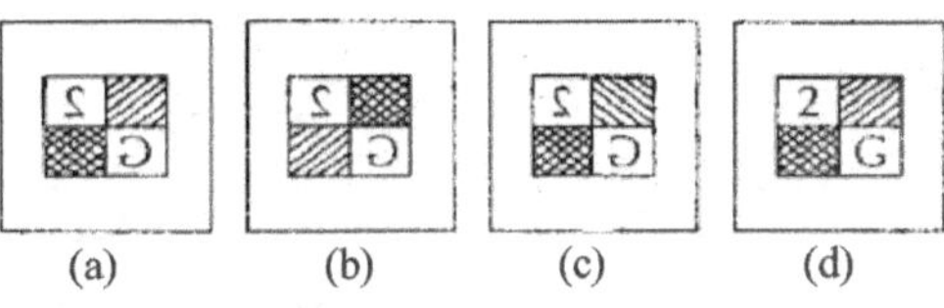

(a)   (b)   (c)   (d)

DIRECTIONS (Qs. 39 & 40) : In each of the following questions, find the missing number/ letters/ figure from the given responses :

---

39. 36, 28, 24, 22 ?
    (a) 18   (b) 19
    (c) 21   (d) 22

40. 7, 9, 13, 21, 37, ?
    (a) 58   (b) 63
    (c) 69   (d) 72

41. If PEAR is written as GFDN, how is REAP written in this code?
    (a) FDNG   (b) NFDG
    (c) DNGF   (d) NDFG

42. Pointing towards a woman in a photograph Vijay said, "She is the daughter of the father of sister of my brother". How is the lady in the photograph related to Vijay?
    (a) Wife   (b) Mother
    (c) Sister   (d) Daughter

43. If P denotes ÷, Q denotes ×, R denotes +, and S denotes –, then, 1 8 Q 1 2 P 4 R 5 S 6 = _?_
    (a) 95　　　　　　(b) 53
    (c) 51　　　　　　(d) 57

44. If $33 + 45 = 30$, $90 + 26 = 40$, then $30 + 45 =$ _?_
    (a) 15　　　　　　(b) 14
    (c) 16　　　　　　(d) 18

45.

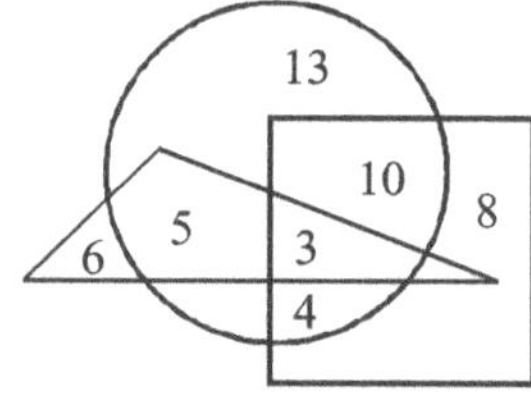

In the above diagram, square represents women, triangle represent the sub-inspectors of police and circle represents the graduates. Which numbered area represents women graduate sub-inspectors of police?
    (a) 5　　　　　　(b) 3
    (c) 8　　　　　　(d) 13

46. In the given figure, how many people study 2 subjects?

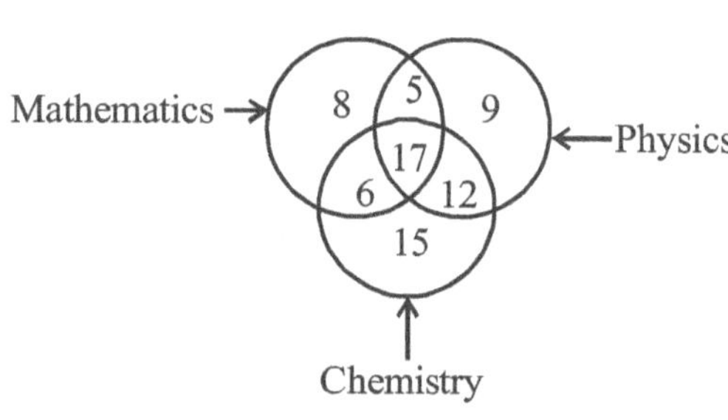

    (a) 11　　　　　　(b) 23
    (c) 12　　　　　　(d) 40

DIRECTIONS (Qs. 47-48) : In each of the questions below are given three statements followed by two conclusions numbered I and II. You have to take the given statements to be true even if they seem to be at variance from commonly known facts and then decide which of the given conclusions logically follows from the statements disregarding commonly known facts.

Give answer (a) if only conclusion I follows.
Give answer (b) if only conclusion II follows.
Give answer (c) if either conclusion I or conclusion II follows.
Give answer (d) if both conclusions I and II follow.

47. **Statements:**
    Some casual are formal.
    All formal are expensive.
    All expensive are elegant.
    Conclusions:
    I.　All formal are elegant.
    II.　Some casual are expensive.

48. **Statements:**
    All roses are red.
    Some red are colour.
    All colour are paints.
    Conclusions:
    I.　Some red are paints.
    II.　All red are roses.

Directions (Qs. 49-50): In each question below is given a statement followed by two conclusions numbered I and II. You have to assume everything in the statement to be true, then consider the two conclusions together and decide which of them logically follows beyond a reasonable doubt from the information given in the statement.

49. **Statements**: People who speak too much against dowry are those who had taken it themselves.
    Conclusions:
    I.　It is easier said than done.
    II.　People have double standards.
    (a) Only conclusion I follows
    (b) Only conclusion II follows
    (c) Either I or II follows
    (d) Both I and II follow

50. **Statements**: The national norm is 100 beds per thousand populations but in this state, 150 beds per thousand are available in the hospitals.
    Conclusions:
    I.　Our national norm is appropriate.
    II.　The state's health system is taking adequate care in this regard.
    (a) Only conclusion I follows
    (b) Only conclusion II follows
    (c) Either I or II follows
    (d) Neither I nor II follows

BASIC SCIENCE AND ENGINEERING

51. Which tool can be used to draw a 90 degree angle?
    (a) 30/60 triangle　　(b) protractor
    (c) drafting machine　(d) all of these

52. Which of the following is a dimensional constant?
    (a) Refractive index
    (b) Poissons ratio
    (c) Strain
    (d) Gravitational constant

53. Mass remains ______ throughout the universe.
    (a) varies   (b) zero
    (c) constant   (d) negative

54. Average speed is
    (a) a measure of how fast something is moving
    (b) the distance covered per unit of time
    (c) always measured in terms of a unit of distance divided by a unit of time
    (d) all of the above

55. Solar energy can also be converted directly into electricity by
    (a) solar cars   (b) mercury
    (c) plasma   (d) solar cells

56. Lamp black absorbs radiant heat which is near about
    (a) 90%   (b) 98%
    (c) 100%   (d) 50%

57. Siemens or Mho ($\mho$) is the unit of __________?
    (a) Conductance   (b) Admittance
    (c) Both 1 & 2   (d) None of the above

58. A Ferris wheel is an example of which kind of simple machine?
    (a) Fixed pulley   (b) Movable pulley
    (c) Wheel and axle (d) Incline plane

59. What increases the risk of accidents involving electricity at your workplace?
    (a) The use of chargeable tools.
    (b) The use of spark-free tools.
    (c) The use of un-insulated tools
    (d) None of these.

60. Which of the following is a natural source of Air pollution?
    (a) Storms
    (b) Acid rain
    (c) Precipitation
    (d) Volcanic eruptions

61. What is the difference between a CD-ROM and a CD-RW?
    (a) They are the same – just two different terms used by different manufacturers
    (b) A CD-ROM can be written to and a CD-RW cannot
    (c) A CD-RW can be read & written to, but a CD-ROM can only be read from CD.
    (d) A CD-ROM holds more information than a CD-RW

62. Pendulum bob cannot attain its initial height because
    (a) it continues to lose energy in thermal form
    (b) it continues to lose energy in sound form
    (c) it continues to lose energy in light form
    (d) it continues to lose energy in potential form

63. An axonometric drawing which has all three axes divided by equal angles is:
    (a) dimetric   (b) trimetric
    (c) orthographic   (d) isometric

64. Dimensional formula of latent heat
    (a) $M^0L^2T^{-2}$ (b) MLT^{-2}
    (c) ML^2T^{-2} (d) ML^2T^{-2}

65. Force due to pull of gravity is called
    (a) Weight   (b) Force
    (c) Mass   (d) Tension

66. When speed of object changes, velocity
    (a) remains same   (b) also changes
    (c) decreases   (d) increases

67. When the distance covered by an object is directly proportional to time, it is said to travel with ________.
    (a) zero velocity
    (b) constant speed
    (c) constant acceleration
    (d) uniform acceleration

68. When force is applied on an object but object does not move, it means that
    (a) no power is used   (b) no work is done
    (c) work is done   (d) power is used

69. A wooden spoon is dipped in a cup of ice cream. Its other end.
    (a) becomes cold by the process of radiation.
    (b) becomes cold by the process of conduction.
    (c) "becomes not become cold".
    (d) becomes cold by the process of convection.

70. In a series circuit with unequal resistances
   (a) the highest resistance has the most of the current through it
   (b) the lowest resistance has the highest voltage drop
   (c) the lowest resistance has the highest current
   (d) the highest resistance has the highest voltage drop

71. Which is an example of a wheel and axle that makes work easier by reducing friction?
   (a) wheelbarrow   (b) screwdriver
   (c) ladder   (d) pencil sharpener

72. What should you do to reduce the amount of effort needed to lift something using a first class lever?
   (a) Move the fulcrum closer to the effort
   (b) move the fulcrum to the middle of the lever
   (c) move the fulcrum closer to the load
   (d) None of these.

73. 'Green House Effect' means
   (a) cultivation of crops in green house to conserve heat
   (b) trapping of solar energy due to carbon dioxide gases
   (c) trapping of solar energy by earth upper surface
   (d) increase of heat due to atmospheric pollution

74. Which of the following is an example of an optical disk?
   (a) Digital versatile disks
   (b) Magnetic disks
   (c) Memory disks
   (d) Data bus disks

75. ______are attempts by individuals to obtain confidential information from you by falsifying their identity
   (a) Phishing trips   (b) Computer viruses
   (c) Phishing scams   (d) Spyware scams

GENERAL AWARENESS AND CURRENT AFFAIR

76. A boat will submerge when it displaces water equal to its own –
   (a) volume   (b) weight
   (c) surface area   (d) density

77. Which organ of Human body is affected by Alzheimer disease?
   (a) Brain   (b) Bone Marrow
   (c) Lung   (d) Intestine

78. What is the chemical name of vitamin E ?
   (a) Calciferol   (b) Tocopherol
   (c) Riboflavin   (d) Phylloquinone

79. According to the Constitution of India, the Right to Property is a –
   (a) Fundamental Right
   (b) Directive Principle
   (c) Legal Right
   (d) Social Right

80. The mirror used in search light is –
   (a) Concave Mirror   (b) Convex Mirror
   (c) Plane Mirror   (d) None of these

81. Photoelectric effect is
   (a) an instantaneous process
   (b) delayed process
   (c) emission of protons
   (d) emission of neutrons

82. The layer of atmosphere close to the earth's surface is called:
   (a) Exosphere   (b) Ionosphere
   (c) Stratosphere   (d) Troposphere

83. Which union ministry has organized the 2nd meeting of National Council on India's Nutrition Challenges under POSHAN Abhiyaan in New Delhi?
   (a) Ministry of Information and Broadcasting
   (b) Ministry of Panchayati Raj
   (c) Ministry of Food Processing Industries
   (d) Ministry of Women and Child Development

84. Which former chairman of Coal India Ltd (CIL) has authored the book "When Coal Turned Gold: The Making of a Maharatna Company"?
   (a) Gopal Singh
   (b) PB Bhattacharyya
   (c) Suresh Kumar
   (d) Sutirtha Bhattacharya

85. Which state government has launched smartphone scheme "Sanchar Kranti Yojna" to the people of the state?
    (a) Madhya Pradesh (b) Chhattisgarh
    (c) Odisha (d) Jharkhand

86. Who is known as the 'Lady with the Lamp'?
    (a) Sarojini Naidu
    (b) Joan of Arc
    (c) Mother Teresa
    (d) Florence Nightingale

87. The government of which state has instituted the 'Tansen Samman' ?
    (a) Uttar Pradesh (b) Madhya Pradesh
    (c) Gujarat (d) Maharashtra

88. In which state the folk painting 'Madhubani' is popular?
    (a) West Bengal (b) Orissa
    (c) Bihar (d) Assam

89. A substance that stimulates the production of antibodies when introduces into a living organism is known as _____
    (a) Carcinogen (b) androgen
    (c) antigen (d) Oestrogen

90. Electron microscope was given by _____
    (a) Knoll and Ruska (b) Robert Koch
    (c) Leeuwenhock (d) C.P. Swanson

91. Convectional rainfall occurs in _____
    (a) Equatorial region (b) Temperate region
    (c) Tropical region (d) Polar region

92. 'Darwin finches' refer to a group of _____
    (a) Fishes (b) Lizards
    (c) Birds (d) Amphibians

93. Where has the world's largest monolithic statue of Buddha been installed?
    (a) Bamiyan (b) Hyderabad
    (c) Kandy (d) Lhasa

94. The largest fresh water lake in India is
    (a) Wular lake (b) Nainital lake
    (c) Dal lake (d) Bhimtal lake

95. The Indian Supercomputer built by CRL, Pune which ranked fourth fastest in the world and most powerful in Asia is called
    (a) EKA (b) SAGA
    (c) Virgo (d) Param

96. A solution is
    (a) a solid dissolved in water
    (b) a mixture of two liquids
    (c) a homogeneous mixture of two or more substances
    (d) a solid dissolved in a liquid

97. The first organic compound synthesised in the laboratory was
    (a) lactic acid (b) glucose
    (c) urea (d) uric acid

98. The buffer action of blood is due to the presence of
    (a) Cl^- and HCO_3^-
    (b) HCO_3^- and H_2CO_3
    (c) HCl and NaCl
    (d) Cl^- and CO_3^{--}

99. Which one of the following contains maximum percentage of carbon ?
    (a) Wrought iron
    (b) High speed steel
    (c) Castiron
    (d) Stainless steel

100. If a body moves with a constant speed in a circle
    (a) no acceleration is produced in it
    (b) its velocity remains constant
    (c) no work is done on it
    (d) no force acts on it

HINTS & EXPLANATIONS

1. (a) Here, $52 - 33 = 78 - 59 = 117 - 98 = 19$
    Now, $52 = 13 \times 2 \times 2$
    $78 = 13 \times 2 \times 3$
    $117 = 13 \times 3 \times 3$
    $\therefore$ LCM $= 13 \times 2 \times 2 \times 3 \times 3 = 468$
    $\therefore$ Required number $= 468 - 19 = 449$
    Hence, the sum of digits is 17.

2. (b) Percentage profit $= \dfrac{15 - 12}{12} \times 100 = 25$

3. (b) Let tub capacity x L.

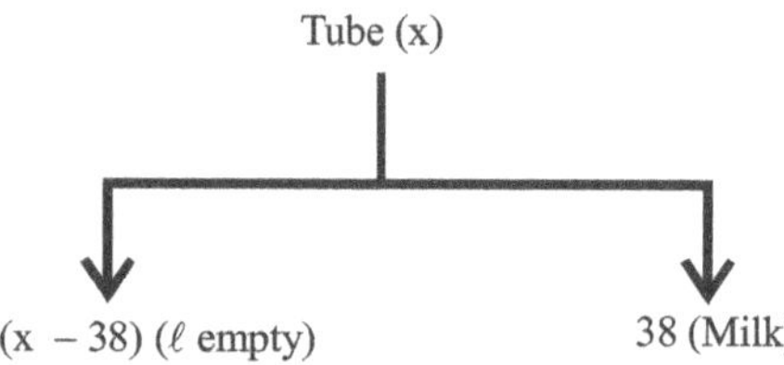

    Now, $x \times \dfrac{95}{100} = 38$
    $x = 40\,L,$
    Additional milk $= 40\,L - 38\,L = 2\,L.$

4. (b) Profit will be shared in the ratio of
    $11 \times 3 : 16.5 \times 3 : 8.25 \times 3$
    $= 11 : 16.5 : 8.25$
    $= 44 : 66 : 33$
    Anil's share in the profit
    $= \dfrac{33}{143} \times 19.5 = ₹4.5$ lakh
    50% of Anil's share $= ₹2.25$ lakh

5. (b) Let the required amount $= p$
    $$\dfrac{P}{2}\left[\left(1 + \dfrac{10}{100}\right)^4 - 1\right] - \dfrac{P \times 4 \times 5}{100} = 3205$$
    $$\dfrac{P}{2}\left[\left(\dfrac{11}{10}\right)^4 - 1\right] - \dfrac{P}{5} = 3205$$
    $$\dfrac{P}{2}\left[\dfrac{14641}{10000} - 1\right] - \dfrac{P}{5} = 3205$$
    $$\dfrac{P}{2}\left[\dfrac{4641}{10000}\right] - \dfrac{P}{5} = 3205$$
    $$\dfrac{4641P}{20000} - \dfrac{P}{5} = 3205$$
    $$\dfrac{641P}{20000} = 3205$$
    $$P = \dfrac{3205}{641} \times 20000 = ₹1,00,000$$

6. (c) Given, $A : B : C = \dfrac{1}{5} : \dfrac{1}{6} : \dfrac{1}{10} = 6 : 5 : 3$
    $\therefore$ Share of A
    $= \dfrac{6}{6 + 5 + 3} \times 8400 = \dfrac{6}{14} \times 8400$
    $= ₹3600$

7. (a) Given that,
    Number of male employees (M) $= 45$
    Number of female employees (F) $= 15$
    Mean salary of male employee $(\overline{x}_M)$
    $= ₹5000$
    Total number of employees $= (M + F)$
    $\qquad\qquad = 45 + 15 = 60$
    Mean salary of employees $(\overline{x}_{MF}) = ₹4800$
    Let mean salary of female employee is $\overline{x}_F$
    By formula,
    $$\overline{x}_{MF} = \dfrac{M\,\overline{x}_M + F\,\overline{x}_F}{(M + F)}$$
    $\Rightarrow \quad 4800 = \dfrac{45 \times 5000 + 15 \times \overline{x}_F}{60}$
    $\Rightarrow \quad 4800 \times 60 - 45 \times 5000 = 15 \times \overline{x}_F$
    $\therefore \quad \overline{x}_F = 4800 \times 4 - 3 \times 5000$
    $\quad = 300(16 \times 4 - 50) = 300 \times 14 = ₹4200.$

8. (a) Given numbers are 10, 7, 8, 5, 6, 8, 5, 8 and 6
    Arrange in ascending order
    $\qquad 5, 5, 6, 6, 7, 8, 8, 8, 10$
    Total term, n $= 9$ (odd)
    Now,

    (i) Mean $= \dfrac{5 + 5 + 6 + 6 + 7 + 8 + 8 + 8 + 10}{9}$
    $\qquad\qquad = \dfrac{63}{9} = 7$

(ii) Median $= \left(\dfrac{n+1}{2}\right)$th term

$\qquad = \left(\dfrac{9+1}{2}\right)$th term

$\qquad = $ 5th term $= 7$

(iii) Mode $= 8$ because of higher frequency term

$\qquad \therefore \quad$ Mean $=$ Median

9. (c) C.P. $= \dfrac{100}{(100+5)} \times 21000$

$\qquad$ C.P $= ₹\,20000$

$\qquad$ New profit $= 15\%$

$\qquad$ New S.P $= \dfrac{(100+15)}{100} \times 20000 = ₹\,23000$

$\qquad \therefore \quad$ To get 15% profit he has to sell an article at ₹23000.

10. (c) 10 men in 15 days

$\qquad \Rightarrow$ 1 man can do the work in 150 days

$\qquad \Rightarrow$ 1 man can do twice the work in 300 days

$\qquad$ Similarly, 18 boys in 15 days

$\qquad \Rightarrow$ 1 boy can do the work in 270 days

$\qquad \Rightarrow$ 1 boy can do twice the work in 540 days

Now, if there are 15 men and 33 boys trying to do twice the work then

$$\left(15\times\dfrac{1}{300}\right)+\left(33\times\dfrac{1}{540}\right)$$

$$=\dfrac{1}{20}+\dfrac{11}{180}=\dfrac{9+11}{180}=\dfrac{20}{180}=\dfrac{1}{9}$$

$\Rightarrow$ It will take 9 days for 15 men and 33 Boys to do twice the work.

11. (a) $2x+3x+5x = 180° - 45° = 135°$

$\qquad \Rightarrow 10x = 135°$

$\qquad \Rightarrow x = \dfrac{135}{10} = \dfrac{27}{2}$

$\qquad \therefore$ Largest angle

$\qquad = 5x+15° = \left(5\times\dfrac{27}{2}\right)°+15°$

$\qquad = \dfrac{135+30}{2} = \dfrac{165°}{2}$

$\qquad \because 180° = \pi$ radian

$\qquad \therefore \dfrac{165°}{2} = \dfrac{\pi}{180}\times\dfrac{165}{2} = \dfrac{11\pi}{24}$ radian

12. (b) Volume of water flowed in an hour

$\qquad = 2000 \times 40 \times 3 \text{ m}^3$

$\qquad = 240000 \text{ m}^3$

$\qquad \therefore$ Volume of water flowed in 1 minute.

$\qquad = \dfrac{240000}{60} = 4000 \text{ m}^3$

$\qquad = 4000000 \text{ litre}$

13. (d) Let the numbers are x, y.

$\qquad x - y = 3 \qquad\qquad\qquad …(1)$

$\qquad x^2 - y^2 = 39$

$\qquad \Rightarrow (x-y)(x+y) = 39$

$\qquad \Rightarrow x+y = 13 \qquad\qquad …(2)$

$\qquad$ Adding eqn (1) and (2)

$\qquad x+y+x-y = 16$

$\qquad \Rightarrow x = 8$

$\qquad \therefore y = 3$

$\qquad$ Hence, 8 is the larger number.

14. (d) $p \times q = \text{HCF} \times \text{LCM}$

$\qquad \therefore$ Second number $= \dfrac{8\times 48}{24} = 16$

15. (a) Expression

$$= \dfrac{\dfrac{7}{3}-\dfrac{13}{11}}{3+\dfrac{1}{3+\dfrac{1}{\dfrac{9+1}{3}}}} = \dfrac{\dfrac{77-39}{33}}{3+\dfrac{1}{3+\dfrac{3}{10}}}$$

$$= \dfrac{\dfrac{38}{33}}{3+\dfrac{1}{\dfrac{30+3}{10}}} = \dfrac{\dfrac{38}{33}}{3+\dfrac{10}{33}}$$

$$= \dfrac{\dfrac{38}{33}}{\dfrac{99+10}{33}} = \dfrac{38}{33}\times\dfrac{33}{109} = \dfrac{38}{109}$$

16. (b) Required average

$$= \dfrac{40\times 5 - 35 + 25}{5} = \dfrac{190}{5} = 38 \text{ years}$$

17. (d) Net increase percentage

$$= \left(10 + 20 + \frac{20 \times 10}{100}\right)\% = 32\%$$

$$\therefore \ x \times \frac{132}{100} = 33$$

$$\Rightarrow x = \frac{33 \times 100}{132} = ₹\,25$$

18. (b) Percentage decrease $= \dfrac{25}{125} \times 100 = 20$

19. (d) Final rate of interest for two pens

$$= x + y + \frac{xy}{100}$$

$$= 10 + 10 + \frac{10 \times 10}{100} = 21\%$$

Let principal be P.

$$\Rightarrow P \times \frac{121}{100} = 12100$$

$$P = 100 \times 100 = ₹\,10000$$

20. (c) $(P + Q)$'s 1 day's work $= \dfrac{1}{12}$ ...(i)

$(Q + R)$'s 1 day's work $= \dfrac{1}{15}$ ...(ii)

$(R + P)$'s 1 day's work $= \dfrac{1}{20}$ ...(iii)

Adding all three equations, $2\,(P + Q + R)$'s 1 day's work

$$= \frac{1}{12} + \frac{1}{15} + \frac{1}{20} = \frac{5 + 4 + 3}{60} = \frac{12}{60} = \frac{1}{5}$$

$\therefore$ $(P + Q + R)$'s 1 day's work $= \dfrac{1}{10}$ ...(iv)

$\therefore$ P's 1 day's work
= Equation (iv) – equation (ii)

$$= \frac{1}{10} - \frac{1}{15} = \frac{3 - 2}{30} = \frac{1}{30}$$

$\therefore$ P alone will complete the work in 30 days,

21. (a) Let the second number be x.

$\therefore$ First number $= 2x$

$\therefore$ Third number $= \dfrac{2x}{3}$

$$\therefore 2x + x + \frac{2x}{3} = 49.5 \times 3$$

$$\Rightarrow 6x + 3x + 2x = 49.5 \times 9 = 445.5$$

$$\Rightarrow 11x = 445.5 \Rightarrow x = \frac{445.5}{11} = 40.5$$

$\therefore$ Required difference

$$= 2x - \frac{2x}{3} = \frac{4x}{3}$$

$$= \frac{4 \times 40.5}{3} = 54$$

22. (a) Number $= x,\ 2x$ and $3x$

$$\therefore \ \frac{x + 5}{2x + 5} = \frac{2}{3}$$

$$\Rightarrow 4x + 10 = 3x + 15$$

$$\Rightarrow x = 5$$

$$\Rightarrow \text{Number} = 5,\ 10 \text{ and } 15,$$

23. (b) Circumradius of a triangle

$$= \frac{abc}{\sqrt{(a + b + c)(a + b - c)(b + c - a)(a + c - b)}}$$

$$= \frac{3 \times 4 \times 5}{\sqrt{(3 + 4 + 5)(3 + 4 - 5)(4 + 5 - 3)(3 + 5 - 4)}}$$

$$= \frac{60}{\sqrt{12 \times 2 \times 6 \times 4}} = 2.5 \text{ cm}$$

24. (d) $5a + \dfrac{1}{3a} = 5$

Multiply by $\dfrac{3}{5}$ on both sides

$$\frac{3}{5}\left(5a + \frac{1}{3a}\right) = 5 \times \frac{3}{5}$$

$$3a + \frac{1}{5a} = 3$$

Squaring on both sides

$$9a^2 + \frac{1}{25a^2} + 2 \times 3a \times \frac{1}{5a} = 9$$

$$\Rightarrow 9a^2 + \frac{1}{25a^2} = 9 - \frac{6}{5} = \frac{39}{5}$$

25. (c) C.P of 1 cow $= ₹\ x$
C.P of a goat $= ₹\ y$
$3x + 8y = 47200$ ...(i)
$\Rightarrow 8x + 3y = 100200$ ...(ii)
By equation (i) $\times 3 - $ (ii) $\times 8$,
$9x + 24y - 64x - 24y$
$= 141600 - 801600$
$\Rightarrow 55x = 660000$

$x = \dfrac{660000}{55} = ₹12000$

26. (a) As, $9 \times 3 - 3 = 24$
$3 \times 3 - 3 = 6$

27. (b) 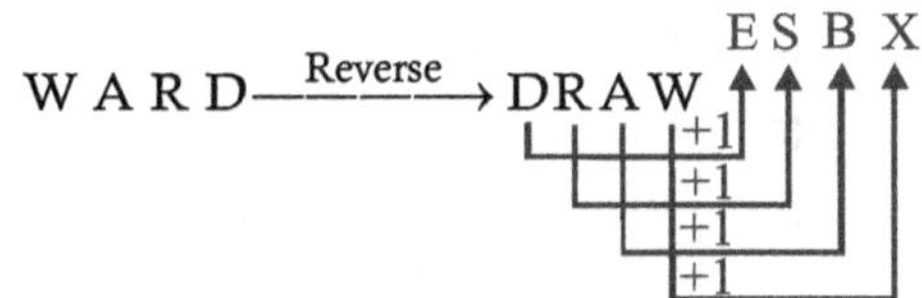

Similarly,

28. (b) The resting place of pig is called Sty. Similarly, the resting place of cow is called Byre.

29. (d)

30. (b) Required distance $= 30\,m + 20\,m = 50\,m$

31. (a) As, $6 \times 5 = 30$
$30 \times 3 + 1 = 91$
$8 \times 7 = 56$
$56 \times 3 + 1 = 169$
$10 \times 7 = 70$
$70 \times 3 + 1 = 211$
Similarly,
$11 \times 10 = 110$
$110 \times 3 + 1 = \boxed{331}$

32. (a)

33. (c) Rahul's present age $= 12$ yrs,
Paras present age $= 4$ yrs
Let Rahul be twice as old as Paras after x yrs from now.
Then, $12 + x = 2\,(4 + x)$
$= 12 + x = 8 + 2x \Rightarrow x = 4$
Hence, Rahul's required age $= 12 + x \Rightarrow 16$ yrs

34. (c) As, $(5 + 4 + 7)/2 = 8$
$(3 + 7 + 2)/2 = 6$
Similarly,
$(6 + 9 + 5)/2 = 10$.

35. (a)
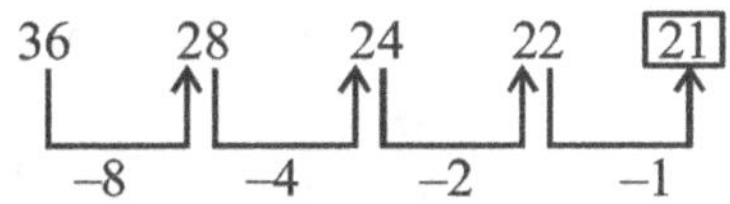

36. (d)
37. (d) 38. (c)
39. (c) The pattern is as follows :
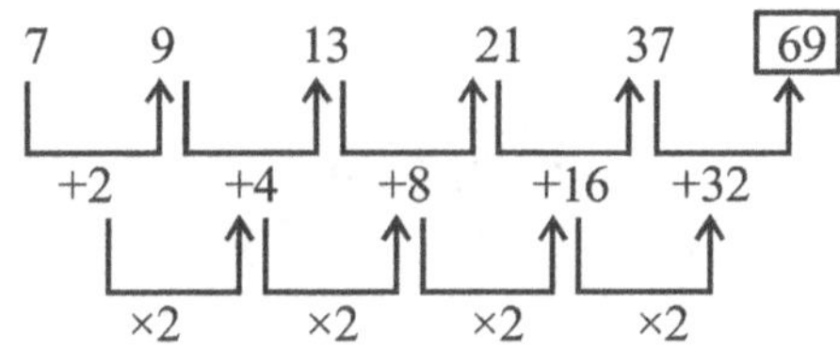

40. (c) The pattern is as follows :

7   9   13   21   37 $\boxed{69}$

$+2$ $+4$ $+8$ $+16$ $+32$

$\times 2$ $\times 2$ $\times 2$ $\times 2$

41. (b) As,

P   E   A   R
↓   ↓   ↓   ↓
G   F   D   N

Therefore,

R   E   A   P
↓   ↓   ↓   ↓
N   F   D   G

42. (c) Sister of my brother = My sister
Father of my sister = My father
Daughter of my father = My sister

43. (b)

$P \Rightarrow \div$	$Q \Rightarrow \times$
$R \Rightarrow +$	$S \Rightarrow -$

$18\,Q\,12\,P\,4\,R\,5\,S\,6 = ?$
$\Rightarrow ? = 18 \times 12 \div 4 + 5 - 6$
$\Rightarrow ? = 18 \times 3 + 5 - 6$
$\Rightarrow ? = 54 + 5 - 6 = \boxed{53}$

44. (a) As, $3 + 3 + 4 + 5 = 15 \Rightarrow 1 + 5 = 6$
    and, $6 \times 5 = 30$
    $9 + 0 + 2 + 6 = 17 \Rightarrow 1 + 7 = 8$
    and, $8 \times 5 = 40$
    Similarly,
    $3 + 0 + 4 + 5 = 12 \Rightarrow 1 + 2 = 3$
    and, $3 \times 5 = \boxed{15}$

45. (b) Women graduate sub–inspectors of police
    can be represented by the region common
    to all the three geometrical figures. Such
    region is marked '3'.

46. (b) Total number of peoples, who study only
    2 subjects
    $\Rightarrow 5 + 12 + 6 = 23$

47. (d)

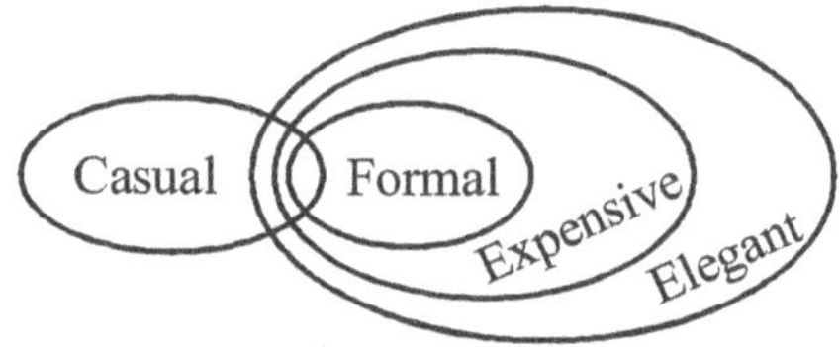

So, Both I and II follow.

48. (a)

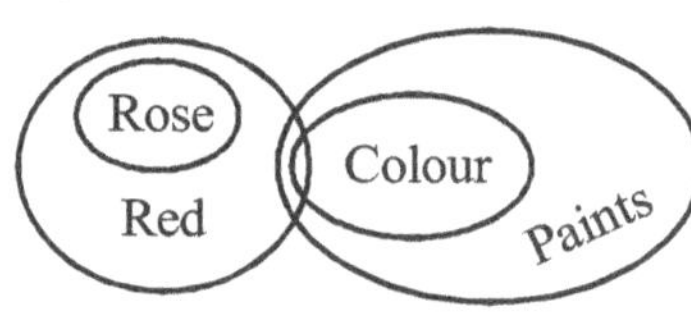

So, Only I follows.

49. (d) The statement clearly implies that it is easier
    to say than to do something and what
    people say is different from what they do.
    So, both I and II follow

50. (b) Whether the national norm is appropriate
    or not cannot be said. So, I does not follow.
    However, more number of beds per
    thousand population are available in the
    state. So, II follows.

51	(d)	52	(d)	53	(c)	54	(d)	55	(d)
56	(b)	57	(c)	58	(c)	59	(c)	60	(d)
61	(c)	62	(a)	63.	(d)	64.	(a)	65.	(a)
66.	(b)	67.	(b)	68.	(b)	69.	(c)	70.	(d)
71.	(b)	72.	(c)	73.	(b)	74.	(a)	75.	(c)
76.	(b)	77.	(a)	78.	(b)	79.	(c)	80.	(d)
81.	(a)	82.	(d)	83.	(d)	84.	(b)	85.	(b)
86.	(d)	87.	(b)	88.	(c)	89.	(c)	90.	(a)
91.	(a)	92.	(d)	93.	(d)	94.	(a)	95.	(a)
96.	(c)	97.	(c)	98.	(b)	99.	(c)	100.	(c)

PRACTICE SET   6

Time: 90 minutes   **Max. Marks - 100**

MATHEMATICS

1. The product of two successive numbers is 9506. Which is the smaller of the two numbers?
   (a) 96   (b) 97
   (c) 98   (d) 99

2. A cricket player after playing 10 tests scored 100 runs in the 11th test. As a result, the average of his runs is increased by 5. The present average of runs is
   (a) 45   (b) 40
   (c) 50   (d) 55

3. Two-thirds of three-fourths of one-fifth of a number is 15. What is 30 per cent of that number?
   (a) 45   (b) 60
   (c) 75   (d) 30

4. The sum of the circumference of a circle and the perimeter of a square is equal to 272 cm. The diameter of the circle is 56 cm. What is the sum of the areas of the circle and the square?
   (a) 2464 sq cm   (b) 2644 sq cm
   (c) 3040 sq cm   (d) Cannot be determined

5. Two persons contested an election of Parliament. The winning candidate secured 57% of the total votes polled and won by a majority of 42,000 votes. The number of total votes polled is
   (a) 4,00,000   (b) 5,00,000
   (c) 6,00,000   (d) 3,00,000

6. The remainder when 3^{21} is divided by 5 is
   (a) 1   (b) 2
   (c) 3   (d) 4

7. The average of 5 consecutive numbers is n. If the next two numbers are also included, the average of the 7 numbers will
   (a) increase by 2   (b) increase by 1
   (c) remain the same   (d) increase by 1.4

8. A shopkeeper allows a discount of 10% to his customers and still gains. 20%. Find the marked price of the article which costs ₹ 450.
   (a) ₹ 600   (b) ₹ 540
   (c) ₹ 660   (d) ₹ 580

9. A team played 40 games in a season and won in 24 of them. What percent of games played did the team win ?
   (a) 70%   (b) 40%
   (c) 60%   (d) 35%

10. A is thrice as good a workman as B and is, therefore, able to finish a piece of work in 60 days less than (b) The time (in days) in which they can do it working together is
   (a) 22   (b) $22\dfrac{1}{2}$
   (c) 23   (d) $23\dfrac{1}{4}$

11. ₹ 700 is divided among A, B, C in such a way that the ratio of the amount of A and B is 2 : 3 and that of B and C is 4 : 5. Find the amounts in ₹ each received, in the order A, B, C
   (a) ₹ 150, 250, 300   (b) ₹ 160, 240, 300
   (c) ₹ 150, 250, 290   (d) ₹ 150, 240, 310

12. The perimeter of a triangle is 40cm and its area is 60 cm^2. If the largest side measures 17cm, then the length (in cm) of the smallest side of the triangle is
   (a) 4   (b) 6
   (c) 8   (d) 15

13. The last digit of $(1001)^{2008} + 1002$ is
   (a) 0   (b) 3
   (b) 4   (d) 6

14. $\sqrt{6 + \sqrt{6 + \sqrt{6 + \ldots}}} = ?$
   (a) 2.3   (b) 3
   (c) 6   (d) 6.3

15. A batsman in his 12th innings makes a score of 63 runs and there by increases his average scores by 2. What is his average after the 12th innings?
   (a) 13   (b) 41
   (c) 49   (d) 87

16. What single discount is equivalent to two successive discounts of 20% and 15%?
    (a) 35%   (b) 32%
    (c) 34%   (d) 30%

17. X sells two articles for ₹ 4,000 each with no loss and no gain in the interaction. If one was sold at a gain of 25% the other is sold at a loss of
    (a) 25%   (b) $18\dfrac{2}{9}\%$
    (c) $16\dfrac{2}{3}\%$ (d) 20%

18. What would be the compound interest of ₹ 25000 for 2 yrs. at 5% per annum
    (a) ₹ 2500   (b) ₹ 2562.5
    (c) ₹ 2425.25   (d) ₹ 5512.5

19. With average speed of 40 km/hour, a train reaches its' destination in time. If it goes with an average speed of 35 km/hour, it is late by 15 minutes. The total journey is
    (a) 30 km   (b) 40 km
    (c) 70 km   (d) 80 km

20. Pipe A alone can fill a tank in 8 hours. Pipe B alone can fill it in 6 hours. If both the pipes are opened and after 2 hours pipe A is closed, then the other pipe will fill the tank in
    (a) 6 hours   (b) $3\dfrac{1}{2}$ hours
    (c) 4 hours   (d) $2\dfrac{1}{2}$ hours

21. The ratio of the quantities of an acid and water in a mixture is 1 : 3. If 5 litres of acid is further added to the mixture, the new ratio becomes 1 : 2. The quantity of new mixture in litres is
    (a) 32   (b) 40
    (c) 42   (d) 45

22. The ratio of monthly incomes of A, B is 6 : 5 and their monthly expenditures are in the ratio 4 : 3. If each of them saves ₹ 400 per month, find the sum of their monthly incomes.
    (a) ₹ 2300   (b) ₹ 2400
    (c) ₹ 2200   (d) ₹ 2500

23. A copper wire is bent in the form of square with an area of 121 cm². It the same wire is bent in the form of a circle, the radius (in cum) of the circle is
    (Take $\pi = \dfrac{22}{7}$)
    (a) 7   (b) 10
    (c) 11   (d) 14

24. A ship is moving at a speed of 30 km/hr. To know the depth of the ocean beneath it, it sends a radiowave which travels at a speed 200 m/s. The ship receives the signal after it has moved 500 m. The depth of the ocean is
    (a) 6 km   (b) 12 km
    (c) $\sqrt{6}$ m   (d) 8 km

25. If 12 men or 18 women can reap a field in 14 days, then working at the same rate, 8 men and 16 women can reap the same field in:
    (a) 9 days   (b) 5 days
    (c) 7 days   (d) 8 days

GENERAL INTELLIGENCE AND REASONING

DIRECTIONS (Qs. 26-28) : In questions below, select the related word/letter/number from the given alternatives.

26. King : Palace :: Eskimo : ?
    (a) Caravan   (b) Asylum
    (c) Monastery   (d) Igloo

27. AFKP : DINS :: WBGL : ?
    (a) ORUX   (b) OSWA
    (c) OTYD   (d) OQSU

28. 12 : 20 :: ?
    (a) 15 : 37   (b) 16 : 64
    (c) 27 : 48   (d) 30 : 42

DIRECTIONS (Qs. 29-30) : Complete the given series.

29. BDF, CFI, DHL, ?
    (a) CJM   (b) EIM
    (c) EJO   (d) EMI

30. 1, 3, 8, 19, 42, 89, ?
    (a) 108   (b) 184
    (c) 167   (d) 97

31. In a certain code DEPUTATION is written as ONTADEPUTI. How is DERIVATION written in that code ?
    (a) ONVADERITI   (b) ONDEVARITI
    (c) ONVAEDIRTI   (d) ONVADEIRIT

32. Sohan ranks seventh from the top and twenty-sixth from the bottom in a class. How many students are there in the class ?
    (a) 33   (b) 34
    (c) 31   (d) 32

33. Seema's younger brother Sohan is older than Seeta. Sweta is younger than Deepti but elder than Seema. Who is the eldest ?
    (a) Seeta   (b) Deepti
    (c) Seema   (d) Sweta

34. Find out which of the diagrams given in the alternatives correctly represents the relationship stated in the question.
Sharks, Whales, Turtles

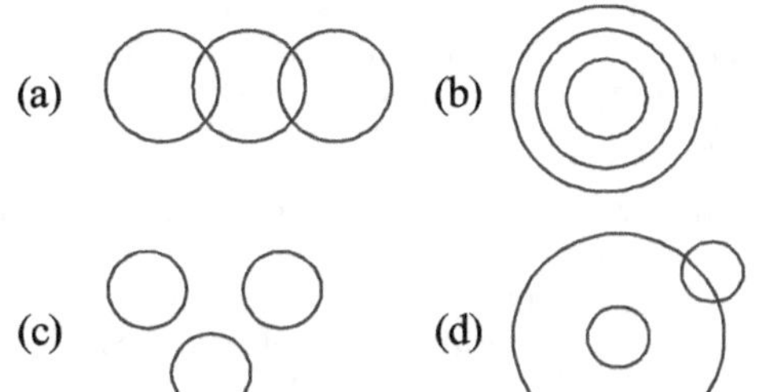

(a) (b)

(c) (d)

35. If a represents ÷, 'b' represents +, 'c' represents – and 'd' represents x then 24a 6d 4b 9c 8 = ?
   (a) 6
   (b) 17
   (c) 20
   (d) 19

36. Mani is double the age of Prabhu. Ramona is half the age of Prabhu. If Mani is sixty, find out the age of Ramona.
   (a) 20 years
   (b) 15 years
   (c) 10 years
   (d) 24 years

37. What number will come at the place of '?' mark.

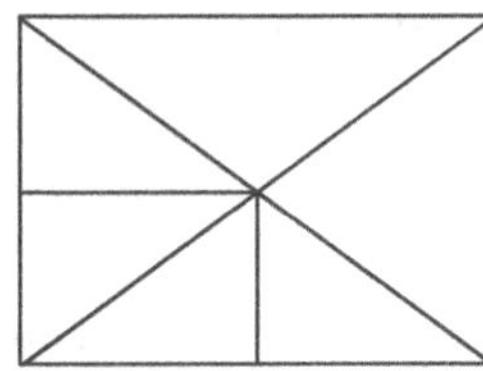

   (a) 53
   (b) 71
   (c) 76
   (d) 68

38. How many triangles are there in the following figure ?

   (a) 12
   (b) 8
   (c) 16
   (d) 15

39. **Statements :**
   1. All students are doctors.
   2. No doctor is leader.
   Conclusions :
   I. All leaders are students.
   II. Some doctors are students.
   (a) Only conclusion I follows
   (b) Only conclusion II follows
   (c) Both conclusions I and II follows
   (d) Neither conclusion I nor II follows

40. In question below, which anwser figure will complete the pattern in the question figure?
   Question figure :

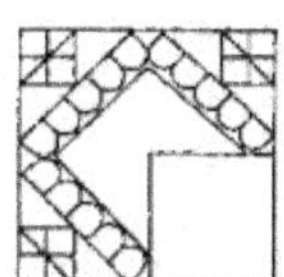

   Answer figures :

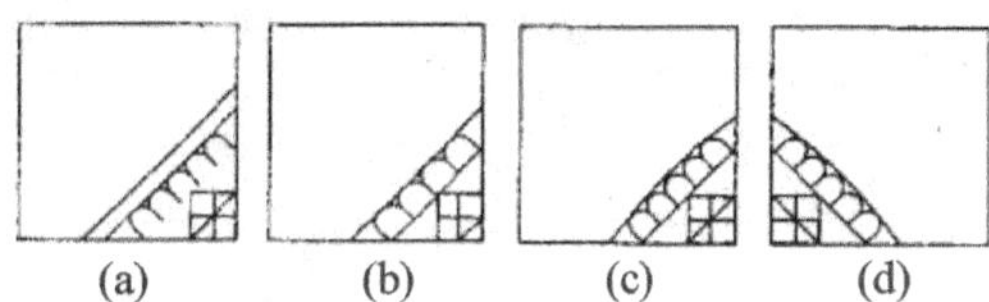

   (a) (b) (c) (d)

41. From the given answer figures, select the one in which the question figure is hidden/embedded.
   Question figure :

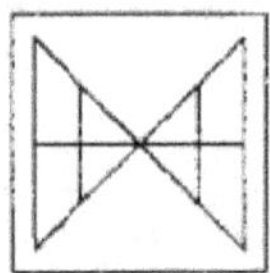

   Answer figures:

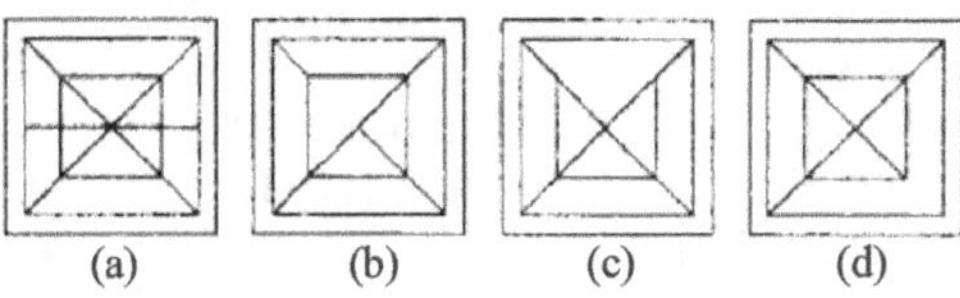

   (a) (b) (c) (d)

42. Nithya is Sam's Sister. Mogan is Sam's Father. Selvan is Rajan's Son. Rajan is Mogan's Brother. How is Nithya related to Selvan?
   (a) Daughter
   (b) Sister
   (c) Cousin
   (d) Wife

43. One evening, Raja started to walk toward the Sun. After walking a while, he turned to his right and again to his right. After walking a while, he again turned right. In which direction is he facing?
   (a) South
   (b) East
   (c) West
   (d) North

44. If + means ÷, – means ×, × means +, ÷ means –, give the value for $45 + 9 – 3 × 15 ÷ 2$
   (a) 40
   (b) 36
   (c) 56
   (d) 28

45. In the given diagram, circle represents professionals, square represents dancers, triangle represents musicians and rectangle

represents Europeans. Different regions in the diagram are numbered 1 to 11. Who among the following is neither a dancer nor a musician but is professional and not a European?

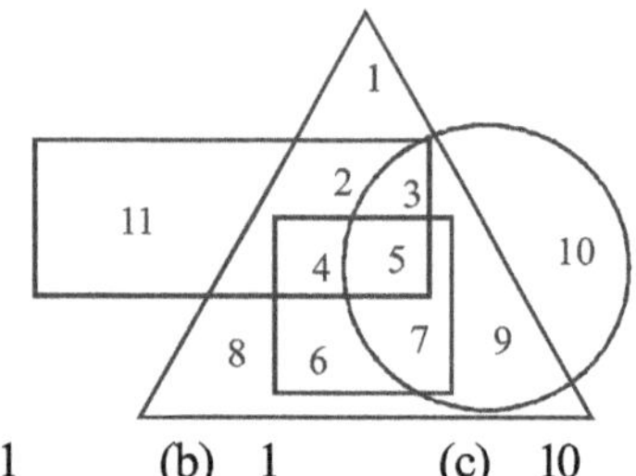

(a) 11   (b) 1   (c) 10   (d) 8

46. In the given figure, how many are musical toys?

(a) 53   (b) 61
(c) 42   (d) 45

DIRECTIONS (Qs. 47 -48) : In each of the questions below are given three statements followed by two conclusions numbered I and II. You have to take the given statements to be true even if they seem to be at variance from commonly known facts and then decide which of the given conclusions logically follows from the statements disregarding commonly known facts.

Give answer (a) if only conclusion I follows.
Give answer (b) if only conclusion II follows.
Give answer (c) if either conclusion I or conclusion II follows.
Give answer (d) if neither conclusion I nor conclusion II follows.

47. **Statements:**
     All towns are cities.
     All cities are urban.
     Some urban are rural.
     Conclusions:
     I.   Some towns are rural.
     II.   All rural are towns.

48. **Statements:**
     All medicines are tablets.
     Some tablets are tonics.
     Some tonics are bitter.
     Conclusions:
     I.   Some tablets are bitter.
     II.   No medicine is a tonic.

DIRECTIONS (Qs. 49-50): In each question below is given a statement followed by two conclusions numbered I and II. You have to assume everything in the statement to be true, then consider the two conclusions together and decide which of them logically follows beyond a reasonable doubt from the information given in the statement.

49   **Statements:** Our securities investments carry market risk. Consult your investment advisor or agent before investing.
     Conclusions:
     I.   One should not invest in securities.
     II.   The investment advisor calculates the market risk with certainty.
     (a)   Only conclusion I follows
     (b)   Only conclusion II follows
     (c)   Either I or II follows
     (d)   Neither I nor II follows

50. **Statements:** Money plays a vital role in politics.
     Conclusions:
     I.   The poor can never become politicians.
     II.   All the rich men take part in politics.
     (a)   Only conclusion I follows
     (b)   Only conclusion II follows
     (c)   Either I or II follows
     (d)   Neither I nor II follows

BASIC SCIENCE AND ENGINEERING

51. Which line type is thick and black?
     (a)   Visible lines
     (b)   center lines
     (c)   construction lines
     (d)   all of the above

52. One Wb/m^2 is equal to
     (a) 10^4 gauss   (b) $4\pi \times 10^{-3}$ gauss
     (c) 10^2 gauss   (d) 10^{-4} gauss

53. Sum of amount of matter in a substance is called its
     (a)   mass   (b)   weight
     (c)   length   (d)   volume

54. The slope of velocity-time graph for motion with uniform velocity is equal to
     (a)   final velocity   (b)   initial velocity
     (c)   zero   (d)   none of these

55. By burning large amount of fuel, we get
     (a)   petrol   (b)   heat
     (c)   sound   (d)   chemicals

56. An example of conductor of heat is
    (a) paper (b) cloth
    (c) air (d) aluminum

57. The energy of a charged capacitor resides in
    (a) the electric field only
    (b) the magnetic field only
    (c) Both the electric and magnetic fields
    (d) Neither in electric nor magnetic field

58. How many basic types of simple machines are there?
    (a) 2 (b) 3
    (c) 5 (d) 6

59. The Occupational Safety and Health Review Commission is a:
    (a) neutral agency
    (b) appellate body
    (c) legislative body
    (d) quasi-judicial agency

60. During green house effect, carbon dioxide and water vapours absorbs,
    (a) UV radiations
    (b) Solar radiation
    (c) Short wave radiations
    (d) Long wave radiations

61. The basic goal of computer process is to convert data into
    (a) files (b) tables
    (c) information (d) graphs

62. A screwdriver can be used to open a can of paint. In this situation, the screwdriver is being used as a
    (a) Wheel and axle. (b) Screw.
    (c) Lever. (d) inclined plane

63. A drawing instrument set usually contains all of the following, except:
    (a) bow compass (b) scale
    (c) dividers (d) extra leads

64. Quantities other than base quantities are termed as
    (a) Derived quantities
    (b) Base quantities
    (c) Professional quantities
    (d) Energetic quantities

65. A bulb weights 500 N, its mass in grams would be
    (a) 50 g (b) 5 g
    (c) 5000 g (d) 500 g

66. When an object is raised to a certain height above ground, it possesses
    (a) Chemical Potential Energy
    (b) Elastic Potential Energy
    (c) Gravitational Potential Energy
    (d) Kinetic energy

67. A car stopped screeching to avoid crash with a van, change is involved in process is
    (a) Kinetic energy is converted into sound energy
    (b) Kinetic Energy is converted into sound and thermal energy
    (c) Potential energy is converted into sound, heat and kinetic energy
    (d) Kinetic and potential energy is converted into thermal and sound energy

68. Freezing point of ethyl alcohol is 156 K, which is equal to
    (a) 426 °C (b) 117 °C
    (c) −426 °C (d) −117 °C

69. Two points used for centigrade scale or Celsius scale are
    (a) Melting point and boiling point
    (b) Condensing point and boiling point
    (c) Ice point and steam point
    (d) Condensation point and freezing point

70. The hot resistance of the bulb's filament is higher than its cold resistance because the temperature co-efficient of the filament is
    (a) zero
    (b) negative
    (c) positive
    (d) about 2 ohms per degree

71. A seesaw on a playground is an example of what type of simple machine?
    (a) wedge (b) lever
    (c) screw (d) wheel and axle

72. In the case of fatal accident, when should be a report filed for nearest OSHA office?
    (a) Within 24 hours (b) Within 48 hours
    (c) Within 8 hours (d) Within 4 hours

73. Which of the following three R's are regarded as environment friendly?
    (a) Reduce, Reuse, Recycle
    (b) Read, Register, Recall
    (c) Random, Reduce, Recall
    (d) Reduce, Rebuild, Restrict

74. In MICR, C stands for...........
    (a) Code (b) Colour
    (c) Computer (d) Character

75. Can an employer appeal against an improvement or prohibition notice?
    (a) Yes, but only against an improvement and not prohibition notice.
    (b) Yes, under Section 24 of the Health and Safety at Work Act 1974.
    (c) Yes, but only against a prohibition and not an improvement notice.
    (d) No, there is no right to appeal.

GENERAL AWARENESS AND CURRENT AFFAIR

76. 'Freon' used as refrigerants is chemically known as
    (a) chlorinated hydrocarbon
    (b) fluorinated hydrocarbon
    (c) chlorofluoro hydrocarbon
    (d) fluorinated aromatic compound
77. The humidity of air measured in percentage is called
    (a) absolute humidity   (b) specific humidity
    (c) relative humidity   (d) All of these above
78. In which of the following years was the first Railway line between Bombay and Thane laid?
    (a) 1853   (b) 1854
    (c) 1856   (d) 1858
79. Who drafted the Constitution of Muslim League, 'The Green Book'?
    (a) Rahamat Ali
    (b) Muhammad Iqbal
    (c) Muhammad Ali Jinnah
    (d) Maulana Muhammad Ali Jauhar
80. Bluetooth technology allows
    (a) wireless communications between equipments
    (b) signal transmission on mobile phones only
    (c) landline to mobile phone communication
    (d) satellite television communication
81. Who among the following was the Viceroy of India at the time of the formation of Indian National Congress?
    (a) Lord Mayo   (b) Lord Ripon
    (c) Lord Dufferin   (d) Lord Lansdowne
82. Whose philosophy is called the Advaita?
    (a) Ramanujacharya (b) Shankaracharya
    (c) Nagarjuna   (d) Vasumitra

83. In which part of the Constitution, details of citizenship are mentioned?
    (a) I   (b) II
    (c) III   (d) IV
84. Which one of the following diseases is caused by virus?
    (a) Tuberculosis   (b) Typhoid
    (c) Influenza   (d) Diphtheria
85. Prokaryotic cells lack
    (a) nucleolus
    (b) nuclear membrane
    (c) membrane bound by organelles
    (d) All of these above
86. Plants that grow in saline water are called
    (a) halophytes   (b) hydrophytes
    (c) mesophytes   (d) thallophytes
87. Which one of the following does not contain Silver?
    (a) German Silver   (b) Horn Silver
    (c) Ruby Silver   (d) Lunar Caustic
88. The soils which are rich in Calcium are known as
    (a) Pedocals   (b) Pedalfers
    (c) Podsols   (d) Laterits
89. Which citizen centric platform has been jointly launched by Atal Innovation Mission (AIM) and MyGov?
    (a) Swachh India Platform
    (b) Educate India Platform
    (c) Innovate India Platform
    (d) Indian culture Platform
90. Which Assamese film bagged the best movie award at the 3rd Love International Film Festival 2018 in Los Angeles?
    (a) Amazon Obhijaan
    (b) Xhoihobote Dhemalite
    (c) Calendar
    (d) Kothanodi
91. Who has been conferred with the Odisha's highest literary award 'Atibadi Jagannath Das Samman' for 2018?
    (a) P K Kunhalikutty
    (b) Ramakanta Rath
    (c) P P Thankachan
    (d) Ramesh Chennithala

92. The waves used in sonography are
    (a) sound waves (b) ultrasonic waves
    (c) micro waves (d) infra-red waves
93. Fifth Generation Computers are
    (a) Data Interpreters
    (b) Data Controllers
    (c) Data Processors
    (d) Knowledge Processors
94. Name the oldest Indian civilization
    (a) Mesopotamian civilization
    (b) Egyptian civilization
    (c) Indus Valley civilization
    (d) None of these
95. Who is the author of 'A Suitable Boy' ?
    (a) Arundhati Roy
    (b) Khushwant Singh
    (c) Vikram Seth
    (d) None of these
96. Who was awarded the first Rajiv Gandhi National Sadbhavana Award ?
    (a) Mother Teresa (b) Moraji Desai
    (c) JRD Tata (d) None of these
97. International Literacy Day is observed on which one of the following days every year ?
    (a) 28th March (b) 18th September
    (c) 8th September (d) 18th March
98. Who among the following Mughal rulers has been called the 'Prince of Builders' ?
    (a) Shah Jahan (b) Babur
    (c) Akbar (d) Jahangir
99. Name the American film cartoonist who created Mickey Mouse and Donald Duck
    (a) Steven Spielberg (b) Hanna Barbera
    (c) Warner Brothers (d) Walt Disney
100. An earthquake is also known as
    (a) tremor (b) temper
    (c) teacher (d) None of these

HINTS & EXPLANATIONS

1. (b) From the given alternatives,

$97 \times 98 = 9506$

$\therefore$ Smaller number $= 97$

2. (c) If the average in 10 tests be x, then,

$$\frac{x \times 10 + 100}{11} = x + 5$$

$x \times 10 + 100 = (x + 5) \times 11$

$\Rightarrow 11x - 10x = 100 - 55$

$\Rightarrow x = 45$

$\therefore$ Required average $= 50$

3. (a) $\dfrac{2}{3} \times \dfrac{3}{4} \times \dfrac{1}{5} \times a = 15$; $a =$ Number

$\Rightarrow a = 150$

Then 30% of $a = \dfrac{30}{100} \times 150 = 45$

4. (c) Circumference of the circle

$= \pi \times$ diameter

$= \dfrac{22}{7} \times 56 = 176 \, \text{cm}$

$\therefore$ Perimeter of the square

$= (272 - 176) = 96 \, \text{cm}$

$\therefore$ Side of the square

$= \left(\dfrac{96}{4}\right) = 24 \, \text{cm}$

$\therefore$ Area of the square

$= (24 \times 24) = 576 \, \text{sq cm}$

$\therefore$ Area of the circle $= \pi r^2$

$= \dfrac{22}{7} \times 28 \times 28 = 2464 \, \text{sq cm.}$

$\therefore$ Required sum

$= (576 + 2464) \, \text{sq cm} = 3040 \, \text{sq cm}$

5. (d)

6. (c) $3^1 = 3$; $3^2 = 9$; $3^3 = 27$; $3^4 = 81$; $3^4 = 243$

i.e. unit's digit is repeated after index 4.

Remainder after dividing 21 by $4 = 1$

$\therefore$ Unit's digit in the expansion of $(3)^{21} = 3$

$\therefore$ Remainder after dividing by $5 = 3$

7. (b) Let the numbers be $n - 2, n - 1, n, n + 1$ and $n + 2$. Their average $= n$.

Next two consecutive numbers are $n + 3$ and $n + 4$.

Therefore the average of 7 consecutive numbers

$$= \frac{(n-2) + (n-1) + n + (n+1) + (n+2) + (n+3) + (n+4)}{7}$$

$$= \frac{5n + 2n + 7}{7} = n + 1$$

8. (a) Let the marked price of the article be ₹ x.

$$\therefore x \times \frac{90}{100} = \frac{450 \times 120}{100}$$

$$\Rightarrow \frac{9x}{10} = 540$$

$$\Rightarrow x = \frac{540 \times 10}{9} = ₹ \, 600$$

9. (c) Required percentage $= \dfrac{24}{40} \times 100 = 60\%$

10. (b) If a completes the work in x days, B will do the same in 3x days.

$\therefore 3x - x = 60$

$\Rightarrow 2x = 60$

$\Rightarrow x = 30$ and $3x = 90$

$\therefore (A + B)$'s day's work

$$= \frac{1}{30} + \frac{1}{90} = \frac{3+1}{90} = \frac{4}{90} = \frac{2}{45}$$

$\therefore$ A and B together will do the work in

$$\frac{45}{2} = 22\frac{1}{2} \text{ days.}$$

11. **(b)** A : B = 2 : 3 = 8 : 12

B : C = 4 : 5 = 12 : 15

$\therefore$ A : B : C = 8 : 12 : 15

Sum of ratio = 35

$$\therefore \text{A's share} = \frac{8}{35} \times 700 = ₹\,160$$

$$\text{B's share} = \frac{12}{35} \times 700 = ₹\,240$$

$$\text{C's share} = \frac{15}{35} \times 700 = ₹\,300$$

12. **(c)** Smallest side of the triangle = x cm (let)

$\therefore$ Second side of triangle

$$= 40 - 17 - x = 23 - x$$

$$\text{Semi-perimeter,} = s = \frac{40}{2} = 20$$

$$\therefore \sqrt{s(s-a)(s-b)(s-c)} = 60$$

$$\Rightarrow \sqrt{20(20-17)(20-x)(20-23+x)} = 60$$

$$\Rightarrow (20-x)(x-3) = 60$$

$$\Rightarrow 20x - 60 - x^2 + 3x = 60$$

$$\Rightarrow x^2 - 23x + 120 = 0$$

$$\Rightarrow x^2 - 15x - 8x + 120 = 0$$

$$\Rightarrow x(x-15) - 8(x-15) = 0$$

$$\Rightarrow (x-8)(x-15) = 0$$

$$\Rightarrow x = 8 \text{ or } 15$$

13. **(b)** Last digit of $(1001)^{2008} + 1002 = 1 + 2 = 3$

14. **(b)** $\sqrt{6 + \sqrt{6 + \sqrt{6 \ldots}}} = x$

$6 = 3 \times 2$

By trick = 3

15. **(b)** Let the average of batsman after 11th innings = A

$$\frac{\text{Total score made by batsman at the end of 11th innings}}{11} = A$$

$\therefore$ Total score after 11th innings = 11 A

Now,

$$\frac{\begin{array}{c}\text{Total score after 11th innings}\\ + \text{ score made in 12th innings}\end{array}}{12} = A + 2$$

$$\Rightarrow 11A + 63 = (A+2) \times 12$$

$$\Rightarrow 11A - 12A = 24 - 63$$

$$\Rightarrow A = 39$$

12th innings average = 39 + 2 = 41

16. **(b)** Single equivalent discount

$$= \left(x + y - \frac{xy}{100}\right)\%$$

$$= \left(20 + 15 - \frac{20 \times 15}{100}\right)\% = 32\%$$

17. **(d)** SP of both articles is same. Profit on one is equal to loss on the other.

If loss per cent be x, then

$$25 - x - \frac{25x}{100} = 0$$

$$\Rightarrow 25 - x - \frac{x}{4} = 0 \Rightarrow 100 - 4x - x = 0$$

$$\Rightarrow 5x = 100$$

$$\Rightarrow x = 20\%$$

18. **(b)** $CI = P\left[1 + \dfrac{R}{100}\right]^t - P$

$$= 25000\left[1 + \frac{5}{100}\right]^2 - 25000$$

$$= 25000\left[\left(\frac{105}{100}\right)^2 - 1\right]$$

$$= 25000 \left[\frac{11025 - 10000}{10000} \right]$$

$$5 \times \frac{1025}{2} = ₹2562.5$$

19. (c) If the total length of journey be x km, then

$$\frac{x}{35} - \frac{x}{40} = \frac{15}{60}$$

$$\Rightarrow \frac{8x - 7x}{280} = \frac{1}{4}$$

$$\Rightarrow \frac{x}{280} = \frac{1}{4}$$

$$\Rightarrow x = \frac{1}{4} \times 280 = 70 \text{ km}$$

20. (d) Part of the tank filled by both pipes in two hours

$$= 2\left(\frac{1}{8} + \frac{1}{6} \right) = 2\left(\frac{3+4}{24} \right) = \frac{7}{12}$$

Remaining part $= 1 - \frac{7}{12} = \frac{5}{12}$

Time taken by B in filling the remaining part

$$= \frac{5}{12} \times 6 = \frac{5}{2} = 2\frac{1}{2} \text{ hours}$$

21. (d) Let the quantity of acid in original mixture be x litre and that of water be 3x litre.

$$\therefore \frac{x+5}{3x} = \frac{1}{2}$$

$$\Rightarrow 2x + 10 = 3x \Rightarrow x = 10$$

$\therefore$ Quantity of new mixture

$$= 4x + 5 = 45 \text{ litres}$$

22. (c) Incomes of A and B

$$= ₹ 6x \text{ and } 5x$$

Expenses of A and B

$$= ₹ 4y \text{ and } 3y$$

$$\therefore 6x - 4y = 400 \text{ ...(i)}$$

$$5x - 3y = 400 \quad \text{...(ii)}$$

By equation (i) × 3 – (ii) × 4

$$\Rightarrow 18x - 12y - 20x + 12y$$

$$= 1200 - 1600$$

$$\Rightarrow 2x = 400 \Rightarrow x = 200$$

$\therefore$ Total income

$$= 6x + 5x = 11x = ₹ 2200.$$

23. (a) Side of square $= \sqrt{121} = 11$ cm

$\therefore$ Length of wire $= 4 \times 11 = 44$ cm

$\therefore 2\pi r = 44$

$$\Rightarrow 2 \times \frac{22}{7} \times r = 44$$

$$\Rightarrow r = \frac{44 \times 7}{2 \times 22} = 7 \text{ cm}$$

24. (a) Speed of ship $= 30$ kmph

$$= \frac{30 \times 5}{18} \text{ m/sec.} = \frac{25}{3} \text{ m/sec.}$$

Time taken in covering 500 metre

$$= \frac{500 \times 3}{25} = 60 \text{ seconds}$$

Speed of radio waves

$$= \frac{200}{1000} \text{ km/sec.} = \frac{1}{5} \text{ km/sec.}$$

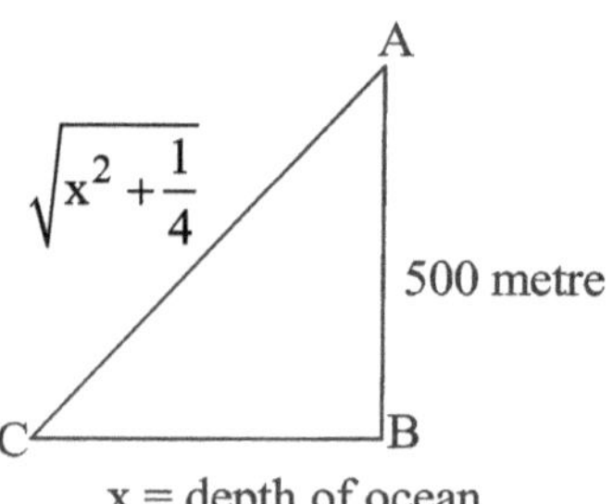

x = depth of ocean

$$\therefore \frac{\sqrt{x^2 + \frac{1}{4}}}{\frac{1}{5}} + \frac{x}{\frac{1}{5}} = 60$$

$$\Rightarrow \sqrt{x^2 + \frac{1}{4}} + x = \frac{1}{5} \times 60 = 12$$

$$\therefore (12 - x)^2 = x^2 + \frac{1}{4}$$

$$\Rightarrow 144 + x^2 - 24x = x^2 + \frac{1}{4}$$

$$\Rightarrow 24x = 144 - \frac{1}{4} = \frac{575}{4}$$

$$\Rightarrow x = \frac{575}{4 \times 24} = 6 \text{ km}$$

25. (a) $\because$ 12 men $\equiv$ 18 women

$\therefore$ 2 men $\equiv$ 3 women

$\therefore$ 8 men + 16 women = 28 women

$\therefore M_1 D_1 = M_2 D_2$

$\Rightarrow 18 \times 14 = 28 \times D_2$

$$\Rightarrow D_2 = \frac{18 \times 14}{28} = 9 \text{ days}$$

26. (d) A palace is the official home of a King.

Similarly,

An igloo is a small round house of an Eskimo.

27. (c) $A \xrightarrow{+5} F \xrightarrow{+5} K \xrightarrow{+5} P$

$D \xrightarrow{+5} I \xrightarrow{+5} N \xrightarrow{+5} S$

$W \xrightarrow{+5} B \xrightarrow{+5} G \xrightarrow{+5} L$

$O \xrightarrow{+5} T \xrightarrow{+5} Y \xrightarrow{+5} D$

28. (d)

$$\begin{array}{cccc} 12 & 20 & \boxed{30} & \boxed{42} \\ \downarrow & \downarrow & \downarrow & \downarrow \\ (3 \times 4) & (4 \times 5) & (5 \times 6) & (6 \times 7) \end{array}$$

29. (c)

$B \xrightarrow{+2} D \xrightarrow{+2} F, \quad C \xrightarrow{+3} F \xrightarrow{+3} I, \quad D \xrightarrow{+4} H \xrightarrow{+4} L,$

$E \xrightarrow{+5} J \xrightarrow{+5} O$

30. (b) Each of the numbers is doubled and 1, 2, 3, 4, 5, 6 is added in turn, so $89 \times 2 + 6 = 184$.

31. (a)

$$\begin{array}{cccc} 1 & 2 & 3 & 4 \\ \boxed{\text{DEPU}} & \boxed{\text{TA}} & \boxed{\text{TI}} & \boxed{\text{ON}} \end{array}$$

Coded $\longrightarrow$

$$\begin{array}{cccc} \boxed{\text{ON}} & \boxed{\text{TA}} & \boxed{\text{DEPU}} & \boxed{\text{TI}} \\ 4 & 2 & 1 & 3 \end{array}$$

Similarly,

$$\begin{array}{cccc} 1 & 2 & 3 & 4 \\ \boxed{\text{DERI}} & \boxed{\text{VA}} & \boxed{\text{TI}} & \boxed{\text{ON}} \end{array}$$

Coded $\longrightarrow$

$$\begin{array}{cccc} \boxed{\text{ON}} & \boxed{\text{VA}} & \boxed{\text{DERI}} & \boxed{\text{TI}} \\ 4 & 2 & 1 & 3 \end{array}$$

32. (d) Clearly, number of students in the class

$$= (6 + 1 + 25) = 32$$

33. (b) Seema > Sohan > Seeta   ...(i)

Deepti > Sweta > Seema   ...(ii)

Combining (i) and (ii) we get

Deepti > Sweta > Seema > Sohan > Seeta

34. (c) Sharks belong to class pisces. Whale is a mammal and Turtle belongs to class reptilia.

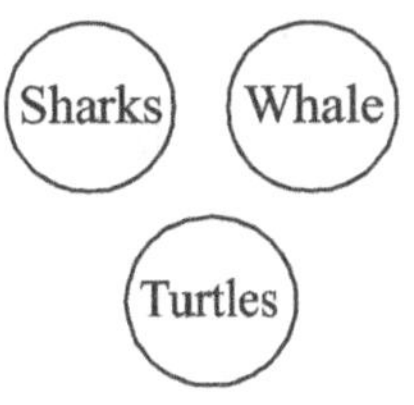

35. (b) $24 \div 6 \times 4 + 9 - 8$

$4 \times 4 + 9 - 8$

$16 + 9 - 8$

$25 - 8 = 17$

36. (b) Mani's Age = 60 years

Prabhu's Age = 60/2 = 30 years

Romana's Age = 30/2 = 15 years

37. (d) $14 + 9 = 23$

$9 \times 5 = 45$

$23 + 45 = 68$

38. (a)   39. (b)   40. (c)   41. (a)

42. (c) Nithya is Sam's Sister and Mogan is Sam's Father $\Rightarrow$

Nithya is Mogan's Daughter.

Selvan is Rajan's Son and Rajan is Mogan's Brother $\Rightarrow$

Selvan is Mogan's Nephew.

So, Nithya is Selvan's Cousin.

43. (a) The direction diagram is as follows :

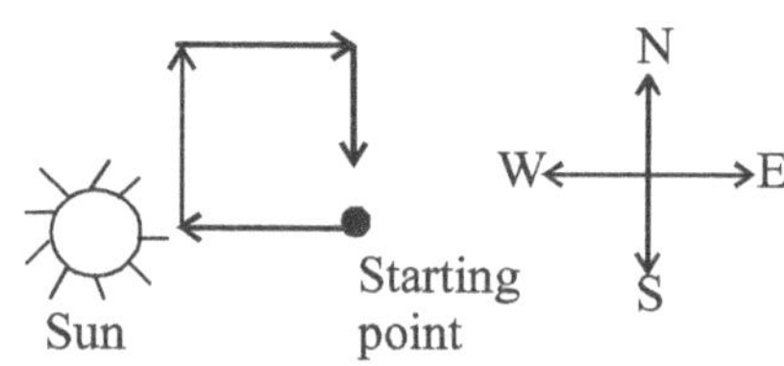

So, raja is facing south direction.

44. (d)

$+ \Rightarrow \div$	$- \Rightarrow \times$
$\times \Rightarrow +$	$\div \Rightarrow -$

$45 + 9 - 3 \times 15 \div 2$

$\Rightarrow ? = 45 \div 9 \times 3 + 15 - 2$

$\Rightarrow ? = 5 \times 3 + 15 - 2$

$\Rightarrow ? = 30 - 2 = \boxed{28}$

45. (c) The required region should be present only in circle. Such region is marked '10'.

46. (c) Total number of musical toys $= 14 + 28 = 42$.

47. (d)

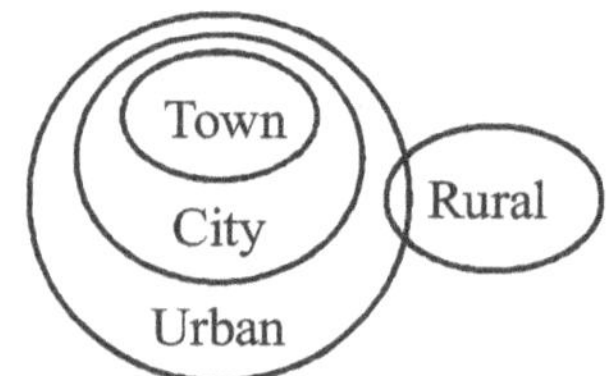

So, Neither I nor II follows.

48. (d)

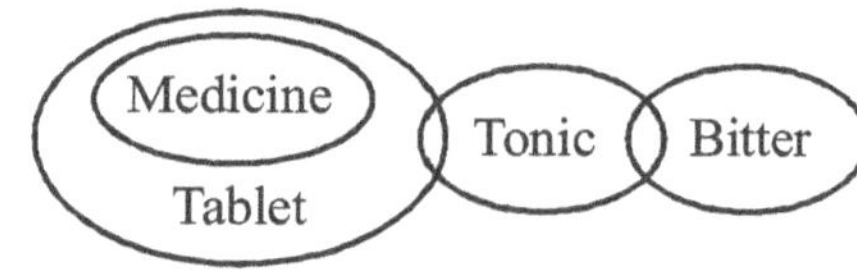

So, Neither I nor II follows.

49. (b) Investment in securities involves risk. This does not mean that one should not invest in securities. So, I does not follow. Since the statement advises one to consult investment advisor before investing, so II follows.

50. (d) Neither the poor nor the rich, but only the role of money in politics is being talked about in the statement. So, neither I nor II follows.

51. (a)   52. (a)   53. (a)   54. (c)   55. (b)

56. (d)   57. (c)   58. (d)   59. (d)   60. (d)

61. (c)   62. (c)   63. (b)   64. (a)   65. (b)

66. (c)   67. (b)   68. (d)   69. (c)   70. (c)

71. (b)   72. (c)   73. (a)   74. (d)   75. (b)

76. (c)   77. (c)   78. (a)   79. (c)   80. (a)

81. (c)   82. (b)   83. (b)   84. (c)   85. (d)

86. (a)   87. (a)   88. (a)   89. (c)   90. (b)

91. (b)   92. (b)   93. (d)   94. (c)   95. (c)

96. (a)   97. (c)   98. (a)   99. (d)   100. (a)

PRACTICE SET 7

MATHEMATICS

1. How many numbers, between 1 and 300 are divisible by 3 and 5 together?
   - (a) 16
   - (b) 18
   - (c) 20
   - (d) 100

2. The value of
$$3 \div \left[(8-5) \div \left\{ (4-2) + \left(2 + \frac{8}{13} \right) \right\} \right] \text{ is}$$
   - (a) $\dfrac{15}{17}$
   - (b) $\dfrac{13}{17}$
   - (c) $\dfrac{15}{19}$
   - (d) $\dfrac{13}{19}$

3. Kamya purchased an item for ₹46,000 and sold it at a loss of 12 per cent. With that amount she purchased another item and sold it at a gain of 12 per cent. What was her overall gain/loss?
   - (a) Loss of ₹662.40
   - (b) Profit of ₹662.40
   - (c) Loss of ₹642.80
   - (d) Profit of ₹642.80

4. The cost price of an article is 64% of the marked price. The gain percentage after allowing a discount of 12% on the marked price is
   - (a) 37.5%
   - (b) 48%
   - (c) 50.5%
   - (d) 52%

5. A 180-metre long train crosses another 270-metre long train running in the opposite direction in 10.8 seconds. If the speed of the first train is 60 kmph, what is the speed of the second train in kmph?
   - (a) 80 km/h
   - (b) 90 km/h
   - (c) 150 km/h
   - (d) Cannot be determined

6. In what time will ₹300000 amount to ₹746496 at 20% compound interest?
   - (a) 3 yrs
   - (b) 4 yrs
   - (c) 5 yrs
   - (d) 6 yrs

7. Two person Ravi and Shyam can do a work in 60 days and 40 days respectively. They began the work together but Ravi left after some time and Shyam finished the remaining work in 10 days. After how many days did Ravi leave?
   - (a) 8 days
   - (b) 12 days
   - (c) 15 days
   - (d) 18 days

8. Divide 81 into three parts so that $\frac{1}{2}$ of 1st, $\frac{1}{3}$ of 2nd and $\frac{1}{4}$ of 3rd are equal.
   - (a) 36, 27, 18
   - (b) 27, 18, 36
   - (c) 18, 27, 36
   - (d) 30, 27, 24

9. The largest and the second largest angles of a triangle are in the ratio of 4 : 3. The smallest angle is half the largest angle. What is the difference between the smallest and the largest angles of the triangle?
   - (a) 30°
   - (b) 60°
   - (c) 40°
   - (d) 20°

10. The mean of 100 values is 45. If 15 is added to each of the first forty values and 5 is subtracted from each of the remaining sixty values, the new mean becomes
    - (a) 45
    - (b) 48
    - (c) 51
    - (d) 55

11. If the number of square centimetres on the surface area of a sphere is three times the number of cubic centimetres in its volume, then what is its diameter?
    - (a) 1 cm
    - (b) 2 cm
    - (c) 3 cm
    - (d) 6 cm

12. If $x * y = (x+3)^2 (y-1)$, then the value of $5 * 4$ is
    - (a) 192
    - (b) 182
    - (c) $\sqrt{2}$
    - (d) 356

13. The average of four consecutive even numbers is 9. Find the largest number.
    (a) 12   (b) 6
    (c) 8   (d) 10

14. If the selling price of 10 articles is equal to the cost price of 11 articles, then the gain percent is
    (a) 10%   (b) 11%
    (c) 15%   (d) 25%

15. If 125% of x is 100, then x is :
    (a) 80   (b) 150
    (c) 400   (d) 125

16. If 9 men or 12 women can reap a field in 18 days, then working at the same rate, 6 men and 16 women can reap the same field in:
    (a) 9 days   (b) 5 days
    (c) 7 days   (d) 8 days

17. The ratio between two numbers is 2 : 3. If each number is increased by 4, the ratio between them becomes 5 : 7. The difference between the numbers is
    (a) 8   (b) 6
    (c) 4   (d) 2

18. If 17^{200} is divided by 18, the remainder is
    (a) 1   (b) 2
    (c) 16   (d) 17

19. The average weight of 12 crewmen in a boat is increased by $\frac{1}{3}$ kg, when one of the crewmen whose weight is 55 kg is replaced by a new man. What is the weight of that new men?
    (a) 58 kg   (b) 60 kg
    (c) 57 kg   (d) 59 kg

20. While selling a watch, a shopkeeper gives a discount of 5%. If he gives a discount of 6%, he earns ₹ 15 less as profit. What is the marked price of the watch?
    (a) ₹ 1,250   (b) ₹ 1,400
    (c) ₹ 1,500   (d) ₹ 750

21. 20% loss on selling price is what per cent loss on the cost price?
    (a) 25%   (b) 15%
    (c) $16\frac{2}{3}\%$ (d) $16\frac{1}{3}\%$

22. A sum of money placed at compound interest double itself at 2 years. The year it will take to amount 4 times itself is
    (a) 6 years   (b) 4 years
    (c) 8 years   (d) 3 years

23. A car covers four successive 6 km stretches at speeds of 25 kmph, 50 kmph, 75 kmph and 150 kmph respectively. Its average speed over this distance is
    (a) 25 kmph   (b) 50 kmph
    (c) 75 kmph   (d) 150 kmph

24. Two men A and B started a job in which A was thrice as good as B and therefore took 60 days less than B to finish the job. How many days will they take to finish the job, if they start working together?
    (a) 15 days   (b) 20 days
    (c) $22\frac{1}{2}$ days   (d) 25 days

25. Monthly incomes of A and B are in the ratio of 4 : 3 and their expenses bear the ratio 3 : 2. Each of them saves ₹ 6,000 at the end of the month, then the monthly income of A is
    (a) ₹ 12,000   (b) ₹ 24,000
    (c) ₹ 30,000   (d) ₹ 60,000

GENERAL INTELLIGENCE AND REASONING

DIRECTIONS (Qs. 26-28) : In questions, select the related word/letters/number from given alternatives.

26. PETAL : FLOWER : : ?
    (a) salt : pepper   (b) tire : bicycle
    (c) base : ball   (d) sandals : shoes

27. 8 : 28 : : 27 : ?
    (a) 28   (b) 8
    (c) 64   (d) 65

28. ACEG : SUWY : : BDFH : ?
    (a) TVZX   (b) RTZV
    (c) TVXZ   (d) RTVZ

29. If FRIEND is coded as HUMJTK, how is CANDLE written in that code ?
    (a) EDRIRL   (b) DCQHQK
    (c) ESJFME   (d) FYOBOC
    (e) DEQJQM

30. Rahim and his uncle differ in their ages by 30 years. After 7 years, if the sum of their ages is 66, what will be the age of the uncle ?
    (a) 39 years   (b) 41 years
    (c) 51 years   (d) 49 years

31. A cyclist goes 30 km to North and then turning East he goes 40 km. Again he turns to his right and goes 20 km. After this, he turns to his right and goes 40 km. How far is he from his starting point ?
    (a) 25 km   (b) 40 km
    (c) 6 km   (d) 10 km

32. Choose the correct figure that represents the given relation:

    Blue eyes, females, doctors

    (a)    (b) 

    (c) 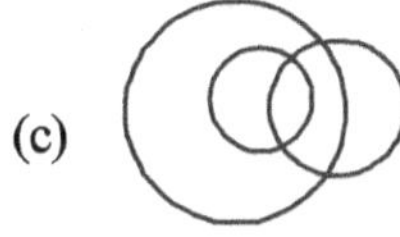   (d) 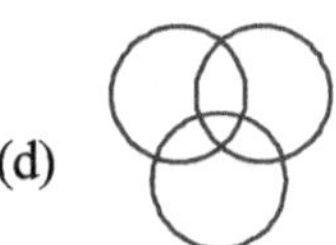

33. A man said to lady, "Your mother's husband's sister is my aunt." How is the lady related to the man?
    (a) Daughter   (b) Grand daughter
    (c) Mother   (d) Sister

34. How many rectangles are there in the question figure ?

    Question figure :

    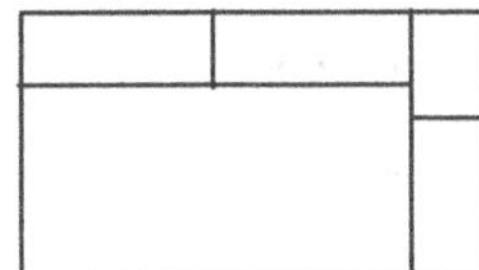

    (a) 6   (b) 7
    (c) 8   (d) 9

35. Find out the two signs to be interchanged for making following equation correct.

    $5 + 3 \times 8 - 12 \div 4 = 3$

    (a) + and −   (b) − and ÷
    (c) + and ×   (d) + and ÷

36. Find the missing number.

7	9	8
2	4	3
5	7	6
16	32	?

    (a) 17   (b) 23
    (c) 47   (d) 73

37. From the given answer figures, select the one in which the question figure is hidden/embedded.

    Question Figure :

    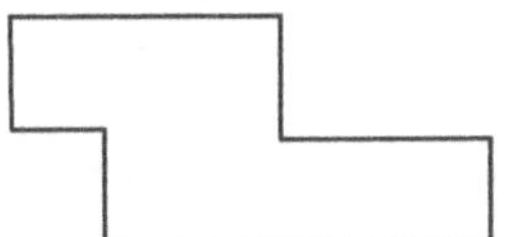

    Answer Figures :

    (a)    (b) 

    (c) 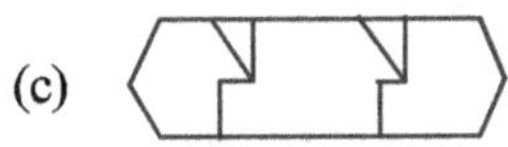 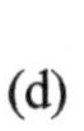   (d) 

38. Complete the given figure.

    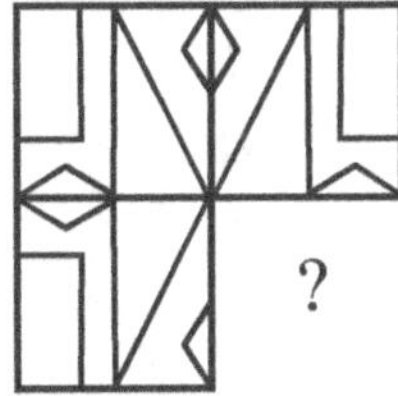

    (a) 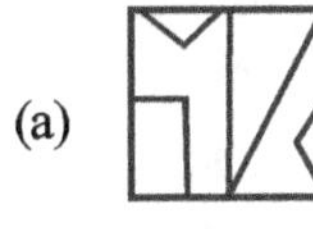   (b) 

    (c)    (d) 

39. If a mirror is placed on the line MN, then which of the answer figure is the right image of given figure?

    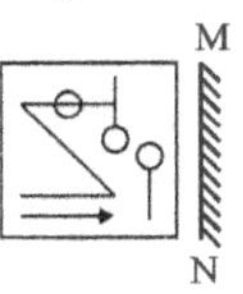 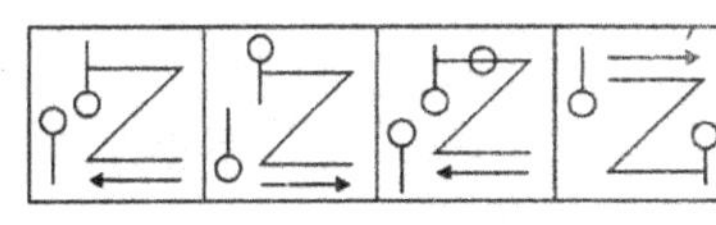

    (X)   (a)   (b)   (c)   (d)

DIRECTIONS (Qs. 40 & 41) : In next two questions, a series is given, with one/two terms(s) missing. Choose the correct alternative from the given ones that will complete the series.

40. 4, 196, 16, 169, ?, 144, 64
    (a) 21   (b) 81
    (c) 36   (d) 32

41. 8, 15, 36, 99, 288, ?
    (a) 368   (b) 676
    (c) 855   (d) 908

42. If FLATTER is coded as 7238859 and MOTHER is coded as 468159, then how is MAMMOTH coded?
    (a) 4344681   (b) 4344651
    (c) 4146481   (d) 4346481

43. Arun said, "This girl is the wife of the grandson of my mother". Who is Arun to the girl ?
    (a) Grandfather   (b) Husband
    (c) Father-in-law   (d) Father

44. If $+$ means $\div$, $-$ means $\times$, $\times$ means $+$, $\div$ means $-$, then
    $90 + 18 - 6 \times 30 \div 4 = ?$
    (a) 64   (b) 65
    (c) 56   (d) 48

45. Read the figure and find the region representing persons who are educated and employed but not confirmed.

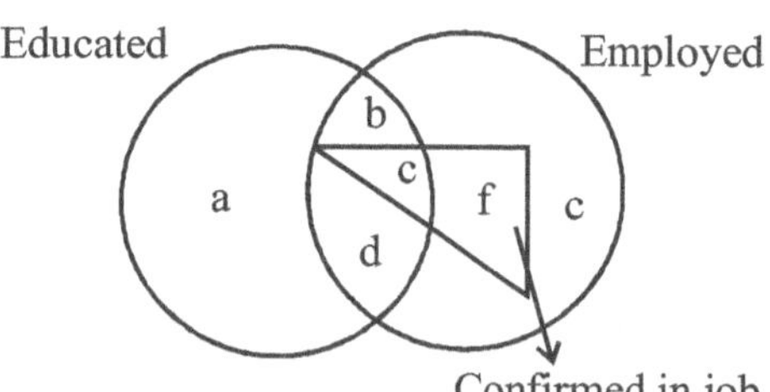

    (a) abc   (b) bd
    (c) adc   (d) ac

46. In the given figure, which letter represents carnivorous plants which are not green?

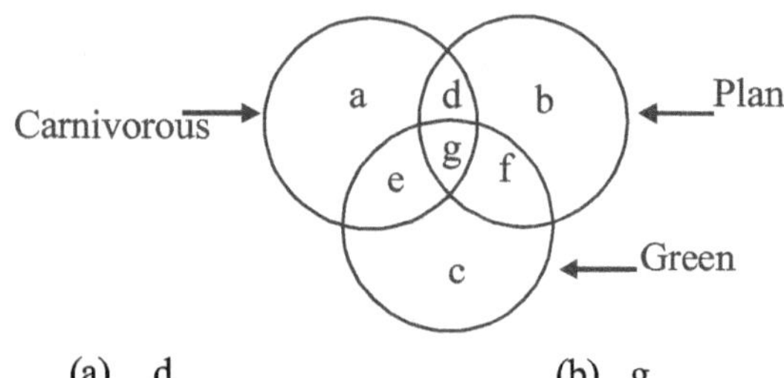

    (a) d   (b) g
    (c) e   (d) f

DIRECTIONS (Qs. 47 & 48) : In each of the questions below are given three statements followed by two conclusions numbered I and II. You have to take the given statements to be true even if they seem to be at variance from commonly known facts and then decide which of the given conclusions logically follows from the statements disregarding commonly known facts.

Give answer (a) if only conclusion I follows.

Give answer (b) if only conclusion II follows.

Give answer (c) if either conclusion I or conclusion II follows.

Give answer (d) if neither conclusion I nor conclusion II follows.

47. **Statements:**
    All petals are flowers.
    Some flowers are not petals.
    Some petals are colours.
    Conclusions:
    I.   Some flowers are colours.
    II.   Some flowers are not colours.

48. **Statements:**
    All desks are tables.
    Some tables are drawers.
    Some drawers are big.
    Conclusions:
    I.   Some tables are big.
    II.   No desk is a drawer.

DIRECTIONS (Qs. 49 & 50): In each question below is given a statement followed by two conclusions numbered I and II. You have to assume everything in the statement to be true, then consider the two conclusions together and decide which of them logically follows beyond a reasonable doubt from the information given in the statement.

49. **Statements:** Vegetable prices are soaring in the market.
    Conclusions:
    I. Vegetables are becoming a rare commodity.
    II. People cannot eat vegetables.
    (a) Only conclusion I follows
    (b) Only conclusion II follows
    (c) Either I or II follows
    (d) Neither I nor II follows

50. **Statements:** The serious accident in which a person was run down by a car yesterday had again focused attention on the most unsatisfactory state of roads.

Conclusions:

I. The accident that occurred was fatal.

II. Several accidents have so far taken place because of unsatisfactory state of roads.

(a) Only conclusion I follows

(b) Only conclusion II follows

(c) Either I or II follows

(d) Neither I nor II follows

BASIC SCIENCE AND ENGINEERING

51. In isometric drawings:
(a) Two axes are perpendicular
(b) True measurements can be made only along or parallel to the isometric axes
(c) All faces are unequally distorted
(d) None of the above

52. The dimensions of potential energy are
(a) $[MLT^{-1}]$ (b) $[ML^2T^{-2}]$
(c) $[ML^{-1}T^{-2}]$ (d) $[ML^{-1}T^{-2}]$

53. The density of water at room temperature is about
(a) $10\,g/cm^3$
(b) $1\,g/cm^3$
(c) $0.1\,g/cm^3$
(d) $0.01\,g/cm^3$

54. The ______ of a distance versus time graph is speed.
(a) slope
(b) y-intercept
(c) origin
(d) none of the answers

55. If the speed of an object is doubled then its kinetic energy is ______
(a) doubled
(b) quadruple
(c) halved
(d) tripled

56. An iron ball at 40°C is dropped in a mug containing water at 40°C. The heat will ______
(a) not flow from iron ball to water or from water to iron ball
(b) flow from iron ball to water
(c) flow from water to iron ball
(d) none of the above

57. When no current is passed through a conductor,
(a) the free electrons do not move
(b) the average speed of a free electron over a large period of time is not zero
(c) the average velocity of a free electron over a large period of time is zero
(d) the average of the velocities of all the free electrons at an instant is non zero

58. Which type of lever always reduces the force applied?
(a) Lever of the first order
(b) Lever of the second order
(c) Lever of the third order
(d) All of these

59. The following is/are physical hazard agent(s)
(a) Falls
(b) Electricity
(c) Inhalation
(d) All of the above

60. Which of the following is a natural source of environmental pollution?
(a) Earthquake
(b) Automobiles
(c) Industries
(d) Sewage

61. A communication network which is used by large organizations over regional, national or global area is called:
(a) LAN (b) WAN
(c) MAN (d) VAN

62. The conductivity of a superconductor is
(a) infinite (b) very large
(c) very small (d) zero

63. When you want to make the letters of a line of text narrower, you would set its:
(a) Aspect (b) Scale
(c) Alignment (d) Font

64. [ML-1T-2] is the dimensional formula of
    (a) Force
    (b) Coefficient of friction
    (c) Modulus of elasticity
    (d) Energy

65. If earth loses its gravity, then for a body
    (a) A weight becomes zero, but not the mass
    (b) Mass becomes zero but not weight
    (c) Neither mass nor weight becomes zero
    (d) Both mass and weight are zero

66. Distance travelled by a body in time 't' is
    (a) instantaneous speed
    (b) average velocity
    (c) average acceleration
    (d) instantaneous acceleration

67. Moving wind and waves, flying bird and spinning bowling ball use
    (a) Potential Energy
    (b) Mechanical Energy
    (c) Kinetic Energy
    (d) Thermal Energy

68. Liquid widely used in thermometer is
    (a) Water
    (b) Lime
    (c) Copper (II) Sulphate
    (d) Mercury

69. Bulbs in street lighting are all connected in
    (a) parallel
    (b) series
    (c) series-parallel
    (d) end-to-end

70. A wheel barrow is an example of a ______ class lever.
    (a) First
    (b) third
    (c) fourth
    (d) second

71. Which act establishes responsibilities and rights for employers and employees?
    (a) SARA
    (b) RCRA
    (c) CERCLA
    (d) OSHA

72. The maximum biological damage is produced by
    (a) X-rays
    (b) beta-rays
    (c) gamma-rays
    (d) alpha-rays

73. All of the logic and mathematical calculations done by the computer happen in/ on the ....
    (a) system board
    (b) central control unit
    (c) central processing unit
    (d) mother board

74. How many hours per week can a worker are required to work on average under the Working Time Regulations 1998?
    (a) 48 hours
    (b) 45 hours
    (c) 35 hours
    (d) None of these

75. What type of sketch incorporates convergence?
    (a) Isometric
    (b) perspective
    (c) oblique
    (d) multi-view

GENERAL AWARENESS AND CURRENT AFFAIR

76. Which of the following is not an algae?
    (a) Blue Algae   (b) Green Algae
    (c) Red Algae   (d) Brown Algae

77. Any session of State Legislature is prorogated by –
    (a) Presiding officer of the house
    (b) The Chief Minister of the State
    (c) The Governor
    (d) None of the above

78. The book 'The man who Divided India' was written by —
    (a) Maulana Abul Kalam Azad
    (b) Dr. Rajendra Prasad
    (c) Rafiq Zakaria
    (d) None of these

79. 'Red Ink' is prepared from –
    (a) Phenol
    (b) Aniline
    (c) Congo red
    (d) Eosin

80. Which one is not micro nutrient?
    (a) Iron
    (b) Zinc
    (c) Sulphur
    (d) Manganese

81. An air bubble inside water behave as an:
    (a) bifocal lens
    (b) convergent lens
    (c) divergent lens
    (d) cylindrical lens

82. "Hopman cup" is related to which sports?
    (a) Football
    (b) Lawn Tennis
    (c) Badminton
    (d) Cricket

83. Which of the following memories is an optical memory?
    (a) Floppy Disk
    (b) Bubble Memories
    (c) CD-ROM
    (d) Core Memories

84. Taxonomy is a science that deals with
    (a) Morphology
    (b) Anatomy
    (c) Classification
    (d) Economic uses

85. The largest reservoir of fresh water is :
    (a) Ground Water
    (b) Ponds
    (c) Lakes
    (d) Glaciers

86. The Central government has launched the National Viral Hepatitis Control programme in collaboration with which organisation to combat the disease by 2030?
    (a) UNICEF
    (b) UNHRC
    (c) WHO
    (d) UNISDR

87. Which country's researchers have developed the world's smallest computer "Michigan Micro Mote"?
    (a) United States
    (b) China
    (c) Japan
    (d) Germany

88. Which Indian swimmer clinched gold in men's 50 meter breaststroke event at 2018 Singapore National Swimming Championships?
    (a) Virdhawal Khade
    (b) Arvind Mani
    (c) M M Sahu
    (d) Sandeep Sejwal

89. Which state Chief Minister has been conferred with 'Chief Minister of the Year' award at the 52nd Skoch Summit 2018?
    (a) Rajasthan   (b) Tamil Nadu
    (c) Assam   (d) Punjab

90. Our atmosphere is divided into .... layers.
    (a) four   (b) five
    (c) two   (d) three

91. Lungs of a plant are
    (a) flowers   (b) roots
    (c) leaves   (d) stems

92. Who has authored the book titled 'Narendra Modi : A Political Biography ?
    (a) Jeffrey Dell
    (b) Kingsley Amis
    (c) Andy Marino
    (d) David Irving

93. Who invented the electric bulb?
    (a) Thomas Alva Edison
    (b) James Watt
    (c) Thomas More
    (d) None of these
94. Who invented aeroplane?
    (a) Hoffman
    (b) Wright Brothers
    (c) Edison
    (d) Stevenson
95. Who is called Rawalpindi Express?
    (a) Rahul Dravid
    (b) Imran Khan
    (c) Sachin Tendulkar
    (d) Shoaib Akhtar
96. Sriharikota Island lies near :
    (a) Chilka lake
    (b) Pulicat lake
    (c) Mahanadi Mouth
    (d) Godavari Mouth

97. The colour of the star is an indication of its :
    (a) distance from the earth
    (b) temperature
    (c) luminosity
    (d) distance from the sun
98. Liver is located in
    (a) Thorax   (b) Abdomen
    (c) Neck   (d) Head
99. 'Elisa' is -
    (a) Fat deposition test
    (b) Immunological test
    (c) Bone malformation test
    (d) None of the above
100. Who discovered the blood group in human being?
    (a) Jennings
    (b) Robert G. Edwards
    (c) Landsteiner
    (d) Pantin and Mast

HINTS & EXPLANATIONS

1. (c) LCM of 3 and 5 = 15

   Number divisible by 15 are 15, 30, 45 .....300.

   Let total numbers are n

   $300 = 15 + (n-1) \times 15$

   $300 = 15 + 15\,n - 15$

   $\Rightarrow n = 20$

2. (b) $3 \div \left[(8-5) \div \left\{ (4-2) \div \left(2 + \dfrac{8}{13} \right) \right\} \right]$

   $\Rightarrow 3 \div \left[(3) \div \left(2 \div \dfrac{34}{13} \right) \right]$

   $\Rightarrow 3 \div \left[(3) \div \left(2 \times \dfrac{13}{34} \right) \right]$

   $\Rightarrow 3 \div \left[\dfrac{3 \times 34}{13 \times 2} \right]$

   $\Rightarrow \dfrac{3 \times 13 \times 2}{3 \times 34} = \dfrac{13}{17}$

3. (a) First S.P. $= \dfrac{46000 \times 88}{100} = ₹\,40480$

   Second S.P. $= \dfrac{40480 \times 112}{100} = ₹\,45337.6$

   $\therefore$ Loss $= ₹(46000 - 45337.6) = ₹\,662.4$

4. (a) Marked price of article $= ₹\,100$ (let)

   $\therefore$ C.P. of article $= ₹\,64$

   $\therefore$ S.P. of article $= ₹\,88$

   $\therefore$ Profit per cent $= \dfrac{88 - 64}{64} \times 100 = 37.5\%$

5. (b) Relative speed of two trains

   $= \dfrac{180 + 270}{10.8}\,\dfrac{m}{s} = \dfrac{4500}{108}\,\dfrac{m}{s}$

   $= \dfrac{4500}{108} \times \dfrac{18}{5}\,\dfrac{km}{h} = 150$ km/hr

   Speed of second train $= 150 - 60 = 90$ km/h.

6. (c) $300000 \left[1 + \dfrac{20}{100} \right]^{t} = 746496$

   $\therefore \left[\dfrac{6}{5} \right]^{t} = \dfrac{746496}{300000} \Rightarrow \left(\dfrac{6}{5} \right)^{t} = \left(\dfrac{6}{5} \right)^{5}$

   $t = 5$

7. (d) Shyam alone worked for 10 days. So work

   done by him $= \dfrac{10}{40} = \dfrac{1}{4}$

   $\therefore$ (Ravi + Shyam) have done

   $1 - \dfrac{1}{4} = \dfrac{3}{4}$ of the work.

   (Ravi + Shyam) do $\dfrac{3}{4}$ of the work in

   $24 \times \dfrac{3}{4} = 18$ days

8. (c) Let lst, 2nd and 3rd part represented by x, y, z

   Let $\dfrac{1}{2}x = \dfrac{1}{3}y = \dfrac{1}{4}z = k$

   $\therefore \quad x = 2k, y = 3k, z = 4k$

   According to question

   $x + y + z = 81$

   $\Rightarrow \quad 2k + 3k + 4k = 81 \Rightarrow 9k = 81 \Rightarrow k = 9$

   Hence, parts are 18, 27, 36.

9. (c) The smallest angle of the triangle is half of the largest angle.

   $\therefore$ Ratio of the three angle $= 4 : 3 : 2$

   $\therefore 4x + 3x + 2x = 180°$

$\therefore 9x = 180°$

$\therefore x = 20°$

$\therefore$ Required difference $= 4x - 2x$

$= 2x = 2 \times 20° = 40°$

10. (b) Given that, mean of 100 values is 45

$\therefore$ Sum of 100 values, i.e. $\sum\limits_{i=1}^{100} x = 45 \times 100$

$= 4500$

According to condition,

$$\sum_{i=1}^{40}(x_i + 15) + \sum_{i=41}^{100}(x_i - 5)$$

$$= \sum_{i=1}^{40} x_i + 15 \times 40 + \sum_{i=41}^{100} x_i - 5 \times 60$$

$$= \left(\sum_{i=1}^{40} x_i + \sum_{i=41}^{100} x_i\right) + 600 - 300$$

$$= \sum_{i=1}^{100} x_i + 300$$

$= 4500 + 300 = 4800$ [from equation (i)]

$\therefore$ New mean $= \dfrac{4800}{100} = 48$

11. (b) According to question,

Surface area of sphere $= 3$ (Volume of sphere)

$\Rightarrow 4\pi r^2 = 3 \times \dfrac{4}{3}\pi r^3 \Rightarrow r = 1$

$\therefore$ Diameter $= 2r = 2$ cm

12. (a) $x \star y = (x+3)^2 (y-1)$

$\therefore 5 \star 4 = (5+3)^2 (4-1)$

$= 64 \times 3 = 192$

13. (a) Let the consecutive even numbers are $2n$, $2n+2$, $2n+4$ and $2n+6$

$\text{Average} = \dfrac{2n + 2n+2 + 2n+4 + 2n+6}{4}$

$8n + 12 = 4 \times 9 \Rightarrow n = 3$

Hence, the numbers are 6, 8, 10 and 12. Largest among them is 12.

14. (a) Let the C.P. of each article be ₹ 1.

$\therefore$ C.P. of articles $= ₹ 10$

and S.P. of 10 articles $= ₹ 11$

$\therefore$ Profit percent $= \dfrac{11-10}{10} \times 100 = 10\%$

15. (a) $\dfrac{125}{100} \times x = 100$

$\Rightarrow x = \dfrac{100 \times 100}{125} = 80$

16. (a) $\because$ 9 men $\equiv$ 12 women

$\therefore$ 3 men $\equiv$ 4 women

$\therefore$ 6 men + 16 women $=$ 24 women

$\therefore M_1 D_1 = M_2 D_2$

$\Rightarrow 18 \times 12 = 24 \times D_2$

$\Rightarrow D_2 = \dfrac{18 \times 12}{24} = 9$ days

17. (a) Let the numbers be $2x$ and $3x$.

$\therefore \dfrac{2x+4}{3x+4} = \dfrac{5}{7}$

$\therefore 15x + 20 = 14x + 28$

$\Rightarrow x = 28 - 20 = 8$ (Required Difference)

18. (a) Remainder when $(x-1)^n$ is divided by x is $(-1)^n$

$\therefore (17)^{200} = (18-1)^{200}$

$\therefore$ Remainder $= (-1)^{200} = 1$

19. (d) **Short-cut method:**

Weight of new crewmen

$=$ Replace man weight $+$ [No. of crew men $\times$ increased average]

$= 55 + 12 \times \dfrac{1}{3} = 59$ kg

20. (c) Difference in discount $= 1\%$

$\dfrac{1}{100} \times x = 15$

$x = 1500$

21. (c) Let SP = 100

    Loss% on SP = 20%

    CP = 100 + 20 = 120

    $$\text{L\% of CP} = \frac{20}{120} \times 100 = 16\frac{2}{3}$$

22. (b) Let the sum be ₹1 which becomes ₹2 after 2 years

    $$\Rightarrow 2 = \left(1 + \frac{R}{100}\right)^2 \qquad \text{...(i)}$$

    Let the sum of ₹1 becomes ₹4 after 'n' years

    $$\Rightarrow 4 = 1\left(1 + \frac{R}{100}\right)^n$$

    $$\Rightarrow 2^2 = 1\left(1 + \frac{R}{100}\right)^n$$

    $$\left[1\left(1 + \frac{R}{100}\right)^2\right]^2 = \left(1 + \frac{R}{100}\right)^n$$

    n = 4 years

23. (b) Average Speed $= \dfrac{\text{Total Distance Covered}}{\text{Total Time Taken}}$

    $$= \frac{6+6+6+6}{\dfrac{6}{25} + \dfrac{6}{50} + \dfrac{6}{75} + \dfrac{6}{150}} \Rightarrow \frac{24}{6\left[\dfrac{1}{25} + \dfrac{1}{50} + \dfrac{1}{75} + \dfrac{1}{150}\right]}$$

    $$= \frac{24 \times 300}{6 \times 24} \Rightarrow 50 \text{ km/hr}$$

24. (c) If time taken by A be x days,

    then time taken by B = 3x days

    $\therefore 3x - x = 60$

    $\Rightarrow 2x = 60$

    $\Rightarrow x = 30$

    Time taken by B = 90 days

    $\therefore$ (A + B)'s 1 day's work

$$= \frac{1}{30} + \frac{1}{90} = \frac{3+1}{90} = \frac{4}{90} = \frac{2}{45}$$

$\therefore$ The work will be completed in

$$\frac{45}{2} \text{ i.e. } 22\frac{1}{2} \text{ days}$$

25. (b) Let salary of A and B be = 4x and 3x

    expenditure = income-saving

    ATQ

    $$\frac{4x - 6000}{3x - 6000} = \frac{3}{2}$$

    $8x - 12000 = 9x - 18000$

    $x = 6000$

    A's salary = 4x = 4 × 6000 = ₹ 24000

26. (b) A petal is a part of a flower; a tire is a part of a bicycle.

27. (d) First number = 8 and the sum of the digits of the second number is 2 + 8 = 10.

    Thus, the difference of the first number and the sum of the digits of second number is 10 - 8 = 2.

    Similarly, the sum of the digits of third number is 2 + 7 = 9.

    Hence, the sum of digits of fourth number should be 2 more than 9 i.e. 11 and 6 + 5 = 11

    Hence, (d) 65 is the correct option.

28. (c)

29. (a)

30. (b) Let uncle's present age = x

    Rahim's present age = y

    $x - y = 30$ ...(i)

    After 7 year

    $(x + 7) + (y + 7) = 66$

    $x + y + 14 = 66$

    $x + y = 52$ ...(ii)

    combining (i) and (ii) we get

    $(x + y = 52) + (x - y = 30)$

    $2x = 82$

    $x = 41$

    Uncle's age is 41 years

31. (d)   32. (d)

33. (d)   Lady's mother's husband → Lady's father
           Lady's father's sister → Lady's Aunt.
           So, Lady's aunt is man's aunt and therefore
           lady is man's sister.

34. (d)

35. (b)   On interchanging − and ÷,
           We get the equation as
           $$5 + 3 \times 8 \div 12 - 4 = 3$$
           or $5 + 3 \times 2/3 - 4 = 3$
           or $3 = 3$, which is true

36. (b) $7 + 2^2 + 5 = 16$
           $9 + 4^2 + 7 = 32$
           $8 + 3^2 + 6 = \boxed{23}$

37. (c)   38. (c)   39. (c)

40. (c)   The pattern is as follows :
           $4 = (2)^2; 16 = (4)^2; 36 = (6)^2;$
           $64 = (8)^2; 196 = (14)^2; 169 = (13)^2;$
           $144 = (12)^2;$

41. (c)   The pattern is as follows :

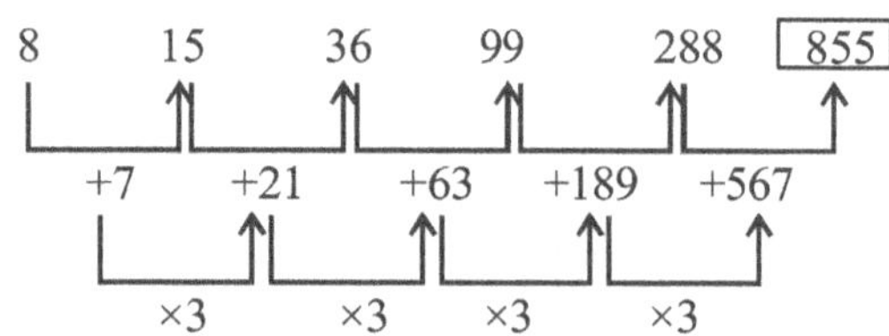

42. (a)   As,

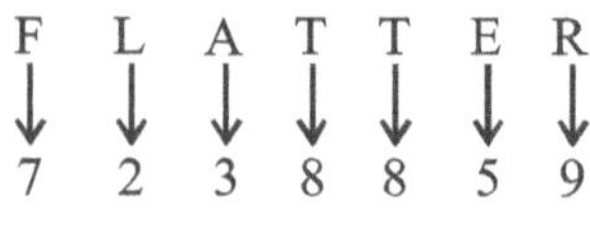

           and,

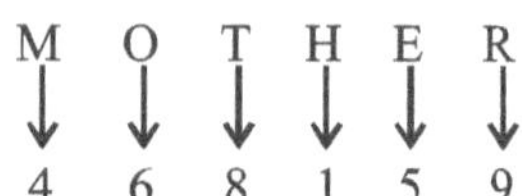

           Therefore,

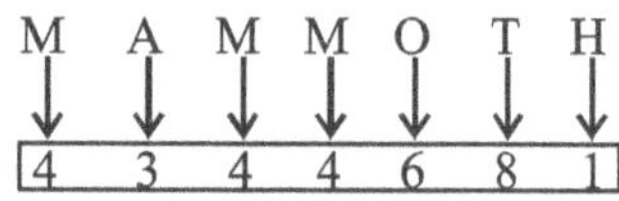

43. (c)   Grandson of Arun's mother means either
           son or nephew of Arun. Therefore, Arun is
           the father-in-law of that girl.

44. (c) $90 \div 18 \times 6 + 30 - 4 = 56$

45. (b)   The letters 'b' and 'd' are present in both
           the circles.

46. (a)   According to figure,
           'd' letter represents carnivorous plants
           which are not green.

47. (a)

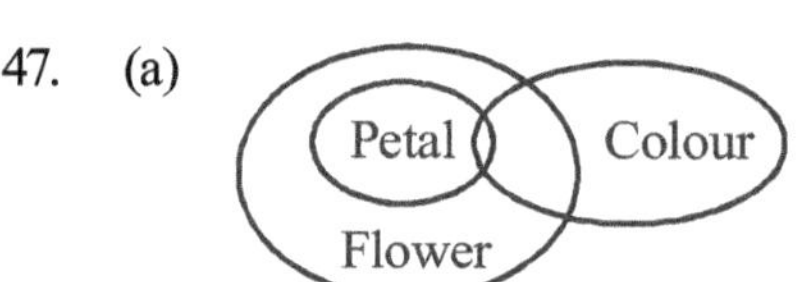

           So, Only I follows.

48. (d)

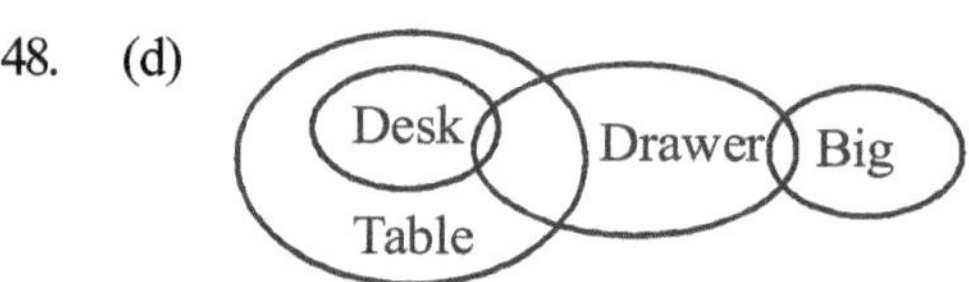

           So, Neither I nor II follows.

49. (d)   The availability of vegetables is not
           mentioned in the given statement. So, I
           does not follow Also, II is not directly
           related to the statement and so it also does
           not follow.

50. (d)   Since the accident has caused concern, it
           must be fatal. So, I follows. The use of the
           word 'again' in the statement justifies the
           fact mentioned in II. So, II also follows.

51. (b) 52. (b) 53. (b) 54. (a) 55. (b)
56. (a) 57. (d) 58. (b) 59. (d) 60. (a)
61. (b) 62. (a) 63. (a) 64. (c) 65. (a)
66. (b) 67. (c) 68. (d) 69. (a) 70. (a)
71. (d) 72. (c) 73. (c) 74. (a) 75. (b)
76. (a) 77. (c) 78. (c) 79. (d) 80. (c)
81. (c) 82. (b) 83. (c) 84. (c) 85. (d)
86. (c) 87. (a) 88. (d) 89. (a) 90. (b)
91. (c) 92. (c) 93. (a) 94. (b) 95. (d)
96. (b) 97. (b) 98. (b) 99. (b) 100. (c)

PRACTICE SET 8

Time: 90 minutes　　　　　　　　　　　　**Max. Marks - 100**

MATHEMATICS

1. A number being successively divided by 3, 5 and 8 leaves 1, 2 and 4 as remainders respectively. What are the remainders if the order of divisors be reversed?
   - (a) 3, 3, 1
   - (b) 3, 1, 3
   - (c) 1, 3, 3
   - (d) None of these

2. The prices of a school bag and a shoe are in the ratio 7 : 5. The price of a school bag is ₹ 200 more than the price of a shoe. Then the price of a shoe is
   - (a) ₹ 500
   - (b) ₹ 1,200
   - (c) ₹ 200
   - (d) ₹ 700

3. A shopkeeper bought 30 kg of wheat at the rate of ₹ 45 per kg. He sold forty per cent of the total quantity at the rate of ₹ 50 per kg. Approximately, at what price per kg should he sell the remaining quantity to make 25 percent overall profit?
   - (a) ₹ 54
   - (b) ₹ 52
   - (c) ₹ 50
   - (d) ₹ 60

4. The average of nine numbers is 50. The average of the first five numbers is 54 and that of the last three numbers is 52. Then the sixth number is
   - (a) 24
   - (b) 44
   - (c) 30
   - (d) 34

5. If two numbers are respectively 20% and 50% of a third number, what is the percentage of the first number to the second ?
   - (a) 10
   - (b) 20
   - (c) 30
   - (d) 40

6. Out of a certain sum, $\frac{1}{3}$ rd is invested at 3%, $\frac{1}{6}$ th at 6% and the rest at 8%. If the simple interest for 2 years from all these investments amounts to ₹ 600, find the original sum.
   - (a) ₹ 4000
   - (b) ₹ 5000
   - (c) ₹ 6000
   - (d) ₹ 7000

7. A contractor undertakes to built a walls in 50 days. He employs 50 peoples for the same. However after 25 days he finds that only 40% of the work is complete. How many more man need to be employed to complete the work in time?
   - (a) 25
   - (b) 30
   - (c) 35
   - (d) 20

8. The length of a rectangular plot is thrice its breadth. If the area of the rectangular plot is 7803 sq. metre, what is the breadth of the rectangular plot?
   - (a) 51 metres
   - (b) 153 metres
   - (c) 104 metres
   - (d) 88 metres

9. The H.CF. and L.CM. of two numebrs are 8 and 48 respectively. If one of the numbers is 24, then the other number is
   - (a) 48
   - (b) 36
   - (c) 24
   - (d) 16

10. The greatest number, which when subtracted from 5834, gives a number exactly divisible by each of 20, 28, 32 and 35, is
    - (a) 1120
    - (b) 4714
    - (c) 5200
    - (d) 5600

11. A number, when divided by 114, leaves remainder 21. If the same number is divided by 19, then the remainder will be
    - (a) 1
    - (b) 2
    - (c) 7
    - (d) 17

12. If $\left(\dfrac{3}{5}\right)^3 \left(\dfrac{3}{5}\right)^{-6} = \left(\dfrac{3}{5}\right)^{2x-1}$, then x is equal to
    - (a) –2
    - (b) 2
    - (c) –1
    - (d) 1

13. A drum of kerosene is $\dfrac{3}{4}$ full. When 30 litres of kerosene is drawn from it, it remains $\dfrac{7}{12}$ full. The capacity of the drum is

(a) 120 *l*   (b) 135 *l*
(c) 150 *l*   (d) 180 *l*

14. By what least number should 5400 be multiplied so as to obtain a perfect cube number ?
    (a) 3   (b) 5
    (c) 24   (d) 40

15. If a and b are two odd positive integers, by which of the following integers is $(a^4 - b^4)$ always divisible ?
    (a) 3   (b) 6
    (c) 8   (d) 12

16. If the ratio of cost price and selling price of an article be as 10 : 11, the percentage of profit is
    (a) 8%   (b) 10%
    (c) 11%   (d) 15%

17. A manufacturer marked an article at ₹50 and sold it allowing 20% discount. If his profit was 25% then the cost price of the article was
    (a) ₹80   (b) ₹70
    (c) ₹64   (d) ₹60

18. A shopkeeper earns a profit of 12% on selling a book at 10% discount on the printed price. The ratio fo the cost price and the printed price of the book is
    (a) 45 : 56   (b) 45 : 51
    (c) 47 : 56   (d) 47 : 51

19. By selling a bicycle for ₹ 5700, A shopkeeper gains 14%. If the profit is reduced to 8%, then the selling price will be
    (a) 5600   (b) 5400
    (c) 5800   (d) 6000

20. If A's income is 50% less than that of B's, then B's income is what per cent more than that of A?
    (a) 125   (b) 100
    (c) 75   (d) 50

21. Two natural numbers are in the ratio 3 : 5 and their product is 2160. The smaller of the numbers is
    (a) 36   (b) 24   (c) 18   (d) 12

22. Two successive price increases of 10% and 10% of an article are equivalent to a single price increase of

(a) 19%   (b) 20%
(c) 21%   (d) 22%

23. An equilateral triangle of side 6 cm has its corners cut off to form a regular hexagon. Area (in cm^2) of this regular hexagon will be
    (a) $3\sqrt{3}$ (b) $3\sqrt{6}$
    (c) $6\sqrt{3}$ (d) $\dfrac{5\sqrt{3}}{2}$

24. If ₹ 4000 is divided between A and B in the ratio 3 : 2, then A will receive
    (a) ₹ 1600   (b) ₹ 2500
    (c) ₹ 2400   (d) ₹ 2800

25. Buses start from a bus terminal with a speed of 20 km/hr at intervals of 10 minutes. What is the speed of a man coming from the opposite directiion towards the bus terminal if he meets the buses at intervals of 8 minutes ?
    (a) 3 km/hr   (b) 4 km/hr
    (c) 5 km/hr   (d) 7 km/hr

GENERAL INTELLIGENCE AND REASONING

DIRECTIONS (Qs. 26-27) : In the questions, select the related word/ letters/numbers from the given alternatives.

26. Saint : Meditation : : Scientist : ?
    (a) Research   (b) Knowledge
    (c) Spiritual   (d) Rational

27. 7 : 56 :: 9 : ?
    (a) 63   (b) 81
    (c) 90   (d) 99

28. In a certain code language NATIONALISM is written as OINTANMSAIL. How is DEPARTMENTS written in that code?
    (a) RADEPTSTMNE
    (b) RADPETSTMNE
    (c) RADPESTMTNE
    (d) RADPETSTNME

29. From the given alternative words, select the word which cannot be formed using the letters of the given word:

    TRIVANDRUM

    (a) RAIN   (b) DRUM
    (c) TRAIN   (d) DRUK

30. A man said to a woman, "Your mother's husband's sister is my aunt." How is the woman related to the man ?

    (a) Granddaughter   (b) Daughter
    (c) Sister   (d) Aunt

31. Rasik walks 20 m North. Then, he turns right and walks 30 m. Then he turns right and walks 35 m. Then he turns left and walks 15 m. Then he again turns left and walks 15 m. In which direction and how many metres away is he from his original position?

    (a) 15 metres West   (b) 30 metres East
    (c) 30 metres West   (d) 45 metres East

32. In a row of boys Akash is fifth from the left and Nikhil is eleventh from the right. If Akash is twenty-fifth from the right then how many boys are there between Akash and Nikhil?

    (a) 14   (b) 13
    (c) 15   (d) 12

33. If '−' stands for division, '+' for multiplication '÷' for subtraction and '×' for addition. Which one of the following equation is correct?

    (a) $6 \div 20 \times 12 + 7 - 1 = 70$
    (b) $6 + 20 - 20 \div 7 \times 1 = 62$
    (c) $6 - 20 \div 12 \times 7 + 1 = 57$
    (d) $6 + 20 - 20 \div 7 - 1 = 38$

34. Choose the diagram which represent the relationship among the following :- Capsules, Antibiotics, Injection.

    (a) ⬭⬭⬭   (b) ⬭⬭
    (c) ⬭⬭   (d) ⬭⬭

DIRECTION (Q. 35) : In the question below are given two statements followed by two conclusions. You have to take the given statements to be true even if they seem to be at variance with commonly known facts. Read all the conclusions and then decide which of the given statements disregarding commonly known facts.

> **Give answer (a)** If only conclusion I follows.
> **Give answer (b)** if only conclusion II follows.
> **Give answer (c)** if either I or II follows.
> **Give answer (d)** if neither I nor II follows.

35. **Statements:**

    All leaders are good team workers.

    All good team workers are good orators.

    Conclusions:

    I.   Some good team workers are leaders.

    II. All good orators are leaders.

DIRECTION (Q. 36): In the following questions, select the missing number from the given response.

36.
2	7	9
7	3	4
9	8	?
126	168	216

    (a) 8   (b) 3
    (c) 6   (d) 36

37. How many triangles are there in the figure ABCDEF?

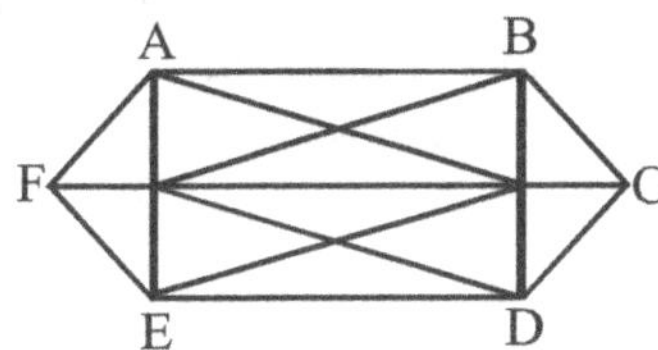

    (a) 24   (b) 26
    (c) 28   (d) 30

DIRECTION (Q. 38): From the given answer figures, select the one which is hidden/embedded in the question figure (X).

38.

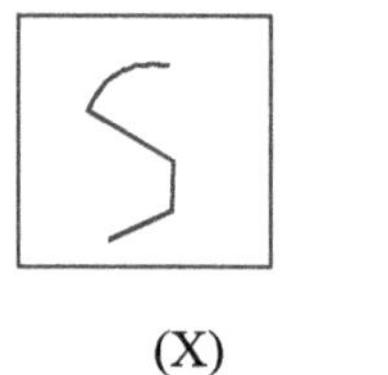

(X)

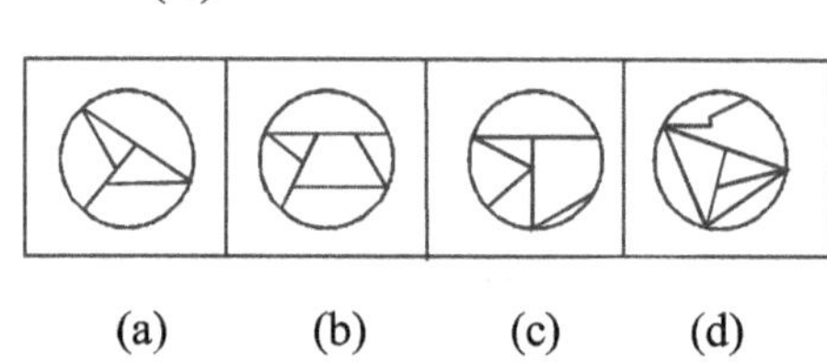

(a)   (b)   (c)   (d)

DIRECTION (Q. 39): In the following question, which answer figure will complete the pattern in the question figure?

---

39. **Question figure:**

(a)

(b)

(c)

(d)

DIRECTIONS (Qs. 40-41): A series is given, with one/two term missing. Choose the correct alternative from the given ones that will complete the series.

---

40. 121, 144, 289, 324, 529, 576, _?_ .
  (a) 961   (b) 841
  (c) 900   (d) 729

41. 5, 21, 69, 213, 645, _?_ .
  (a) 1670   (b) 1941
  (c) 720   (d) 1320

42. Pointing to a man, a lady said "His mother is the only daughter of my mother". How is the lady related to the man?

  (a) Mother   (b) Daughter
  (c) Sister   (d) Aunt

43. Vivek and Ashok start from a fixed point. Vivek moves 3 km north and turns right and then covers 4 km. Ashok moves 5 km west and turns right and walks 3 km. Now how far are they apart?
  (a) 10 km   (b) 9 km
  (c) 8 km   (d) 6 km

44. If Q means add to, J means multiply by, T means subtract from, K means divided by, then
  30 K 2 Q 3 J 6 T 5 = ?
  (a) 18   (b) 28
  (c) 31   (d) 103

45. In the given figure, circles represent students studying three different subjects. How many students study all the three subjects?

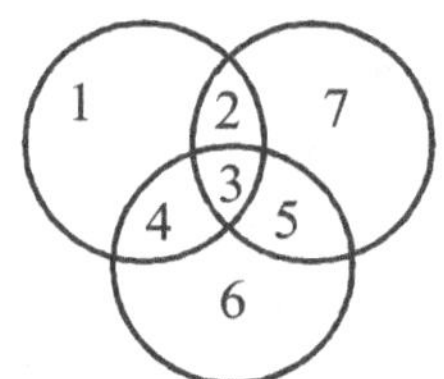

  (a) 2   (b) 3   (c) 4   (d) 1

46. In the given figure, how many yellow birds are there?

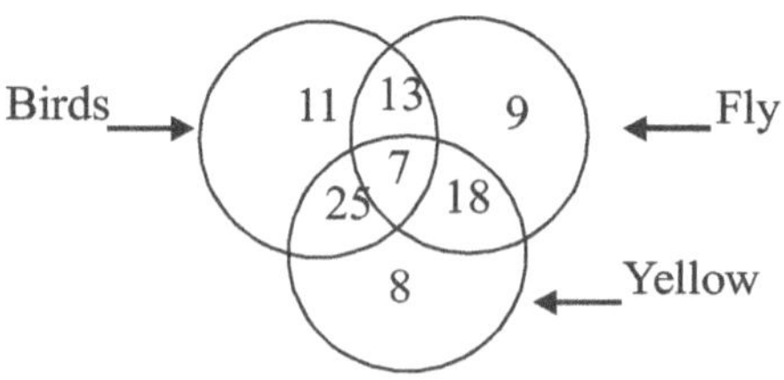

  (a) 25   (b) 32
  (c) 18   (d) 20

DIRECTIONS (Qs. 47-48) : In each of the questions below are given three statements followed by two conclusions numbered I and II. You have to take the given statements to be true even if they seem to be at variance from commonly known facts and then decide which of the given conclusions logically follows from the statements disregarding commonly known facts.

Give answer **(a)** if only conclusion I follows.

Give answer **(b)** if only conclusion II follows.

Give answer **(c)** if either conclusion I or conclusion II follows.

Give answer **(d)** if neither conclusion I nor conclusion II follows.

47. **Statements:**

    All colleges are buildings.

    All buildings are concrete.

    Some concrete are strong.

    Conclusions :

    I.   Some colleges are strong.

    II.   At least some strong are concrete.

48. **Statements:**

    Some trees are tall.

    All tall are healthy.

    All healthy are not tall.

    Conclusions:

    I.   Some healthy are tall.

    II.   Some trees are not tall.

DIRECTIONS (Qs. 49-50): In each question below is given a statement followed by two conclusions numbered I and II. You have to assume everything in the statement to be true, then consider the two conclusions together and decide which of them logically follows beyond a reasonable doubt from the information given in the statement.

49. **Statements:** In a recent survey report, it has been stated that those who undertake physical exercise for at least half an hour a day are less prone to have any heart ailments.

    Conclusions:

    I.   Moderate level of physical exercise is necessary for leading a healthy life.

    II.   All people who do desk-bound jobs definitely suffer from heart ailments.

    (a)   Only conclusion I follows

    (b)   Only conclusion II follows

    (c)   Either I or II follows

    (d)   Neither I nor II follows

50. **Statements:** A bird in hand is worth two in the bush.

    Conclusions:

    I.   We should be content with what we have.

    II.   We should not crave for what is not.

    (a)   Only conclusion I follows

    (b)   Only conclusion II follows

    (c)   Either I or II follows

    (d)   Both I and II follow

BASIC SCIENCE AND ENGINEERING

51. The following are the Solids of revolution except

    (a)   Prism   (b)   Sphere

    (c)   Cone   (d)   Cylinder

52. If length of pendulum is increased by 2%. The time period will

    (a)   Increases by 1%

    (b)   Decreases by 1%

    (c)   Increases by 2%

    (d)   Decreases by 2%

53. Which of these has the lowest density?

    (a)   cork   (b)   glass

    (c)   water   (d)   aluminum

54. The ratio of the numerical values of the average velocity and average speed of a body is

    (a)   unity   (b)   unity or less

    (c)   unity or more   (d)   less than unity

55. In process of rubbing hands, mechanical energy is converted into

    (a)   sound energy   (b)   electrical energy

    (c)   thermal energy   (d)   heat energy

56. Which of the following is not a unit of heat energy ?

    (a)   joule   (b)   kelvin

    (c)   calorie   (d)   None of these

57. What is the suitable material for electric fuse?

    (a)   Cu   (b)   Constantan

    (c)   Tin-lead alloy   (d)   Nichrome

58. A ramp is a simple inclined plane that allows one to apply an input force ___________ the output force.
    (a) perpendicular to   (b) less than
    (c) equal to   (d) greater than

59. What is important in an accident investigation?
    (a) To clean up the site of the accident as quickly as possible in order to prevent new accidents.
    (b) To only interview the victim.
    (c) To collect all facts and information at the location of the accident.
    (d) None of these.

60. Amount of carbon dioxide present in atmospheric air is
    (a) 0.318%   (b) 0.383%
    (c) 21%   (d) 78%

61. Holding the mouse button down while moving an object of text is known as –
    (a) moving   (b) dragging
    (c) dropping   (d) highlighting

62. Metals are best
    (a) insulators of heat
    (b) conductors of heat
    (c) sharers of heat
    (d) insulators of electricitys

63. The primary unit of measurement for engineering drawings and design in the mechanical industries is the
    (a) Millimeter   (b) Centimeter
    (c) Meter   (d) Kilometer

64. Precision of micrometer screw gauge is
    (a) 0.1 cm   (b) 0.01 mm
    (c) 0.1 mm   (d) 0.01 m

65. SI unit for density is
    (a) $kg\,cm^{-3}$ (b) $g\,cm^{-3}$
    (c) $kg\,m^{-3}$ (d) $g\,m^{-3}$

66. In the case of a rectilinear uniform motion, distance-time graph is a
    (a) parabola   (b) straight line
    (c) curved line   (d) rectangle

67. When direction of applied force and direction in which object moves are perpendicular to each other, then
    (a) no power is used   (b) no work is done
    (c) work is done   (d) power is used

68. A constant force on an object given by product of force and distance moved by object in direction of force is termed as
    (a) Work done   (b) Efficiency
    (c) Power   (d) Energy

69. It is the process of heat transfer from a hot body to a colder body without heating the space between the two is called as:
    (a) Conduction   (b) Radiation
    (c) Convection   (d) Absorption

70. The insulation on a current carrying conductor is provided
    (a) to prevent leakage of current
    (b) to prevent shock
    (c) both of above factors
    (d) none of above factors

71. Which could help a person in a wheelchair get from the street onto the sidewalk?
    (a) screw   (b) lever
    (c) wheel and axle   (d) inclined plane

72. OSHA (occupational safety and health act), was created to ______
    (a) Data analysis
    (b) to reduce hazards
    (c) Ecological development
    (d) EIA analysis

73. Of the following man-made disasters, which is socially induced?
    (a) Arson
    (b) Ozone depletion
    (c) Debris Avalanche
    (d) Salt Water Intrusion

74. The first computer was programmed using ....
    (a) Assembly language
    (b) Machine language
    (c) Spaghetti code
    (d) Source code

75. A moving coil instrument can be used to measure
    (a) Low frequency alternating current
    (b) High frequency alternating current
    (c) Direct current
    (d) Direct current and alternating current both

GENERAL AWARENESS AND CURRENT AFFAIR

76. Which of the following is not evident at Mohenjodaro?
    (a) Pasupati seal
    (b) Great granary and great bath
    (c) Multi-pillared assembly hall
    (d) Evidence of double burials

77. Total schedules in Indian Constitution are:
    (a) 22   (b) 10
    (c) 16   (d) 12

78. Who was the President of the Constituent Assembly?
    (a) Rajendra Prasad (b) B. R. Ambedkar
    (c) K. M. Munshi   (d) G. V. Mavlankar

79. Which one of the following is a vector quantity?
    (a) Momentum   (b) Pressure
    (c) Energy   (d) Work

80. The working principle of a washing machine is :
    (a) centrifugation (b) dialysis
    (c) reverse osmosis (d) diffusion

81. Acid rain is caused by the pollution of environment by
    (a) carbon dioxide and nitrogen
    (b) carbon monoxide and carbon dioxide
    (c) ozone and carbon dioxide
    (d) nitrous oxide and sulphur dioxide

82. The wine is prepared by the process of
    (a) fermentation   (b) catalysation
    (c) conjugation   (d) displacement

83. Which one of the following hormones contains iodine?
    (a) Thyroxine   (b) Testosterone
    (c) Insulin   (d) Adrenaline

84. The major component of honey is
    (a) glucose   (b) sucrose
    (c) maltose   (d) fructose

85. In eye donation, which one of the following parts of donor's eye is utilized?
    (a) Iris   (b) Lens
    (c) Cornea   (d) Retina

86. Octopus is
    (a) an arthropod   (b) an echinoderm
    (c) a hemichordate (d) a mollusc

87. Who is the author of the book 'Harry Potter' and the 'Half-Blood Prince'?
    (a) Mark Twain
    (b) J. K. Rowling
    (c) William Shakespeare
    (d) Jules Verne

88. The term 'brown air' is used for
    (a) Photochemical smog
    (b) Sulfurous smog
    (c) Industrial smog
    (d) Acid fumes

89. Which state police have launched a mobile-based messenger application "Cop Connect" to provide real time information to police officers across the State?
    (a) Karnataka   (b) Tamil Nadu
    (c) Kerala   (d) Telangana

90. Which country to host the high-level Conference on "International Decade for Action: Water for Sustainable Development, 2018-2028"?
    (a) Tajikistan   (b) Russia
    (c) India   (d) Sri Lanka

91. What was/were the official mascots of the 2018 Asian Games?
    (a) Bhin Bhin   (b) Kaka
    (c) Atung   (d) All (a), (b), and (c)

92. Primary source of biological energy is -
    (a) Green plants   (b) Non green plants
    (c) Sun   (d) Animals

93. Plague is a -
    (a) Bacterial disease
    (b) Viral disease
    (c) Mineral deficiency disease
    (d) Fungal disease

94. The substance most commonly used as a food preservative is -
    (a) Tartaric acid
    (b) Acetic acid
    (c) Sodium salt of benzoic acid
    (d) Sodium carbonate

95. The largest irrigated area in India is occupied by -
    (a) Cotton   (b) Wheat
    (c) Rice   (d) Sugarcane

96. Which part of human body is first highly affected by nuclear radiations?
    (a) Skin   (b) Bone marrow\
    (c) Lungs   (d) Eyes

97. Gobar Gas contains chiefly -
    (a) NH_3 (b) NH_4
    (c) $C2H_4$ (d) CH_4

98. The Central Tobacco Research institute is located at-
    (a) Kolkata
    (b) Vijayawada
    (c) Hyderabad
    (d) Rajmundary

99. Lothal and Kalibangan are associated with
    (a) Harappan Civilization
    (b) Egyptian Civilization
    (c) Babylonian Civilization
    (d) Chinese Civilization

100. Who were the immediate successors of the Mauryas in Magadha?
    (a) Kushanas   (b) Pandyas
    (c) Satavahanas   (d) Sungas

HINTS & EXPLANATIONS

1. (a) Complete remainder $= d_1 d_2 r_3 + d_1 r_2 + r_1$
$= 3 \times 5 \times 4 + 3 \times 2 + 1 = 67$
Divided 67 by 8, 5 and 3, the remainders are 3, 3, 1.

2. (a) $7x - 5x = 200$
$\Rightarrow 2x = 200 \Rightarrow x = 100$
$\therefore$ Price of a pair of shoes $= 5x = 500$

3. (d) CP of wheat $= 30 \times 45 = ₹1350$
40% of 30 kg = 12 kg
SP of 12 kg $= 12 \times 50 = ₹600$
For 25% profit, total SP of all the wheat is

$$1350 \times \frac{125}{100} = 1350 \times \frac{5}{4} = ₹\frac{6750}{4} = ₹1687.5$$

Remaining wheat $(30 - 12) = 18$ kg.
Rate of remaining wheat

$$= \frac{1087.5}{18} \approx ₹60$$

4. (a) The sixth number $= 9 \times 50 - 5 \times 54 - 3 \times 52$
$= 450 - 270 - 156 = 24$

5. (d) Let the third number be 100. Then, the first and second numbers will be 20 and 50, respectively.

$$\text{Required \%} = \frac{20}{50} \times 100 = 40\%$$

6. (b) Rest part $= 1 - \left(\frac{1}{3} + \frac{1}{6}\right) = \frac{1}{2}$

Rate % per annum on total sum

$$= \left(\frac{1}{3} \times 3\right) + \left(\frac{1}{6} \times 6\right) + \left(\frac{1}{2} \times 8\right) = 6\%$$

$$\therefore \ P = \frac{600 \times 100}{6 \times 2} = ₹5,000$$

7. (a) 50 men complete 0.4 work in 25 days.
Applying the work rule,

$$m_1 \times d_1 \times w_2 = m_2 \times d_2 \times w_1$$
we have,
$$50 \times 25 \times 0.6 = m_2 \times 25 \times 0.4$$

$$\text{or } m_2 = \frac{50 \times 25 \times 0.6}{25 \times 0.4} = 75 \text{ men}$$

Number of additional men required
$= (75 - 50) = 25$

8. (a) Let the breadth of the rectangular plot be x metre.
$\therefore$ Length $= 3x$ metre
According to the question,
$3x \times x = 7803$

$$\Rightarrow x^2 = \frac{7803}{3} = 2601$$

$$\therefore x = \sqrt{2601} = 51 \text{ metre}$$

9. (d) $p \times q = \text{HCF} \times \text{LCM}$

$$\therefore \text{ Second number } = \frac{8 \times 48}{24} = 16$$

10. (b)

2	20,	28,	32,	35
2	10,	14,	16,	35
5	5,	7,	8,	35
7	1,	7,	8,	7
	1,	1,	8,	1

$\therefore \text{LCM} = 2 \times 2 \times 5 \times 7 \times 8 = 1120$
$\therefore$ Required number
$= 5834 - 1120 = 4714$

11. (b) If the first divisor is a multiple of second divisor.
Then, remainder by the second divisor.
$\therefore$ Remainder $= 21 \div 19 = 2$

12. (c) $\left(\dfrac{3}{5}\right)^3 \left(\dfrac{3}{5}\right)^{-6} = \left(\dfrac{3}{5}\right)^{2x-1}$

$$\Rightarrow \left(\frac{3}{5}\right)^3 \left(\frac{3}{5}\right)^{-3} \left(\frac{3}{5}\right)^{-3} = \left(\frac{3}{5}\right)^{2x-1}$$

$$\Rightarrow \left(\frac{3}{5}\right)^0 \left(\frac{3}{5}\right)^{-3} = \left(\frac{3}{5}\right)^{2x-1}$$

$$\Rightarrow 2x - 1 = -3$$
$$\Rightarrow 2x = -3 + 1 = -2$$
$$\Rightarrow x = -1$$

13. (d) Let the capacity of the drum be x litres.

$$\therefore \frac{3x}{4} - 30 = \frac{7x}{12}$$

$$\Rightarrow \frac{3x}{4} - \frac{7x}{12} = 30$$

$$\Rightarrow \frac{9x - 7x}{12} = 30$$

$$\Rightarrow \frac{x}{6} = 30$$

$$= x = 6 \times 30 = 180 \text{ litres}$$

14. (b) $5400 = 5 \times 5 \times 3 \times 3 \times 3 \times 2 \times 2 \times 2 = 5$
No to be multiplied by 5.

15. (c) $a^4 - b^4 = (a^2 + b^2)(a + b)(a - b)$
$\therefore$ Required number $= (3 + 1)(3 - 1) = 8$

16. (b) Gain $= 11x - 10x = ₹x$

$$\therefore p\% = \frac{p \times 100}{CP} \times 100$$

$$= \frac{x}{10x} \times 100 = 10\%$$

17. (c) Marked price $= ₹ 100$
S.P. after discount $= 80\%$ of 100
$= ₹ 80$
If the CP of article be $₹x$, then

$$\frac{125 \times x}{100} = 80$$

$$\Rightarrow x = \frac{80 \times 100}{125} = ₹ 64$$

18. (a) Let the CP be $₹100$.
$\therefore SP = ₹112$
If the marked price be $₹x$, then
90% of $x = 112$

$$\Rightarrow x = \frac{112 \times 100}{90} = ₹ \frac{1120}{9}$$

$\therefore$ Required ratio

$$= 100 : \frac{1120}{9}$$

$$= 900 : 1120 = 45 : 56$$

19. (b) C.P. of bicycle

$$= \frac{100}{114} \times 5700 = ₹ 5000$$

S.P. for a profit of 8%

$$= \frac{108}{100} \times 5000 = ₹ 5400$$

20. (b) Required precentage

$$= \frac{50}{100 - 50} \times 100$$

$$= 100\%$$

21. (a) Let the numbers be $3x$ and $5x$.
$\therefore 3x \times 5x = 2160$

$$\Rightarrow x^2 = \frac{2160}{3 \times 5} = 144 = 12 \times 12$$

$$\Rightarrow x = 12$$

$\therefore$ Smaller number
$= 3x = 3 \times 12 = 36$

22. (c) Single equivalent percentage increase in price

$$= \left(10 + 10 + \frac{10 \times 10}{100}\right)\% = 21\%$$

23. (c) 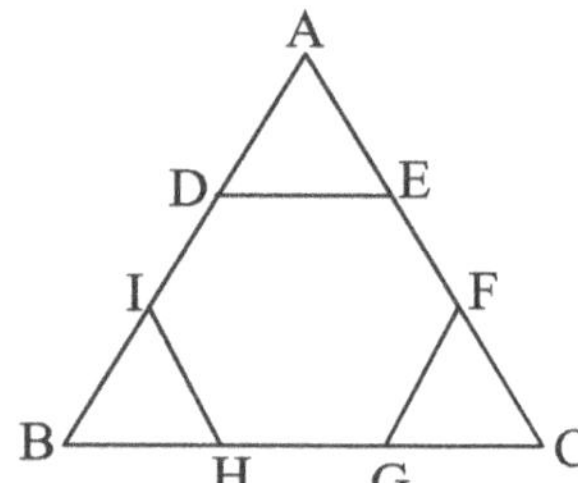

Side of the regular hexagon

$$= \frac{1}{3} \times 6 = 2 \text{ cm}$$

$$\therefore \text{ Area of the hexagon} = \frac{3\sqrt{3}}{2} a^2$$

$$= \frac{3\sqrt{3}}{2} \times 2 \times 2$$

$$= 6\sqrt{3} \text{ sq. cm.}$$

24. (c) A's share

$$= ₹\left(\frac{3}{5} \times 4000\right) = ₹2400$$

25. (c) Distance coverd in 10 minutes at 20kmph = distance covered in 8 minutes at $(20 + x)$ kmph

$$\Rightarrow 20 \times \frac{10}{60} = \frac{8}{60}(20 + x)$$

$\Rightarrow 200 = 160 + 8x$

$\Rightarrow 8x = 40$

$\Rightarrow x = \dfrac{40}{8} = 5$ kmph

26. (a) A saint practices meditation. While, a scientist does research.

27. (c) The relationship is $x : x\,(x+1)$

28. (b) 

Reverse order

```
                          unchanged
        N A T I O  N  A L I S M
Reverse order ←         ↓     ←
        O I T A N  N  M S I L A
        ↓ ↓  ↘↙ ↓  ↓  ↓ ↓  ↘↙
        O I N T A  N  M S A I L
```

Similarly,

```
                          unchanged
        D E P A R  T  M E N T S
Reverse order ←         ↓     ←
        R A P E D  T  S T N E M
        ↓ ↓  ↘↙ ↓  ↓  ↓ ↓  ↘↙
        R A D P E  T  S T M N E
```

29. (d) DRUK cannot be formed using TRIVANDRUM as it does not contain letter 'K'.

30. (c) Woman's Mother's husband

$\downarrow$

Woman's father

Woman's father's sister $\longrightarrow$ Woman's Aunt.

Since, woman's aunt is man's aunt

$\therefore$ Woman is sister of man.

31. (d) The movements of Rasik from A to F are as shown in figure.
Since $CD = AB + EF$, so F lies in line with A.
Rasik's distance from original position $A = AF$
$= (AG + GF) = (BC + DE) = (30 + 15)\,m = 45\,m$.
Also, F lies to the east of A.

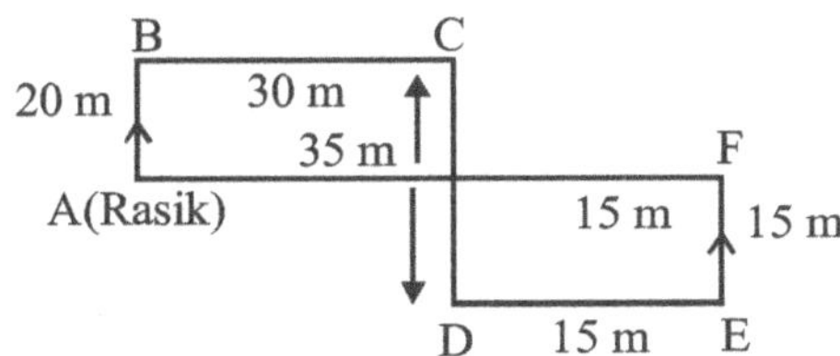

32. (b) There are $(25 - 11 - 1) = 13$ boys are between Akash and Nikhil.

33. (a)

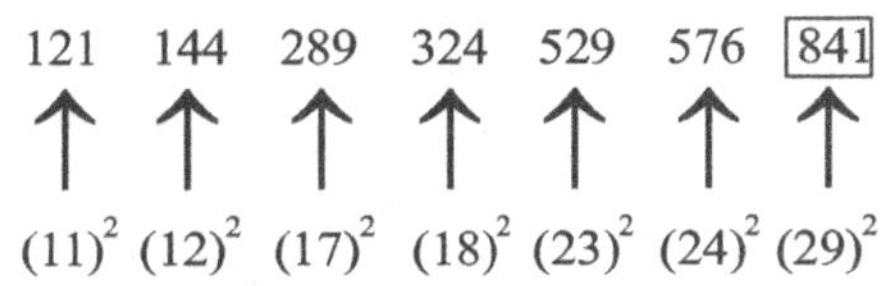

$$- \Rightarrow \div,\ + \Rightarrow \times$$
$$\div \Rightarrow -,\ \times \Rightarrow +$$

Option (a) : $6 \div 20 \times 12 + 7 - 1 = 70$
L.H.S. $= 6 - 20 + 12 \times 7 \div 1$
$= 6 - 20 + 84$
$= 90 - 20 = 70$ R. H.S.

34. (c) Capsules are different from injection but both are uses as antibiotics.

35. (a)

36. (c) $2 \times 7 \times 9 = 126$
$7 \times 3 \times 8 = 168$
$9 \times 4 \times x = 216$
$\Rightarrow \quad x = 6$

37. (c)   38. (b)

39. (c)

40. (b) The pattern is as follows :

$$121 \quad 144 \quad 289 \quad 324 \quad 529 \quad 576 \quad \boxed{841}$$
$$\uparrow \qquad \uparrow \qquad \uparrow \qquad \uparrow \qquad \uparrow \qquad \uparrow \qquad \uparrow$$
$$(11)^2\ (12)^2\ (17)^2\ (18)^2\ (23)^2\ (24)^2\ (29)^2$$

So, 841 will complete the series.

41. (b) The pattern is as follows :
$21 - 5 = 16 \Rightarrow 16 \times 3 = 48$
$69 - 21 = 48 \Rightarrow 48 \times 3 = 144$
$213 - 69 = 144 \Rightarrow 144 \times 3 \Rightarrow 432$
$645 - 213 \Rightarrow 432 \Rightarrow 432 \times 3 = 1296$
and
$\boxed{1941} - 645 = 1296$

42. (a)

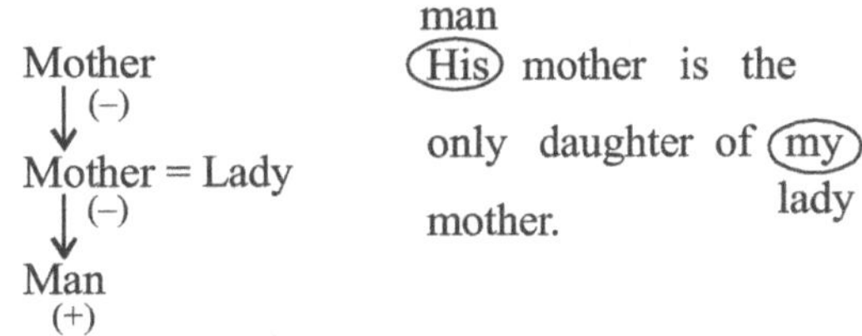

43. (b) The direction diagram is as follows :

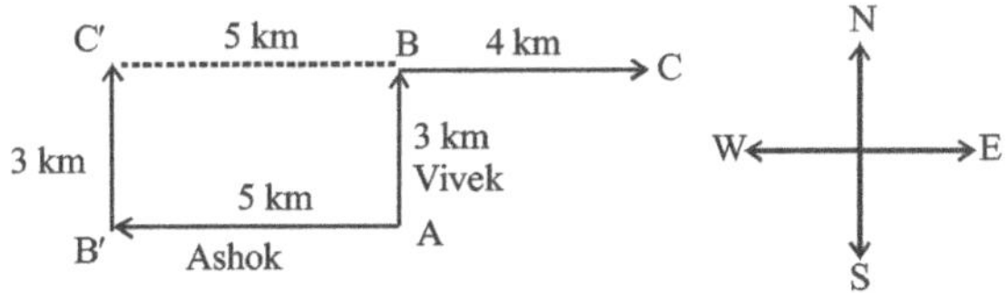

Here, C'B = B'A = 5 km
So, C'B + BC = 5 + 4 = 9 km
Therefore, they are 9 km far apart each other.

44. (b) The expression is :
30 K 2 Q 3 J 6 T 5
$\Rightarrow 30 \div 2 + 3 \times 6 - 5$
$\Rightarrow 15 + 3 \times 6 - 5$
$\Rightarrow 15 + 18 - 5$
$\Rightarrow 33 - 5 = 28$

45. (b) The number '3' is common to all the three circles.

46. (b) According to question,
Total number of yellow birds = (25 + 7) = 32.

47. (b)

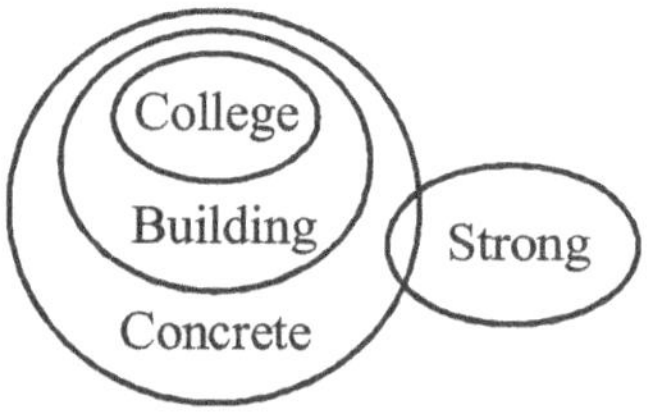

So, Only II follows.

48. (a)

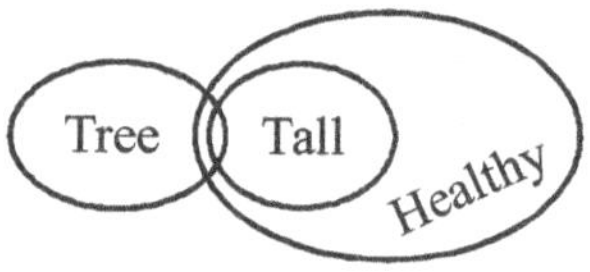

So, Only I follows.

49. (a) The statement mentions that chances of heart ailments are greatly reduced by a regular half-hour exercise. So, I follows. However, it talks of only reducing the probability which does not mean that persons involved in sedentary jobs shall definitely suffer from heart ailments. So, II does not follow.

50. (d) Both the given conclusions clearly bring out the central theme of the proverb given in the statement. So, both I and II follow.

51.	(a)	52.	(a)	53.	(a)	54.	(b)	55.	(d)
56.	(b)	57.	(a)	58.	(b)	59.	(c)	60.	(a)
61.	(b)	62.	(b)	63.	(a)	64.	(b)	65.	(c)
66.	(b)	67.	(b)	68.	(a)	69.	(b)	70.	(c)
71.	(d)	72.	(b)	73.	(a)	74.	(b)	75.	(c)
76.	(d)	77.	(d)	78.	(a)	79.	(a)	80.	(a)
81.	(a)	82.	(a)	83.	(a)	84.	(d)	85.	(c)
86.	(d)	87.	(a)	88.	(a)	89.	(d)	90.	(a)
91.	(d)	92.	(c)	93.	(a)	94.	(c)	95.	(c)
96.	(d)	97.	(d)	98.	(d)	99.	(a)	100.	(d)

PRACTICE SET 9

MATHEMATICS

1. If $3\frac{4}{5}$ is subtracted from $6\frac{3}{5}$ and difference is multiplied by 355 then what will be the final number?
   - (a) 1004
   - (b) 884
   - (c) 774
   - (d) 994

2. In a class of 65 students and 4 teachers, each student got sweets that are 20% of the total number of students and each teacher got sweets that are 40% of the total number of students. How many sweets were there?
   - (a) 845
   - (b) 897
   - (c) 949
   - (d) 104

3. In a mixture of milk and water the proportion of water by weight was 75% if in the 60 gms mixture 15 gms water was added, what would be the percentage of water in the new mixture?
   - (a) 75%
   - (b) 80%
   - (c) 90%
   - (d) 100%

4. The sum of five numbers is 290. The average of the first two numbers is 48.5 and the average of last two numbers is 53.5. What is the third number?
   - (a) 72
   - (b) 84
   - (c) 96
   - (d) 86

5. The average weight of a class of 15 boys and 10 girls is 38.4 kg. If the average weight of the boys is 40 kg, then what is the average weight of the girls?
   - (a) 36.5 kg
   - (b) 35 kg
   - (c) 36 kg
   - (d) 34.6 kg

6. Marked price of an article is ₹275. Shopkeeper allows a discount of 5% and he gets a profit of 4.5%. The actual cost of the article is
   - (a) 250
   - (b) 225
   - (c) 215
   - (d) 210

7. X borrowed some money from a source at 8% simple interest and lent it to Y at 12% simple interest on the same day and gained ₹ 4,800 after 3 years. The amount X borrowed, in ₹, is
   - (a) 42,000
   - (b) 60,000
   - (c) 1,20,000
   - (d) 40,000

8. What annual payment will discharge a debt of ₹6,450 due in 4 years at 5% per annum simple interest ?
   - (a) ₹1,400
   - (b) ₹1,500
   - (c) ₹1,550
   - (d) ₹1,600

9. The average of the first 100 positive integers is
   - (a) 100
   - (b) 51
   - (c) 50.5
   - (d) 49.5

10. In a family, the average age of a father and a mother is 35 years. The average age of the father, mother and their only son is 27 years. What is the age of the son ?
    - (a) 12 years
    - (b) 11 years
    - (c) 10.5 years
    - (d) 10 years

11. If 5 men or 7 women can earn ₹ 5,250 per day, how much would 7 men and 13 women earn per day ?
    - (a) ₹11,600
    - (b) ₹11,700
    - (c) ₹16,100
    - (d) ₹17,100

12. If A and B together can complete a piece of work in 15 days and B alone in 20 days, in how many days can A alone complete the work ?
    - (a) 60
    - (b) 45
    - (c) 40
    - (d) 30

13. By walking at $\frac{3}{4}$ of his usual speed, a man reaches his office 20 minutes later than his usual time. The usual time taken by him to reach his office is
    - (a) 75 minutes
    - (b) 60 minutes
    - (c) 40 minutes
    - (d) 30 minutes

14. A can complete a piece of work in 18 days, B in 20 days and C in 30 days, B and C together start the work and are forced to leave after 2 days. The time taken by A alone to complete the remaining work is
    (a) 10 days (b) 12 days
    (c) 15 days (d) 16 days

15. A train, 300 m long, passed a man, walking along the line in the same direction at the rate of 3 km/hr in 33 seconds. The speed of the train is
    (a) 30 km/hr (b) 32 km/hr
    (c) $32\dfrac{8}{11}$ km/hr (d) $35\dfrac{8}{11}$ km/hr

16. In how many years will a sum of ₹ 800 at 10% per annum compound interest, compounded semi-annually becomes ₹ 926.10 ?
    (a) $1\dfrac{1}{2}$ years (b) $1\dfrac{2}{3}$ years
    (c) $2\dfrac{1}{3}$ years (d) $2\dfrac{1}{2}$ years

17. In a 100m race, Kamal defeats Bimal by 5 seconds. If the speed of Kamal is 18 kmph, then the speed of Bimal is
    (a) 15.4 kmph (b) 14.5 kmph
    (c) 14.4 kmph (d) 14 kmph

18. A train, 240 m long crosses a man walking along the line in opposite direction at the rate of 3 kmph in 10 seconds. The speed of the train is
    (a) 63 kmph (b) 75 kmph
    (c) 83.4 kmph (d) 86.4 kmph

19. A boatman rows 2 km in 5 minutes, along the stream and 16 km in 1 hour against the stream. The speed of the stream is
    (a) 4 kmph (b) 6 kmph
    (c) 10 kmph (d) 12 kmph

20. A can compete $\dfrac{1}{3}$ of a work in 5 days and B, $\dfrac{2}{5}$ of the work in 10 days. In how many days both A and B together can complete the work ?
    (a) 10 (b) $9\dfrac{3}{8}$
    (c) $8\dfrac{4}{5}$ (d) $7\dfrac{1}{2}$

21. 7 men can complete a piece of work in 12 days. How many additional men will be required to complete double the work in 8 days ?
    (a) 28 (b) 21
    (c) 14 (d) 7

22. In an examination, a student scores 4 marks for every correct answer and loses 1 mark for every wrong answer. A student attempted all the 200 questions and scored, in all 200 marks. The number of questions, he answered correctly was
    (a) 82 (b) 80
    (c) 68 (d) 60

23. If A's income is 25% less than B's income, by how much percent is B's income more than that of A?
    (a) 25 (b) 30
    (c) $33\dfrac{1}{3}$ (d) $66\dfrac{2}{3}$

24. Two number are in the ratio 7 : 11. If 7 is added to each of the numbers, the ratio becomes 2 : 3. The smaller number is
    (a) 39 (b) 49
    (c) 66 (d) 77

25. A 4–digit number is formed by repeating a 2–digit number such as 1515, 3737, etc. Any number of this form is exactly divisible by
    (a) 7 (b) 11
    (c) 13 (d) 101

GENERAL INTELLIGENCE & REASONING

26. 'Hygrometer' is related to 'Humidity' in the same way as 'Sphygmomanometer' is related to
    (a) Pressure (b) Blood Pressure
    (c) Precipitation (d) Heart Beat

DIRECTIONS (Qs. 27-28): In questions, select the related word/letters/numbers from the given alternatives.

27. HEATER : KBDQHO : : COOLER : ?
    (a) ALRHV (b) FLRIHO
    (c) FLIRHO (d) FRLIHO

28. 12 : 30 : : 20 : ?
    (a) 25 (b) 32
    (c) 35 (d) 42

29. In a certain code language OUTCOME is written as OQWWEQOE. How is REFRACT written in that code?
    (a) RTGITCET   (b) RTGTICET
    (c) RTGITECT   (c) RTGICTET
30. Introducing Rajesh, Neha said, "His brother's father is the only son of my grand father". How Neha is related to Rajesh?
    (a) Sister   (b) Daughter
    (c) Mother   (d) Niece
31. Ruchi's house is to the right of Vani's house at a distance of 20 metres in the same row facing North. Shabana's house is in the North- East direction of Vani's house at a distance of 25 metres. Determine that Ruchi's house is in which direction with respect of Shabana's house?
    (a) North-East   (b) East
    (c) South   (d) West
32. Some boys are sitting in a line. Mahendra is on 17th place from left and Surendra is on 18th place from right. There are 8 boys in between them. How many boys are there in the line?
    (a) 43   (b) 42
    (c) 41   (d) 44
33. Ravi has spent a quarter $\left(\dfrac{1}{4}\right)$ of his life as a boy, one–fifth $\left(\dfrac{1}{5}\right)$ as a youth, one-third $\left(\dfrac{1}{3}\right)$ as man and thirteen (13) years in old age. What is his present age?
    (a) 70 years   (b) 80 years
    (c) 60 years   (d) 65 years
34. Select the missing number from the given responses.

21	24	36
11	14	12
3	?	4
77	112	108

    (a) 2   (b) 4
    (c) 3   (d) 5

Give answer (a) If only conclusion I follows.
Give answer (b) if only conclusion II follows.
Give answer (c) if either I or II follows.
Give answer (d) if neither I nor II follows.

35. **Statements:**
    All terrorists are human.
    All humans are bad.
    Conclusions:
    I. All terrorists are bad.
    II. No human can be a terrorist.
36. Which of the following diagrams represents the relationship among Sun, Moon and Star?

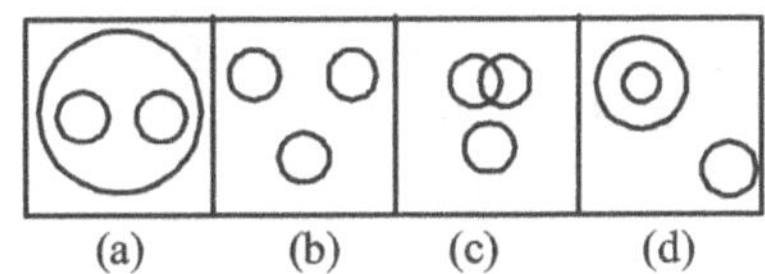

   (a)   (b)   (c)   (d)

37. If '–' stands for '+', '+' stands for '×', '×' stands for '–' then which one of the following is not correct ?
    (a) $22 + 7 - 3 \times 9 = 148$
    (b) $33 \times 5 - 10 + 20 = 228$
    (c) $7 + 28 - 3 \times 52 = 127$
    (d) $44 - 9 + 6 \times 11 = 87$
38. From the given answer figures, select the one in which the question figure is hidden/embedded.
    Question Figure:

    Answer Figures:

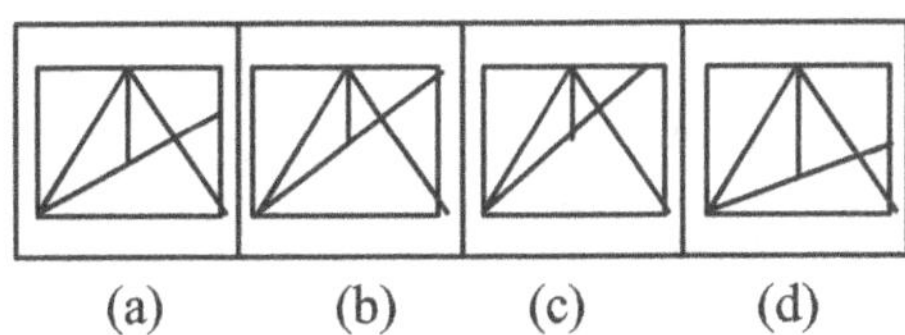

   (a)   (b)   (c)   (d)

39. Which answer figure will complete the pattern in the question figure ?

(a) 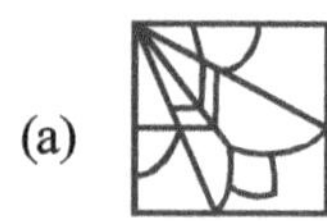   (b) 

(c)    (d) 

DIRECTIONS (Qs. 40-41): In questions, identify the wrong number in the series.

40. 9, 19, 40, 83, 170, 340
    (a) 83   (b) 40
    (c) 340   (d) 170
41. 21, 28, 33, 35, 37, 36
    (a) 21   (b) 36
    (c) 33   (d) 35
42. In a certain code, "CERTAIN" is coded as "XVIGZRM", "SEQUENCE" is coded as "HVJFVMXV". How would "REQUIRED" be coded?
    (a) FJIVWVIR   (b) VJIFWTRV
    (c) WVJRIFVI   (d) IVJFRIVW
43. If LUXOR is coded as 30, then GUILDS will be coded as?
    (a) 40   (b) 36
    (c) 38   (d) 24
44. Seema's younger brother Sohan is older than Seeta. Sweta is younger than Deepti but elder than Seema. Who is the eldest ?
    (a) Seeta   (b) Deepti
    (c) Seema   (d) Sweta
45. A person walks 9 km to the South. From there he walks 5 km to the North. After this he walks 3 km to the West. In which direction and how far is he now from the starting point?
    (a) 4 km South
    (b) 4 km North
    (c) 5 km North West
    (d) 5 km South West

46. If I means '×', You means '÷', We means '–' and He means '+', then what will be the value of 8 I 12 He 16 You 2 We 10?
    (a) 45   (b) 94
    (c) 96   (d) 112
47. The diagram represents Teachers, Singers and Players. Study the diagram and find out how many teachers are also singers.

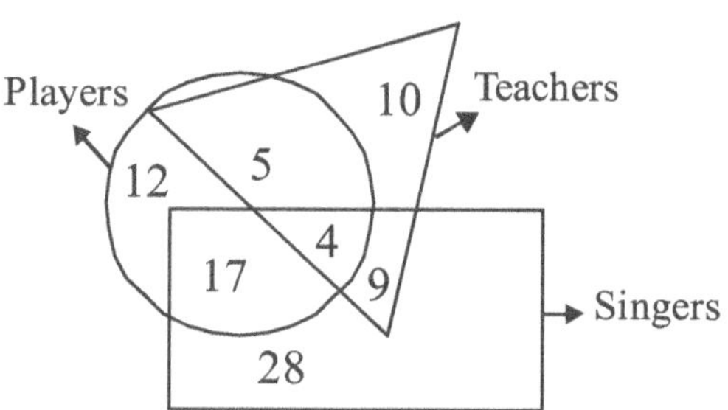

    (a) 4   (b) 5
    (c) 9   (d) 13
48. In the given figure, How many water are either tap or shower?

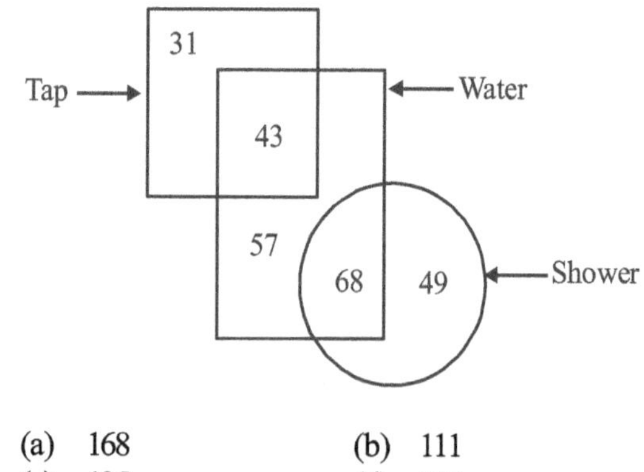

    (a) 168   (b) 111
    (c) 125   (d) 108

DIRECTIONS (Qs. 49-50): In each question below is given a statement followed by two conclusions numbered I and II. You have to assume everything in the statement to be true, then consider the two conclusions together and decide which of them logically follows beyond a reasonable doubt from the information given in the statement.

49. **Statements**: This world is neither good nor evil; each man manufactures a world for himself.
    Conclusions:
    I.   Some people find this world quite good.
    II. Some people find this world quite bad.

(a) Only conclusion I follows
(b) Only conclusion II follows
(c) Either I or II follows
(d) Both I and II follow

50. **Statements**: Any student who does not behave properly while in the school brings bad name to himself and also for the school.
Conclusions:
I. Such student should be removed from the school.
II. Stricter discipline does not improve behaviour of the students.
(a) Only conclusion I follows
(b) Only conclusion II follows
(c) Either I or II follows
(d) Neither I nor II follows

BASIC SCIENCE AND ENGINEERING

51. An axonometric drawing which has two axes divided by equal angles is:
(a) dimetric   (b) trimetric
(c) orthographic   (d) isometric

52. The dimensional formula for magnetic flux is
(a) $[ML^2T^{-2}A^{-1}]$ (b) $[ML^3T^{-2}A^{-2}]$
(c) $[M^0L^{-2}T^2A^{-2}]$ (d) $[ML^2T^{-1}A^2]$

53. When air is cooled, its density
(a) increases   (b) decreses
(c) remains same   (d) None of these

54. Velocity-time curve for a body projected vertically upwards is
(a) parabola   (b) ellipse
(c) hyperbola   (d) straight line

55. When a body vibrates, it produces
(a) sound   (b) water
(c) heat   (d) electricity

56. Heat content of a body depends on
(a) mass of the body
(b) temperature of the body
(c) specific heat capacity
(d) all of the above

57. Which of the following is an ohmic conductor?
(a) Copper   (b) Silver
(c) Gold   (d) All of these

58. A good example of a second class lever is the...
(a) Can-opener   (b) Wheelbarrow
(c) Hammer   (d) Tongs

59. Which of the following is NOT a factor that influences health and safety?
(a) Occupational factors e.g. work risks
(b) Environmental factors e.g. workplace noise
(c) Superstition factors e.g. walking under ladders, black cats etc
(d) Human factors e.g error or haste

60. Cow dung can be used
(a) as manure
(b) for production of biogas
(c) both (a) and (b)
(d) none of these

61. Super computer developed by Indian scientists
(a) Param   (b) Super301
(c) Compaq Presario   (d) Cray YMP

62. Food we eat contains
(a) Chemical Potential Energy
(b) Elastic Potential Energy
(c) Gravitational Potential Energy
(d) Kinetic energy

63. Which of the following pencil leads is hardest?
(a) HB   (b) H
(c) B   (d) F

64. SI unit for light intensity is
(a) Candela   (b) Watts
(c) Joules   (d) Kelvin

65. Which method of determining mass involves measuring how much an object resists acceleration?
(a) Inertial mass   (b) Atomic mass
(c) Gravitational mass (d) Newton mass

66. What is the weight of a 1kg mass object on planet Earth?
(a) 9.8 pound   (b) 1 Newton
(c) 5 Newtons   (d) 9.8 Newtons

67. The main difference between speed and velocity is that velocity includes this:
(a) there is no difference
(b) units
(c) magnitude
(d) direction

68. The speed-time graph for a particle moving at constant speed is a straight-line _________ to the time axis.
    - (a) parallel
    - (b) perpendicular
    - (c) aligned
    - (d) inclined

69. The energy possessed by an oscillating pendulum of a clock is
    - (a) Kinetic energy
    - (b) Potential energy
    - (c) Restoring energy
    - (d) Mechanical energy

70. Centigrade (Celsius) scale can be converted into Kelvin scale by formula
    - (a) $\Omega\ ^\circ C$ = Temperature in Kelvin + 273
    - (b) $\Omega\ ^\circ C$ = Temperature in Kelvin − 273
    - (c) $\Omega\ ^\circ C$ = Temperature in Fahrenheit + 273
    - (d) $\Omega\ ^\circ C$ = Temperature in Fahrenheit − 273

71. An electric filament bulb can be worked from
    - (a) D.C. supply only
    - (b) A.C. supply only
    - (c) Battery supply only
    - (d) All of the above

72. The resistance of a few meters of wire conductor in closed electrical circuit is
    - (a) Practically zero
    - (b) Low
    - (c) High
    - (d) Very high

73. Simple machines make work easier by trading ______ for force.
    - (a) motion
    - (b) distance
    - (c) work
    - (d) friction

74. Hazard communication in OSHA conducts ______
    - (a) Chemical analysis
    - (b) Toxic exposure
    - (c) Strength analysis
    - (d) Hazard evaluations of the products

75. The set of ecosystems is called a
    - (a) Biome
    - (b) Climate
    - (c) Subsystem
    - (d) Structure

GENERAL AWARENESS AND CURRENT AFFAIR

76. The Prime Minister of India is the head of the
    - (a) State Government
    - (b) Central Government
    - (c) Both the State and Central Government
    - (d) None of them

77. The Green Revolution in India has contributed to
    - (a) inter-regional inequality
    - (b) inter-class inequality
    - (c) inter-crop inequality
    - (d) All of the above

78. Which zone of a candle flame is the hottest ?
    - (a) Dark innermost zone
    - (b) Outermost zone
    - (c) Middle luminous zone
    - (d) Central zone

79. Which one of the following is used to remove Astigmatism for a human eye?
    - (a) Concave lens
    - (b) Convex lens
    - (c) Cylindrical lens
    - (d) Prismatic lens

80. Which one of the following is a mixed fertilizer?
    - (a) Urea
    - (b) CAN
    - (c) Ammonium sulphate
    - (d) NPK

81. The most reactive among the halogens is
    - (a) Fluorine
    - (b) Chlorine
    - (c) Bromine
    - (d) Iodine

82. Which one of the following is a modified stem?
    - (a) Carrot
    - (b) Sweet potato
    - (c) Coconut
    - (d) Potato

83. 'Athlete's Foot' is a disease caused by
    - (a) Bacteria
    - (b) Fungus
    - (c) Protozoan
    - (d) Nematode

84. 'India of our Dreams' is a book written by
    - (a) Dr. S. Radhakrishnan
    - (b) Dr. C. Subramanian
    - (c) M.V. Kamath
    - (d) Dr. Rajendra Prasad

85. The antibiotic penicillin is obtained from which of the following ?
    - (a) synthetic process
    - (b) a bacterium
    - (c) fungus
    - (d) virus infected cells

86. Petrology is the study of
    (a) rocks   (b) soils
    (c) earth   (d) minerals
87. In Asian Games 2018, total how many Gold Medals were won by India?
    (a) 10   (b) 24
    (c) 15   (d) 30
88. The National Sports Day is celebrated every year in India on ____________ .
    (a) 29 August   (b) 22 August
    (c) 15 August   (d) 18 August
89. Bajrang Punia is related with which of the following sports?
    (a) Boxing   (b) Arm Wrestling
    (c) Weight Lifting   (d) Wrestling
90. Which one among the following has the highest energy?
    (a) Blue light   (b) Green light
    (c) Red light   (d) Yellow light
91. When water is heated from 0° C to 10° C its volume
    (a) Increases
    (b) Decreases
    (c) Does not change
    (d) First decreases then increases
92. The offending substance in the liquor tragedies leading to blindness etc, is –
    (a) ethyl alcohol   (b) amyl alcohol
    (c) benzyl alcohol   (d) methyl alcohol
93. Which is a celestial phenomenon occurring due to stars?
    (a) Ozone hole   (b) Black hole
    (c) Rainbow   (d) Comet
94. The minimum forest cover to maintain ecological balance in the plains is –
    (a) 50%   (b) 40%
    (c) 33%   (d) 25%
95. Which one of the following is the busiest ocean route in the world?
    (a) Indian Ocean
    (b) North Atlantic Ocean
    (c) South Atlantic Ocean
    (d) Pacific Ocean
96. Which one of the following rivers flows in a rift valley?
    (a) Amazon
    (B) Indus
    (C) Volga
    (d) Rhine
97. The oldest mountain ranges in India are –
    (a) The Himalayas
    (b) The Nilgiris
    (c) The Vindhyas
    (d) The Aravalli Hills
98. One astronomical unit is the average distance between
    (a) Earth and Sun
    (B) Earth and Moon
    (C) Jupiter and Sun
    (D) Pluto and Sun
99. One astronomical unit is the average distance between
    (a) The Earth and the Sun
    (b) The Earth and the Moon
    (c) The Jupiter and the Sun
    (d) The Pluto and the Sun
100. Comets are luminous celestial bodies moving around
    (a) Jupiter
    (b) Sun
    (c) Moon
    (d) Earth

HINTS & EXPLANATIONS

1. (d) Required number

$$= \left(6\frac{3}{5} - 3\frac{4}{5}\right) \times 355$$

$$= \left(\frac{33}{5} - \frac{19}{5}\right) \times 355$$

$$= \frac{14}{5} \times 355 = 994$$

2. (c) Total number of sweets

$$= 65 \times 65 \times \frac{20}{100} + 4 \times 65 \times \frac{40}{100}$$

$$= 845 + 104 = 949$$

3. (b) In 60 gm. of mixture,

Quantity of water $= 60 \times \dfrac{75}{100} = 45$ gm

Quantity of milk $= 15$ gm
After mixing 15 gm of more water, Quantity of water in new mixture
$= 45 + 15 = 60$ gm

∴ Quantity of water in 75 gm of mixture
$$= 60 \text{ gm}$$

∴ 100 gm of mixture will contain

$$= \frac{60}{75} \times 100 = 80\% \text{ of water}$$

4. (d) Third number
$$= 290 - 2 \times 48.5 - 2 \times 53.5$$
$$= 290 - 97 - 107 = 86$$

5. (c) Let average weight of girls $= x$
Total weight of the boys $= 40\,\text{kg} \times 15$
$$= 600 \text{ kg.}$$
Average weight of a class

$$= \frac{\text{Total weight of girls} + \text{Total weight of boys}}{\text{No. of boys} + \text{No. of girls}}$$

$$\Rightarrow 38.4 = \frac{600 + 10 \times x}{15 + 10}$$

$$\Rightarrow 38.4 = \frac{600 + 10x}{25}$$

$$\Rightarrow 38.4 \times 25 = 600 + 10x$$

∴ $\quad x = 36\,\text{kg}$

6. (a) MP $= 275$

SP after Discount of 5% $= \dfrac{95}{100} \times 275$

CP where P % of 4.5 $= \dfrac{100}{104.5} \times \dfrac{95}{100} \times 275$
$$= ₹250$$

7. (d) Let X borrow ₹ P
He has to return total amount,

$$A = P + \frac{P \times 8 \times 3}{100}$$

Total amount x get from y, A′

$$= P + \frac{P \times 12 \times 3}{100}$$

According to question
$$A' - A = 4800$$

$$\left(P + \frac{36P}{100}\right) - \left(P + \frac{24P}{100}\right) = 4800$$

$$\frac{12P}{100} = 4800$$

$$\Rightarrow P = \frac{4800 \times 100}{12} = 40,000$$

8. (b) Let the annual instalment be ₹x.

$$\therefore \left(x + \frac{x \times 3 \times 5}{100}\right)$$

$$+ \left(x + \frac{x \times 2 \times 5}{100}\right) + \left(x + \frac{x \times 1 \times 5}{100}\right) + x = 6450$$

$$\Rightarrow \frac{115x}{100} + \frac{110x}{100} + \frac{105x}{100} + x = 6450$$

$$\Rightarrow 115x + 110x + 105x + 100x$$
$$= 6450 \times 100$$
$$\Rightarrow 430x = 6450 \times 100$$

$$\therefore x = \frac{6450 \times 100}{430} = ₹1500$$

9. (c) $1 + 2 + 3 + \ldots + n = \dfrac{n(n+1)}{2}$

∴ Average of these numbers

$$\therefore \text{Average} = \frac{n+1}{2} = \frac{100+1}{2} = 50.5$$

10. (b) Father + mother
$= 2 \times 35 = 70$ years
Father + mother + son
$= 27 \times 3 = 81$ years
$\therefore$ Son's age $= 81 - 70 = 11$ years

11. (d) 5 men $\equiv$ 7 women

$\therefore$ 7 men $\equiv \dfrac{7}{5} \times 7 = \dfrac{49}{5}$ women

$\therefore$ 7 men + 13 women

$= \dfrac{49}{5} + 13 = \dfrac{114}{5}$ women

Now,

$\because$ 7 women $\equiv ₹5250$

$\therefore \dfrac{114}{5}$ women $\equiv \dfrac{5250}{7} \times \dfrac{114}{5} = ₹17100$

12. (a) $(A + B)$'s 1 day's work $= \dfrac{1}{15}$

B's 1 day's work $= \dfrac{1}{20}$

$\therefore$ A's 1 day's work

$= \dfrac{1}{15} - \dfrac{1}{20} = \dfrac{4-3}{60} = \dfrac{1}{60}$

$\therefore$ A alone will do the work in 60 days.

13. (b) $\dfrac{4}{3}$ of usual time = Usual time + 20 minutes

$\therefore \dfrac{1}{3}$ rd of usual time = 20 minutes

$\therefore$ Usual time $= 20 \times 3 = 60$ minutes

14. (c) $(B + C)$'s 2 days' work

$= 2\left(\dfrac{1}{20} + \dfrac{1}{30}\right) = 2\left(\dfrac{3+2}{60}\right)$

$= \dfrac{1}{6}$ part

Remaining work $= 1 - \dfrac{1}{6} = \dfrac{5}{6}$ part

$\therefore$ Time taken by A to complete this part of

work $= \dfrac{5}{6} \times 18 = 15$ days

15. (d) If the speed of the train be x kmph, then
relative speed
$= (x - 3)$ kmph.

$= (x - 3) \times \dfrac{5}{18}$ m / sec

$\therefore \dfrac{300}{(x-3) \times \dfrac{5}{18}} = 33$

$\Rightarrow 5400 = 33 \times 5\,(x - 3)$
$\Rightarrow 360 = 11\,(x - 3)$
$\Rightarrow 11x - 33 = 360$

$\Rightarrow x = \dfrac{393}{11} = 35\dfrac{8}{11}$ kmph

16. (a) Rate $= 10\%$ per annum $= 5\%$ half yearly

$A = P\left(1 + \dfrac{R}{100}\right)^T$

$\Rightarrow 926.10 = 800\left(1 + \dfrac{5}{100}\right)^T$

$\Rightarrow \dfrac{9261}{8000} = \left(\dfrac{21}{20}\right)^T$

$\Rightarrow \left(\dfrac{21}{20}\right)^3 = \left(\dfrac{21}{20}\right)^T$

$\therefore$ Time = 3 half years = $1\dfrac{1}{2}$ years

17. (c) Time taken by Kamal

$= \dfrac{100}{18 \times \dfrac{5}{18}} = 20$ sec

$\therefore$ Time taken by Bimal $= 20 + 5 = 25$ sec

$\therefore$ Bimal's speed $= \dfrac{100}{25} = 4$ m/sec

$= \dfrac{4 \times 18}{5}$ kmph $= 14.4$ kmph.

18. (c) Let train speed be x
relative speed $= (x + 3)$ kmph

$\therefore$ Time $= \dfrac{\text{Length of the train}}{\text{Relative speed}}$

$\Rightarrow \dfrac{10}{3600} = \dfrac{\dfrac{240}{1000}}{(x+3)} = \dfrac{240}{1000(x+3)}$

$\Rightarrow x + 3 = 86.4$
$\Rightarrow x = 83.4$ kmph

19. (a) Speed of current

$$= \frac{1}{2} \text{ (Rate downstream} - \text{Rate upstream)}$$

$$= \frac{1}{2} (24 - 16) \text{ kmph} \quad [\text{Rate downstream}]$$

$$= 4 \text{ kmph}$$

20. (b) Total time taken by A = 15 days

Total time taken by B $= \dfrac{10 \times 5}{2} = 25$ days

$\therefore$ (A + B)'s 1 day's work

$$= \frac{1}{15} + \frac{1}{25} = \frac{5+3}{75} = \frac{8}{75}$$

$\therefore$ the work will be completed in $\dfrac{75}{8} = 9\dfrac{3}{8}$ days.

21. (c) $M_1 D_1 W_2 = M_2 D_2 W_1$

$\Rightarrow 7 \times 12 \times 2 = M_2 \times 8 \times 1$

$$\Rightarrow M_2 = \frac{7 \times 12 \times 2}{8} = 21$$

$\therefore$ No. of additional men = $21 - 7 = 14$

22. (b) If the number of correct answers be x, then

$x \times 4 - 1. (200 - x) = 200$

$\Rightarrow 4x - 200 + x = 200$

$\Rightarrow 5x = 400$

$$\Rightarrow x = \frac{400}{5} = 80$$

23. (c) Required percentage

$$= \frac{25}{100 - 25} \times 100 = \frac{100}{3} = 33\frac{1}{3}\%$$

24. (b) Let the numbers be 7x and 11x respectively.

$$\therefore \quad \frac{7x + 7}{11x + 7} = \frac{2}{3}$$

$\therefore 22x + 14 = 21x + 21$

$\Rightarrow x = 7$

$\therefore$ Smaller number

$= 7x = 7 \times 7 = 49$

25. (d) $xyxy = xy \times 100 + xy$

$= xy(100 + 1) = 101 \times xy$

Hence, the number is exactly divisible by 101.

26. (b) First is an instrument to measure the second.

27. (b)

$$
\begin{array}{cccccc}
H & E & A & T & E & R \\
{\scriptstyle +3}\downarrow & {\scriptstyle -3}\downarrow & {\scriptstyle +3}\downarrow & {\scriptstyle -3}\downarrow & {\scriptstyle +3}\downarrow & {\scriptstyle -3}\downarrow \\
K & B & D & Q & H & O
\end{array}
$$

Similarly,

$$
\begin{array}{cccccc}
C & O & O & L & E & R \\
{\scriptstyle +3}\downarrow & {\scriptstyle -3}\downarrow & {\scriptstyle +3}\downarrow & {\scriptstyle -3}\downarrow & {\scriptstyle +3}\downarrow & {\scriptstyle -3}\downarrow \\
F & L & R & I & H & O
\end{array}
$$

28. (d) $12 = 3^2 + 3,$ $30 = 5^2 + 5 :$

$20 = 4^2 + 4 :$ $? = 6^2 + 6$

29. (a)

$$
\begin{array}{ccccccc}
O & U & T & C & O & M & E \\
{\scriptstyle +2}\downarrow & {\scriptstyle +2}\downarrow & {\scriptstyle +3}\downarrow & {\scriptstyle +2}\downarrow & {\scriptstyle +2}\downarrow & {\scriptstyle +2}\downarrow & {\scriptstyle +0}\downarrow
\end{array}
$$

Coded as $\longrightarrow$ O Q W W E Q O E

$$
\begin{array}{ccccccc}
R & E & F & R & A & C & T \\
{\scriptstyle +2}\downarrow & {\scriptstyle +2}\downarrow & {\scriptstyle +3}\downarrow & {\scriptstyle +2}\downarrow & {\scriptstyle +2}\downarrow & {\scriptstyle +2}\downarrow & {\scriptstyle +0}\downarrow
\end{array}
$$

Coded as $\longrightarrow$ R T G I T C E T

30. (a) Father of Rajesh's brother is the father of Rajesh. Rajesh's father is the only son of Neha's grandfather. Hence, Rajesh's father is Neha's father. So, Neha is the sister of Rajesh.

31. (c)

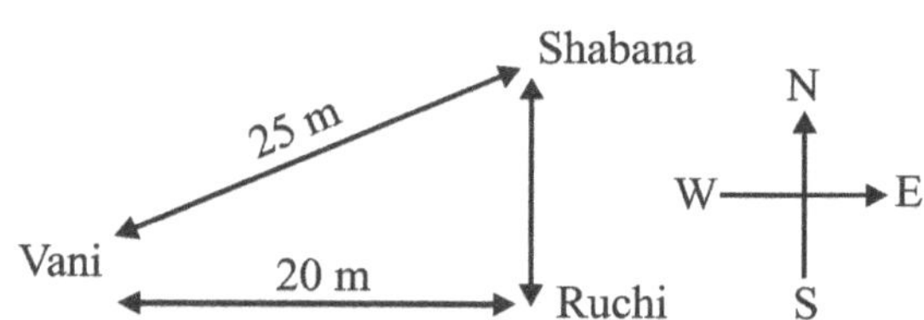

32. (a) Total boys

$$= \left[\begin{array}{ccc} \text{Mahendra's} \\ \text{place} & + & \text{Surendra's} \\ \text{from left} & & \text{place} \\ & & \text{from right} \end{array} \right] +$$

$$\left[\begin{array}{c} \text{Boys between} \\ \text{them} \end{array} \right] = [17 + 18] + 8 = 43$$

33. (c) Suppose his present age is x years.
According to question

$$\frac{x}{4}+\frac{x}{5}+\frac{x}{3}=x-13$$

$$\Rightarrow \frac{15x+12x+20x}{60}=x-13$$

$$\Rightarrow 47x=60x-780$$
$$\Rightarrow 60x-47x=780$$
$$\Rightarrow 13x=780$$

$$\therefore x=\frac{780}{13}=60 \text{ years}$$

34. (c) As, $3 \times 7 = 21$, $11 \times 7 = 77$
$4 \times 9 = 36$, $12 \times 9 = 108$
Therefore, $14 \times 8 = 112$
$? \times 8 = 24$

$$\boxed{? = 3}$$

35. (a) 36. (d)

37. (c) $7 \times 28 + 3 - 52 = 127$
$196 + 3 - 52$
$199 - 52 = 147$ (incorrect)

38. (c) 39. (b)

40. (c) $9 \times 2 + 1 = 18 + 1 = 19$
$19 \times 2 + 2 = 38 + 2 = 40$
$40 \times 2 + 3 = 80 + 3 = 83$
$83 \times 2 + 4 = 166 + 4 = 170$

$$170 \times 2 + 5 = 340 + 5 = \boxed{345}$$

Therefore, the number 340 is wrong in the series.

41. (d) $21 + 7 = 28$
$28 + 5 = 33$

$$33 + 3 = \boxed{36}$$

$36 + 1 = 37$
$37 - 1 = 36$

Therefore, the number 35 is wrong in the series.

42. (d) C E R T A I N
$\updownarrow$ $\updownarrow$ $\updownarrow$ $\updownarrow$ $\updownarrow$ $\updownarrow$
X V I G Z R M
Pairs of Opposite Letters

S E Q U E N C E
$\updownarrow$ $\updownarrow$ $\updownarrow$ $\updownarrow$ $\updownarrow$ $\updownarrow$ $\updownarrow$ $\updownarrow$
H V J F V M X V
Therefore,

R E Q U I R E D
$\updownarrow$ $\updownarrow$ $\updownarrow$ $\updownarrow$ $\updownarrow$ $\updownarrow$ $\updownarrow$ $\updownarrow$
I V J F R I V W

43. (d) As,

L   U   X   O   R
$\downarrow$ $\downarrow$ $\downarrow$ $\downarrow$ $\downarrow$
$12 + 21 + 24 + 15 + 18 = 90$

$$\frac{90}{3} = 30$$

Similarly,

G   U   I   L   D   S
$\downarrow$ $\downarrow$ $\downarrow$ $\downarrow$ $\downarrow$ $\downarrow$
$7 + 21 + 9 + 12 + 4 + 19 = 72$

$$\frac{72}{3} = \boxed{24}$$

44. (b) Seema > Sohan > Seeta   ...(i)
Deepti > Sweta > Seema   ...(ii)
Combining (i) and (ii) we get
Deepti > Sweta > Seema > Sohan > Seeta

45. (d)

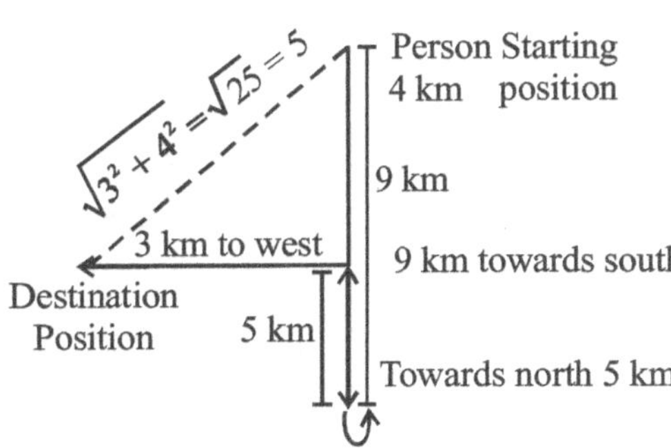

Person is in south west direction & 5 km from the starting point.

46. (b) The expression is :
8 I 12 He 16 You 2 we 10
$$\Rightarrow 8 \times 12 + 16 \div 2 - 10$$
$$\Rightarrow 8 \times 12 + 8 - 10$$
$$\Rightarrow 104 - 10 = 94$$

47. (c)

Persons	Numbers						
	4	5	9	10	12	17	28
◯ Players	✓	✓	✗	✗	✓	✓	✗
△ Teachers	✓	✓	✓	✓	✗	✗	✗
▢ Singers	✓		✓	✗	✗	✓	✓

Number of teachers who are also singers = 9

48. (b) According to figure,

Total number of water are either tap or shower = (43 + 68) = 111.

49. (d) The statement mentions that the world for a man is as he makes it himself. So, some people might find it good and some quite bad. Thus, both I and II follow.

50. (d) Clearly, I cannot be deduced from the statement. Also, nothing about discipline is mentioned in the statement. So, neither I nor II follows.

51. (a) 52. (a) 53. (a) 54. (d) 55. (a)
56. (d) 57. (d) 58. (b) 59. (c) 60. (c)
61. (a) 62. (a) 63. (a) 64. (a) 65. (a)
66. (d) 67. (d) 68. (a) 69. (d) 70. (b)
71. (d) 72. (a) 73. (b) 74. (d) 75. (a)
76. (b) 77. (d) 78. (d) 79. (c) 80. (d)
81. (a) 82. (d) 83. (b) 84. (c) 85. (d)
86. (a) 87. (c) 88. (a) 89. (d) 90. (a)
91. (d) 92. (d) 93. (b) 94. (c) 95. (b)
96. (d) 97. (d) 98. (a) 99. (a) 100. (b)

PRACTICE SET 10

MATHEMATICS

1. A certain number is divided by 385 by division by factors. The quotient is 102, the first remainder is 4, the second is 6 and the third is 10. Find the number.
   - (a) 39654
   - (b) 32754
   - (c) 38554
   - (d) None of these

2. The smallest positive integer which when multiplied by 392, gives a perfect square is
   - (a) 2
   - (b) 3
   - (c) 5
   - (d) 7

3. A shopkeeper fixes the marked price of an item 20% above the cost price. He allows his customers a discount and makes a profit of 8%. Find the rate of discount.
   - (a) 8%
   - (b) 9%
   - (c) 10%
   - (d) 11%

4. The difference between C. I. (Compound Interest) and S.I. (Simple Interest) on a sum of ₹ 4,000 for 2 years at 5% p.a. payable yearly is
   - (a) ₹ 20
   - (b) ₹ 10
   - (c) ₹ 50
   - (d) ₹ 60

5. A, B and C are partners. A receives 9/10 of the profit and B and C share the remaining profit equally. A's income is increased by ₹ 270 when the profit rises from 12 to 15%. Find the capital invested by B and C each
   - (a) ₹ 5000
   - (b) ₹ 1000
   - (c) ₹ 500
   - (d) ₹ 1500

6. A sum of ₹ 300 is divided among P, Q and R in such a way that Q gets ₹ 30 more than P and R gets ₹ 60 more than Q. The ratio of their share is
   - (a) 3 : 2 : 5
   - (b) 2 : 5 : 3
   - (c) 5 : 3 : 2
   - (d) 2 : 3 : 5

7. A man walks half of the journey at 4 km/h by cycle does one third of journey at 12 km/h and rides the remainder journey in a horse cart at 9 km/h, thus completing the whole journey in 6 hours and 12 minutes. The length of the journey is
   - (a) 36 km
   - (b) 39 km
   - (c) 40 km
   - (d) 28 km

8. If $2^x = 3^y = 6^{-z}$ then $\left(\dfrac{1}{x} + \dfrac{1}{y} + \dfrac{1}{z} \right)$, is equal to
   - (a) 0
   - (b) 1
   - (c) $\dfrac{3}{2}$
   - (d) $-\dfrac{1}{2}$

9. The monthly salaries of A and B together amount to ₹ 40,000. A spends 85% of his salary and B, 95% of his salary. If now their savings are the same, then the salary (in ₹) of A is
   - (a) 10,000
   - (b) 12,000
   - (c) 16,000
   - (d) 18,000

10. The least among the fractions $\dfrac{15}{16}, \dfrac{19}{20}, \dfrac{24}{35}, \dfrac{34}{35}$ is
    - (a) $\dfrac{34}{35}$
    - (b) $\dfrac{15}{16}$
    - (c) $\dfrac{19}{20}$
    - (d) $\dfrac{24}{25}$

11. Out of six consecutive natural numbers, if the sum of first three is 27, what is the sum of the other three ?
    - (a) 36
    - (b) 35
    - (c) 25
    - (d) 24

12. The H.C.F. and L.C.M. of two numbers are 12 and 336 respectively. If one of the numbers is 84, the other is
    - (a) 36
    - (b) 48
    - (c) 72
    - (d) 96

13. $\left\{ \dfrac{(0.1)^2 - (0.01)^2}{0.0001} + 1 \right\}$ is equal to
    - (a) 1010
    - (b) 110
    - (c) 101
    - (d) 100

14. If there is a profit of 20% on the cost price of an article, the percentage of profit calculated on its selling price will be

(a) 24% (b) $16\frac{2}{3}$ %

(c) $8\frac{1}{3}$ % (d) 20%

15. If the cost price of 15 books is equal to the selling price of 20 books, the loss percent is
(a) 16% (b) 20%
(c) 24% (d) 25%

16. If on a marked price, the difference of selling prices with a discount of 25% and two successive discounts of 15% and 10% is ₹ 72, then the marked price (in rupees) is
(a) 3,600 (b) 3,000
(c) 2,500 (d) 4,800

17. If an electricity bill is paid before due date, one gets a reduction of 4% on the amount of the bill. By paying the bill before due date a person got a reduction of ₹ 13. The amount of his electricity bill was
(a) ₹ 125 (b) ₹ 225
(c) ₹ 325 (d) ₹ 425

18. The price of an article was first increased by 10% and then again by 20%. If the last increased price be ₹ 33, the original price was
(a) ₹ 30 (b) ₹ 27.50
(c) ₹ 26.50 (d) ₹ 25

19. The ratio of milk and water in mixtures of four containers are 5 : 3, 2 : 1, 3 : 2 and 7 : 4 respectively, in which container is the quantity of milk, relative to water, minimum ?
(a) First (b) Second
(c) Third (d) Fourth

20. Two numbers are in the ratio 1 : 3. If their sum is 240, then their difference is
(a) 120 (b) 108
(c) 100 (d) 96

21. The ratio of income and expenditure of a person is 11 : 10. If he saves ₹ 9,000 per annum, his monthly income is
(a) ₹ 8,000 (b) ₹ 8,800
(c) ₹ 8,500 (d) ₹ 8,250

22. If the length of a rectangle is increased by 10% and its breadth is decreased by 10%, the change in its area will be
(a) 1% increase (b) 1% decrease
(c) 10% increase (d) No change

23. A sum of ₹ 12,000, deposited at compound interest becomes double after 5 years. How much will it be after 20 years ?

(a) ₹ 1,44,000 (b) ₹ 1,20,000
(c) ₹ 1,50,000 (d) ₹ 1,92,000

24. If the sum of two numbers be multiplied by each number separately, the products so obtained are 247 and 114. The sum of the numbers is
(a) 19 (b) 20
(c) 21 (d) 23

25. Find a number, one–seventh of which exceeds its eleventh part by 100.
(a) 1925 (b) 1825
(c) 1540 (d) 1340

GENERAL INTELLIGENCE AND REASONING

DIRECTIONS (Qs. 26 - 28) : In question, select the related word/letters/numbers from the given alternatives.

26. Foresight : Anticipation :: Insomnia : ?
(a) Treatment (b) Disease
(c) Sleeplessness (d) Unrest

27. PAPER : SCTGW : : MOTHER : ?
(a) ORVLGW (b) PQVIGT
(c) PQXJJT (d) PQXKJV

28. 182 : ? : : 210 : 380
(a) 342 (b) 272
(c) 240 (d) 156

DIRECTIONS (Qs. 29 - 30) : Complete the given series.

29. ABD, DGK, HMS, MTB, SBL, ?
(a) ZAB (b) XKW
(c) ZKU (d) ZKW

30. 165, 195, 255, 285, 345, ?
(a) 375 (b) 390
(c) 420 (d) 435

31. In a code, CORNER is written as GSVRIV. How can CENTRAL be written in that code?
(a) DFOUSBM (b) GIRXVEP
(c) GJRYVEP (d) GNFJKER

32. A is B's sister. C is B's mother. D is C's father. E is D's mother. Then, how is A related to D?
(a) Grandmother (b) Grandfather
(c) Daughter (d) Granddaughter

33. M is to the East of D, F is to the South of D and K is to the West of F. M is in which direction with respect to K?
(a) South-West (b) North-West
(c) North-East (d) South-East

34. If '−' stand for addition, '+' stands for subtraction, '÷' stands for multiplication and '×' stands for division, then which one of the following equations is correct?
    (a) $25 \times 5 \div 20 - 27 + 7 = 120$
    (b) $25 + 5 \times 20 - 27 \div 7 = 128$
    (c) $25 + 5 - 20 + 27 \times 7 = 95$
    (d) $25 - 5 + 20 \times 27 \div 7 = 100$

35. Shan is 55 years old, Sathian is 5 years junior to Shan and 6 years senior to Balan. The youngest brother of Balan is Devan and he is 7 years junior to him. So what is the age difference between Devan and Shan?
    (a) 18 years   (b) 15 years
    (c) 13 years   (d) 7 years

36. Malay Pratap is on 13th position from the starting and on 17th position from the end in his class. He is on 8th position from the starting and on 13th position from the end among the students who passed. How many students failed?
    (a) 7
    (b) 8
    (c) 9
    (d) Cannot be determined

37. In the following questions find the missing number

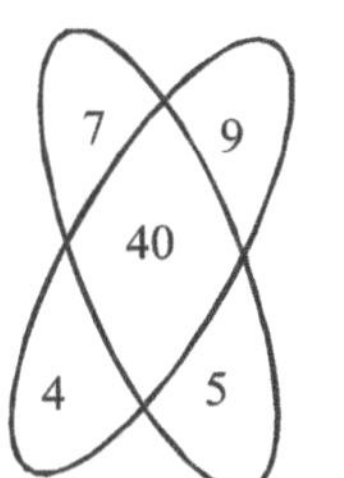

    (a) 60   (b) 62
    (c) 64   (d) 66

38. Which one of the following diagrams represents the correct relationship among 'Judge', 'Thief' and 'Criminal'?

    (a)    (b) 

    (c)    (d) 

39. From the given answer figures, select the one in which the question figure is hidden/ embedded.
    Question Figure

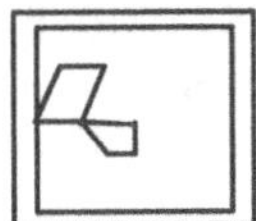

    Answer Figures

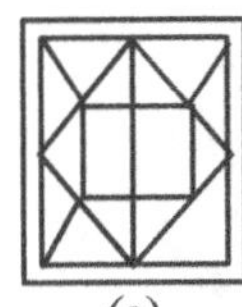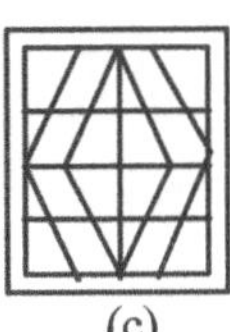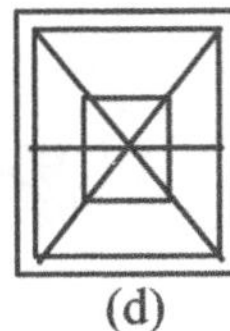
    (a)   (b)   (c)   (d)

40. How many triangles are there in the given figure below?

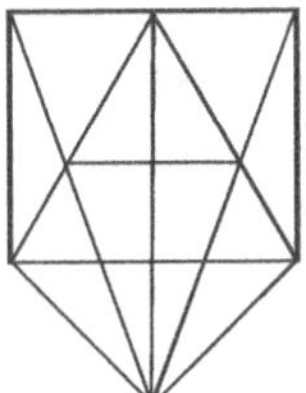

    (a) 20   (b) 21
    (c) 26   (d) 28

41. In the following question, choose the correct water image of the figure (X) from amongst the four alternatives (a), (b), (c), (d) given alongwith it.

    a b s e n c e
    ?
    (a) ９ｐ２６ＵＣ６
    (b) ９ｑ２６∩Ｃ６
    (c) ９ｐ２∂∩Ｃ∂
    (d) ９ｐＳ６∩Ｃ６

42. In the following question, which answer figure will complete the question figure?
    Question Figure

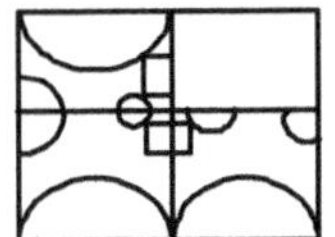

    Answer Figures

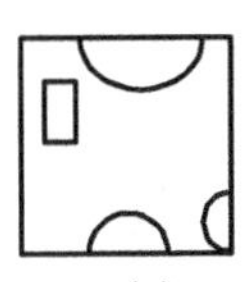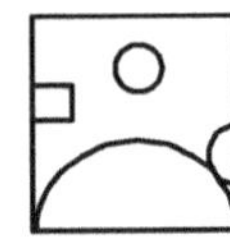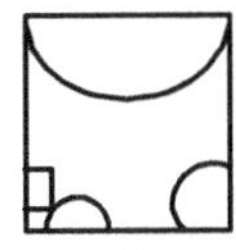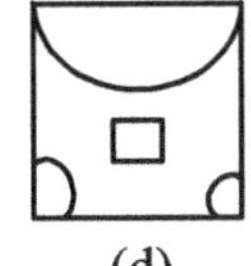
    (a)   (b)   (c)   (d)

43. If SEASONAL is written as ESSANOLA, how can SEPARATE be written in that code?
    (a) SEAPARET   (b) ESPARATE
    (c) ESPAARTE   (d) ESAPARET

44. The figure represents three classes of youth in a village. How many educated youth are poor?

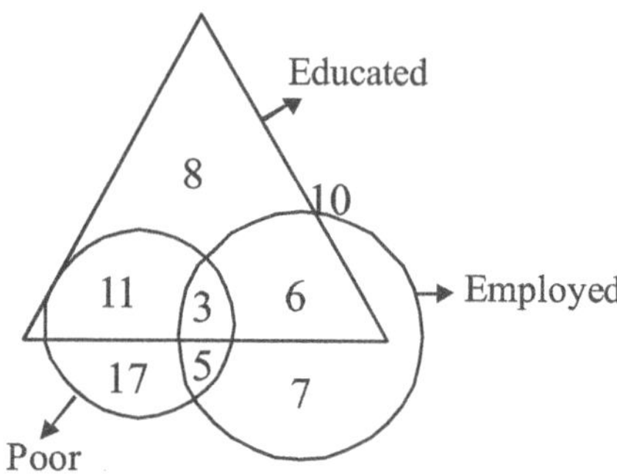

    (a) 14   (b) 9   (c) 6   (d) 19

45. In the given figure, how many players are quick and fat?

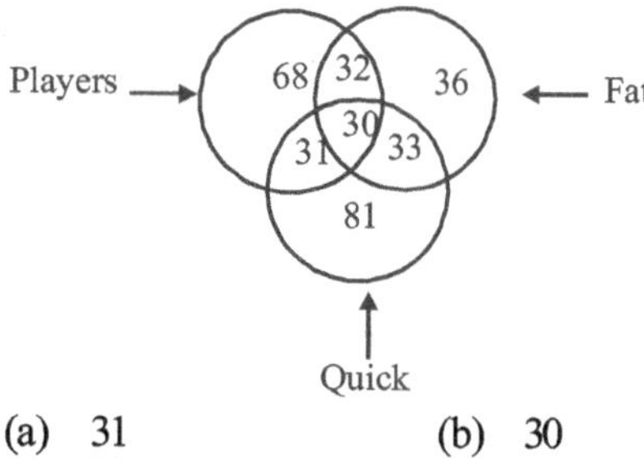

    (a) 31   (b) 30
    (c) 32   (d) 33

DIRECTIONS (Qs. 46 - 48): In each question below are two statements followed by two conclusions numbered I and II. You have to take the two given statements to be true even if they seem to be at variance from commonly known facts and then decide which of the given conclusions logically follows from the given statements disregarding commonly known facts.

(a) if only conclusion I follows.
(b) if only conclusion II follows.
(c) if either conclusion I or II follows.
(d) if both conclusions I and II follow.

46. **Statements:** No plane is hill.
    Some hills are towns.
    Conclusions: I. No town is plane.
    II. Some towns are planes.

47. **Statements:** All metals are liquids.
    All liquids are gases.
    Conclusions:
    I. All metals are gases.
    II. Atleast some gases are liquids.

48. **Statements:**
    Some books are pens.
    No pen is pencil.
    Conclusions:
    I. Some books are pencils.
    II. No book is pencil.

DIRECTIONS (Qs. 49 - 50) : In each question below is given a statement followed by two conclusions numbered I and II. You have to assume everything in the statement to be true, then consider the two conclusions together and decide which of them logically follows beyond a reasonable doubt from the information given in the statement.

49. **Statements:** To cultivate interest in reading, the school has made it compulsory from June this year for each student to read two books per week and submit a weekly report on the books.
    Conclusions:
    I.   Interest in reading can be created by force.
    II. Some students will eventually develop interest in reading.
    (a) Only conclusion I follows
    (b) Only conclusion II follows
    (c) Either I or II follows
    (d) Neither I nor II follows

50. **Statements:** Recent trends also indicate that the number of child migrants in large cities is increasing. These children leave their families to join the ranks of urban poor doing odd jobs in markets, workshops, hotels or in service sectors.
    Conclusions:
    I.   Migration to big cities should be checked.
    II. The plight of poor children should be thoroughly studied.
    (a) Only conclusion I follows
    (b) Only conclusion II follows
    (c) Either I or II follows
    (d) Neither I nor II follows

BASIC SCIENCE AND ENGINEERING

51. Which type of line is particular to section drawings?
    (a) break lines   (b) phantom lines
    (c) extension lines   (d) cutting plane lines

52. The dimensional formula for angular momentum is
    (a) $[M^0L^2T^{-2}]$ (b) $[ML^2T^{-1}]$
    (c) $[MLT^{-1}]$ (d) $[ML^2T^{-2}]$

53. Specific weight of water at 20°C is
    (a) 9810kg/m^3 (b) 9810N/m^3
    (c) 9.81kg/m^3 (d) all the above
54. Speed of a body in particular direction can be called
    (a) acceleration   (b) displacement
    (c) velocity   (d) distance
55. When spring or rubber band is released it converts potential energy into
    (a) Mechanical Energy
    (b) Electrical Energy
    (c) Thermal energy
    (d) Kinetic energy
56. The temperature at which liquid changes into vapour is called as:
    (a) melting point
    (b) boiling point
    (c) expansion point
    (d) expansion point
57. At temperature 0°K, the germanium behaves as a/an
    (a) conductor   (b) insulator
    (c) super-conductor   (d) ferromagnetic
58. A lever or pulley connected to a shaft
    (a) wheel and axle
    (b) block and tackle
    (c) wheelbarrow
    (d) screw
59. Which of the following is not a type of health hazard?
    (a) Chemical   (b) Biological
    (c) Magical   (d) Ergonomic
60. Global warming affects
    (a) Climate change   (b) Food production
    (c) Melting of glaciers   (d) All of these
61. An error is also known as
    (a) bug   (b) debug
    (c) cursor   (d) icon
62. An electric lamp produces
    (a) light energy
    (b) heat energy
    (c) both A and B
    (d) electrical energy
63. A drafter helps in drawing
    (a) parallel and perpendicular lines
    (b) concentric circles
    (c) smooth curves
    (d) all of above

64. The projection showing the front in the true shape and size is
    (a) isometric   (b) perspective
    (c) oblique   (d) axonometric
65. Minimum length an instrument can measure is called its
    (a) accuracy
    (b) estimate
    (c) precision
    (d) limitations
66. Mass of dry air is 12.175 kg and volume is 5 m^3, its density is
    (a) $24.425 \, \text{kg m}^{-3}$ (b) $2.435 \, \text{kg m}^{-3}$
    (c) $243.5 \, \text{kg m}^{-3}$ (d) $0.435 \, \text{kg m}^{-3}$
67. When an object is moving with uniform velocity, what is its acceleration?
    (a) zero
    (b) uniform
    (c) non-uniform
    (d) negative
68. A fan keeps working for 30 minutes and uses energy of 90000 J, power consumed by bulb is
    (a) 3000 W
    (b) 50 W
    (c) 500 W
    (d) 300 W
69. The four bulbs of 40W each are connected in series swift a battery across them, which of the following statement is true
    (a) The current through each bulb in same
    (b) The voltage across each bulb is not same
    (c) The power dissipation in each bulb is not same
    (d) None of the above
70. Which answer lists only simple machines?
    (a) lever, screw, wheel
    (b) screw, car, tires
    (c) television, computers, levers
    (d) lawn mower, edger, leaf blower
71. The main statute governing health and safety at work is the_____?
    (a) The Health and Safety of Employees Act 1974.
    (b) The Health and Safety at Work Act 1974.
    (c) The Health and Safety of Independent Contractors Act 2005.
    (d) The Health and Safety of Workers Act 2011.

72. Energy _____ in an Ecosystem
    (a) Is released
    (b) Is absorbed
    (c) Flows
    (d) None of the above

73. Which key is used in combination with another key to perform a specific task?
    (a) Function
    (b) Spacebar
    (c) Arrow
    (d) Control

74. Instrument used to measure temperature is termed as
    (a) Barometer
    (b) Thermometer
    (c) Manometer
    (d) Galvanometer

75. Which of the following statement is true?
    (a) A galvanometer with low resistance in series is an ammeter
    (b) A galvanometer with high resistance in series is an ammeter
    (c) A galvanometer with high resistance in parallel is a voltmeter
    (d) A galvanometer with low resistance in parallel is a voltmeter

GENERAL AWARENESS AND CURRENT AFFAIR

76. Which among the following parts of a plant is involved in gaseous exchange?
    (a) Stomata
    (b) Lenticels
    (c) Vacuoles
    (d) Stomata and Lenticels

77. Graphite is used in nuclear reactors for –
    (a) reducing the speed of fast neutrons
    (b) cooling the reactor
    (c) absorbing neutrons
    (d) None of the above

78. How many members are nominated by the governor in the Legislative Council of the State?
    (a) 1/3rd of the total membership
    (b) 1/6th of the total membership
    (c) 1/12th of the total membership
    (d) 12 members

79. Which of the following book is centred on "Environment"?
    (a) The Late, Great Planet Earth
    (b) Silent Spring
    (c) Here I stand
    (d) And then One Day

80. If an insect that feeds on feces sits on the food you are going to eat, you are most likely to be infected by which disease?
    (a) Tuberculosis
    (b) Cholera
    (c) Typhoid
    (d) Hepatitis B

81. Which of the following is not an antibiotics?
    (a) Penicilin
    (b) Ampicilin
    (c) Streptomycin
    (d) Aspirin

82. Mitosis is a type of cell division in which –
    (a) The chromosomes maintain their original number.
    (b) The chromosome number is reduced to half.
    (c) The Chromosome number is doubled.
    (d) The chromosome number is reduced to one fourth.

83. WiMax stands for – Wimax
    (a) Worldwide interoperability for Microwave Access
    (b) Wireless Maximum
    (c) Wireless international Microwave Access
    (d) Worldwide Microwave Access

84. Ginger is an example of–
    (a) Modified Node
    (b) Modified Root
    (c) Modified Stem
    (d) Tap Root

85. The first death anniversary day of Sri Rajiv Gandhi was observed as the —
    (a) National Integration Day
    (b) Peace and love Day
    (c) Secularism Day
    (d) Anti-terrorism Day

86. If the length of a simple pendulum is halved then its period of oscillation is –
    (a) doubled
    (b) halved
    (c) increased by a factor $\sqrt{2}$
    (d) decreased by a factor $\sqrt{2}$

87. Brass contains
    (a) Copper and Zinc   (b) Copper and Tin
    (c) Copper and Silver   (d) Copper and Nickel

88. Name the Indian javelin thrower who became the first-ever Indian to win a gold medal at the Asian Games.
    (a) Rajesh Bind
    (b) Neeraj Chopra
    (c) Devendra Jhajharia
    (d) Kashinath Naik

89. The First South Asian Association for Regional Cooperation (SAARC) Agri Cooperative Business Forum has begun in _____________.
    (a) Colombo
    (b) New Delhi
    (c) Thimpu
    (d) Kathmandu

90. The National Sports Day is celebrated every year to mark the birthday of _______.
    (a) Rajiv Gandhi
    (b) IM Vijayan
    (c) Major Dhyan Chand
    (d) Milkha Singh

91. Willy willy is
    (a) A type of tree in temperate regions
    (b) A tropical cyclone of North West Australia
    (c) A wind that blows in a desert
    (d) A kind of common fish found near Lakshadweep Islands

92. Which strait connects Red Sea and Indian Ocean?
    (a) Bab-el-Mandeb
    (b) Hormuz
    (c) Bosporus
    (d) Malacca

93. The dry wind 'Santa Ana' blows in
    (a) Siberia
    (b) Argentina
    (c) Switzerland
    (d) California

94. The largest exporter of wood pulp is
    (a) Canada
    (b) Sweden
    (c) Finland
    (d) Norway

95. Xerophytes can tolerate and withstands
    (a) The drought conditions
    (b) Severe cold
    (c) Humidity
    (d) High temperature

96. Golden revolution refers to the development of
    (a) Oilseeds
    (b) Pulses
    (c) Horticulture
    (d) Cereals

97. Which state in India has the world's largest deposit of 'thorium'?
    (a) Kerala
    (b) Karnataka
    (c) Andhra Pradesh
    (d) Assam

98. Raniganj coal field is in
    (a) Bihar
    (b) Odissa
    (c) West Bengal
    (d) Madhya Pradesh

99. The world's largest Railway Platform is at
    (a) Gorakhpur
    (b) New York
    (c) Kharagpur
    (d) Chieago

100. The orbital speed of Jupiter is
    (a) Greater than the orbital speed of the earth
    (b) Less than the orbital speed of the earth
    (c) Equal to the orbital speed of the earth
    (d) Zero

HINTS & EXPLANATIONS

1. (a) Let the number be z. Now $385 = 5 \times 7 \times 11$

5	z	Remainders
7	y	4
11	x	6
	102	10

$x = 11 \times 102 + 10 = 1132$

$y = 7x + 6 = 7 \times 1132 + 6 = 7930$

$z = 5y + 4 = 5 \times 7930 + 4 = 39654$

2. (a) $392 \times 2 = 784 \Rightarrow (27)^2$

Hence, 2 can be multiplied by 392 which gives perfect square.

3. (c) Let C.P. = ₹ 100. Then M.P. = ₹ 120 and S.P. = ₹ 108

$$\% \text{ discount} = \left(\frac{12}{120} \times 100\right)\% = 10\%$$

4. (b) Required difference $= \dfrac{PR^2}{(100)^2}$

$$\Rightarrow \frac{4000 \times 5 \times 5}{100 \times 100} = ₹10$$

5. (c) Let the profit $= x$

Profit of $A = \dfrac{9x}{10}$, Remaining profit $= \dfrac{x}{10}$

Profit of $B = \dfrac{x}{20}$

Profit of $C = \dfrac{x}{20}$

Ratio of profit $= \dfrac{9}{10} : \dfrac{1}{20} : \dfrac{1}{20}$

$$= 18 : 1 : 1$$

A's income is increased by ₹ 270 . When profit rises 3%

Investment of $A = \dfrac{270}{3} \times 100 = ₹9000.$

If investment of A, B and C = 18x, x and x

$18x = 9000$

$x = 500$

B's investment = ₹ 500.

C's investment = ₹ 500.

6. (d) $Q = P + 30 \Rightarrow Q - P = 30$ and

$R - Q = 60 = 2 \times 30$

∴ Required ratio $= 2 : 3 : 5$

look : $3 - 2 = 1, 5 - 3 = 2$

7. (a) Let the length of the journey $= x$ km.

∴ Journey rides by horse cart

$$= x\left(1 - \frac{1}{2} - \frac{1}{3}\right) = \frac{1}{6}x \text{ km.}$$

Then, total time taken to complete journey

$$= \frac{31}{5} \text{ hr}$$

$$\Rightarrow t_1 + t_2 + t_3 = \frac{31}{5}$$

$$\Rightarrow \frac{x}{2} \times \frac{1}{4} + \frac{x}{3} \times \frac{1}{12} + \frac{x}{6 \times 9} = \frac{31}{5}$$

$$\Rightarrow x = \frac{31}{5} \times \frac{216}{37} = 36.2 \text{km} \approx 36 \text{km}$$

8. (a) $2^x = 3^y = 6^{-z} = k$

$$\Rightarrow 2 = k^{\frac{1}{x}} ; 3 = k^{\frac{1}{y}} ; 6 = k^{-\frac{1}{z}}$$

∵ $2 \times 3 = 6$

$$\Rightarrow k^{\frac{1}{x}} \times k^{\frac{1}{y}} = k^{-\frac{1}{z}} \Rightarrow k^{\frac{1}{x}+\frac{1}{y}} = k^{-\frac{1}{z}}$$

$$\Rightarrow \frac{1}{x} + \frac{1}{y} = -\frac{1}{z} \Rightarrow \frac{1}{x} + \frac{1}{y} + \frac{1}{z} = 0$$

9. (a) Let the monthly salary of A be x,, monthly salary of B is (40000 − x).

Savings of A = $(100 − 85)\%$ of x $= 0.15x$

Savings of B = $(100 − 95)\%$ of $(40000 − x)$

$$= 0.05 (40000 − x)$$

$0.15\,x = 0.05\,(40000 - x)$

$0.15x + 0.05x = 40000 \times 0.05$

$0.2x = 2000$

$x = ₹10000$

10. (b) $\dfrac{15}{16} = 0.94;\quad \dfrac{19}{20} = 0.95$

$\dfrac{24}{25} = 0.96;\quad \dfrac{34}{35} = 0.97$

11. (a) $8 + 9 + 10 = 27$

$11 + 12 + 13 = 36$

So, let 3 consecutive no $x, x+1, x+2$

Next 3 consecutive no $x+3; x+4, x+5$

i.e. sum of last 3 consecutive no. is 9 more than sum of first 3.

$= 27 + 9 = 36$

12. (b) First number × second number

$= HCF \times LCM$

$\Rightarrow 84 \times \text{second number} = 12 \times 336$

∴ Second number

$= \dfrac{12 \times 336}{84} = 48$

13. (d) $\dfrac{0.01 - 0.0001}{0.0001} + 1 = \dfrac{0.0099}{0.0001} + 1$

$= 99 + 1 = 100$

14. (b) If the CP = ₹100, then SP = ₹120 and gain = ₹20

$\text{Gain \%} = \dfrac{20}{120} \times 100$

$= \dfrac{50}{3} = 16\dfrac{2}{3}\%$

15. (d) If the CP of each book be ₹1, then

SP of 20 books = ₹15

CP of 20 books = ₹20

∴ $L\% = \dfrac{20 - 15}{20} \times 100 = 25\%$

16. (d) Let the marked price be ₹ x.

∴ In case I, SP = ₹ $\dfrac{75x}{100}$

Single discount equivalent to successive discounts of 15% and 10%.

$= \left(15 + 10 - \dfrac{15 \times 10}{100}\right)\% = 23.5\%$

∴ S.P. in this case = ₹ $\dfrac{76.5x}{100}$

∴ $\dfrac{76.5x}{100} - \dfrac{75x}{100} = ₹72$

$\Rightarrow \dfrac{1.5x}{100} = 72$

∴ $x = \dfrac{72 \times 100}{1.5} = ₹4800$

17. (c) Let the amount of the bill be ₹ x.

∴ $\dfrac{4x}{100} = 13$

$\Rightarrow x = \dfrac{1300}{4} = ₹325$

18. (d) Net increase percentage

$= \left(10 + 20 + \dfrac{20 \times 10}{100}\right)\% = 32\%$

∴ $x \times \dfrac{132}{100} = 33$

$\Rightarrow x = \dfrac{33 \times 100}{132} = ₹25$

19. (c) Milk in $V_1 = \dfrac{5}{8} = 0.625$

Milk in $V_2 = \dfrac{2}{3} = 0.66$

Milk in $V_3 = \dfrac{3}{5} = 0.6$

Milk in $V_4 = \dfrac{7}{11} = 0.636$

20. (a) Let the numbers be $3x$ and x.

$3x + x = 240$

$\Rightarrow 4x = 240$

$\Rightarrow x = \dfrac{240}{4} = 60$

$\therefore$ Difference $= 3x - x = 2x$
$= 2 \times 60 = 120$

21. (d) Let the income of man be Rs. $= 11x$ and his expenditure be ₹ $10x$.
$\therefore$ Savings $x = ₹\,9000$

$\therefore$ Monthly income of man $= \dfrac{11 \times 9000}{12}$

$= ₹\,8250$

22. (b) Required change in area

$$\boxed{\text{trick} = \dfrac{-x^2}{100}}$$

Negative sign shows a decrease.

$= 10 - 10 - \dfrac{10 \times 10}{100}$

$= -1\%$

or 1% decreasing.

23. (d) $A = P\left(1 + \dfrac{R}{100}\right)^{T}$

$\Rightarrow 24000 = 12000\left(1 + \dfrac{R}{100}\right)^{5}$

$\Rightarrow 2 = \left(1 + \dfrac{R}{100}\right)^{5}$

$\Rightarrow 2^4 = \left(1 + \dfrac{R}{100}\right)^{20}$

$= 16$ times
i.e. The sum amounts to ₹192000.

24. (a) Let the numbers be x and y.
$\therefore x(x+y) = 247$
and $y(x+y) = 114$
$\Rightarrow x^2 + xy = 247$ and $xy + y^2 = 114$
On adding;
$x^2 + xy + xy + y^2 = 247 + 114$
$\Rightarrow x^2 + 2xy + y^2 = 361$
$\Rightarrow (x+y)^2 = 19^2 \Rightarrow x + y = 19$

25. (a) Let the number be x.

$\therefore \dfrac{x}{7} - \dfrac{x}{11} = 100$

$\Rightarrow \dfrac{11x - 7x}{11 \times 7} = 100$

$\Rightarrow 4x = 77 \times 100$

$\Rightarrow x = \dfrac{77 \times 100}{4} = 1925$

26. (c) The words in each pair are synonyms.

27. (c)

P	A	P	E	R
+3	+2	+4	+2	+5
↓	↓	↓	↓	↓
S	C	T	G	W

Similarly,

M	O	T	H	E	R
+3	+2	+4	+2	+5	+2
↓	↓	↓	↓	↓	↓
P	Q	X	J	J	T

28. (a) $210 = (15)^2 - 15$ $\qquad 15 + 5 = 20$

$380 = (20)^2 - 20$

$182 = (14)^2 - 14$

$(19)^2 - 19 = 342 \quad\Big] 14 + 5$

29. (d)

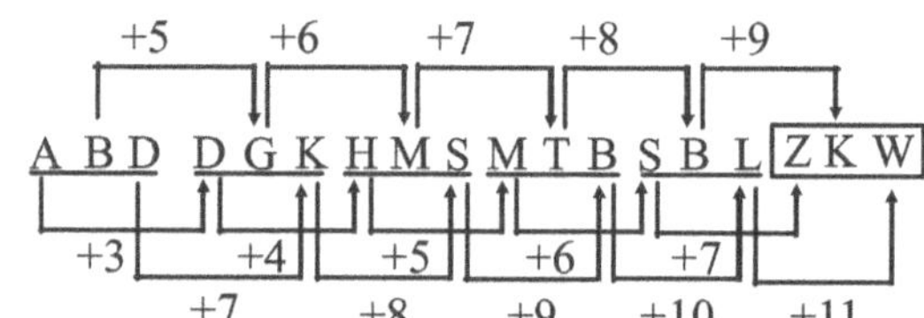

30. (d) Each number is 15 multiplied by a prime number i.e. 15×11, 15×13, 15×17, 15×19, 15×23, ...

So, missing term $= 15 \times 29 = 435$.

31. (b)

C	O	R	N	E	R
+4	+4	+4	+4	+4	+4
↓	↓	↓	↓	↓	↓

Coded as: G S V R I V

Similarly,

C	E	N	T	R	A	L
+4	+4	+4	+4	+4	+4	+4
↓	↓	↓	↓	↓	↓	↓
G	I	R	X	V	E	P

32. (d) A is the sister of B and B is the son/daughter of C. So, A is the daughter of C.

Also, D is the father of C.

Thus, A is the granddaughter of D.

33. (c)

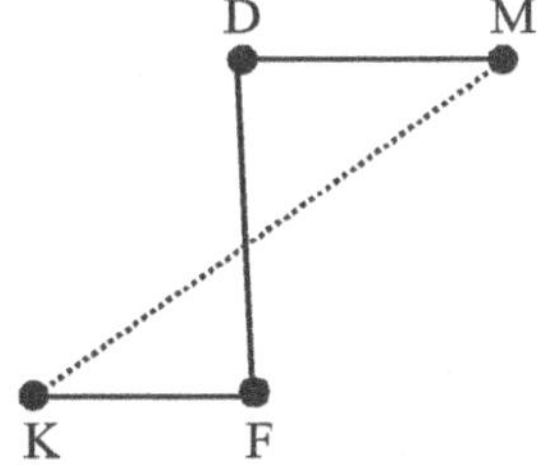

M is to the North-East of K.

34. (a) Solve by options, we can check all the options one by one.

$25 \div 5 \times 20 + 27 - 7 \Rightarrow 5 \times 20 + 27 - 7$

$\Rightarrow 100 + 27 - 7$

$120 = 120$

35. (a) Age of Shan = 55 years

Age of Sathian = 55 – 5 = 50 years

Age of Balan = 50 – 6 = 44 years

Age of Devan = 44 – 7 = 37 years

Difference between the ages of Shan and Devan = 55 – 37 = 18 years.

36. (c) Total students

= [Malay's place from starting + Malay's place from end] –1

= [13 + 17] – 1 = 29

Number of passed students

= [Malay's place from starting + Malay's place from end] –1

= [8 + 13] – 1 = 20

∴ Number of failed students = 29 – 20 = 9

37. (b) $(7 + 9 + 5 + 4) \times 2 - 10 = 40$

$(17 + 8 + 3 + 6) \times 2 - 14 = 54$

$(10 + 21 + 6 + 3) \times 2 - 18 = 62$

38. (c)   39. (c)

40. (d)

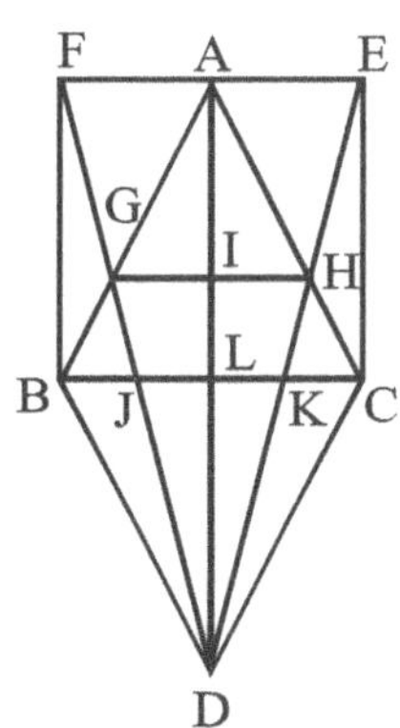

ΔFDE, ΔACD, ΔABD,
ΔFBD, ΔABC, ΔBCD,
ΔBKD, ΔBLD, ΔBJD,
ΔJCD, ΔJKD, ΔLDJ, ΔLCD,
ΔLKD, ΔHDC, ΔKDC, ΔEDC,
ΔHKC, ΔEKC, ΔAEC, ΔEHC,
ΔAEH, ΔAGH, ΔAIH, ΔAGI.
ΔAFB, ΔAGF, ΔFBG.

∴ Total 28 triangles.

41. (a) The water image of 'a' is 'ɒ', 'b' is 'p', 'S' is 'Ƨ', 'e' is 'ɘ', 'n' is 'ʋ', 'c' is 'ɔ' and 'e' is 'ɘ'.

42. (c)

43. (d)

| S | E | A | S | O | N | A | L |

| E | S | S | A | N | O | L | A |

Therefore,

| S | E | P | A | R | A | T | E |

| E | S | A | P | A | R | E | T |

44. (a)

Persons	Numbers						
	3	5	6	7	8	11	17
Educated	✓	✗	✓	✗	✓	✓	✗
Employed	✓	✓	✓	✓	✗	✗	✗
Poor	✓	✓	✓	✗	✗	✓	✓

Number of educated youth are poor = 11 + 3 = 14

45. (b) Total number of players are quick and fat = 30.

46. (c)

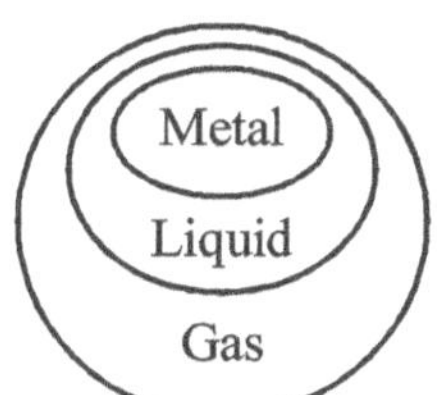

So, Either I or II follows.

47. (d)

So, Both I and II follow.

48. (c)

49. (b) Clearly, the new scheme intends to develop interest in reading by

incorporating the habit in their routine. So, only II follows while I does not.

50. (d) The statement mentions the problem of increased migration of children to cities. But the ways to deal with the problem cannot be deduced from it. So, neither I nor II follows.

51. (d)	52. (b)	53. (b)	54. (c)
55. (d)	56. (b)	57. (b)	58. (a)
59. (c)	60. (d)	61. (a)	62. (c)
63. (d)	64. (c)	65. (c)	66. (b)

67. (a)	68. (b)	69. (a)	70. (a)
71. (b)	72. (c)	73. (d)	74. (b)
75. (a)	76. (a)	77. (a)	78. (b)
79. (b)	80. (c)	81. (d)	82. (c)
83. (a)	84. (c)	85. (d)	86. (d)
87. (a)	88. (b)	89. (d)	90. (c)
91. (b)	92. (a)	93. (d)	94. (a)
95. (a)	96. (c)	97. (a)	98. (b)
99. (a)	100. (b)		

PRACTICE SET　11

MATHEMATICS

1. The H.C.F. and L.C.M. of two numebrs are 8 and 48 respectively. If one of the numbers is 24, then the other number is
   - (a) 48
   - (b) 36
   - (c) 24
   - (d) 16

2. The average of the first 100 positive integers is
   - (a) 100
   - (b) 51
   - (c) 50.5
   - (d) 49.5

3. If the ratio of cost price and selling price of an article be as 10 : 11, the percentage of profit is
   - (a) 8%
   - (b) 10%
   - (c) 11%
   - (d) 15%

4. Krishna purchased a number of articles at ₹10 for each and the same number for ₹14 each. He mixed them together and sold them for ₹13 each. Then his gain or loss percent is
   - (a) Loss $8\dfrac{1}{3}\%$
   - (b) Gain $8\dfrac{2}{3}\%$
   - (c) Loss $8\dfrac{2}{3}\%$
   - (d) Gain $8\dfrac{1}{3}\%$

5. Ram borrows a certain sum of money at 8% per annum simple interest and Rahim borrows ₹2,000 at 5% per annum simple interest. If the interest at the end of 3 years is equal, then the amount borrowed by Ram is
   - (a) ₹1,250
   - (b) ₹1,500
   - (c) ₹2,000
   - (d) ₹1,000

6. If 5 men or 7 women can earn ₹5,250 per day, how much would 7 men and 13 women earn per day ?
   - (a) ₹11,600
   - (b) ₹11,700
   - (c) ₹16,100
   - (d) ₹17,100

7. A drum of kerosene is $\dfrac{3}{4}$ full. When 30 litres of kerosene is drawn from it, it remains $\dfrac{7}{12}$ full. The capacity of the drum is
   - (a) 120 ℓ
   - (b) 135 ℓ
   - (c) 150 ℓ
   - (d) 180 ℓ

8. In a business partnership among A, B, C and D, the profit is shared as follows:
   $$\frac{\text{A's share}}{\text{B's share}} = \frac{\text{B's share}}{\text{C's share}} = \frac{\text{C's share}}{\text{D's share}} = \frac{1}{3}$$
   If the total profit is ₹4,00,000, the share of C is
   - (a) ₹1,12,500
   - (b) ₹1,37,500
   - (c) ₹90,000
   - (d) ₹2,70,000

9. An equilateral triangle of side 6 cm has its corners cut off to form a regular hexagon. Area (in cm^2) of this regular hexagon will be
   - (a) $3\sqrt{3}$
   - (b) $3\sqrt{6}$
   - (c) $6\sqrt{3}$
   - (d) $\dfrac{5\sqrt{3}}{2}$

10. If $(a-b) = 3$, $(b-c) = 5$ and $(c-a) = 1$, then the value of $\dfrac{a^3 + b^3 + c^3 - 3abc}{a+b+c}$ is
    - (a) 17.5
    - (b) 20.5
    - (c) 10.5
    - (d) 15.5

11. In an examination a student scores 4 marks for every correct answer and loses 1 mark for every wrong answer. If he attempts all 75 questions and secures 125 marks, the number of questions he attempts correctly is
    - (a) 35
    - (b) 40
    - (c) 42
    - (d) 46

12. The traffic lights at three different road crossings change after 24 seconds, 36 seconds and 54 seconds respectively. If they all change

simultaneously at 10 : 15 :00 AM, then at what time will they again change simultaneously?
(a) 10 : 16 : 54 AM   (b) 10 : 18 : 36 AM
(c) 10 : 17 : 02 AM   (d) 10 : 22 : 12 AM

13. A can do a work in 12 days. When he had worked for 3 days, B joined him. If they complete the work in 3 more days, in how many days can B alone finish the work?
(a) 6 days   (b) 12 days
(c) 4 days   (d) 8 days

14. X is 3 times as fast as Y and is able to complete the work in 40 days less than Y. Then the time in which they can complete the work together is
(a) 15 days   (b) 10 days
(c) $7\dfrac{1}{2}$ days   (d) 5 days

15. A river 3 m deep and 40 m wide is flowing at the rate of 2 km per hour. How much water (in litres) will fall into the sea in a minute?
(a) 4,00,000   (b) 40,00,000
(c) 40,000   (d) 4,000

16. The perimeter of a triangle is 40cm and its area is 60 cm^2. If the largest side measures 17cm, then the length (in cm) of the smallest side of the triangle is
(a) 4   (b) 6   (c) 8   (d) 15

17. A shopkeeper allows a discount of 10% to his customers and still gains. 20%. Find the marked price of the article which costs ₹ 450.
(a) ₹ 600   (b) ₹ 540
(c) ₹ 660   (d) ₹ 580

18. In a business partnership among A, B, C and D, the profit is shared as follows:

$$\dfrac{\text{A's share}}{\text{B's share}} = \dfrac{\text{B's share}}{\text{C's share}} = \dfrac{\text{C's share}}{\text{D's share}} = \dfrac{1}{3}$$

If the total profit is ₹ 4,00,000, the share of C is
(a) ₹ 1,12,500   (b) ₹ 1,37,500
(c) ₹ 90,000   (d) ₹ 2,70,000

19. What number should be added to or subtracted from each term of the ratio 17 : 24 so that it becomes equal to 1 : 2?
(a) 5 is subtracted   (b) 10 is added
(c) 7 is added   (d) 10 is subtracted

20. The ratio of weekly incomes of A and B is 9 : 7 and the ratio of their expenditures is 4 : 3. If each saves ₹ 200 per week, then the sum of their weekly incomes is
(a) ₹ 3,600   (b) ₹ 3,200
(c) ₹ 4,800   (d) ₹ 5,600

21. Among three numbers, the first is twice the second and thrice the third. If the average of the three numbers is 49.5, then the difference between the first and the third number is
(a) 54   (b) 28
(c) 39.5   (d) 41.5

22. The mean of 50 numbers is 30. Later it was discovered that two entries were wrongly entered as 82 and 13 instead of 28 and 31. Find the correct mean.
(a) 36.12   (b) 30.66
(c) 29.28   (d) 38.21

23. While selling a watch, a shopkeeper gives a discount of 5%. If he gives a discount of 6%, he earns ₹ 15 less as profit. What is the marked price of the watch?
(a) ₹ 1,250   (b) ₹ 1,400
(c) ₹ 1,500   (d) ₹ 750

24. Krishna purchased a number of articles at ₹10 for each and the same number for ₹ 14 each. He mixed them together and sold them for ₹13 each. Then his gain or loss percent is
(a) Loss $8\dfrac{1}{3}$%   (b) Gain $8\dfrac{2}{3}$%
(c) Loss $8\dfrac{2}{3}$%   (d) Gain $8\dfrac{1}{3}$%

25. A trader bought two horses for ₹19,500. He sold one at a loss of 20% and the other at a profit of 15%. If the selling price of each horse is the same, then their cost prices are respectively.
(a) ₹ 10,000 and ₹ 9,500
(b) ₹ 11,500 and ₹ 8,000
(c) ₹ 12,000 and ₹ 7,500
(d) ₹ 10,500 and ₹ 9,000

GENERAL INTELLIGENCE & REASONING

DIRECTIONS (Qs. 26-28) : In each of the following questions, select the related letters/word/number from the given alternatives.

26. $\dfrac{M}{AC} : \dfrac{N}{AD} :: \dfrac{O}{AE} : ?$

(a) $\dfrac{P}{AF}$ (b) $\dfrac{Q}{AB}$

(c) $\dfrac{P}{AC}$ (d) $\dfrac{R}{AD}$

27. $6:11::11:?$
    (a) 6   (b) 17
    (c) 21   (d) 30
28. Patrol : Security : : Insurance : ?
    (a) Money   (b) Policy
    (c) Savings   (d) Risk
29. M is the son of P. Q is the grand daughter of O who is the husband of P. How is M related to O?
    (a) Son   (b) Daughter
    (c) Mother   (d) Father
30. In a row of boys, Srinath is 7th from the left and Venkat is 12th from the right. If they interchange their positions, Srinath becomes 22nd from the left. How many boys are there in the row ?
    (a) 19   (b) 31
    (c) 33   (d) 34
31. If SPARK is coded as TQBSL, what will be the code for FLAME ?
    (a) GMBNF   (b) GNBNF
    (c) GMCND   (d) GMBMF
32. If '−' stands for '÷' '+' stands for '×' , '÷' stands for '−' and stands ×' for '+', which one of the following equations is correct?
    (a) $30-6+5 \times 4 \div 2 = 27$
    (b) $30+6-5 \div 4 \times 2 = 30$
    (c) $30 \times 6 \div 5 - 4 + 2 = 32$
    (d) $30 \div 6 \times 5 + 4 - 2 = 40$
33. If $841 = 3, 633 = 5, 425 = 7$ then $217 = ?$
    (a) 6   (b) 7
    (c) 8   (d) 9
34. Find the missing number from the given responses:

5	6	12
4	3	4
2	3	?
18	27	96

    (a) 4   (b) 5
    (c) 3   (d) 6

DIRECTION (Q. 35) : In the following question, two statements P and Q are given followed by four conclusions I, II, III and IV. You have to consider the two statements to be true even if they seem to be at variance from commonly known facts. You have to decide which of the given conclusions, if any, follow the given statements.

35. **Statements :**
    P. All men are women.
    Q. All women are crazy.
    Conclusions :
    I. All men are crazy.
    II. All the crazy are men.
    III. Some of the crazy are men
    IV. Some of the crazy are women
    (a) None of the conclusions follows
    (b) All the conclusions follow
    (c) Only I, III and IV follow
    (d) Only II and III follow
36. How many triangles are there in the given figure?

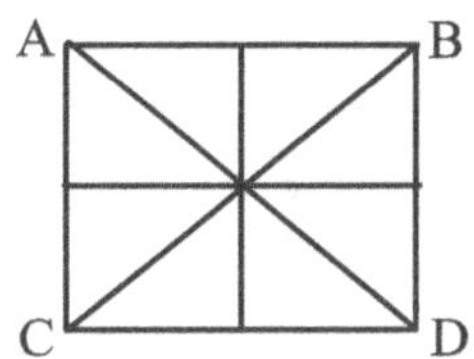

    (a) 16   (b) 14
    (c) 8   (d) 12
37. Which of the answer figure indicates the best relationship between milk, goat, cow, hen ?
    Answer figures :

(a)   (b)

(c)   (d)

DIRECTION (Q. 38) : In the following question which answer figure will complete the question figure?

38. **Question Figure :**

Answer Figures :

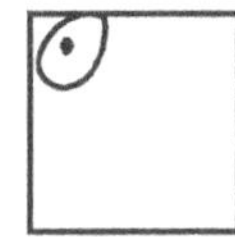 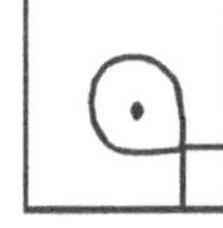 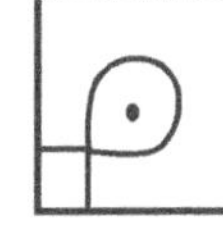 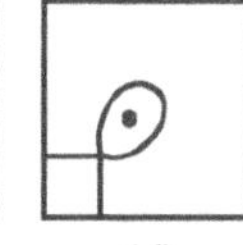

     (a)   (b)   (c)   (d)

DIRECTION (Q. 39) : If a mirror is placed on the line MN, then which of the answer figures is the correct image of the given question figure ?

39. **Question Figure:**

Answer Figures:

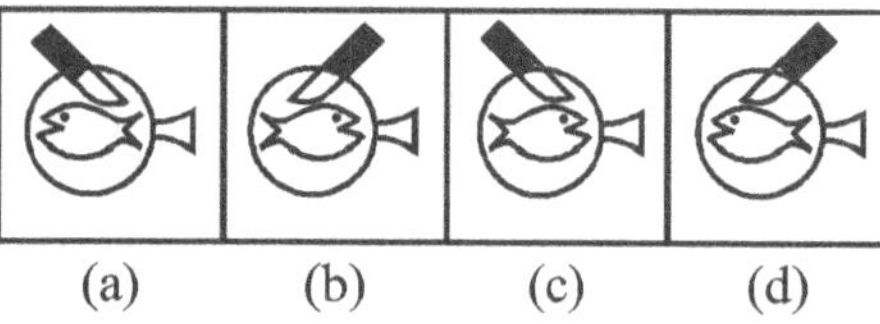

(a)   (b)   (c)   (d)

DIRECTIONS (Qs. 40–41): In each of the following questions, select the missing number from the given responses.

40. 500, 484, 459, _?_, 374
    (a) 384   (b) 432
    (c) 418   (d) 423

41. 60, 69, 85, _?_, 146
    (a) 110   (b) 117
    (c) 109   (d) 120

42. In a certain code language, GRAPE is written as 27354 and FOUR is written as 1687. How is GROUP written in that code?
    (a) 27384   (b) 27684
    (c) 27685   (d) 27658

43. WAYIN is written as TXVFX. How LBUK can be written in that code?
    (a) IYRH   (b) KATJ
    (c) JZSI   (d) NDWM

44. Sunil is the son of Kesav. Simran, Kesav's sister, has a son Maruti and daughter Sita. Prem is the maternal uncle of Maruti. How is Sunil related to Maruti?
    (a) Uncle   (b) Brother
    (c) Nephew   (d) Cousin

45. Satish starts from A and walks 2 km east upto B and turns southwards and walks 1 km upto C. At C he turns to east and walks 2 km upto D. He then turns northwards and walks 4 km to E. How far is he from his starting point ?
    (a) 5 km (b) 6 km (c) 3 km (d) 4 km

46. Select the correct combination of mathematical signs to replace * signs and to balance the given equation.
    5 * 5 * 5 * 3 * 10
    (a) × + = ×   (b) + – × =
    (c) + ÷ = ×   (d) + ÷ × =

47. In a group of persons, 11 persons speak Kannada, 20 persons speak Tamil and 11 persons speak Telugu. In that group, if two persons speak two languages and one person speak all the languages, then how many persons are there in the group?

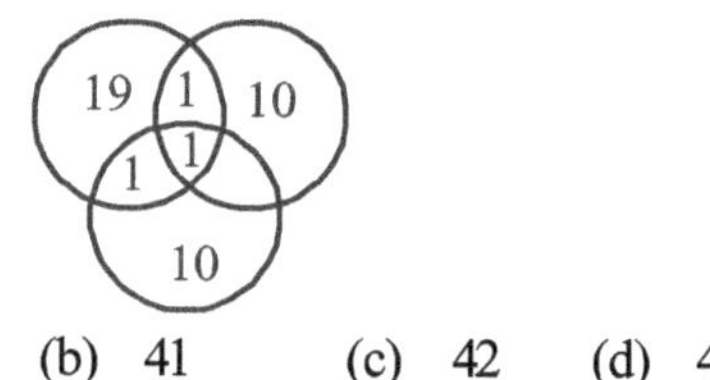

    (a) 40   (b) 41   (c) 42   (d) 43

DIRECTIONS (Qs. 48–49): In each question below are given two statements followed by two conclusions numbered I and II. You have to take the two given statements to be true even if they seem to be at variance with commonly known facts. Read both the statement and then decide which of the given conclusions logically follows from the given statements disregarding commonly known facts. Give answer

(a) if only conclusion I follows.
(b) if only conclusion II follows.
(c) if either conclusion I or II follows.
(d) if neither conclusion I nor II follows.

48. **Statements:**   All cards are sheets.
                 All files are cards.
    Conclusions: **I.** All cards are files.
                 II. All files are sheets.

49. **Statements :** Some questions are answers.
                All questions are issues.
    Conclusions : **I.** At least some answers are issues.
                II. Some answers are definitely not questions.

DIRECTION (Q. 50): In each question below is given a statement followed by two conclusions numbered I and II. You have to assume everything in the statement to be true, then consider the two conclusions together and decide which of them logically follows beyond a reasonable doubt from the information given in the statement.

50. **Statements:** No country is absolutely self-dependent these days.
    Conclusions:
    I.   It is impossible to grow and produce all that a country needs.
    II. Countrymen in general have become lazy.
    (a) Only conclusion I follows
    (b) Only conclusion II follows
    (c) Either I or II follows
    (d) Neither I nor II follows

BASIC SCIENCE AND ENGINEERING

51. The following line is used for dimension line
    (a) Continuous thick
    (b) Continuous thin
    (c) Chain thin line
    (d) Short zigzag thin

52. The dimensions of gravitational constant G are
    (a) $[MLT^{-2}]$ (b) $[ML^3 T^{-2}]$
    (c) $[M^{-1}L^3 T^{-2}]$ (d) $[M^{-1}LT^{-2}]$

53. In Newton's second law of motion, what is the relationship between acceleration and mass? Acceleration
    (a) Is directly proportional to mass.
    (b) Is inversely proportional to mass.
    (c) Does not depend on mass.
    (d) It is dividing by mass.

54. Acceleration is described as rate of change of
    (a) distance with time
    (b) velocity with distance
    (c) velocity with time
    (d) distance with velocity

55. Energy can be converted into some other forms but cannot be
    (a) destroyed   (b) decrease
    (c) increase   (d) none of above

56. The water is poor conductors of heat so do not heated by:
    (a) absorption   (b) conduction
    (c) radiation   (d) convection

57. The resistance of a straight conductor does not depend upon its
    (a) shape of cross–section
    (b) temperature
    (c) material
    (d) length

58. Which of these is an example of a wedge?
    (a) skateboard   (b) broom
    (c) stairs   (d) butter knife

59. What is the best way to prevent injury at work?
    (a) Remove the hazard or redesign the task
    (b) Restrict access to the hazard
    (c) Provide gloves and a bobble hat
    (d) Send all employees home - they'll much safer there

60. Environmental education is targeted to
    (a) General public
    (b) Professional social groups
    (c) Technicians and scientists
    (d) All of these

61. Integrated Chips or IC's were started to be in use from which generation of Computers?
    (a) 1st Generation   (b) 2nd Generation
    (c) 3rd Generation   (d) 4th Generation

62. Appliances based on heating effect of current work on
    (a) only a.c.   (b) only d.c.
    (c) both a.c. and d.c. (d) None of these

63. Which one is not correct for scale in engineering drawing?
    (a) 1:2   (b) 1:20
    (c) 1:1/2   (d) 1/2

64. In pendulum, heavy metal ball is called
    (a) String   (b) Gong
    (c) Hook   (d) Bob

65. The law of __________ of mass states that the mass of a closed system must remain constant over time.
    (a) Conservation   (b) Density
    (c) Weight   (d) Elasticity

66. An object that is not accelerating could be sitting still or doing this:
    (a) turning a corner
    (b) moving at a constant speed
    (c) increasing its velocity
    (d) moving slowling

67. With reference to equation of W = F.s, where 'W' is work done, 'F' is force and 's' is displacement, we can conclude that 1 Joule is equal to
    (a) $1 \, N \, m^{-2}$, where N is Newton and m is meter
    (b) $1 \, N \, m$, where N is Newton's and m is meter
    (c) $1 \, W \, m$, where W is watts and m is meter
    (d) $1 \, W \, m^{-1}$, where W is watt and m is meter

68. Ice point is equal to 273 K, which is equal to
    (a) –273 °C   (b) 273 °C
    (c) 0 °C   (d) 100 °C
69. Electric current passing through the circuit produces
    (a) magnetic effect   (b) luminous effect
    (c) thermal effect   (d) chemical effect
70. Which part of the lever is the part you are trying to move?
    (a) Load   (b) effort
    (c) fulcrum   (d) None of these.
71. Which of the following does not form part of an employer's common law duty to take care?
    (a) Safe work equipment.
    (b) Safe work premises.
    (c) Competent fellow employees.
    (d) Reasonable salaries.
72. In which of the following ecosystems large volumes of air are purified?
    (a) Unsubsidized Natural Solar powered ecosystems
    (b) Naturally Subsidized Solar powered ecosystems
    (c) Man Subsidized Solar powered ecosystems
    (d) Fuel powered ecosystems
73. The instructions for starting the computer are housed in _____
    (a) RAM   (b) CD-ROM
    (c) ROM Chip   (d) None of these
74. What type of sketch uses a miter line?
    (a) a two-view multiview
    (b) an isometric pictorial
    (c) a three-point perspective pictorial
    (d) a three-view multiview
75. A closed switch has a resistance of
    (a) zero   (b) about 50 ohms
    (c) about 500 ohms   (d) infinity

GENERAL AWARENESS AND CURRENT AFFAIR

76. Who was the founder of The Servants of India Society?
    (a) G.K. Gokhale   (b) M.G. Ranade
    (c) B.G. Tilak   (d) Bipin Chandra Pal

77. A concave lens always forms an image which is?
    (a) real and erect
    (b) virtual and erect
    (c) real and inverted
    (d) virtual and inverted
78. Optical fibres are based on the phenomenon of
    (a) Interference
    (b) Dispersion
    (c) Diffraction
    (d) Total Internal Reflection
79. A vitamin requires cobalt for its activity. The vitamin is
    (a) Vitamin B_{12} (b) Vitamin D
    (c) Vitamin B_2 (d) Vitamin A
80. One of the constituents of tear gas is
    (a) Ethane   (b) Ethanol
    (c) Ether   (d) Chloropicrin
81. In coriander, the useful parts are
    (a) roots & leaves
    (b) leaves & flowers
    (c) leaves & dried fruits
    (d) flowers & dried fruits
82. The disease that kills more people than lung cancer as a consequence of air pollution is:
    (a) chronic bronchitis (b) asthma
    (c) emphesema   (d) heart attack
83. The Konkan Railway connects:
    (a) Goa – Mangalore
    (b) Roha – Mangalore
    (c) Kanyakumari – Mangalore
    (d) Kanyakumari – Mumbai
84. The book titled 'The Indian War of Independence' was written by
    (a) Krishna Verma   (b) Madame Cama
    (c) B.G. Tilak   (d) V.D. Savarkar
85. The Central Drug Research Institute of India is located at
    (a) Madras   (b) Lucknow
    (c) Delhi   (d) Bangalore
86. India's first Indian human mission will be launched by Indian Space Research Organisation (ISRO) by _______.
    (a) 2022   (b) 2018
    (c) 2020   (d) 2024

87. Name the North-eastern state, which will host the 2022 National Games coinciding with its 50 years of statehood.
    (a) Assam   (b) Manipur
    (c) Meghalaya   (d) Mizoram
88. Name the Indian State, which has decided to set up pilot corridor for an innovative concept of 'Caterpillar Train'?
    (a) Maharashtra   (b) Kerala
    (c) Goa   (d) Haryana
89. Name the State, which has launched Nagar Uday Abhiyan Scheme, recently?
    (a) Uttar Pradesh
    (b) Arunachal Pradesh
    (c) Himachal Pradesh
    (d) Madhya Pradesh
90. When air is saturated, it cannot hold
    (a) More water vapour (b) More air
    (c) More CO_2 (d) More O_2
91. Which one of the following is used to remove astigmatism for a human eye?
    (a) Concave lens   (b) Convex lens
    (c) Cylindrical lens (d) Prismatic lens
92. Compton effect is associated with
    (a) Positive rays   (b) β-rays
    (c) γ-rays   (d) X-rays
93. Formic acid is obtained from
    (a) red ants   (b) fats
    (c) vinegar   (d) orange

94. The most common lanthanide is
    (a) Lanthanum   (b) Cerium
    (c) Plutonium   (d) Samarium
95. Paraldehyde is used as
    (a) Drug   (b) Good fuel
    (c) Polymer   (d) Dye
96. Enzyme catalysis is an example of______?
    (a) Auto catalysts
    (b) Heterogeneous
    (c) Homogeneous catalysts
    (d) Induced catalysts
97. India War of Independence 1857' is written by
    (a) S. N. Sen   (b) R. C. Majumdar
    (c) V. D. Savarkar   (d) S. B. Chaudhari
98. Rotation of the earth causes deflection of wind by
    (a) Coriolis force   (b) Dynamic force
    (c) Gradient force   (d) Gravity force
99. What does happens when water is condensed into ice?
    (a) Heat is absorbed
    (b) Heat is released
    (c) Quantity of heat remains unchanged
    (d) None of the above
100. The highest grade and best quality coal is
    (a) Lignite   (b) Peat
    (c) Bituninous   (d) Anthracite

HINTS & EXPLANATIONS

1. (d) $p \times q = \text{HCF} \times \text{LCM}$

   $\therefore$ Second number $= \dfrac{8 \times 48}{24} = 16$

2. (c) $1 + 2 + 3 + \ldots\ldots + n = \dfrac{n(n+1)}{2}$

   $\therefore$ Average of these numbers

   $\therefore$ Average $= \dfrac{n+1}{2}$

   $= \dfrac{100+1}{2} = 50.5$

3. (b) Gain $= 11x - 10x = ₹x$

   $\therefore p\% = \dfrac{p \times 100}{p} \times 100 = \dfrac{x}{10x} \times 100 = 10\%$

4. (a) Average cost of $= \dfrac{10+14}{2} = 12$

   QP $= 13$

   $P\% = \dfrac{13-12}{12} \times 100 = 8\dfrac{1}{3}$

5. (a) Let Ram borrowed $₹P$

   $\dfrac{P \times 8 \times 3}{100} = \dfrac{2000 \times 5 \times 3}{100}$

   $P = \dfrac{2000 \times 5}{8} = ₹1,250$

6. (d) 5 men $\equiv$ 7 women

   $\therefore$ 7 men $\equiv \dfrac{7}{5} \times 7 = \dfrac{49}{5}$ women

   $\therefore$ 7 men + 13 women

   $= \dfrac{49}{5} + 13 = \dfrac{114}{5}$ women

   Now,

   $\because$ 7 women $\equiv ₹5250$

   $\therefore \dfrac{114}{5}$ women

   $\equiv \dfrac{5250}{7} \times \dfrac{114}{5} = ₹17100$

7. (d) Let the capacity of the drum be x litres.

   $\therefore \dfrac{3x}{4} - 30 = \dfrac{7x}{12}$

   $\Rightarrow \dfrac{3x}{4} - \dfrac{7x}{12} = 30 \quad \Rightarrow \dfrac{9x - 7x}{12} = 30$

   $\Rightarrow \dfrac{x}{6} = 30 = x = 6 \times 30 = 180$ litres

8. (c) $A : B = 1 : 3$

   $B : C = 1 : 3 = 3 : 9$

   $C : D = 1 : 3 = 9 : 27$

   $\therefore A : B : C : D = 1 : 3 : 9 : 27$

   Sum of ratios $= 1 + 3 + 9 + 27 = 40$

   $\therefore$ C's share of profit

   $= \dfrac{9}{40} \times 400000 = ₹90000$

9. (c)

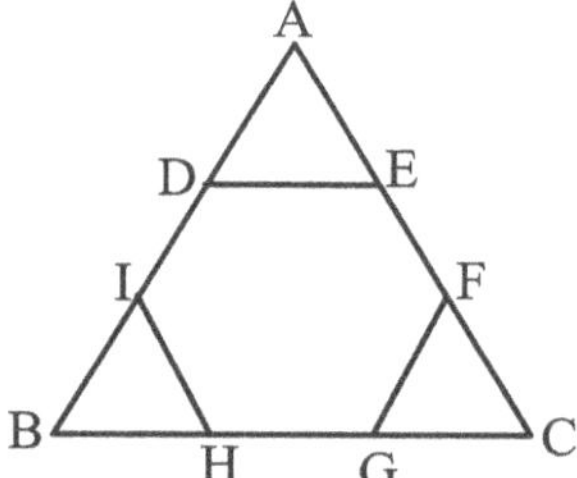

   Side of the regular hexagon

   $= \dfrac{1}{3} \times 6 = 2$ cm

   $\therefore$ Area of the hexagon $= \dfrac{3\sqrt{3}}{2} a^2$

   $= \dfrac{3\sqrt{3}}{2} \times 2 \times 2 = 6\sqrt{3}$ sq. cm.

10. (a) $a^3 + b^3 + c^3 - 3abc$

    $= \dfrac{1}{2}(a+b+c)\left[(a-b)^2 + (b-c)^2 + (c-a)^2\right]$

$$\therefore \ \frac{a^3+b^3+c^3-3abc}{a+b+c}$$

$$=\frac{1}{2}\left[(a-b)^2+(b-c)^2+(c-a)^2\right]$$

$$=\frac{1}{2}(9+25+1)\ =\frac{35}{2}=17.5$$

11. **(b)** Let the number of correct answers be x.

$$\therefore\ 4x-(75-x)\times 1=125$$
$$\Rightarrow 4x-75+x=125$$
$$\Rightarrow 5x=125+75=200$$
$$\therefore\ x=\frac{200}{5}=40$$

12. **(b)** LCM of 24, 36 and 54 seconds
$$=216\ \text{seconds}$$
$$=3\ \text{minutes}\ 36\ \text{seconds}$$
$$\therefore\ \text{Required time}=10:15:00+$$
3 minutes 36 seconds
$$=10:18:36\ \text{a.m.}$$

13. **(a)** ATQ

$$\frac{3}{A}+\frac{3}{A}+\frac{3}{B}=1$$

$$\frac{6}{12}+\frac{3}{B}=1$$

$$\frac{3}{B}=\frac{1}{2}$$

B = 6 days

14. **(a)** If X completes a work in x days, Y will do the same in 3x days.
$$\therefore\ 3x-x=40\Rightarrow x=20$$
$$\therefore\ \text{Y will finish the work in 60 days.}$$
$$\therefore\ (X+Y)\text{'s 1 days work}$$

$$=\frac{1}{20}+\frac{1}{60}=\frac{3+1}{60}=\frac{1}{15}$$

$\therefore$ Both together will complete the work in 15 days.

15. **(b)** Volume of water flowed in an hour
$$=2000\times 40\times 3\ \text{m}^3$$
$$=240000\ \text{m}^3$$
$\therefore$ Volume of water flowed in 1 minute.

$$=\frac{240000}{60}=4000\ \text{m}^3=4000000\ \text{litre}$$

16. **(c)** Smallest side of the triangle = x cm (let)
$\therefore$ Second side of triangle
$$=40-17-x=23-x$$

$$\text{Semi-perimeter,}=s=\frac{40}{2}=20$$

$$\therefore\ \sqrt{s(s-a)(s-b)(s-c)}=60$$

$$\Rightarrow \sqrt{20(20-17)(20-x)(20-23+x)}=60$$

$$\Rightarrow (20-x)(x-3)=60$$
$$\Rightarrow 20x-60-x^2+3x=60$$
$$\Rightarrow x^2-23x+120=0$$
$$\Rightarrow x^2-15x-8x+120=0$$
$$\Rightarrow x(x-15)-8(x-15)=0$$
$$\Rightarrow (x-8)(x-15)=0$$
$$\Rightarrow x=8\ \text{or}\ 15$$

17. **(a)** Let the marked price of the article be ₹ x.

$$\therefore\ x\times\frac{90}{100}=\frac{450\times 120}{100}$$

$$\Rightarrow \frac{9x}{10}=540$$

$$\Rightarrow x=\frac{540\times 10}{9}=₹\,600$$

18. **(c)** A : B = 1 : 3
B : C = 1 : 3 = 3 : 9
C : D = 1 : 3 = 9 : 27
$\therefore$ A : B : C : D = 1 : 3 : 9 : 27
Sum of ratios = 1 + 3 + 9 + 27 = 40
$\therefore$ C's share of profit

$$=\frac{9}{40}\times 400000=₹\,90000$$

19. **(d)** Let the number x be added

$$\therefore\ \frac{17+x}{24+x}=\frac{1}{2}$$

$$\Rightarrow 34+2x=24+x$$
$$\Rightarrow 2x-x=24-34$$
$$\Rightarrow x=-10$$

Hence, 10 should be subtracted.

20. **(b)** Let monthly income of A and B be 9x and 7x
Expenditure = Income – Saving

ATQ

$$\frac{9x-200}{7x-200}=\frac{4}{3}$$

$$27x-6.00=28x-800$$

$$x=200$$

Sum $=200\times16=₹3200$

21. (a) Let the second number be x.

∴ First number $=2x$

∴ Third number $=\dfrac{2x}{3}$

∴ $2x+x+\dfrac{2x}{3}=49.5\times3$

$\Rightarrow 6x+3x+2x=49.5\times9=445.5$

$\Rightarrow 11x=445.5 \Rightarrow x=\dfrac{445.5}{11}=40.5$

∴ Requried difference

$=2x-\dfrac{2x}{3}=\dfrac{4x}{3}$

$=\dfrac{4\times40.5}{3}=54$

22. (c) Requried average

$=30+\dfrac{(28+31-82-13)}{50}$

$=30+\left(-\dfrac{36}{50}\right)=30-0.72=29.28$

23. (c) Difference in discount $=1\%$

$\dfrac{1}{100}\times x=15$

$x=₹1500$

24. (d) Average cost of $=\dfrac{10+14}{2}=12$

QP $=13$

$P\%=\dfrac{13-12}{12}\times100=8\dfrac{1}{3}\%$

25. (b) The sum of cost prices of two articles is ₹ x. One of them is sold at a loss of a% and other is sold at a gain of b% and their S.P. is same.

∴ C.P. of article sold at a loss of a%

$=\dfrac{100+b}{200-a+b}\times x$

$=\dfrac{100+15}{200-20+15}\times19500$

$=\dfrac{115}{195}\times19500=₹11500$

∴ C.P. of second article $=₹8000$

26. (a) As,

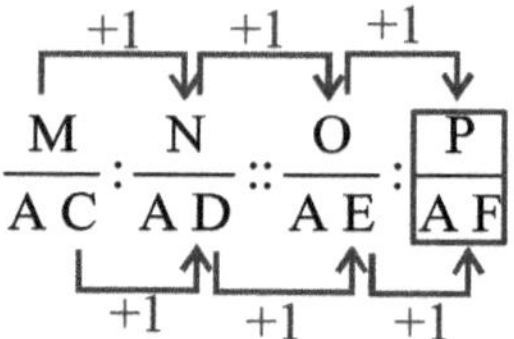

27. (c) As, $6\times2-1=11$

Similarly, $11\times2-1=\boxed{21}$

28. (d) In order to ensure security, police or defence personnel patrol the area. Similarly, to cover risk, insurance is done.

29. (a) O is the husband of P. M is the son of P. Therefore, M is the son of O.

30. (c)
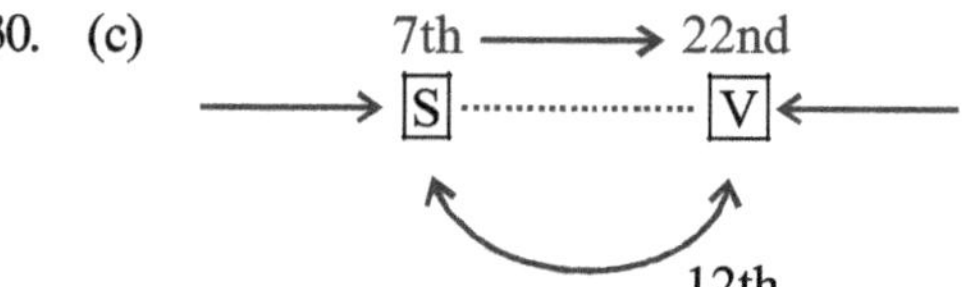

Total number of boys in the row

$=22+12-1=\boxed{33}$

31. (a)
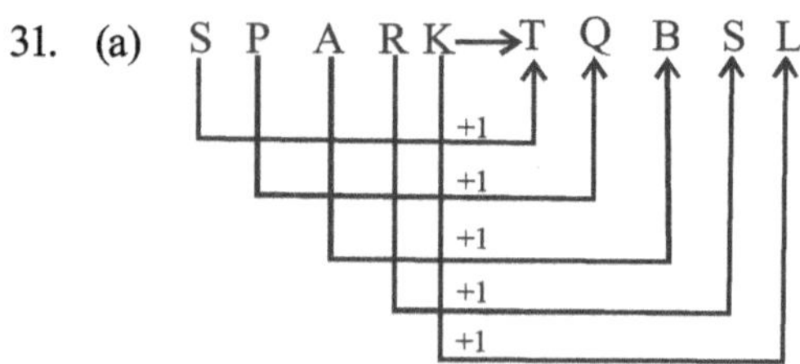

Similarly,

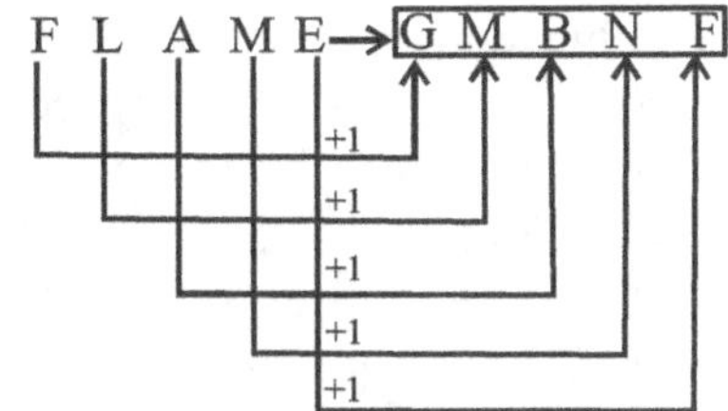

32. (a)
$30 - 6 + 5 \times 4 \div 2 = 27$
$\Rightarrow 30 \div 6 \times 5 + 4 - 2 = 27$
$\Rightarrow 25 + 4 - 2 = 27$
$30 + 6 - 5 \div 4 \times 2 = 30$
$\Rightarrow 30 \times 6 \div 5 - 4 + 2 = 30$
$\Rightarrow 36 - 4 + 2 \neq 30$
$30 \times 6 \div 5 - 4 + 2 = 32$
$\Rightarrow 30 + 6 - 5 \div 4 \times 2 \neq 32$

33. (d) As, $\dfrac{8}{4} = 2; 2 + 1 = 3$

$\dfrac{6}{3} = 2; 2 + 3 = 5$

$\dfrac{2}{1} = 2; 2 + 7 = 9$

34. (d) $5 + 4 = 9$ and $9 \times 2 = 18$
$6 + 3 = 9$ and $9 \times 3 = 27$
$12 + 4 = 16$ and ?

$= \dfrac{96}{16} = \boxed{6}$

35. (c)   36. (a)

37. (c)

Milk
Cow   Goat   Hen

38. (d)

39. (c)

40. (d) $500 - (4)^2 = 484$
$484 - (5)^2 = 459$
$459 - (6)^2 = \boxed{423}$
$423 - (7)^2 = 374$

41. (a) $60 + (3)^2 = 69$
$69 + (4)^2 = 85$
$85 + (5)^2 = \boxed{110}$
$110 + (6)^2 = 146$

42. (c) GRAPE $= 2\,7\,3\,5\,4$
FOUR $= 1\,6\,8\,7$
So, $G = 2, R = 7, A = 3, P = 5, E = 4, F = 1,$
$O = 6, U = 8, R = 7$
GROUP $= 2\,7\,6\,8\,5$

43. (a) As

W	A	Y	I	N
$-3\downarrow$	$-3\downarrow$	$-3\downarrow$	$-3\downarrow$	$-3\downarrow$
T	X	V	F	K

	L	B	U	K
Similarly,	$-3\downarrow$	$-3\downarrow$	$-3\downarrow$	$-3\downarrow$
	I	Y	R	H

44. (d)

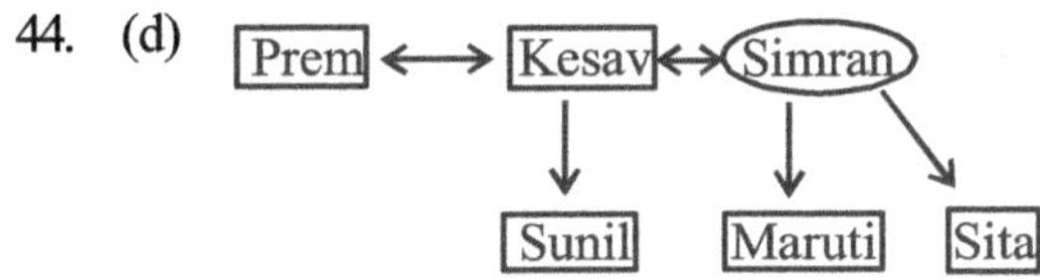

Sunil   Maruti   Sita

Hence, Sunil is the cousin of Maruti.

45. (a)

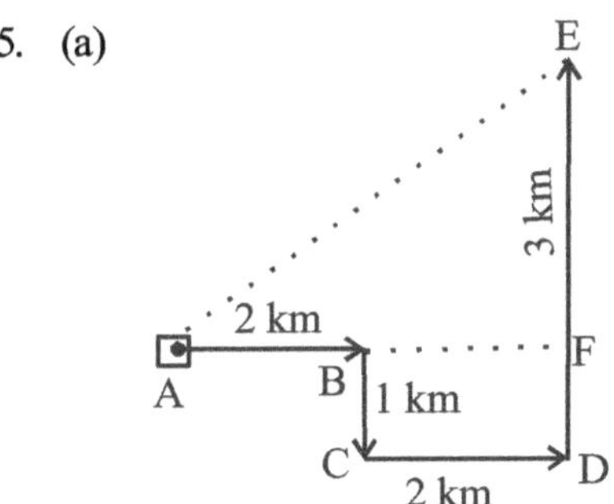

$\therefore$ Required distance AE,

$= \sqrt{(AF)^2 + (EF)^2}$

$= \sqrt{(4)^2 + (3)^2} = \sqrt{16 + 9} = \sqrt{25} = \boxed{5 \text{ km}}$

46. (a) $5 * 5 * 5 * 3 * 10$
$\Rightarrow 5 \times 5 + 5 = 3 \times 10$
$\Rightarrow 30 = 30$

47. (c)

48. (b)

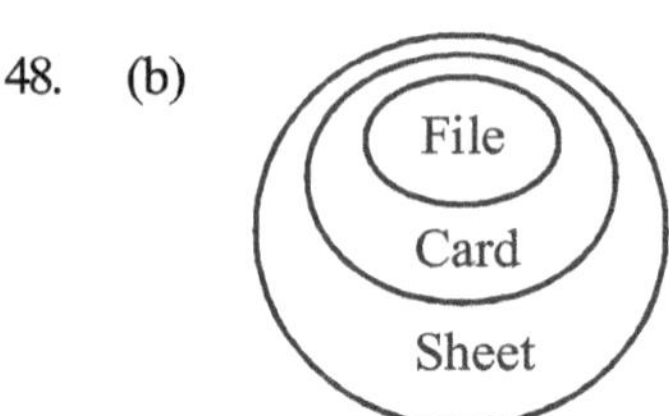

So, Only II follows.

49. (a)

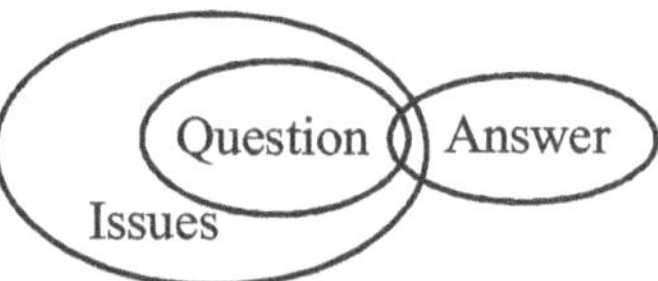

So, Both I and II follow.

50. (a) Clearly, only I provides a suitable explanation to the given statement. So, only I follows.

51. (b) 52. (c) 53. (b) 54. (c) 55. (a)
56. (b) 57. (a) 58. (d) 59. (a) 60. (d)
61. (c) 62. (c) 63. (d) 64. (d) 65. (a)
66. (b) 67. (b) 68. (c) 69. (c) 70. (b)
71. (d) 72. (a) 73. (c) 74. (d) 75. (a)
76. (a) 77. (b) 78. (d) 79. (a) 80. (d)
81. (c) 82. (c) 83. (b) 84. (d) 85. (b)
86. (a) 87. (c) 88. (d) 89. (d) 90. (a)
91. (c) 92. (d) 93. (a) 94. (b) 95. (a)
96. (b) 97. (c) 98. (b) 99. (a) 100. (d)

PRACTICE SET 12

MATHEMATICS

1. In a family, the average age of a father and a mother is 45 years. The average age of the father, mother and their only son is 37 years. What is the age of the son ?
   - (a) 22 years
   - (b) 21 years
   - (c) 20.5 years
   - (d) 20 years

2. A manufacturer marked an article at ₹50 and sold it allowing 20% discount. If his profit was 25% then the cost price of the article was
   - (a) ₹40
   - (b) ₹35
   - (c) ₹32
   - (d) ₹30

3. The population of a town is 15000. If the number of males increases by 8% and that of females by 10%, then the population would increase to 16300. Find the number of females in the town.
   - (a) 4000
   - (b) 6000
   - (c) 3000
   - (d) 5000

4. A sum amounts double in 8 years by simple interest. Then the rate of simple interest p.a. is
   - (a) 10%
   - (b) 12.5%
   - (c) 15%
   - (d) 20%

5. By walking at $\dfrac{3}{4}$ of his usual speed, a man reaches his office 20 minutes later than his usual time. The usual time taken by him to reach his office is
   - (a) 75 minutes
   - (b) 60 minutes
   - (c) 40 minutes
   - (d) 30 minutes

6. If P and Q together can complete a piece of work in 30 days and Q alone in 40 days, in how many days can P alone complete the work ?
   - (a) 120
   - (b) 145
   - (c) 140
   - (d) 130

7. If ₹1000 is divided between A and B in the ratio 3 : 2, then A will receive
   - (a) ₹400
   - (b) ₹500
   - (c) ₹600
   - (d) ₹800

8. In $\triangle ABC$, $\angle B = 60°$, $\angle C = 40°$. If AD bisects $\angle BAC$ and $AE \perp BC$, then $\angle EAD$ is
   - (a) 40°
   - (b) 80°
   - (c) 10°
   - (d) 20°

9. If each intetior angle is double of each exterior angle of a regular polygon with n sides, then the value of n is
   - (a) 8
   - (b) 10
   - (c) 5
   - (d) 6

10. The length (in metres) of the longest rod that can be put in a room of dimensions 10 m × 10 m × 5 m is
    - (a) $15\sqrt{3}$
    - (b) 15
    - (c) $10\sqrt{2}$
    - (d) $5\sqrt{3}$

11. When the price of sugar decreases by 10%, a man could buy 1 kg more for ₹ 540. Then the original price of sugar per kg is
    - (a) ₹ 50
    - (b) ₹ 60
    - (c) ₹ 54
    - (d) ₹ 64

12. If the price of sugar is raised by 25%, find by how much percent a householder must reduce his consumption of sugar so as not to increase his expenditure?
    - (a) 10
    - (b) 20
    - (c) 18
    - (d) 25

13. A man can row 6 km/h in still water. If the speed of the current is 2 km/h, it takes 3 hours more in upstream than in the down–stream for the same distance. The distance is
    - (a) 30 km
    - (b) 24 km
    - (c) 20 km
    - (d) 32 km

14. A sum of money placed at compound interest doubles itself in 4 years. In how many years will it amount to four times itself?
    - (a) 12 years
    - (b) 13 years
    - (c) 8 years
    - (d) 16 years

15. X sells two articles for ₹ 4,000 each with no loss and no gain in the interaction. If one was sold at a gain of 25% the other is sold at a loss of

(a) 25%   (b) $18\frac{2}{9}\%$

(c) $16\frac{2}{3}\%$ (d) 20%

16. A reduction of 20% in the price of sugar enables me to purchase 5 kg more for ₹ 600. Find the price of sugar per kg before reduction of price.
(a) ₹ 24   (b) ₹ 30
(c) ₹ 32   (d) ₹ 36

17. The price of a commodity rises from ₹ 6 per kg to ₹ 7.50 per kg. If the expenditure cannot increase, the percentage of reduction in consumption is
(a) 15   (b) 20
(c) 25   (d) 30

18. First and second numbers are less than a third number by 30% and 37% respectively. The second number is less than the first by
(a) 7%   (b) 4%
(c) 3%   (d) 10%

19. Walking at 5 km/hr a student reaches his school from his house 15 minutes early and walking at 3 km/hr he is late by 9 minutes. What is the distance between his school and his house?
(a) 5 km   (b) 8 km
(c) 3 km   (d) 2 km

20. The difference between the compound interest and simple interest for the amount ₹ 5,000 in 2 years is ₹ 32. The rate of interest is
(a) 5%   (b) 8%
(c) 10%   (d) 12%

21. The least number, which is to be added to the greatest number of 4 digits so that the sum may be divisible by 345, is
(a) 50   (b) 6
(c) 60   (d) 5

22. A student was asked to divide a number by 6 and add 12 to the quotient. He, however, first added 12 to the number and then divided it by 6, getting 112 as the answer. The correct answer should have been
(a) 124   (b) 122
(c) 118   (d) 114

23. Four runners started running simultaneously from a point on a circular track. They took 200 seconds, 300 seconds, 360 seconds and 450 seconds to complete one round. After how much time they meet at the starting point for the first time?
(a) 1800 seconds   (b) 3600 seconds
(c) 2400 seconds   (d) 4800 seconds

24. 'x' number of men can finish a piece of work in 60 days. If there were 12 men more, the work could be finished in 20 days less. The original number of men is
(a) 26   (b) 20
(c) 24   (d) 25

25. A work can be completed by P and Q in 12 days, Q and R in 15 days, R and P in 20 days. In how many days P alone can finish the work?
(a) 10   (b) 20
(c) 30   (d) 60

GENERAL INTELLIGENCE AND REASONING

DIRECTIONS (Qs. 26-27) : In each of the following questions, select the related letters/word/number from the given alternatives.

26. ABE : 8 : : KLO : ?
(a) 37   (b) 39   (c) 38   (d) 36

27. Fox : Cunning : : Rabbit : ?
(a) Courageous   (b) Dangerous
(c) Timid   (d) Ferocious

DIRECTIONS (Qs. 28-29) : In each of the following questions find the odd word/letters/number/ figure from the given responses.

28. (a) Mouth Organ   (b) Electric Guitar
(c) Keyboard   (d) Sonata

29. (a) CAFD   (b) TSWV
(c) IGLJ   (d) OMRP

DIRECTIONS (Qs. 30-31) : In Question, a series is given, with one/two term missing. Choose the correct alternative from the given ones that will complete the series.

30. BMRG, DLTF, FKVE, HJXD, __ ? __
(a) JIZC   (b) JZIB
(c) GIFB   (d) MOLC

31. 7, 9, 13, 21, 37, ?
(a) 58   (b) 63   (c) 69   (d) 72

32. X and Y are brothers. R is the father of Y. S is the brother of T and maternal uncle of X. What is T to R?
    (a) Mother (b) Wife
    (c) Sister (d) Brother

33. In a certain code SISTER is written as RHRSDQ. How is UNCLE written in that code ?
    (a) TMBKD (b) TBMKD
    (c) TVBOD (d) TMKBD

34. If L denotes ×; M denotes ÷ ; P denotes + ; Q denotes – then 16 P 24 M 8 Q 6 M 2 L 3 = ?
    (a) 10 (b) 9 (c) 12 (d) 11

35. Some equations have been solved on the basis of a certain system. Find the correct answer for the unsolved equation on that basis. If 9 * 7 = 32, 13 * 7 = 120, 17 * 9 = 208, then 19 * 11 = ?
    (a) 150 (b) 180 (c) 210 (d) 240

36. Select the missing number from the given responses :

7	3	2
4	9	6
2	1	5
69	91	?

    (a) 58 (b) 51 (c) 65 (d) 64

37. Two statements are given followed by four conclusions, I, II, III and IV. You have to consider the statements to be true, even if they seem to be at variance from commonly known facts. You are to decide which of the given conclusions can definitely be drawn from the given statements. Indicate your answer.
    Statements :
    (A) No cow is a chair
    (B) All chairs are tables.
    Conclusions :
    I. Some tables are chairs.
    II. Some tables are cows
    III. Some chairs are cows
    IV. No table is a cow
    (a) Either II or III follow
    (b) Either II or IV follow
    (c) Only I and either II or IV follow.
    (d) All conclusions follow

38. How many triangles are there in the figure ABCDEF?

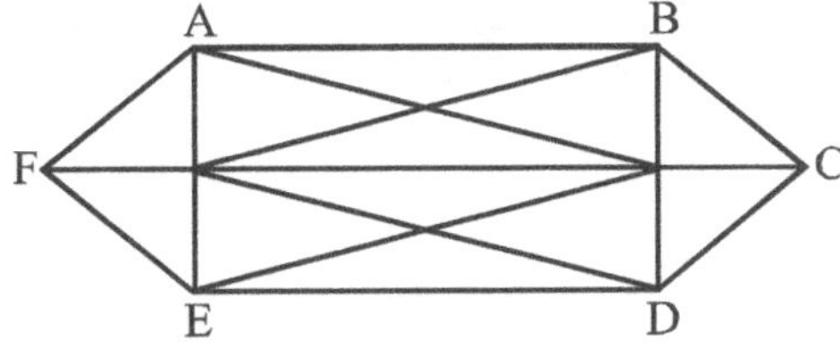

    (a) 24 (b) 26
    (c) 28 (d) 30

39. Identify the figure which best represents the relationship among Tree, Plant, and House.
    Answer figures :

(a) 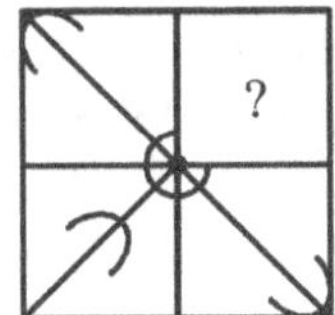 (b) 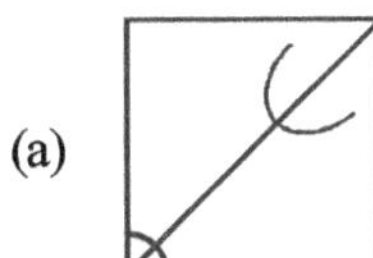

(c)  (d) 

DIRECTION (Q. 40): Which answer figure completes the pattern given in the question figure?

---

40. **Question Figure :**

    Answer Figures :

DIRECTION (Q. 41) : If a mirror is placed on the line MN, then which of the answer figures is the right image of the given figure?

41.　**Question Figure :**

Answer Figures :

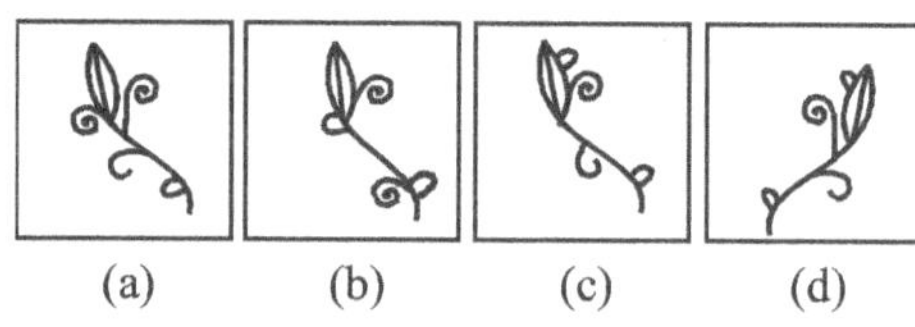

　　(a)　　　　(b)　　　　(c)　　　　(d)

42.　If DOCTOR is written as FQEVQT; how PATIENT can be written in that code?

　　(a)　RVKGPV

　　(b)　RCKPGVV

　　(c)　RCVKGPV

　　(d)　RVCKGVP

43.　If DEGI is equal to 25, what is FEHD equal to?

　　(a)　32　　　　　　　(b)　25

　　(c)　52　　　　　　　(d)　23

44.　A boy introduced a girl as the daughter of the son of the father of his uncle. How is the girl related to the boy?

　　(a)　Aunt

　　(b)　Grand-daughter

　　(c)　Niece

　　(d)　Sister

45.　If '+' means '÷', '×' means '+', '–' means '×' and '÷' means '–', then which of the following equations is correct?

　　(a)　$36 + 6 - 3 \times 2 = 20$

　　(b)　$36 \times 6 + 3 - 2 < 20$

　　(c)　$36 \times 6 + 3 \times 2 > 20$

　　(d)　$36 + 6 \times 3 + 2 = 20$

46.　In the following figure, the boys who are cricketer and sober are indicated by which number?

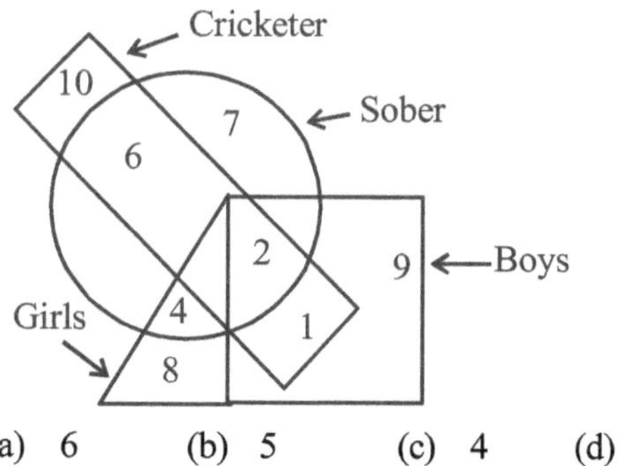

　　(a)　6　　　(b)　5　　　(c)　4　　　(d)　2

DIRECTIONS (Qs. 47–48): In each question below are given two statements followed by two conclusions numbered I and II. You have to take the two given statements to be true even if they seem to be at variance with commonly known facts. Read both the statement and then decide which of the given conclusions logically follows from the given statements disregarding commonly known facts. Give answer

　　(a)　if only conclusion I follows.

　　(b)　if only conclusion II follows.

　　(c)　if either conclusion I or II follows.

　　(d)　if neither conclusion I nor II follows.

47.　**Statements:**　All roads are streets.
　　　　　　　　　　No road is a highway.
　　Conclusions: I　　No highway is street.
　　　　　　　　　II.　　All streets are roads.

48.　**Statements:**　No book is library.
　　　　　　　　　　Some books are diaries.
　　Conclusions: I　　At least some libraries are diaries.
　　　　　　　　　II.　　No diary is library.

DIRECTIONS (Qs. 49-50): In each question below is given a statement followed by two conclusions numbered I and II. You have to assume everything in the statement to be true, then consider the two conclusions together and decide which of them logically follows beyond a reasonable doubt from the information given in the statement.

49.　**Statements:** Players who break various records in a fair way get special prizes. Player X broke the world record but was found to be under the influence of a prohibited drug.

　　Conclusions:

　　I.　　X will get the special prize.

　　II.　　X will not get the special prize.

(a) Only conclusion I follows
(b) Only conclusion II follows
(c) Either I or II follows
(d) Neither I nor II follows

50. **Statements:** Company X has marketed the product. Go ahead; purchase it if price and quality are your considerations.
Conclusions:
I. The product must be good in quality.
II. The price of the product must be reasonable.
(a) Only conclusion I follows
(b) Only conclusion II follows
(c) Either I or II follows
(d) Both I and II follow

BASIC SCIENCE AND ENGINEERING

51. Which of the following is not a pictorial drawing?
(a) isometric   (b) multiview
(c) perspective   (d) axonometric

52. Number of fundamental units in SI system is
(a) 4   (b) 7
(c) 3   (d) 5

53. What is Mass?
(a) The amount of space an object takes up
(b) The amount of matter in an object
(c) The pull of gravity on an object
(d) Mass divided by volume

54. What determines the nature of the path followed by the particle?
(a) Speed   (b) Velocity
(c) Acceleration   (d) Both (b) and (c)

55. Water stored in a dam possesses:
(a) No energy   (b) Electrical energy
(c) Kinetic energy (d) Potential energy

56. Heat capacity depends on
(a) change in temperature
(b) Mass of body
(c) Nature of substance
(d) All the above

57. The unit of specific resistance is
(a) $\Omega\,m^{-1}$ (b) $\Omega^{-1}\,m^{-1}$
(c) Ω^{-1} (d) $2.5\Omega m^{2}$

58. An example of a lever is a...
(a) pulley   (b) Bicycle
(c) Scissors   (d) Screw

59. What is the best safety rule?
(a) Immediately sort the waste generated during the work by type.
(b) Keep the workplace tidy and keep passages clear.
(c) Mark all hazards at the workplace with red-white tape.
(d) None of these.

60. Global warming means:
(a) Increase in Earth's Body Temperature
(b) Increase in solar radiation
(c) Acid Rain
(d) All the above

61. Which of the following refers to the fastest, biggest and most, expensive computers?
(a) Notebooks
(b) Personal computers
(c) Laptops
(d) Super computers

62. Velocity time curve for a body projected vertically upwards is
(a) parabola   (b) ellipse
(c) hyperbola   (d) straight line

63. A common instrument to measure diameter of a circle is known as
(a) rule   (b) measuring tape
(c) calipers   (d) inch tape

64. Density is equal to
(a) m/v, where m is mass and v is volume
(b) m/a, where m is mass and a is area
(c) v/m, where v is volume and m is mass
(d) w/v, where w is weight and v is volume

65. To tell if something is moving it must be compared to this type of point:
(a) vector   (b) magnitude
(c) axis   (d) reference

66. Two quantities that have same SI unit are
(a) Efficiency and Power
(b) Efficiency and Work
(c) Work and Energy
(d) Energy and Power

67. Volume of a fixed mass of liquid is a physical property of
(a) Mercury-in-glass thermometer
(b) Thermocouple thermometer
(c) resistance thermometer
(d) Constant-volume gas thermometer

68. Conductance : mho : :
    (a) resistance : ohm
    (b) capacitance : henry
    (c) inductance : farad
    (d) lumen : steradian

69. Mohan needs to split a log. What simple machine would help him?
    (a) a wedge   (b) a fulcrum
    (c) a pulley   (d) a lever

70. The full form of R.F. is
    (a) Reducing fraction
    (b) Representative fraction
    (c) Reduction factor
    (d) Representative factor

71. Which organization is responsible for the enforcement of the Health and Safety at Work Act 1974?
    (a) The Health and Safety Commission
    (b) Acas
    (c) The Health and Safety Executive
    (d) The Equality and Human Rights Commission

72. Every Ecosystem has ___ major component(s).
    (a) One   (b) Two
    (c) Three   (d) Four

73. Environmental pollution can be controlled by:
    (a) Checking atomic blasts
    (b) Manufacturing electric vehicles
    (c) Sewage treatment
    (d) All of the above

74. Three 60 W bulbs are in parallel across the 60 V power line. If one bulb burns open
    (a) there will be heavy current in the main line
    (b) rest of the two bulbs will not light
    (c) all three bulbs will light
    (d) the other two bulbs will light

75. In Microsoft Word, when a file is saved for the first time
    (a) A copy is automatically printed
    (b) It must be given a name to identify it.
    (c) It does not need a name
    (d) It only needs a name if it is not going to be printed

GENERAL AWARENESS AND CURRENT AFFAIR

76. The term 'Greater India' denotes
    (a) Political unity   (b) Cultural unity
    (c) Religious unity   (d) Social unity

77. The study of population is known as.
    (a) Demography   (b) Climatology
    (c) Petrology   (d) Hydrology

78. 'Mirage' is an example of
    (a) refraction of light only
    (b) total internal reflection of light only
    (c) refraction and total internal reflection of light
    (d) dispersion of light only

79. An stomic clock is based on transitions in
    (a) Sodium   (b) Caesium
    (c) Magnesium   (d) Aluminium

80. The element which is used for vulcanizing rubber
    (a) Sulphur   (b) Bromine
    (c) Silicon   (d) Phosphorus

81. Plasma membrane in eukaryotic celle is made up of
    (a) Phospholipid
    (b) Lipoprotein
    (c) Phospholpo-protein
    (d) Phospho-protein

82. Which plant is called Herbal Indian Doctor?
    (a) Amla   (b) Mango
    (c) Neem   (d) Tulsi

83. 'Eutrophication' is associated with
    (a) Nitrates and Phosphates
    (b) Sewage
    (c) Silt load
    (d) Vegetation

84. The land of maximum biodiversity is
    (a) Tropical   (b) Temperate
    (c) Monsoonal   (d) Equatorial

85. Bark of this tree is used as a condiment–
    (a) Cinnamon   (b) Clove
    (c) Neem   (d) Palm

86. The G20 Digital Economy Ministerial Meeting was held recently in ______
    (a) India   (b) France
    (c) Russia   (d) Argentina

87. World No Tobacco Day is observed around the world every year on _______________ .
    (a) 21 August   (b) 24 May
    (c) 31 May   (d) 14 July

88. Hirakud Dam built over which of the following river?
    (a) Tapti River   (b) Ganga River
    (c) Mahanadi River   (d) Kaveri River

89. Energy that is produced commercially from coal is called
    (a) Light energy   (b) Kinetic energy
    (c) Thermal energy   (d) Potential energy

90. The island of Corsica is associated with
    (a) Mussolini
    (b) Hitler
    (c) Napolean Bonaparte
    (d) Winston Churchill

91. Who among the following Mughal Emperors had the longest reign?
    (a) Bahadur Shah   (b) Jahandar Shah
    (c) Farrukhsiyar   (d) Mohammad Shah

92. The article of Indian Constitution related to abolition of untouchability is
    (a) Article 15   (b) Article 16
    (c) Article 17   (d) Article 18

93. X-rays were discovered by
    (a) Roentgen   (b) Becquere
    (c) Curie   (d) Van lane

94. Which one of the following is not electromagnetic in nature?
    (a) Cathode rays   (b) X-rays
    (c) Gamma-rays   (d) Infrared rays

95. C, BASIC, COBOL and Java are example of language?
    (a) low-level
    (b) computer
    (c) system programming
    (d) high level

96. Which is used in storage batteries?
    (a) Copper   (b) Lead
    (c) Tin   (d) Zinc

97. Which one of the following elements is the poorest conductor of heat?
    (a) sodium   (b) lead
    (c) zinc   (d) mercury

98. Healing of wounds is hastened by vitamin
    (a) A   (b) E
    (c) C   (d) K

99. Which of the following is an air-borne disease?
    (a) Measles   (b) Pink eye
    (c) Typhoid   (d) Tuberculosis

100. Wait of human brain in gram is?
    (a) 1350   (b) 1230
    (c) 1100   (d) 1500

HINTS & EXPLANATIONS

1. (b) Father + mother
$$= 2 \times 45 = 90 \text{ years}$$
Father + mother + son
$$= 37 \times 3 = 111 \text{ years}$$
$$\therefore \text{ Son's age} = 111 - 90 = 21 \text{ years}$$

2. (c) Marked price = ₹50
S.P. after discount = 80% of 50 = ₹40
If the CP of article be ₹x, then
$$\frac{125 \times x}{100} = 40$$
$$\Rightarrow x = \frac{40 \times 100}{125} = ₹32$$

3. (d) If the number of females be x, then, number of males = 15000 − x
$$\therefore x \times \frac{10}{100} + (15000 - x) \times \frac{8}{100} = 16300 - 15000$$
$$\Rightarrow 10x + 120000 - 8x = 1300 \times 100$$
$$\Rightarrow 2x = 130000 - 120000 = 10000$$
$$\Rightarrow x = 5000$$

4. (b) Let P be the principle amount and R be rate of interest.
$$2P = P + \frac{P \times R \times 8}{100}$$
$$R = \frac{100}{8} = 12.5\%$$

5. (b) $\dfrac{4}{3}$ of usual time = Usual time + 20 minutes
$$\therefore \frac{1}{3}\text{rd of usual time}$$
$$= 20 \text{ minutes}$$
$$\therefore \text{ Usual time} = 20 \times 3$$
$$= 60 \text{ minutes}$$

6. (a) (P's + Q's) 1 day's work $= \dfrac{1}{30}$

Q's 1 day's work $= \dfrac{1}{40}$

$$\therefore \text{ P's 1 day's work} = \frac{1}{30} - \frac{1}{40} = \frac{4-3}{120} = \frac{1}{120}$$

7. (c) A's share
$$= ₹\left(\frac{3}{5} \times 1000\right) = ₹600$$

8. (c)

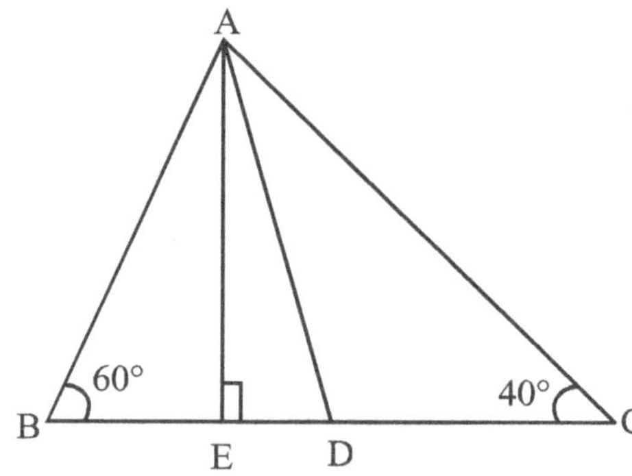

In $\triangle ABC$,
$$\angle A + \angle B + \angle C = 180°$$
$$\angle A + 60° + 40° = 180°$$
$$\angle A = 180° - 60° - 40° = 80°$$
AD bisects $\angle BAC$
$$\therefore \angle A = \angle BAD + \angle DAC$$
$$\angle BAD = \angle DAC = 40°$$
Now, In $\triangle ABE$
$$\angle B + \angle E + \angle BAE = 180°$$
$$60° + 90° + \angle BAE = 180°$$
$$\angle BAE = 30°$$
$$\therefore \angle EAD = \angle BAD - \angle BAE = 40° - 30° = 10°$$

9. (d) Let exterior $\angle$ be = x
interior $\angle$ be = 2x
$$x + 2x = 180$$
$$3x = 180$$

$$x = 60°$$

$$\frac{360°}{60°} = 6$$

10. (b) Length of the longest rod

$$\sqrt{a^2 + b^2 + c^2}$$

$$= \sqrt{10^2 + 10^2 + 5^2}$$

$$= \sqrt{225} = 15 \text{ metre}$$

11. (b) Let the original price of sugar be ₹ x/kg.

$$\therefore \text{New price} = ₹ \frac{9x}{10} \text{ /kg}$$

$$\therefore \frac{540}{\frac{9x}{10}} - \frac{540}{x} = 1$$

$$\Rightarrow \frac{600}{x} - \frac{540}{x} = 1 \Rightarrow \frac{60}{x} = 1$$

$$\Rightarrow x = ₹ 60/kg$$

12. (b) Percentage decrease $= \frac{25}{125} \times 100 = 20\%$

13. (b) Let the required distance be x km.

$$\therefore \frac{x}{6-2} - \frac{x}{6+2} = 3$$

$$\Rightarrow \frac{x}{4} - \frac{x}{8} = 3$$

$$\Rightarrow \frac{2x - x}{8} = 3$$

$$\Rightarrow x = 3 \times 8 = 24 \text{ km}.$$

14. (c) $A = P\left(1 + \frac{R}{100}\right)^T$

$$\Rightarrow 2 = 1\left(1 + \frac{R}{100}\right)^4$$

$$\Rightarrow 2^2 = \left(1 + \frac{R}{100}\right)^8$$

$$= 8 \text{ yrs}$$

15. (d) SP of both articles is same. Profit on one is equal to loss on the other.

If loss per cent be x, then

$$25 - x - \frac{25x}{100} = 0$$

$$\Rightarrow 25 - x - \frac{x}{4} = 0 \Rightarrow 100 - 4x - x = 0$$

$$\Rightarrow 5x = 100$$

$$\Rightarrow x = 20$$

16. (b) Let CP = x, Total ₹ = 600, Sugar bought

$$= \frac{600}{x}$$

$$\text{ATQ } \frac{80x}{100}\left[\frac{600}{x} + 5\right] = 600$$

$$480 + 4x = 600$$

$$4x = 120$$

$$x = 30$$

17. (b) Percentage increase

$$= \frac{7.50 - 6}{6} \times 100 = 25\%$$

$$\therefore \text{Percentage decrease in consumption}$$

$$= \frac{25}{125} \times 100 = 20\%$$

18. (d) Let the third number = 100.

First number = 70

Second number = 63

$$\therefore \text{Required per cent}$$

$$= \frac{70 - 63}{70} \times 100 = 10\%$$

19. (c) Let the required distance be x km.

$$\therefore \frac{x}{3} - \frac{x}{5} = \frac{24}{60}$$

$$\Rightarrow \frac{5x - 3x}{15} = \frac{2}{5} \Rightarrow \frac{2x}{3} = 2$$

$$\Rightarrow 2x = 2 \times 3 \Rightarrow x = 3 \text{ km}$$

20. (b) Difference of 2 years =

$$P\left(\frac{r}{100}\right)^2$$

$$\Rightarrow 32 = \frac{5000 \times r^2}{10000}$$

$$\Rightarrow r^2 = \frac{32 \times 10000}{5000} = 64$$

$$\Rightarrow r = \sqrt{64} = 8\%$$

21. (b) The largest 4-digit number = 9999

$$345)9999(28$$
$$\underline{690}$$
$$3099$$
$$\underline{2760}$$
$$339$$

$\therefore$ Required number = $345 - 339 = 6$

22. (b) Let the number be x

$$\therefore \frac{x+12}{6} = 112$$

$$\Rightarrow x + 12 = 672$$

$$\Rightarrow x = 672 - 12 = 660$$

$$\therefore \text{Correct answer} = \frac{660}{6} + 12$$

$$= 110 + 12 = 122$$

23. (a) Required time = LCM of 200, 300, 360 and 450 seconds = 1800 seconds.

24. (c) $m_1 d_1 = m_2 d_2$
$x \times 60 = (x + 12) \times 40$
$60x = 40x + 480$
$\therefore x = 24$ men

25. (c) (P + Q)'s 1 day's work

$$= \frac{1}{12} \qquad \qquad ...(i)$$

$$(Q + R)\text{'s 1 day's work} = \frac{1}{15} \qquad ...(ii)$$

$$(R + P)\text{'s 1 day's work} = \frac{1}{20} \qquad ...(iii)$$

Adding all three equations, 2 (P + Q + R)'s 1 day's work

$$= \frac{1}{12} + \frac{1}{15} + \frac{1}{20} = \frac{5+4+3}{60}$$

$$= \frac{12}{60} = \frac{1}{5}$$

$$\therefore (P + Q + R)\text{'s 1 day's work} = \frac{1}{10} \;...(iv)$$

$\therefore$ P's 1 day's work
= Equation (iv) – equation (ii)

$$= \frac{1}{10} - \frac{1}{15} = \frac{3-2}{30} = \frac{1}{30}$$

$\therefore$ P alone will complete the work in 30 days,

26. (c) As, $A + B + E \Rightarrow 1 + 2 + 5 = 8$
Similarly,

$$K + L + O \Rightarrow 11 + 12 + 15 = \boxed{38}$$

27. (c) Here, animal-behaviour relationship has been shown. Fox is characterised by its cunningness. Similarly, rabbit is considered as timid.

28. (d) Except Sonata, all others are instruments. Sonata is a piece of music composed for one instrument or two.

29. (b) TSWV does not have any vowel

$$\begin{array}{cccc} & +1 & & +1 \\ C & A & F & D \\ & -2 & & -2 \end{array} \quad , \quad \begin{array}{cccc} & +1 & & +1 \\ I & G & L & J \\ & -2 & & -2 \end{array}$$

$$\text{and} \begin{array}{cccc} & +1 & & \\ O & M & R & P \\ & -2 & & -2 \end{array} \quad \text{but,} \begin{array}{cccc} & +2 & & \\ T & S & W & V \\ & -1 & & -1 \end{array}$$

So, TSWV is odd one out.

30. (a) The pattern is as follows :

$$B \xrightarrow{+2} D \xrightarrow{+2} F \xrightarrow{+2} H \xrightarrow{+2} J$$
$$M \xrightarrow{-1} L \xrightarrow{-1} K \xrightarrow{-1} J \xrightarrow{-1} I$$
$$R \xrightarrow{+2} T \xrightarrow{+2} V \xrightarrow{+2} X \xrightarrow{+2} Z$$
$$G \xrightarrow{-1} F \xrightarrow{-1} E \xrightarrow{-1} D \xrightarrow{-1} C$$

So, JIZC will complete the series.

31. (c) The pattern is as follows :

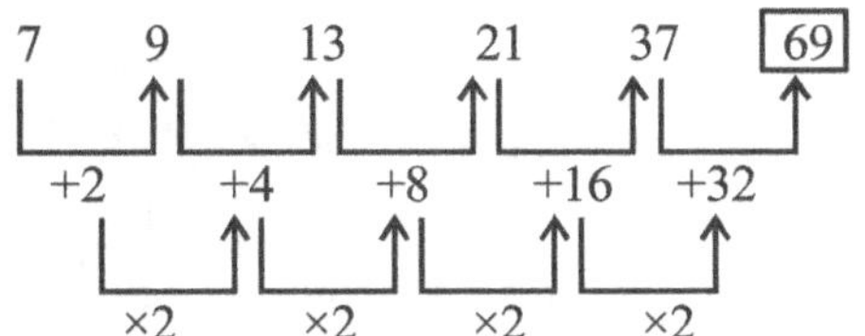

32. (b) R is father of X and Y.

S is maternal uncle of X and Y Considering the given options, it may be assumed that T is wife of R.

33. (a) As,

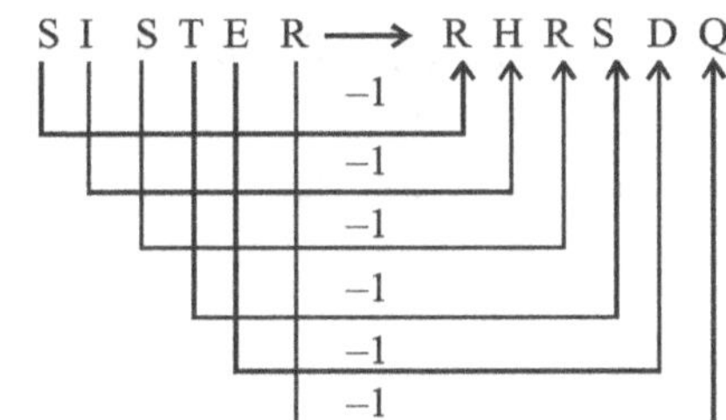

Similarly,

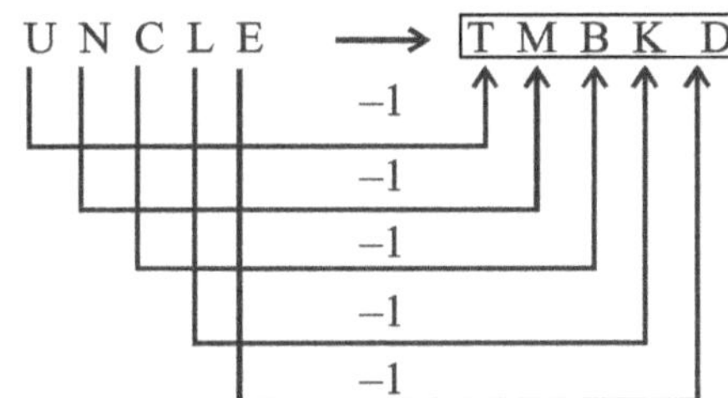

34. (a)

35. (d) $9 + 7 = 16;$ $9 - 7 = 2$
$16 \times 2 = 32$
$13 + 7 = 20;$ $13 - 7 = 6$
$20 \times 6 = 120$
$17 + 9 = 26;$ $17 - 9 = 8$
$26 \times 8 = 208$
$19 + 11 = 30;$ $19 - 11 = 8$
$30 \times 8 = \boxed{240}$

36. (c) Column wise:
First Column,
$(7)^2 + (4)^2 + (2)^2 = 49 + 16 + 4 = 69$
Second Column,
$(3)^2 + (9)^2 + (1)^2 = 9 + 81 + 1 = 91$
Similarly, In third column,
$(2)^2 + (6)^2 + (5)^2 = 4 + 36 + 25 = \boxed{65}$

37. (c)

38. (c) There are 28 triangles are formed in given figure.

39. (c)   40. (a)   41. (b)

42. (c) As,

D	O	C	T	O	R
+2↓	+2↓	+2↓	+2↓	+2↓	+2↓
F	Q	E	V	Q	T

Similarly,

P	A	T	I	E	N	T
+2↓	+2↓	+2↓	+2↓	+2↓	+2↓	+2↓
R	C	V	K	G	P	V

43. (d) The place value of
D E G I
↓ ↓ ↓↓
$4 \; 5 \; 7 \; 9 \Rightarrow 4 + 5 + 7 + 9 = 25$
Similarly, $F E H D \Rightarrow 6 + 5 + 8 + 4 = 23$

44. (c)

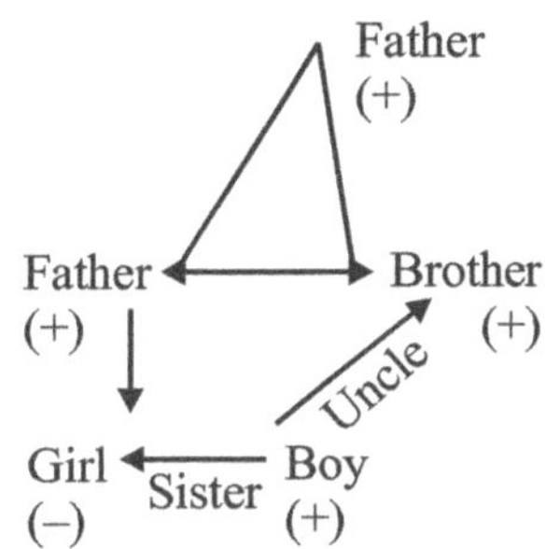

There is no option of cousin sister.

45. (a) By checking options
$36 \div 6 \times 3 + 2 = 6 \times 3 + 2 \Rightarrow 20 = 20$

46. (d)

Regions →	1	2	4	6	7	8	9	10
Persons ↓								
Boys ☐	✓	✓	×	×	×	×	✓	×
Girls △	×	×	✓	×	×	✓	×	×
Sober ○	×	✓	✓	✓	✓	×	×	×
Cricketer ▭	✓	✓	×	✓	×	×	×	✓

Region 2 presents the boys who are cricketer and sober.

47. (d) 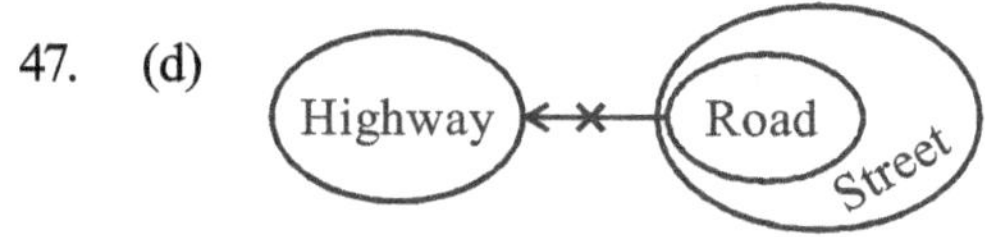

So, Neither I nor II follows.

48. (c) 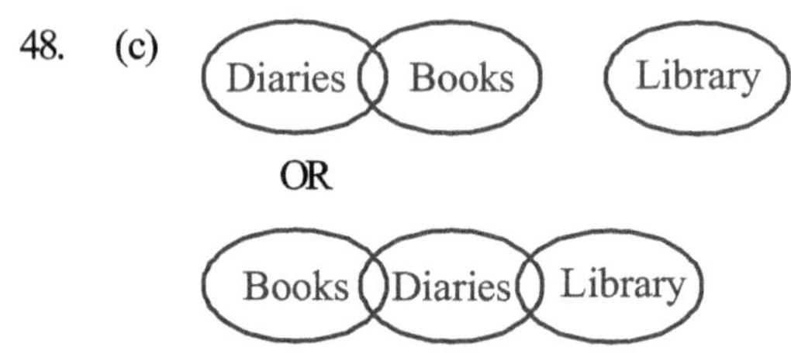

Conclusions :

I. False ⎤
II. False ⎦ Either

49. (b) Clearly, X will not get the special prize because although he broke the world record, he was found to use unfair means. So, II follows while I does not.

50. (d) It is mentioned in the statement that one who considers price and quality before buying a product should buy the product of company X. So, both I and II follow.

51.	(b)	52.	(b)	53.	(b)	54.	(d)	55.	(d)
56.	(d)	57.	(c)	58.	(c)	59.	(b)	60.	(a)
61.	(d)	62.	(d)	63.	(c)	64.	(a)	65.	(c)
66.	(c)	67.	(a)	68.	(a)	69.	(a)	70.	(b)
71.	(c)	72.	(b)	73.	(d)	74.	(d)	75.	(b)
76.	(b)	77.	(a)	78.	(c)	79.	(b)	80.	(a)
81.	(a)	82.	(a)	83.	(a)	84.	(a)	85.	(a)
86.	(d)	87.	(c)	88.	(c)	89.	(c)	90.	(c)
91.	(d)	92.	(b)	93.	(a)	94.	(a)	95.	(d)
96.	(b)	97.	(b)	98.	(c)	99.	(a)	100.	(a)

PRACTICE SET 13

Time: 90 minutes **Max. Marks - 100**

MATHEMATICS

1. The greatest number, which when subtracted from 5834, gives a number exactly divisible by each of 20, 28, 32 and 35, is
   (a) 1120 (b) 4714
   (c) 5200 (d) 5600

2. A shopkeeper earns a profit of 12% on selling a book at 10% discount on the printed price. The ratio for the cost price and the printed price of the book is
   (a) 45 : 56 (b) 45 : 51
   (c) 47 : 56 (d) 47 : 51

3. A trader bought two horses for ₹19,500. He sold one at a loss of 20% and the other at a profit of 15%. If the selling price of each horse is the same, then their cost prices are respectively.
   (a) ₹ 10,000 and ₹ 9,500
   (b) ₹ 11,500 and ₹ 8,000
   (c) ₹ 12,000 and ₹ 7,500
   (d) ₹ 10,500 and ₹ 9,000

4. Rekha invested a sum of ₹ 12000 at 5% per annum compound interest. She received an amount of ₹ 13230 after n years. Find n.
   (a) 2.8 years (b) 3.0 years
   (c) 2.5 years (d) 2.0 years

5. A train, 300 m long, passed a man, walking along the line in the same direction at the rate of 3 km/hr in 33 seconds. The speed of the train is
   (a) 30 km/hr (b) 32 km/hr
   (c) $32\dfrac{8}{11}$ km/hr (d) $35\dfrac{8}{11}$ km/hr

6. A can complete a piece of work in 18 days, B in 20 days and C in 30 days, B and C together start the work and are forced to leave after 2 days. The time taken by A alone to complete the remaining work is
   (a) 10 days (b) 12 days
   (c) 15 days (d) 16 days

7. What must be added to each term of the ratio 7 : 11, so as to make it equal to 3 : 4 ?
   (a) 8 (b) 7.5
   (c) 6.5 (d) 5

8. The cost of a piece of diamond varies with the square of its weight. A diamond of ₹5,184 value is cut into 3 pieces whose weights are in the ratio 1 : 2 : 3. Find the loss involved in the cutting.
   (a) ₹3, 068 (b) ₹3, 088
   (c) ₹3, 175 (d) ₹3, 168

9. If the circumference of a circle is decreased by 50% then the percentage of decrease in its area is
   (a) 25% (b) 50%
   (c) 60% (d) 75%

10. If $a = \dfrac{\sqrt{3}-\sqrt{2}}{\sqrt{3}+\sqrt{2}}$, $b = \dfrac{\sqrt{3}+\sqrt{2}}{\sqrt{3}-\sqrt{2}}$, then the value of $\dfrac{a^2}{b}+\dfrac{b^2}{a}$ is:
    (a) 900 (b) 970
    (c) 1030 (d) 930

11. The sides of a triangles are in the ratio 2:3:4. the perimeter of the triangle is 18cm. The area (in cm^2) of the triangle is
    (a) 9 (b) 36
    (c) $\sqrt{42}$ (d) $3\sqrt{15}$

12. Marked price of an article is ₹275. Shopkeeper allows a discount of 5% and he gets a profit of 4.5%. The actual cost of the article is
    (a) 250 (b) 225
    (c) 215 (d) 210

13. The difference between a discount of 40% on ₹500 and two successive discounts of 36%, 4% on the same amount is
    (a) ₹ 0 (b) ₹ 2
    (c) ₹ 1.93 (d) ₹ 7.20

14. The ratio between two numbers is 2 : 3. If each number is increased by 4, the ratio between them becomes 5 : 7. The difference between the numbers is

(a)   8   (b)   6
(c)   4   (d)   2

15. Monthly incomes of A and B are in the ratio of 4 : 3 and their expenses bear the ratio 3 : 2. Each of them saves ₹ 6,000 at the end of the month, then the monthly income of A is
(a) ₹ 12,000   (b) ₹ 24,000
(c) ₹ 30,000   (d) ₹ 60,000

16. The average of three consecutive odd numbers is 12 more than one third of the first of these numbers. What is the last of the three numbers ?
(a)   15   (b)   17
(c)   19   (d)   Data inadequate

17. The average of 18 observations is recorded as 124. Later it was found that two observations with values 64 and 28 were entered wrongly as 46 and 82. Find the correct average of the 18 observations.
(a) $111\dfrac{7}{9}$ (b)   122
(c)   123   (d) $137\dfrac{3}{7}$

18. The cost price of an article is 64% of the marked price. The gain percentage after allowing a discount of 12% on the marked price is
(a)   37.5%   (b)   48%
(c)   50.5%   (d)   52%

19. A man purchased some eggs at 3 for ₹ 5 and sold them at 5 for ₹ 12. Thus he gained ₹ 143 in all. The number of eggs he bought is
(a)   210   (b)   200
(c)   195   (d)   190

20. The average age of four boys, five years ago was 9 years. On including a new boy, the present average age of all the five is 15 years. The present age of the new boy is
(a)   14 years   (b)   6 years
(c)   15 years   (d)   19 years

21. Two train of length 300 m and 250 m running with speed 60 kmph and 50 kmph in same direction. After what time they will cross each other.
(a)   2 m 48 sec   (b)   2 m 12 sec
(c)   3 m 12 sec   (d)   3 m 18 sec

22. The population of a town is 15000. If the number of males increases by 8% and that of females by 10%, then the population would increase to 16300. Find the number of females in the town.
(a)   4000   (b)   6000
(c)   3000   (d)   5000

23. If ₹5,000 becomes ₹5,700 in a year's time, what will ₹7,000 become at the end of 5 years at the same rate of simple interest?
(a)   ₹10,500   (b)   ₹11,900
(c)   ₹12,700   (d)   ₹7, 700

24. 'A' sells an article to 'B' at a profit of 20% and 'B' sells it to 'C' at a profit of 25%. If 'C' pays ₹1200, the cost price of the article originally (in ₹) is
(a)   700   (b)   600
(c)   1,000   (d)   800

25. A farmer divides his herd of n cows among his four sons, so that the first son gets one–half the herd, the second one–fourth, the third son $\dfrac{1}{5}$ and the fourth son 7 cows. Then the value of n is
(a)   240   (b)   100
(c)   180   (d)   140

GENERAL INTELLIGENCE & REASONING

DIRECTIONS (Qs. 26-28) : In each of the following questions, select the related letters/word/number from the given alternatives.

26. ADBC : EHFG : : ILJK : ?
(a)   MOPN   (b)   MPNO
(c)   ORPQ   (d)   MPON

27. Flexible : Rigid : : Confidence : ?
(a)   Diffidence   (b)   Indifference
(c)   Cowardice   (d)   Scare

28. 1 : 8 : : 27 : ?
(a)   37   (b)   47
(c)   57   (d)   64

DIRECTIONS (Qs. 29-30) : In questions, a series is given, with one term missing. Choose the correct alternative from the given ones that will complete the series.

29. YX, UTS, ONML, __?__ .
(a)   FEDCB   (b)   GFEDC
(c)   IHGFE   (d)   HGFED

30. 8, 15, 36, 99, 288, __?__
(a)   368   (b)   676
(c)   855   (d)   908

31. Vinod introduces, Vishal as the son of the only brother of his father's wife. How is Vinod related to Vishal?
    (a) Cousin
    (b) Brother
    (c) Son
    (d) Uncle

32. If in a certain code HYDROGEN is written as JCJZYSSD, then how can ANTIMONY be written in that code?
    (a) CPVKOQPA
    (b) CRZQWABO
    (c) ERXMQSRC
    (d) GTZOSUTE

33. If $64 \div 14 = 5$, $92 \div 31 = 7$, $26 \div 11 = 6$, then $56 \div 22 = \underline{\ ?\ }$
    (a) 11
    (b) 39
    (c) 7
    (d) 36

34. Some equations have been solved on the basis of certain system. Find the correct answer for the unsolved equation on that basis.
    If $94 + 16 = 42$, $89 + 23 = 78$, then $63 + 45 = ?$
    (a) 18
    (b) 28
    (c) 38
    (d) 48

DIRECTION (Q. 35): Select the missing number from the given responses.

35.

10	11	15
12	12	8
4	12	10
10	5	13
18	20	?

(a) 21
(b) 20
(c) 23
(d) 22

DIRECTION(Q. 36): In the following question/two statements are given, followed by two conclusions I and II. You have to consider the statements to be true, even if they seem to be at variance from commonly known facts. You have to decide which of the given conclusions, if any follow from the given statement.

---

36. **Statements :**
    1. Temple is a place of worship.
    2. Church is also a place of worship.
    Conclusions :
    I. Hindus and Christians use the same place for worship.
    II. All churches are temples.

(a) Neither conclusion I nor II follows
(b) Both conclusion I nor II follows
(c) Only conclusion I follows
(d) Only conclusion II follows

37. How many triangles are there in this figure?

Question figure :

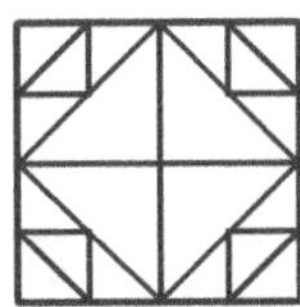

(a) 24
(b) 26
(c) 28
(d) 20

38. Which figure represents the relationship among Sun, Moon, Molecule ?

(a)  (b) 

(c) 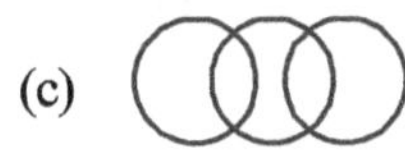 (d) 

DIRECTION (Q.39): Which answer figure completes the pattern given in the question figure?

---

39. **Question Figure :**

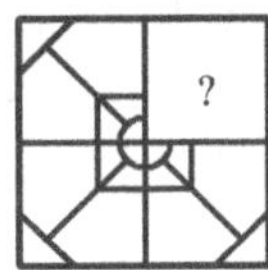

Answer Figures :

(a) 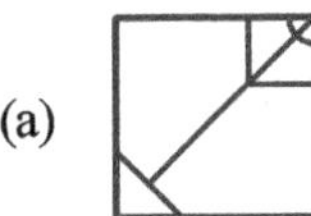 (b) 

(c)  (d) 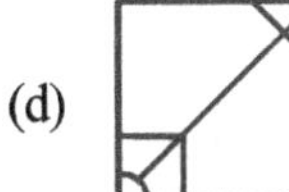

DIRECTION (Q. 40): In the following questions, which answer figure will complete the question figure?

40. From the given answer figures, select the one in which the question figure is hidden/ embedded.

Question Figure

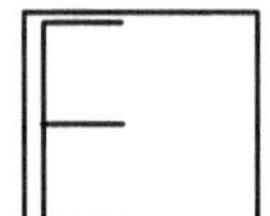

Answer Figures

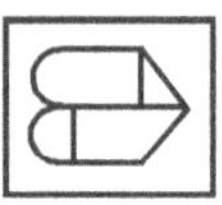  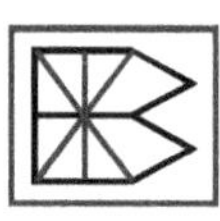 

   (a)   (b)   (c)   (d)

41. If PALE is written as RCNG, how can LEAP be written in that code?
    (a) NGCR   (b) RCGN
    (c) CRNG   (d) NCRG

42. If GARMENT is written as 202691422137, how is INDULGE written in that code?
    (a) 9144211275   (b) 914211275
    (c) 1813326152022   (d) 1813236152022

43. A family consisted of a man, his wife, his three sons, their wives and three children in each son's family. How many members are there in the family?
    (a) 12   (b) 13
    (c) 15   (d) 17

44. Ram and Sham start walking in opposite directions. Ram covers 6 kms and Sham 8 kms. Then Ram turns right and walks 8 kms and Sham turns left and walks 6 kms. How far each is from the starting point?
    (a) 11 kms   (b) 8 kms
    (c) 9 kms   (d) 10 kms

45. If × stands for addition, < for subtraction, + stands for division, > stands for multiplication, − stands for equal, ÷ stands for greater than, and = stands for less than, state which of the following is true ?
    (a) $3 \times 2 < 4 \div 16 > 2 + 4$
    (b) $5 > 8 + 4 = 10 < 4 \times 8$
    (c) $3 \times 4 > 2 - 9 + 3 < 3$
    (d) $5 \times 3 < 3 \div 8 + 4 \times 1 -$ None is true

46. 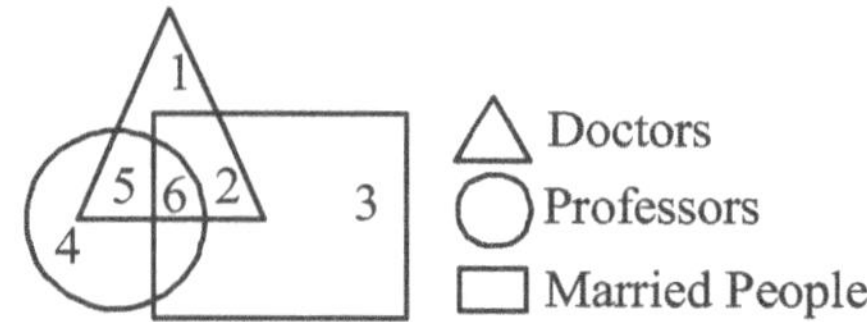

Which number indicates doctors who are not married ?
    (a) 6   (b) 4   (c) 2   (d) 1

DIRECTIONS (Qs.47-48): In each question below are two statements followed by two conclusions numbered I and II. You have to take the two given statements to be true even if they seem to be at variance from commonly known facts and then decide which of the given conclusions logically follows from the given statements disregarding commonly known facts. Give answer

(a) if only conclusion I follows.
(b) if only conclusion II follows.
(c) if either conclusion I or II follows.
(d) if neither conclusion I nor II follows.

47. **Statements:** No holiday is a vacation.
               Some vacations are trips.
    Conclusions:
        I. No trip is a holiday.
        II. Some holidays are definitely not trips.

48. **Statements:** Some kites are birds.
               No kite is an aeroplane.
    Conclusions:
        I. All aeroplanes are birds.
        II. Some birds are definitely not kites

DIRECTIONS (Qs. 49-50): In each question below is given a statement followed by two conclusions numbered I and II. You have to assume everything in the statement to be true, then consider the two conclusions together and decide which of them logically follows beyond a reasonable doubt from the information given in the statement.

---

49. **Statements:** Quality has a price tag. India is allocating lots of funds to education.
    Conclusions:
    I. Quality of education in India would improve soon.
    II. Funding alone can enhance quality of education.

(a) Only conclusion I follows
(b) Only conclusion II follows
(c) Either I or II follows
(d) Neither I nor II follows

50. **Statements:** All the organised persons find time for rest. Sunita, in spite of her very busy schedule, finds time for rest.
Conclusions:
I. Sunita is an organised person.
II. Sunita is an industrious person.
(a) Only conclusion I follows
(b) Only conclusion II follows
(c) Either I or II follows
(d) Both I and II follow

BASIC SCIENCE AND ENGINEERING

51. The internal angle of regular pentagon is ___ degree.
(a) 72 (b) 108
(c) 120 (d) 150

52. Unit of surface tension is
(a) Nm^{-1} (b) Nm^{-2}
(c) N^2m^{-1} (d) Nm^{-3}

53. The dimensions of coefficient of self inductance are
(a) $[ML^2 T^{-2} A^{-2}]$ (b) $[ML^2 T^{-2} A^{-1}]$
(c) $[MLT^{-2} A^{-2}]$ (d) $[MLT^{-2} A^{-1}]$

54. Choose the wrong statement from the following.
(a) The motion of an object along a straight line is a rectilinear motion
(b) The speed in general is less than the magnitude of the velocity
(c) The slope of the displacement-time graph gives the velocity of the body
(d) The area under the velocity-time graph gives the displacement of the body

55. A compressed spring possesses
(a) Kinetic Energy
(b) Elastic Potential Energy
(c) Gravitational Potential Energy
(d) Sound Energy

56. When water is heated from 0°C to 4°C, its volume
(a) increases
(b) decreases
(c) does not change
(d) first decreases and then increases

57. The temperature coefficient of resistance of some material is negative. The material is
(a) silicon (b) aluminium
(c) arsenide (d) germanium

58. Which of the following is NOT a simple machine?
(a) a screw (b) a lever
(c) a pair of scissors (d) a wheel and axle

59. The Occupational Safety and Health Act applies to all employees who work for an employer that is engaged in a business affecting:
(a) internal security.
(b) interstate commerce.
(c) surrounding environment and natural ecosystems.
(d) overall health and safety of civilians.

60. Thickness of the Ozone layer is measured in................
(a) Db(decibel) (b) DU(Dobson Unit)
(c) PPB (d) PPM

61. BCC in the Email refer to
(a) Blind Carbon Copy
(b) Black Carbon Copy
(c) Blank Carbon Copy
(d) Blue Carbon Copy

62. Energy that causes water to evaporate from surface to form water vapors is known as
(a) electrical energy (b) thermal energy
(c) chemical energy (d) heat energy

63. The intersection of a plane surface with the profile plane is line and is call
(a) Horizontal Trace (b) Vertical Trace
(c) Profile Trace (d) Trace

64. Range of measuring tape is
(a) one meter (b) several meters
(c) two meters (d) half meter

65. Spring balance is used to measure
(a) Mass (b) Time
(c) Weight (d) acceleration

66. On a speed graph, this is impossible:
(a) having a perfectly vertical line
(b) having a line slopped down
(c) have a line curving up
(d) having a perfectly horizontal line

67. Which form of energy does the flowing water possess?
(a) gravitational energy
(b) potential energy
(c) electrical energy
(d) kinetic energy

68. Light coloured clothes are preferred during
    (a) a winter   (b) a summer
    (c) a day   (d) a night
69. Absolute zero is equal to -273°C, which is equal to
    (a) 546 K   (b) 546 K
    (c) 0 K   (d) 1 K
70. When electric current passes through a bucket full of water, lot of bubbling is observed. This suggests that the type of supply is
    (a) A.C.   (b) D.C.
    (c) any of above two   (d) None of the above
71. Which of the following simple machines are combined to make scissors?
    (a) wedge and pulley   (b) gear and pulley
    (c) lever and gear   (d) lever and wedge
72. OSHA ensures that employees have been provided with _____
    (a) Job
    (b) personal protective equipment
    (c) Insurance
    (d) Security
73. The following type of ecosystem is of utmost importance from human point of view
    (a) Unsubsidized Natural Solar powered ecosystems
    (b) Naturally Subsidized Solar powered ecosystems
    (c) Man Subsidized Solar powered ecosystems
    (d) Fuel powered ecosystems
74. A 40 w bulb is connected is series with a room heater. If now 40 w bulb is replaced by 100 w bulb, the heater output will
    (a) decrease
    (b) increase
    (c) remain same
    (d) heater will burn out
75. What is Windows XP?
    (a) The computer's operating system
    (b) A program for displaying images on the screen
    (c) A system for displaying photos and images on the computer
    (d) A hard drive

GENERAL AWARENESS AND CURRENT AFFAIR

76. Which of the following cereals was among the first to be used by man?
    (a) Rye   (b) Wheat
    (c) Barley   (d) Oat
77. Who is rightly called the "Father of Local Self Government" in India ?
    (a) Lord Mayo   (b) Lord Ripon
    (c) Lord Curzon   (d) Lord Clive
78. Who was the President of the Constituent Assembly?
    (a) Pt. Jawahar Lal Nehru
    (b) Sardar Patel
    (c) Dr. Rajendra Prasad
    (d) Dr. B.R. Ambedkar
79. The propagation of sound waves in a gas involves
    (a) adiabatic compression and refraction
    (b) isothermal compression and rarefaction
    (c) isochoric compression and rarefaction
    (d) isobaric compression and rarefaction
80. What is the chemical name of vinegar ?
    (a) Citric acid   (b) Acetic acid
    (c) Pyruvic acid   (d) Malic acid
81. Which one of the following is also called the 'power plants' of the cell ?
    (a) Golgi body   (b) Mitochondrion
    (c) Ribosome   (d) Lysosome
82. Which amongst the following is largest endocrine gland in the body?
    (a) Thyroid   (b) Parathyroid
    (c) Adrenal   (d) Pituitary
83. Which of the following is an endemic species?
    (a) Nicobar pigeon   (b) Horn bill
    (c) Indian Rhino   (d) Pink head duck
84. Exercise Shanghai Cooperation Organization (SCO) Peace Mission 2018, the latest in 'Peace Mission' series formally started in __________.
    (a) India   (b) China
    (c) Kazakhstan   (d) Russia
85. Name the Operation that was successfully launched by Indian Air Force during Kargil war.
    (a) Operation Vijay
    (b) Safed Sagar
    (c) Operation Parakram
    (d) Operation Neela Samunder

86. The 10th edition of BRICS Summit had begun recently in which of the following city?
    (a) Beijing   (b) New Delhi
    (c) Moscow   (d) Johannesburg
87. Which country has recently announced to launch Mars Mission "HOPE" by 2020?
    (a) Oman   (b) UAE
    (c) Iran   (d) Israel
88. Which state government has decided to provide free mobile phones to women of BPL families?
    (a) Rajasthan   (b) Gujarat
    (c) Himachal Pradesh   (d) Uttar Pradesh
89. Which day is celebrated as 'Hindi-Divas'?
    (a) 12 march   (b) 14 September
    (c) 2 June   (d) 25 December
90. DOTS is a treatment given to patients suffering from ________
    (a) Polio   (b) AIDS
    (c) Hepatitis   (d) Tuberculosis
91. Polyploidy arises due to change in the
    (a) number of chromatids
    (b) structure of genes
    (c) number of chromosomes
    (d) structure – of chromosomes
92. Sariska and Ranthambore are the reserves for which of the following
    (a) Lion   (b) Deer
    (c) Tiger   (d) Bear
93. Radian is used to measure
    (a) Temperature   (b) Intensity of Flame
    (c) Angle   (d) Solid Angle
94. newton is used to measure
    (a) Speed   (b) Volume
    (c) Force   (d) Area
95. The World's largest island is
    (a) Greenland   (b) Iceland
    (c) New Guinea   (d) Madagascar
96. The suicidal bags of the cell are
    (a) Lysosomes   (b) Ribosomes
    (c) Dictyosomes   (d) Phagosomes
97. The wavelength of visible light are between
    (a) $0.4\,\mu m$ to $0.7\,\mu m$ (b) $3000\mu m$ to $0.4\mu m$
    (c) $0.7\mu m$ to $1000\mu m$ (d) $0.1\,cm$ to $30\,cm$
98. The laws of reflection are for
    (a) Concave mirror
    (b) Convex mirror
    (c) Plane mirror
    (d) All reflecting surfaces
99. Who among the following is credited with starting the work on plant tissue culture?
    (a) F.C. Steward   (b) P. Maheshwari
    (c) P.R. White   (d) Haberlandt
100. Which of the following uses the spawn mechanism to duplicate itself?
    (a) Trojan horse   (b) Worm
    (c) Keystroke logger   (d) Logic bomb

HINTS & EXPLANATIONS

1. (b)

$$\begin{array}{r|llll}
2 & 20, & 28, & 32, & 35 \\
\hline
2 & 10, & 14, & 16, & 35 \\
\hline
5 & 5, & 7, & 8, & 35 \\
\hline
7 & 1, & 7, & 8, & 7 \\
\hline
 & 1, & 1, & 8, & 1
\end{array}$$

$\therefore$ LCM $= 2 \times 2 \times 5 \times 7 \times 8 = 1120$

$\therefore$ Required number

$= 5834 - 1120 = 4714$

2. (a) Let the CP be ₹100.

$\therefore$ SP $= ₹112$

If the marked price be ₹x, then

90% of x $= 112$

$$\Rightarrow x = \frac{112 \times 100}{90} = ₹\frac{1120}{9}$$

$\therefore$ Required ratio $= 100 : \dfrac{1120}{9}$

$= 900 : 1120 = 45 : 56$

3. (b) The sum of cost prices of two articles is ₹x. One of them is sold at a loss of a% and other is sold at a gain of b% and their S.P. is same.

$\therefore$ C.P. of article sold at a loss of a%

$$= \frac{100 + b}{200 - a + b} \times x =$$

$$\frac{100 + 15}{200 - 20 + 15} \times 19500$$

$$= \frac{115}{195} \times 19500 = ₹11500$$

$\therefore$ C.P. of second article $= ₹8000$

4. (d) P $= ₹12000$, Rate $= 5\%$, Time (n) $= ?$, Amount $= 13230$

$$A = P\left(1 + \frac{R}{100}\right)^T \Rightarrow 13230 = 12000\left(1 + \frac{5}{100}\right)^n$$

$$\Rightarrow \frac{13230}{12000} = \left(\frac{21}{20}\right)^n \Rightarrow \frac{1323}{1200} = \left(\frac{21}{20}\right)^n$$

$$\Rightarrow \frac{441}{400} = \left(\frac{21}{20}\right)^n$$

$$\left(\frac{21}{20}\right)^2 = \left(\frac{21}{20}\right)^n$$

$\therefore$ n $= 2$ years

5. (d) If the speed of the train be x kmph, then relative speed

$= (x - 3)$ kmph.

$$= (x - 3) \times \frac{5}{8} \, \text{m/sec}$$

$$\therefore \frac{300}{(x - 3) \times \dfrac{5}{18}} = 33$$

$\Rightarrow 5400 = 33 \times 5 \, (x - 3)$

$\Rightarrow 360 = 11 \, (x - 3)$

$\Rightarrow 11x - 33 = 360$

$$\Rightarrow x = \frac{393}{11} = 35\frac{8}{11} \, \text{kmph}$$

6. (c) (B + C)'s 2 days' work

$$= 2\left(\frac{1}{20} + \frac{1}{30}\right) = 2\left(\frac{3 + 2}{60}\right) = \frac{1}{6} \text{part}$$

Remaining work $= 1 - \dfrac{1}{6} = \dfrac{5}{6}$ part

$\therefore$ Time taken by A to complete this part of work

$$= \frac{5}{6} \times 18 = 15 \, \text{days}$$

7. (d) Let the required number be x.

$$\therefore \frac{7 + x}{11 + x} = \frac{3}{4}$$

$\Rightarrow 28 + 4x = 33 + 3x$

$\Rightarrow x = 33 - 28 = 5$

8. (d) If the weight of a piece of diamond be 6 x units, then

Original price $\alpha \, (6x)^2 = 36kx^2$

$\therefore 36. \, kx^2 = 5184$ .....(i)

Again,

New price $= k(x^2 + 4x^2 + 9x^2) = 14\,kx^2$

$$= \frac{14 \times 5184}{36} = ₹\,2016$$

$\therefore$ Loss $= 5184 - 2016$

$= ₹3168$

9. (d) Circumference $= 2\pi r$ (one variable)

$\therefore$ The decrease in area $= 100 - 50 + \dfrac{50 \times 50}{100}$

$$= 75\%$$

10. (b) $a = \dfrac{\sqrt{3} - \sqrt{2}}{\sqrt{3} + \sqrt{2}} = \dfrac{\sqrt{3} - \sqrt{2}}{\sqrt{3} + \sqrt{2}} \times \dfrac{\sqrt{3} - \sqrt{2}}{\sqrt{3} - \sqrt{2}}$

$$= \frac{\left(\sqrt{3} - \sqrt{2}\right)^2}{3 - 2} = 3 + 2 - 2\sqrt{6} = 5 - 2\sqrt{6}$$

$\therefore b = \dfrac{\sqrt{3} + \sqrt{2}}{\sqrt{3} - \sqrt{2}} = 5 + 2\sqrt{6}$

$\Rightarrow a + b = 10;$

$ab = (5 - 2\sqrt{6})(5 + 2\sqrt{6}) = 25 - 24 = 1$

$\therefore \dfrac{a^2}{b} + \dfrac{b^2}{a} = \dfrac{a^3 + b^3}{ab}$

$$= \frac{(a + b)^3 - 3ab(a + b)}{ab}$$

$= 10^3 - 3 \times 10 = 1000 - 30 = 970$

11. (d) Ratio $= 2 : 3 : 4$

$= 4 : 6 : 8$

Perimeter $= 18$ cm

$\therefore$ Semi-perimeter(s) $= \dfrac{4 + 6 + 8}{2} = 9$

$\therefore$ Area of triangle

$= \sqrt{s(s - a)(s - b)(s - c)}$

$= \sqrt{9(9 - 4)(9 - 6)(9 - 8)}$

$= \sqrt{9 \times 5 \times 3 \times 1} = 3\sqrt{15}$ sq. cm.

12. (a) MP $= 275$

SP after Discount of 5% $= \dfrac{95}{100} \times 275$

CP where P % of 4.5 $= \dfrac{100}{104.5} \times \dfrac{95}{100} \times 275$

$= ₹250$

13. (d) Single equivalent discount for 36% and 4%

$= \left(36 + 4 - \dfrac{36 \times 4}{100}\right)$

$= (40 - 1.44)\% = 38.56\%$

$\therefore$ Required difference $= 1.44\%$ of 500

$$= \frac{500 \times 1.44}{100} = ₹7.20$$

14. (a) Let the numbers be 2x and 3x.

$\therefore \dfrac{2x + 4}{3x + 4} = \dfrac{5}{7}$

$\therefore 15x + 20 = 14x + 28$

$\Rightarrow x = 28 - 20 = 8 =$ Required Difference

15. (b) Let salary of A and B be $= 4x$ and $3x$

expenditure $=$ income-salary

ATQ

$$\frac{4x - 6000}{3x - 6000} = \frac{3}{2}$$

$8x - 12000 = 9x - 18000$

$x = 6000$

A's salary $= 4x = 4 \times 6000 = ₹24000$

16. (c) Let 3 consecutive odd no. be $x, x + 2$ and $x + 4$ ATQ

$$\frac{x + x + 2 + x + 4}{3} = 12 + \frac{1}{3}x$$

$$\frac{3x + 6}{3} - \frac{x}{3} = 12$$

$= 2x + 6 = 36 \quad \Rightarrow \quad x = \dfrac{36 - 6}{2} = 15$

last no $= 15 + 4 = 19$

17. (b) Difference in observations

$= 64 + 28 - 46 - 82 = -36$

$\therefore$ Correct average

$= 124 - \dfrac{36}{18} = 122$

18. (a) Marked price of article $= ₹\,100$ (let)

$\therefore$ C.P. of article $= ₹\,64$

$\therefore$ S.P. of article $= ₹\,88$

$\therefore$ Profit per cent

$= \dfrac{88 - 64}{64} \times 100 = 37.5\%$

19. (c) Let he buy 15 eggs.

$\therefore$ CP of 15 eggs = ₹ 25

$\therefore$ SP of 15 eggs = ₹ 36

$\therefore$ Gain = 36 − 25 = ₹ 11

$\because$ ₹ 11 ≡ 15 eggs

$\therefore$ ₹ 143 ≡ $\dfrac{15}{11} \times 143$

= 195 eggs.

20. (d) Sum of the present ages of four boys

= 9 × 4 + 20 = 56 years

Sum of the present ages of five boys

= 15 × 5 = 75 years

$\therefore$ Present age of new boy

= 75 − 56 = 19 years

21. (d) Total length = 300 + 250 = 550 m = 0.55 km

Time required to cross each other

$$= \frac{0.55}{(60-50)} = 0.055 = 198 \text{ sec} = 3 \text{ m } 18 \text{ sec}$$

22. (d) If the number of females be x, then, number of males = 15000 − x

$$\therefore \text{x} \times \frac{10}{100} + (15000 - \text{x}) \times \frac{8}{100}$$

= 16300 − 15000

$\Rightarrow$ 10x + 120000 − 8x

= 1300 × 100

$\Rightarrow$ 2x = 130000 − 120000

= 10000

$\Rightarrow$ x = 5000

23. (b) Interest = 5700 − 5000 = ₹ 700

$$\therefore \text{Rate} = \frac{700 \times 100}{5000 \times 1} = 14\%$$

Case II,

Interest

$$= \frac{\text{Principal} \times \text{Time} \times \text{Rate}}{100}$$

$$\frac{7000 \times 5 \times 14}{100} = ₹4900$$

Amount = 7000 + 4900 = ₹ 11900

24. (d) Effective profit percent

$$= \left(20 + 25 + \frac{20 \times 25}{100} \right) = 50\%$$

$\therefore$ Original cost price

$$= \frac{100}{150} \times 1200 = ₹800$$

25. (d) According to the question,

$$\frac{\text{n}}{2} + \frac{\text{n}}{4} + \frac{\text{n}}{5} + 7 = \text{n}$$

$$\Rightarrow \frac{10\text{n} + 5\text{n} + 4\text{n}}{20} + 7 = \text{n}$$

$$\Rightarrow \frac{19\text{n}}{20} + 7 = \text{n} \Rightarrow \text{n} - \frac{19\text{n}}{20} = 7$$

$$\Rightarrow \frac{\text{n}}{20} = 7 \Rightarrow \text{n} = 20 \times 7 = 140$$

26. (b) As,

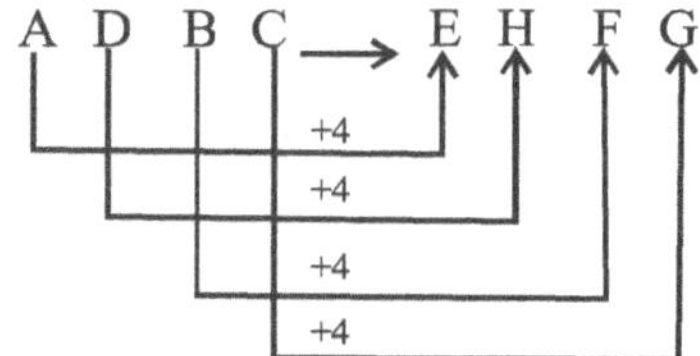

Similarly,

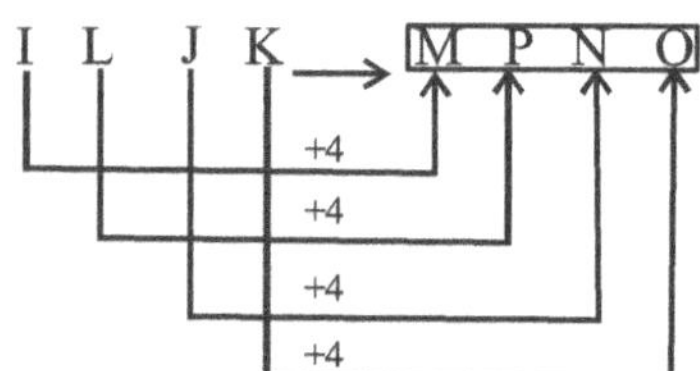

27. (a) Flexible is antonym of Rigid. Similarly, Confidence is antonym of Diffidence.

28. (d) As, $(1)^3 = 1$; $(2)^3 = 8$

$(3)^3 = 27$; $(4)^3 = \boxed{64}$

29. (b) The pattern is as follows :

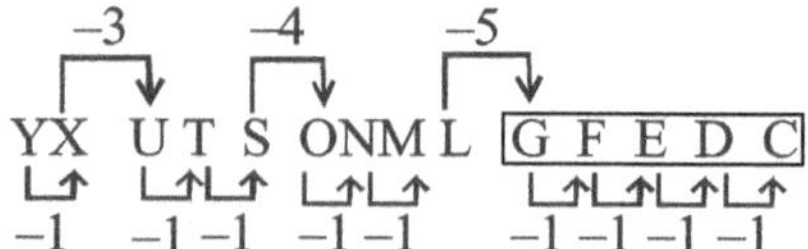

30. (c) The pattern is as follows :

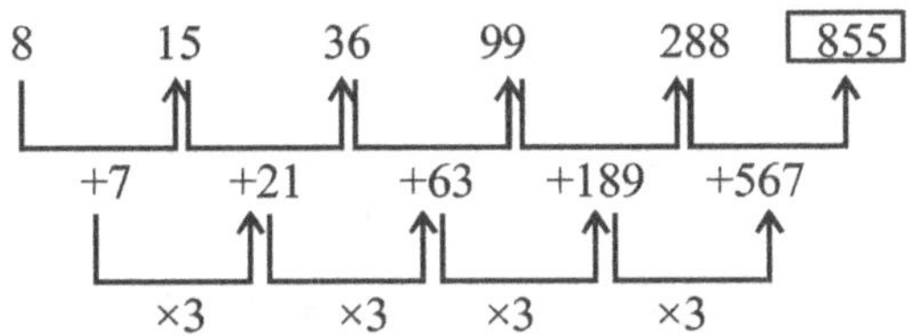

31. (a) Wife of Vinod's father means the mother of Vinod.
Only brother of Vinod's mother means maternal uncle of Vinod.
Therefore, Vinod is cousin of Vishal.

32. (b) Difference is $+2, +4, +6, +8, +10, +12, +14, +16$

33. (c) $6 + 4 = 10; 1 + 4 = 5; 10 - 5 = 5$
$9 + 2 = 11; 3 + 1 = 4; 11 - 4 = 7$
$2 + 6 = 8; 1 + 1 = 2; 8 - 2 = 6$
$5 + 6 = 11; 2 + 2 = 4, 11 - 4 = \boxed{7}$

34. (c) $9 \times 4 + 1 \times 6 = 36 + 6 = 42$
$8 \times 9 + 2 \times 3 = 72 + 6 = 78$
Similarly
$6 \times 3 + 4 \times 5 = 18 + 20 = \boxed{38}$

35. (c) First Column
$10 + 12 + 4 + 10 = 36$
$$\frac{36}{2} = 18$$
Second Column
$$11 + 12 + 12 + 5 = 40 = \frac{40}{2} = 20$$
Third Column
$$15 + 8 + 10 + 13 = 46 = \frac{46}{2} = \boxed{23}$$

36. (a) Temple and Church are places of worship. It does not imply that Hindus and Christians use the same place for worship. Church is different from temple. Therefore, neither Conclusion I nor II follows.

37. (c) 38. (d) 39. (b) 40. (c)

41. (a)
```
P    A    L    E
+2↓  +2↓  +2↓  +2↓
R    C    N    G
```
Similarly,
```
     L    E    A    P
    +2↓  +2↓  +2↓  +2↓
     N    G    C    R
```

42. (d) This question comes under the category of sum 27. Here G's position is written in reverse order.

Therefore, G A R M E N T
20 26 9 14 22 13 7

Similarly, I N D U L G E
18 13 23 6 15 20 22

43. (d) A man + his wife = 1 + 1 = 2
His three sons + their wives = 3 + 3 = 6
Three children in each one's family
= 3 × 3 = 9
Total members = 2 + 6 + 9 = 17

44. (d)

$$OB = \sqrt{(AB)^2 + (AO)^2} = \sqrt{(8)^2 + (6)^2}$$
$$= \sqrt{64 + 36} = \sqrt{100} = 10 \text{km}$$

45. (b)

$\times \Rightarrow +$	$< \Rightarrow -$	$+ \Rightarrow \div$	$> \Rightarrow \times$
$- \Rightarrow =$	$\div \Rightarrow >$	$= \Rightarrow <$	

Option (a)
$3 \times 2 < 4 \div 16 > 2 + 4$
$\Rightarrow 3 + 2 - 4 > 16 \times 2 \div 4$
$\Rightarrow 5 - 4 > \dfrac{16 \times 2}{4} \Rightarrow 1 > 8 \text{ (not possible)}$

Option (b)
$5 > 8 + 4 = 10 < 4 \times 8$
$\Rightarrow 5 \times 8 \div 4 < 10 - 4 + 8$
$\Rightarrow 5 \times 2 < 18 - 4 \Rightarrow 10 < 14$

Option (c)
$3 \times 4 > 2 - 9 + 3 < 3$
$\Rightarrow 3 + 4 \times 2 = 9 \div 3 - 3$
$\Rightarrow 3 + 8 \neq 3 - 3$

option (b) is correct.

46. (d)

Persons	Numbers					
	1	2	3	4	5	6
△ Doctors	✓	✓	✗	✗	✓	✓
○ Professors	✗	✗	✗	✓	✓	✓
□ Married	✗	✓	✓	✗	✗	✓

Number 1 indicates doctors who are not married

47. (b)

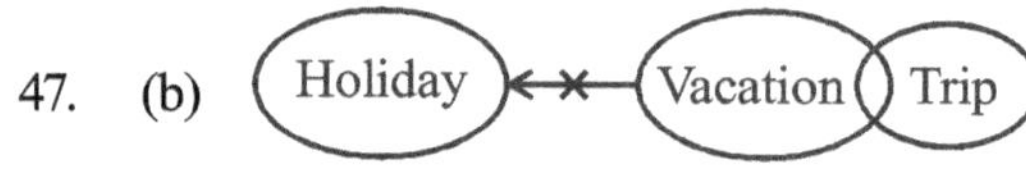

So, Only II follows.

48. (d)

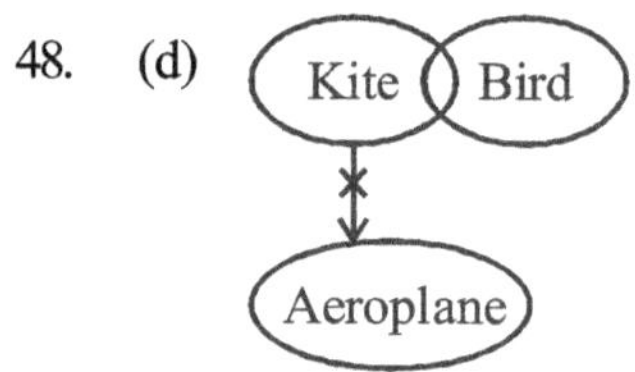

So, Neither I nor II follows.

49. (a) According to the statement, funding is necessary to improve quality and India is allocating funds to education. This means that quality of education will improve in India. So, I follows. But funding alone is sufficient to enhance quality, is not true. So, II does not follow.

50. (d) Sunita has a very busy schedule. This means that she is industrious. But still she finds time for rest. This means that she is an organised person. So, both I and II follow.

51. (a)	52. (a)	53. (a)	54. (b)	55. (b)
56. (d)	57. (d)	58. (c)	59. (b)	60. (b)
61. (a)	62. (b)	63. (c)	64. (b)	65. (c)
66. (a)	67. (d)	68. (b)	69. (c)	70. (b)
71. (d)	72. (b)	73. (a)	74. (b)	75. (a)
76. (b)	77. (b)	78. (c)	79. (a)	80. (b)
81. (b)	82. (a)	83. (a)	84. (d)	85. (b)
86. (d)	87. (b)	88. (a)	89. (b)	90. (d)
91. (a)	92. (c)	93. (c)	94. (c)	95. (a)
96. (a)	97. (a)	98. (d)	99. (d)	100 (b)

PRACTICE SET 14

Time: 90 minutes **Max. Marks - 100**

MATHEMATICS

1. A number, when divided by 114, leaves remainder 21. If the same number is divided by 19, then the remainder will be
   - (a) 1
   - (b) 2
   - (c) 7
   - (d) 17

2. By what least number should 675 be multiplied so as to obtain a perfect cube number ?
   - (a) 3
   - (b) 5
   - (c) 24
   - (d) 40

3. The mean of 50 numbers is 30. Later it was discovered that two entries were wrongly entered as 82 and 13 instead of 28 and 31. Find the correct mean.
   - (a) 36.12
   - (b) 30.66
   - (c) 29.28
   - (d) 38.21

4. By selling a bicycle for ₹ 2,850, Aa shopkeeper gains 14%. If the profit is reduced to 8%, then the selling price will be
   - (a) ₹ 2,600
   - (b) ₹ 2,700
   - (c) ₹ 2,800
   - (d) ₹ 3,000

5. The population of a village increases by 5% annually. If its present population is 4410, then its population 2 years ago was
   - (a) 4500
   - (b) 4000
   - (c) 3800
   - (d) 3500

6. In a 200m race, Kamal defeats Bimal by 10 seconds. If the speed of Kamal is 36 kmph, then the speed of Bimal is
   - (a) 25.4 kmph
   - (b) 24.5 kmph
   - (c) 24 kmph
   - (d) 34 kmph

7. A can complete $\dfrac{1}{3}$ of a work in 10 days and B, $\dfrac{2}{5}$ of the work in 20 days. In how many days both A and B together can complete the work ?
   - (a) 20
   - (b) $18\dfrac{6}{8}$
   - (c) $18\dfrac{4}{5}$
   - (d) $17\dfrac{1}{2}$

8. Two number are in the ratio 7 : 11. If 7 is added to each of the numbers, the ratio becomes 2 : 3. The larger number is
   - (a) 39
   - (b) 49
   - (c) 66
   - (d) 77

9. A and B are partners in a business. A contributes $\dfrac{1}{4}$ of the capital for 15 months and B received $\dfrac{2}{3}$ of the profit. Find for how long B's money was used?
   - (a) 6 months
   - (b) 8 months
   - (c) 10 months
   - (d) 12 months

10. If the ratio of areas of two similar triangles is 9 : 16, then the ratio of their corresponding sides is
    - (a) 3 : 5
    - (b) 3 : 4
    - (c) 4 : 5
    - (d) 4 : 3

11. If each side of a square is increased by 10%, its area will be increased by
    - (a) 10%
    - (b) 21%
    - (c) 44%
    - (d) 100%

12. If $5a + \dfrac{1}{3a} = 5$, the value of $9a^2 + \dfrac{1}{25a^2}$ is
    - (a) $\dfrac{34}{5}$
    - (b) $\dfrac{39}{5}$
    - (c) $\dfrac{42}{5}$
    - (d) $\dfrac{52}{5}$

13. A three-digit number 4a3 is added to another three-digit number 984 to give the four digit number 13b7 which is divisible by 11. Then the value of (a + b) is:
    (a) 11   (b) 12
    (c) 9   (d) 10

14. By decreasing 15° of each angle of a triangle, the ratio of their angles are 2 : 3 : 5. The radian measure of greatest angle is:
    (a) $11\pi/24$ (b) $\pi/12$
    (c) $\pi/24$ (d) $5\pi/24$

15. A watch is sold at a profit of 30%. Had it been sold for ₹ 80 less, there would have been a loss of 10%. What is the cost price of rupees?
    (a) 150   (b) 200
    (c) 400   (d) 800

16. If a commission of 10% is given on the marked price of a work, the publisher gains 20%. If the commission is increased to 15%, the gain present is:

    (a) 15%   (b) $16\frac{2}{3}\%$

    (c) $13\frac{1}{3}\%$ (d) $15\frac{1}{6}\%$

17. If 12 men or 18 women can reap a field in 14 days, then working at the same rate, 8 men and 16 women can reap the same field in:
    (a) 9 days   (b) 5 days
    (c) 7 days   (d) 8 days

18. By selling 9 articles for a rupee, a man incurred a loss of 4%. To make a gain of 44%, the number of articles to be sold for a rupee is:
    (a) 5   (b) 3
    (c) 4   (d) 6

19. The least multiple of 13 which when divided by 4, 5, 6, 7 leaves remainder 3 in each case is
    (a) 3780   (b) 3783
    (c) 2520   (d) 2522

20. If 21 is added to a number, it becomes 7 less than thrice of the number. Then the number is
    (a) 14   (b) 16
    (c) 18   (d) 19

21. Two men A and B started a job in which A was thrice as good as B and therefore took 60 days less than B to finish the job. How many days will they take to finish the job, if they start working together?
    (a) 15 days   (b) 20 days

    (c) $22\frac{1}{2}$ days   (d) 25 days

22. A rectangular garden is 100 m × 80 m. There is a path along the garden and just outside it. Width of path is 10 m. The area of the path is
    (a) 1900 sq m   (b) 2400 sq m
    (c) 3660 sq m   (d) 4000 sq m

23. A dealer offered a machine for sale for ₹27,500 but even if he had charged 10% less, he would have made a profit of 10% . The actual cost of the machine is
    (a) ₹22,000   (b) ₹24,250
    (c) ₹22,500   (d) ₹22,275

24. An employer reduces the number of employees in the ratio 8: 5 and increases their wages in the ratio 7:9. As a result, the overall wages bill is
    (a) Increased in the ratio 56 : 69
    (b) Decreased in the ratio 56 : 45
    (c) Increased in the ratio 13 : 17
    (d) Decreased in the ratio 17 : 13

25. The average age of a jury of 5 is 40. If a member aged 35 resigns and a man aged 25 becomes a member, then the average age of the new jury is
    (a) 30   (b) 38
    (c) 40   (d) 42

GENERAL INTELLIGENCE & REASONING

DIRECTIONS (Qs. 26-28) : In each of the following questions, select the related word/letters/ number/ figure from the given alternatives.

26. AZCX : BYDW : : HQJO : ?
    (a) GRFP   (b) IPKM
    (c) IPKN   (d) GRJP

27. 24 : 126 : : 48 : ?
    (a) 433   (b) 192
    (c) 240   (d) 344

28. Fish : Scales : : Bear : ?
    (a) Feathers   (b) Leaves
    (c) Fur   (d) Skin
29. Pointing towards a woman in a photograph Vijay said, "She is the daughter of the father of sister of my brother". How is the lady in the photograph related to Vijay?
    (a) Wife   (b) Mother
    (c) Sister   (d) Daughter
30. Suresh is 7 ranks ahead of Ashok in the class of 39 students. If Ashok's rank is 17th from the last, what is Suresh's rank from the start ?
    (a) 16th   (b) 23th
    (c) 24th   (d) 15th
31. If in a certain code, RAMAYANA is written as PYKYWYLY, then how MAHABHARATA can be written in that code?
    (a) NBIBCIBSBUB
    (b) LZGZAGZQZSZ
    (c) MCJCDJCTCVC
    (d) KYFYZFYPYRY
32. If P denotes ÷, Q denotes ×, R denotes +, and S denotes –, then, 1 8 Q 1 2 P 4 R 5 S 6 = _?_
    (a) 95   (b) 53
    (c) 51   (d) 57
33. If $54 + 43 = 2$, $60 + 51 = 10$, then $62 + 72 = ?$
    (a) 30   (b) 18
    (c) 20   (d) 9
34. Select the missing number from the given responses.

7	6	9
2	8	4
4	3	?
36	42	26

    (a) 5   (b) 2
    (c) 3   (d) 4
35. If a man on a moped starts from a point and rides 4 km South, then turns left and rides 2 km to turn again to the right to ride 4 km more, towards which direction is he moving?
    (a) North   (b) West
    (c) East   (d) South

36. **Statement :**
    The human organism grows and develops through stimulation and action.
    Conclusions :
    I. Inert human organism cannot grow and develop.
    II. Human organisms do not react to stimulation and action.
    (a) Neither conclusion I nor II follows
    (b) Both conclusion I nor II follows
    (c) Only conclusion I follows
    (d) Only conclusion II follows
37. How many rectangles are there in the question figure?
    Question figure :

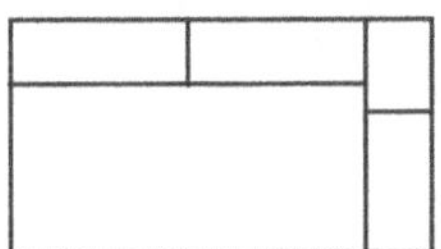

    (a) 6   (b) 7
    (c) 8   (d) 9
38. Which one of the following diagrams best depicts the relationship among Earth, Sea, Sun?

    (a)    (b) 

    (c)    (d) 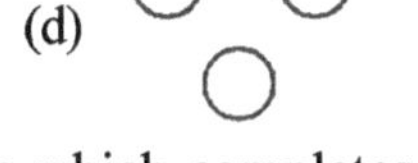

39. Find the answer figure which completes the question figure.
    Question Figure :

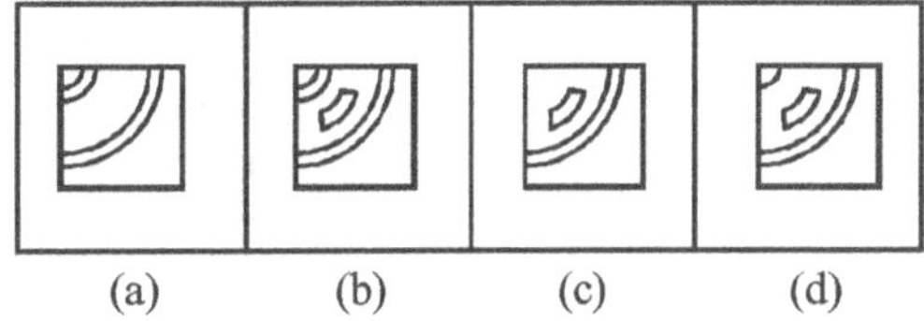

    Answer Figures :

(a)	(b)	(c)	(d)

40. In the question, if a mirror is placed on the line MN, then which of the answer figures is the right image of the given figure?

Question Figure :

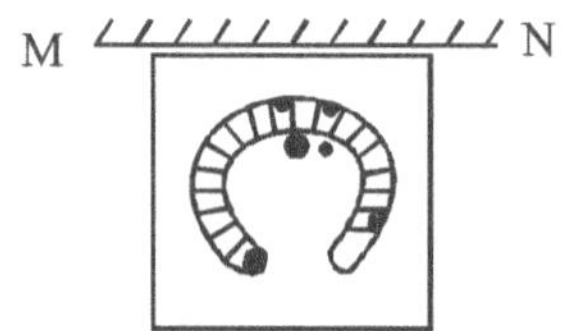

Answer Figures :

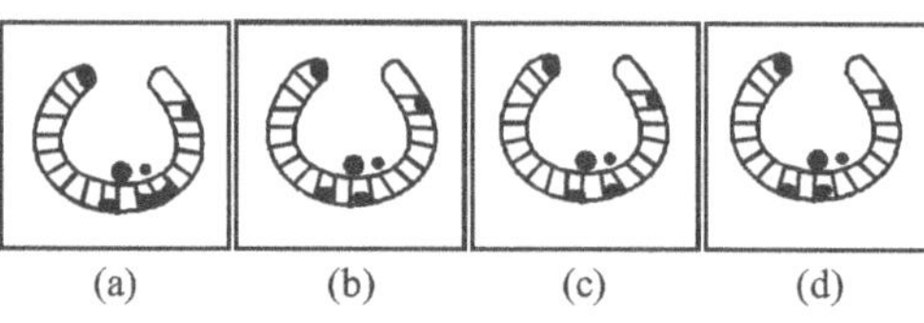

  (a)   (b)   (c)   (d)

DIRECTIONS (Qs. 41-42) : In the following questions a series is given, with one term missing. Choose the correct alternative from the given ones that will complete the series.

41.   2, 3, 6, 7, 14, 15, ?
    (a) 16   (b) 30
    (c) 31   (d) 32

42.   3120, ? , 122, 23, 4
    (a) 488   (b) 621
    (c) 610   (d) 732

43.   If A = 1, ACE = 9, then ART = ?
    (a) 29   (b) 38
    (c) 10   (d) 39

44.   Introducing a man, a woman said "His mother is the only daughter of my father'. How is the man related to the woman?
    (a) Son   (b) Father
    (c) Brother   (d) Uncle

45.   If '+' stands for 'multiplication', '<' stands for 'division', '÷' stands for 'subtraction', '−' stands for 'addition' and '×' stands for 'greater than', identify which expression is correct.
    (a) $20 - 4 \div 4 + 8 < 2 \times 26$
    (b) $20 \times 8 + 15 < 5 \div 9 - 8$
    (c) $20 < 2 + 10 \div 4 - 6 \times 100$
    (d) $20 < 5 + 25 \div 10 - 2 \times 96$

46. 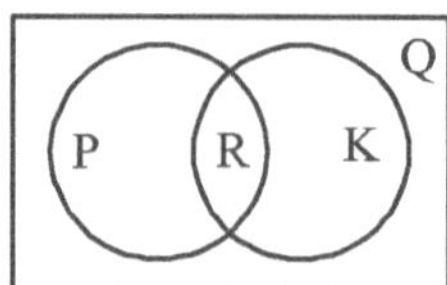

In the fig.

Q represents all quadrilaterals

K represents all Kites

R represents all Rhombus

P represents all Parallelogram

The statement 'Rhombus is also a Kite' can be described as

    (a) P and K is nothing but R
    (b) P or K is nothing but R
    (c) P and R is nothing but K
    (d) P or R is nothing but K

DIRECTIONS (Qs. 47-48): In each question below are two statements followed by two conclusions numbered I and II. You have to take the two given statements to be true even if they seem to be at variance from commonly known facts and then decide which of the given conclusions logically follows from the given statements disregarding commonly known facts. Give answer

---

(a)   if only conclusion I follows.
(b)   if only conclusion II follows.
(c)   if either conclusion I or II follows.
(d)   if neither conclusion I nor II follows.

47. **Statements:**   All metals are plastics.
                            All plastics are fibres.
    Conclusions:
                   I.   Atleast some fibres are metals.
                   II. Some metals are not fibres.

48. **Statements:**   All roads are streets.
                            No street is a highway.
    Conclusions: **I.**   No highway is a road.
                      II. All streets are roads.

DIRECTIONS (Qs. 49-50): In each question below is given a statement followed by two conclusions numbered I and II. You have to assume everything in the statement to be true, then consider the two conclusions together and decide which of them logically follows beyond a reasonable doubt from the information given in the statement.

49. **Statements**: Domestic demand has been increasing faster than the production of indigenous crude oil.

 Conclusions:

 I. Crude oil must be imported.

 II. Domestic demand should be reduced.

 (a) Only conclusion I follows

 (b) Only conclusion II follows

 (c) Either I or II follows

 (d) Neither I nor II follows

50. **Statements:** He stressed the need to stop the present examination system and its replacement by other methods which would measure the real merit of the students.

 Conclusions:

 I. Examinations should be abolished.

 II. The present examination system does not measure the real merit of the students.

 (a) Only conclusion I follows

 (b) Only conclusion II follows

 (c) Either I or II follows

 (d) Neither I nor II follows

BASIC SCIENCE AND ENGINEERING

51. In an axonometric drawing, the projection rays are drawn _____ to each other and _____ to the plane of projection.

 (a) Parallel...oblique

 (b) oblique...parallel

 (c) parallel...perpendicular

 (d) parallel...parallel

52. The dimensions of Planck's constant are same as

 (a) energy

 (b) power

 (c) momentum

 (d) angular momentum

53. When water is heated, it expands and

 (a) rises upward

 (b) moves downward

 (c) remain at the same place

 (d) None of these

54. The speed at any instant of time is known as

 (a) average speed

 (b) velocity

 (c) given speed

 (d) instantaneous speed

55. The work done on an object does not depend on the:

 (a) Displacement

 (b) Angle between force and displacement

 (c) Force applied

 (d) Initial velocity of the object

56. A cold steel spoon is dipped in a cup of hot milk. It transfers heat to its other end by the process of _____

 (a) Convection

 (b) Conduction

 (c) Absorption

 (d) Radiation

57. The example of non–ohmic resistance is

 (a) copper wire

 (b) nichrome wire

 (c) diode

 (d) tungsten wire

58. A pulley is a simple machine used to:

 (a) multiply force

 (b) apply a force at a convenient point

 (c) apply a force in a convenient direction

 (d) None of these

59. The Occupational Safety and Health Act created three federal agencies for administration and enforcement. Which of the following is not one of them?

 (a) The Occupational Safety and Health Administration (OSHA)

 (b) The National Institute of Occupational Safety and Health (NIOSH)

 (c) State Employee Health Commission (SEHC)

 (d) The Occupational Safety and Health Review Commission (OSHRC)

60. The objective of environmental studies is to

 (a) Create environmental ethics that foster awareness about the ecological inter - dependence of economic, social and political factors in a human community and the environment

(b) Acquiring skills to help the concerned individuals in identifying and solving environmental problems

(c) Raise consciousness about environmental conditions

(d) All of the above

61. A hard disk drive is considered as a __________ storage.
(a) flash
(b) non volatile
(c) temporary
(d) non-permanent

62. An object of mass 'm' raised to a height '2h' above ground level possesses a gravitational potential energy of
(a) $1/2 \times mgh$
(b) mgh
(c) 2mgh
(d) $m \times g / 2h$

63. The top and right side views have what common dimension(s)?
(a) height and width
(b) width and depth
(c) height
(d) depth

64. An axonometric drawing which has all three axes divided by equal angles is:
(a) diametric
(b) trimetric
(c) orthographic
(d) isometric

65. Digital stopwatches show reading up to
(a) 2 decimal places
(b) 3 decimal places
(c) 1 decimal place
(d) 4 significant figures

66. Weight is the measure of the force of ______ on an object.
(a) Density
(b) Mass
(c) Matter
(d) Gravity

67. Which of the following is speed and direction of motion?
(a) acceleration
(b) motion
(c) speed
(d) velocity

68. A spring or rubber possess
(a) Chemical Potential Energy
(b) Elastic Potential Energy
(c) Gravitational Potential Energy
(d) Kinetic energy

69. The process of transfer of heat in solids in called as:
(a) Convection
(b) Radiation
(c) Conduction
(d) None of the above

70. If a parallel circuit is opened in the main line, the current
(a) increases in the branch of the lowest resistance
(b) increases in each branch
(c) is zero in all branches
(d) is zero in the highest resistive branch

71. Which simple machine is used to hold objects together?
(a) pulley   (b) screw
(c) hammer   (d) wedge

72. Safety and Health Achievement Recognition Program (SHARP) recognizes ______
(a) Small employers who operate safety and health management system.
(b) Large employers who operate safety and health management system
(c) All employers who operate safety and health management system
(d) Workers who operate safety and health management system

73. What does 'Ozone Layer' absorb?
(a) g-rays
(b) X-rays
(c) Infrared rays
(d) Ultraviolet rays

74. For testing appliances, the wattage of test lamp should be
(a) very low   (b) low
(c) high   (d) any value

75. What page view can you use to see what it will look like when printed?
Discuss
    (a) Draft View
    (b) Outline View
    (c) Print View
    (d) Reading View

GENERAL AWARENESS AND CURRENT AFFAIR

76. The Lodi dynasty was founded by
    (a) Ibrahim Lodi
    (b) Sikandar Lodi
    (c) Bahlol Lodi
    (d) Khizr Khan

77. The first speaker of Lok Sabha was:
    (a) S. Radhakrishnan
    (b) M. Ananthasayanam Ayyangar
    (c) Sardar Hukum Singh
    (d) G. V. Mavlankar

78. Lens is made up of
    (a) Pyrex glass
    (b) Flint glass
    (c) Ordinary glass
    (d) Cobalt glass

79. The noble gas used for the treatment of cancer is
    (a) Helium   (b) Argon
    (c) Krypton   (d) Radon

80. The base used as an antacid is
    (a) Calcium hydroxide
    (b) Barium hydroxide
    (c) Magnesium hydroxide
    (d) Silver hydroxide

81. In which of the following processes is energy released?
    (a) Respiration
    (b) Photosynthesis
    (c) Ingestion
    (d) Absorption

82. Which amongst the following is the largest mammal?
    (a) Elephant
    (b) Whale
    (c) Dinosaur
    (d) Rhinoceros

83. The sex of a child is determined
    (a) six to seven weeks after conception
    (b) in the third month of pregnancy
    (c) at the time of sperm's entry
    (d) at the time of fertilisation of ovum

84. Blood group was discovered by :
    (a) Alexander Fleming
    (b) William Harvey
    (c) Landsteiner
    (d) Pavlov

85. Which is the second nearest star to the Earth after the Sun?
    (a) Vega
    (b) Sirius
    (c) Proxima Centauri
    (d) Alpha Centauri

86. The book "281 and Beyond" is the autobiography of which of the following cricketer?
    (a) Saurav Ganguly
    (b) VVS Laxman
    (c) Virender Sehwag
    (d) MS Dhoni

87. The Behdienkhlam Festival was celebrated recently in which of the following Indian state?
    (a) Assam
    (b) Odisha
    (c) Meghalaya
    (d) Chhattisgarh

88. Name the country that will host the European Union Film Festival (EUFF) 2018.
    (a) Germany   (b) Italy
    (c) France   (d) India

89. What is the main purpose of white blood corpuscles?
    (a) to carry nutrients
    (b) to combat infection
    (c) to carry oxygen
    (d) to give strength

90. A plane mirror reflects a beam of light to form a real image. The incident beam is
    (a) Divergent
    (b) Convergent
    (c) Parallel
    (d) None of these

91. The amount of light reflected depends upon the
    (a) Nature of the surface
    (b) Smoothness of the surface
    (c) Nature of material of object
    (d) All of the above
92. Which of these is a dwarf planet?
    (a) Neptune   (b) Titan
    (c) Eris   (d) Hydra
93. Nuclear sizes are expressed in a unit named
    (a) Fermi   (b) Angstrom
    (c) Newton   (d) Tesla
94. A well cut diamond appears bright because of
    (a) Dispersion
    (b) Total internal reflection
    (c) Its emit light
    (d) Radioactive
95. When a ray or light enters a glass slab from air
    (a) Its wavelength increase
    (b) Its wavelength decrease
    (c) Its frequency increase
    (d) Both are increases
96. Light year is a unit of
    (a) Time   (b) Light
    (c) Distance   (d) Intensity of light

97. Which one of the following is not a non-conventional source of energy?
    (a) Solar Energy
    (b) Natural Gas
    (c) Wind Energy
    (d) Tidal Power
98. The layer where the decrease in temperature with increasing altitude is totally absent is
    (a) Troposphere
    (b) Ionosphere
    (c) Stratosphere
    (d) Mesosphere
99. Siderosis is a disease caused by the inhalation of
    (a) silica dust   (b) iron dust
    (c) zinc dust   (d) coal dust
100. RADAR is used for
    (a) locating submerged submarines
    (b) receiving a signals in a radio receiver
    (c) locating geostationary satellites
    (d) detecting and locating the position of objects such as aeroplanes

HINTS & EXPLANATIONS

1. (b) If the first divisor is a multiple of second divisor.
   Then, remainder by the second divisor.
   $\therefore$ Remainder $= 21 \div 19 = 2$

2. (b) $675 = 5 \times 5 \times 3 \times 3 \times 3 = 5$
   No to be multiplied by 5.

3. (c) Required average

   $$= 30 + \frac{(28 + 31 - 82 - 13)}{50}$$

   $$= 30 + \left(-\frac{36}{50}\right) = 30 - 0.72 = 29.28$$

4. (b) C.P. of bicycle $= \dfrac{100}{114} \times 2850 = ₹2500$

   S.P. for a profit of 8% $= \dfrac{108}{100} \times 2500 = ₹2700$

5. (b) Population 2 years ago

   $$= \frac{4410}{\left(1 + \dfrac{5}{100}\right)^2} = \frac{4410}{441} \times 400 = 4000$$

6. (c) Time taken by Kamal $= \dfrac{200}{36 \times \dfrac{5}{18}} = 20$

   $\therefore$ Time taken by Bimal
   $= 20 + 10 = 30$

   $\therefore$ Bimal's speed $= \dfrac{200}{30} = \dfrac{20}{3}$ m/sec

   $= \dfrac{20}{3} \times \dfrac{18}{5}$ kmph $= 24$ kmph.

7. (b) Total time taken by A $= 30$ days

   Total time taken by B $= \dfrac{20 \times 5}{2} = 50$ days

   $\therefore$ (A + B)'s 1 day's work

   $= \dfrac{1}{30} + \dfrac{1}{50} = \dfrac{5+3}{150} = \dfrac{8}{150}$

   $\therefore$ the work will be completed in

   $\dfrac{150}{8} = 18\dfrac{6}{8}$ days.

8. (d) Let the numbers be 7x and 11x respectively.

   $\therefore \dfrac{7x + 7}{11x + 7} = \dfrac{2}{3}$

   $\therefore 22x + 14 = 21x + 21$

   $\Rightarrow x = 7$

   $\therefore$ Larger number $= 11x = 11 \times 7 = 77$

9. (c) A's profit : B's profit

   $= \dfrac{1}{3} : \dfrac{2}{3} = 1 : 2$

   $\therefore \dfrac{A's \text{ equivalent capital}}{B's \text{ equivalent capital}} = \dfrac{1}{2}$

   $\Rightarrow \dfrac{\dfrac{x}{4} \times 15}{\dfrac{3x}{4} \times n} = \dfrac{1}{2} \Rightarrow \dfrac{15}{3n} = \dfrac{1}{2}$

   $\Rightarrow n = 10$ months

10. (b) Ratio of corresponding sides

    $= \sqrt{\dfrac{9}{16}} = \dfrac{3}{4}$

11. (b) Increase percent in area

    $= \left(10 + 10 + \dfrac{10 \times 10}{100}\right)\% = 21\%$

12. (b) $5a + \dfrac{1}{3a} = 5$

    On multiplying by $\dfrac{3}{5}$,

$$3a + \frac{1}{5a} = 5 \times \frac{3}{5} = 3$$

On squaring,

$$9a^2 + \frac{1}{25a^2} + 2 \times 3a \times \frac{1}{5a} = 9$$

$$\Rightarrow 9a^2 + \frac{1}{25a^2}$$

$$= 9 - \frac{6}{5} = \frac{45-6}{5} = \frac{39}{5}$$

13. (d)

$$\begin{array}{ccc} 4 & a & 3 \\ 9 & 8 & 4 \\ \hline 13 & b & 7 \end{array}$$

$\because$ $13b7$ is exactly divisible by 11.

$\therefore b = 9 \therefore a = 1$

$\therefore a + b = 9 + 1 = 10$

14. (a) $2x + 3x + 5x = 180° - 45° = 135°$

$$\Rightarrow 10x = 135°$$

$$\Rightarrow x = \frac{135}{10} = \frac{27}{2}$$

$\therefore$ Largest angle

$$= 5x + 15° = \left(5 \times \frac{27}{2}\right)° + 15°$$

$$= \frac{135+30}{2} = \frac{165°}{2}$$

$\because 180° = \pi$ radian

$$\therefore \frac{165°}{2} = \frac{\pi}{180} \times \frac{165}{2} = \frac{11\pi}{24} \text{ radian}$$

15. (b) Difference of P% and L% $= 30 - (-10) = 40\%$

$$\frac{40}{100} x = 80$$

$$x = 200 \quad \therefore \text{C.P.} = 200$$

16. (c) C.P. of article $= ₹ 100$

$$\therefore \text{Marked price} = \frac{100 \times 120}{90} = ₹ \frac{400}{3}$$

$$\therefore 85\% \text{ of } \frac{400}{3} = \frac{400}{3} \times \frac{85}{100} = ₹ \frac{340}{3}$$

$$\text{Gain} = \frac{340}{3} - 100 = \frac{40}{3} = 13\frac{1}{3}\%$$

17. (a) $\because$ 12 men $\equiv$ 18 women

$\therefore$ 2 men $\equiv$ 3 women

$\therefore$ 8 men + 16 women $=$ 28 women

$\therefore M_1 D_1 = M_2 D_2$

$$\Rightarrow 18 \times 14 = 28 \times D_2$$

$$\Rightarrow D_2 = \frac{18 \times 14}{28} = 9 \text{ days}$$

18. (d) C.P. of 9 articles $= \frac{100}{96} = ₹ \frac{25}{24}$

$\therefore$ S.P. for a gain of 44 %

$$= \frac{25}{24} \times \frac{144}{100} = ₹ \frac{3}{2}$$

$\therefore$ Required number of articles

$$= 9 \times \frac{2}{3} = 6$$

19. (b) LCM of 4, 5, 6 and 7 $= 420$

$\therefore$ Required number

$= 420k + 3$ which is exactly divisible by 13.

$= 32 \times 13k + 4k + 3$

Hence, $4k + 3$ should be divisible by 13 for some value of k.

For $k = 9$, $4k + 3 = 39$ which is divisible by 13.

$\therefore$ Required number

$= 420 \times 9 + 3 = 3783$

20. (a) If the number be x, then

$x + 21 = 3x - 7$

$\Rightarrow 3x - x = 21 + 7$

$\Rightarrow 2x = 28$

$\Rightarrow x = 14$

21. (c) If time taken by A be x days,

then time taken by B $= 3x$ days

$\therefore 3x - x = 60$

$\Rightarrow 2x - 60$

$\Rightarrow x = 30$

Time taken by B $= 90$ days

$\therefore$ (A + B)'s 1 day's work

$$= \frac{1}{30} + \frac{1}{90} = \frac{3+1}{90} = \frac{4}{90} = \frac{2}{45}$$

$\therefore$ The work will be completed in

$\dfrac{45}{2}$ i.e. $22\dfrac{1}{2}$ days

22. (d) 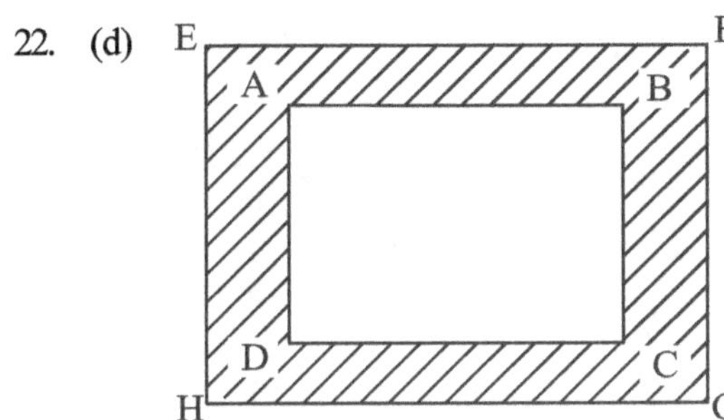

Area of the shaded region
$= (100 + 2 \times 10)(80 + 2 \times 10) - 100 \times 80$
$= 120 \times 100 - 8000$
$= 4000$ sq. metre

23. (c) If the C.P. of machine by ₹x, then

$$x \times \frac{110}{100} = \frac{27500 \times 90}{100}$$

$$\Rightarrow \frac{11x}{10} = 275 \times 90$$

$$\Rightarrow x = \frac{275 \times 900}{11} = ₹22500$$

24. (b) Required ratio $= 8 \times 7 : 5 \times 9 = 56 : 45$

25. (b) Required average

$$= \frac{40 \times 5 - 35 + 25}{5}$$

$$= \frac{190}{5} = 38 \text{ years}$$

26. (c)

27. (d) $5^2 - 1 = 24;\ 5^3 + 1 = 126$

$7^2 - 1 = 48;\ 7^3 + 1 = \boxed{344}$

28. (c) The body of fish remains covered with scales externally. Similarly, the body of bear remains covered with fur.

29. (c) Sister of my brother = My sister
Father of my sister = My father
Daughter of my father = My sister

30. (a)

31. (d)   32. (b)

33. (d) $5 - 4 = 1;\ 4 - 3 = 1$
$1 + 1 = 2$
$6 - 0 = 6;\ 5 - 1 = 4$
$6 + 4 = 10$
$6 - 2 = 4;\ 7 - 2 = 5$
$4 + 5 = \boxed{9}$

34. (b) First column $(7 + 2) \times 4 = 36$
Second Column $(6 + 8) \times 3 = 42$
Third Column $(9 + 4) \times ? = 26$

$$\Rightarrow 13 \times ? = 26 \ \therefore ? = \frac{26}{13} = 2$$

35. (d) The direction diagram is as follows:
Starting point

It is clearly shown that he is moving south direction.

36. (a) Growth and development of human organism is a continuous process. Some changes take place in human body now and then. Therefore, neither Conclusion I nor II follows.

37. (d)   38. (c)   39. (b)   40. (c)

41. (b)

42. (b) 4th term $23 = 5 \times 4 + 3 = 23$
3rd term $122 = 5 \times 23 + 7 = 122$
2nd term $? = 5 \times 122 + 11 = 621$
1st term $3120 = 5 \times \boxed{621} + 15 = 3120$

43. (d) $A = 1,\ A + C + E = 1 + 3 + 5 = 9$
$A + R + T = 1 + 18 + 20 = 39$

44. (a)   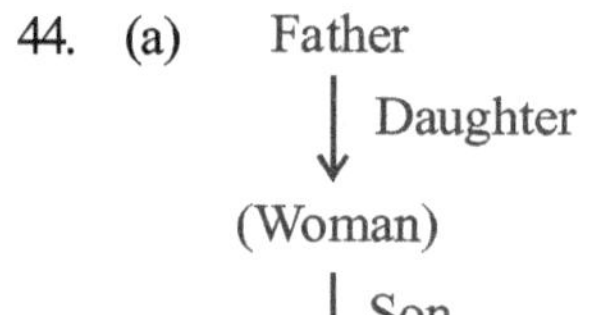

Father
↓ Daughter
(Woman)
↓ Son
Man

Hence, man is son of the woman.

45. (c)

$+ \Rightarrow \times$	$< \Rightarrow \div$	
$- \Rightarrow +$	$\times \Rightarrow >$	$\div \Rightarrow -$

Option (a)

$20 - 4 \div 4 + 8 < 2 \times 26$

$\Rightarrow 20 + 4 - 4 \times 8 \div 2 > 26$

$\Rightarrow 20 + 4 - 4 \times 4 > 26$

$\Rightarrow 24 - 16 > 26 \Rightarrow 8 > 26$ (not possible)

Option (b)

$20 \times 8 + 15 < 5 \div 9 - 8$

$\Rightarrow 20 > 8 \times 15 \div 5 - 9 + 8$

$\Rightarrow 20 > 8 \times 3 - 9 + 8$

$\Rightarrow 20 > 24 - 9 + 8 \qquad \Rightarrow 20 > 23$ (not possible)

Option (c)

$20 < 2 + 10 \div 4 - 6 \times 100$

$\Rightarrow 20 \div 2 \times 10 - 4 + 6 > 100$

$\Rightarrow 10 \times 10 - 4 + 6 > 100$

$\Rightarrow 100 - 4 + 6 > 100$

$\Rightarrow 106 - 4 > 100 \Rightarrow 102 > 100$

Option (d)

$20 < 5 + 25 \div 10 - 2 \times 96$

$\Rightarrow 20 \div 5 \times 25 - 10 + 2 > 96$

$\Rightarrow 4 \times 25 - 10 + 2 > 96$

$\Rightarrow 100 - 10 + 2 > 96$

$\Rightarrow 102 - 10 > 96 \Rightarrow 92 > 96$ (not possible)

46. (a) P and K is nothing but R.

47. (a) 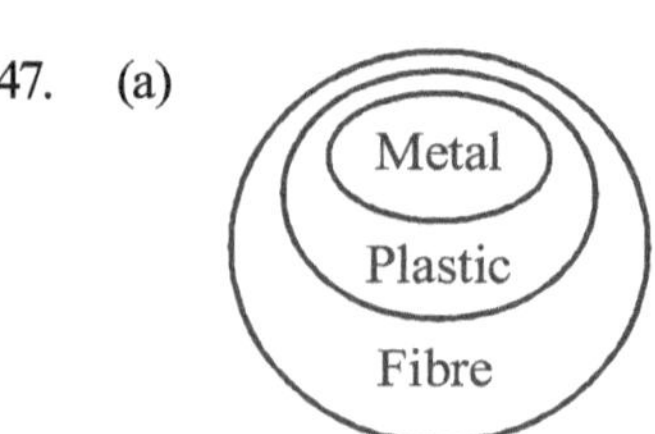

So, Only I follows.

48. (a) 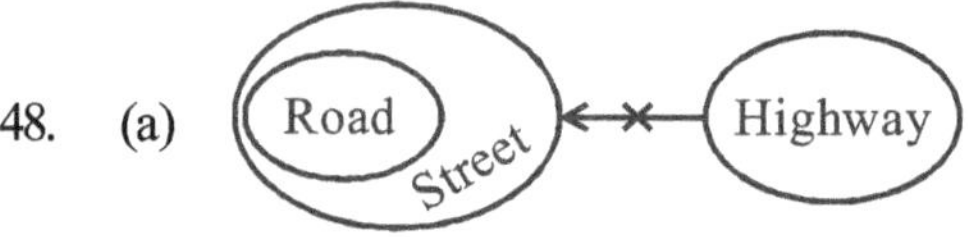

So, Only I follows.

49. (c) The statement mentions that demand for oil is increasing faster than the production. So, either the demand must be reduced or oil must be imported to cope with the increasing demand. Thus, either I or II follows.

50. (b) The statement stresses the need to adopt a new method of examination. So, I does not follow. However, II directly follows from the given statement.

51. (c)	52. (d)	53. (a)	54. (d)	55. (d)
56. (b)	57. (c)	58. (c)	59. (c)	60. (d)
61. (b)	62. (c)	63. (d)	64. (d)	65. (a)
66. (d)	67. (d)	68. (b)	69. (c)	70. (c)
71. (b)	72. (a)	73. (d)	74. (c)	75. (c)
76. (c)	77. (d)	78. (b)	79. (d)	80. (c)
81. (a)	82. (b)	83. (d)	84. (c)	85. (c)
86. (b)	87. (c)	88. (d)	89. (b)	90. (b)
91. (d)	92. (c)	93. (a)	94. (b)	95. (b)
96. (c)	97. (b)	98. (c)	99. (b)	100. (d)

PRACTICE SET 15

MATHEMATICS

1. Two numbers are in the ratio 3 : 4. Their L.C.M. is 84. The greater number is
   - (a) 21
   - (b) 24
   - (c) 28
   - (d) 84

2. The average of three consecutive odd numbers is 12 more than one third of the first of these numbers. What is the last of the three numbers ?
   - (a) 15
   - (b) 17
   - (c) 19
   - (d) Data inadequate

3. By selling an article, a man makes a profit of 25% of its selling price. His profit per cent is
   - (a) 20
   - (b) 25
   - (c) $16\frac{2}{3}$
   - (d) $33\frac{1}{3}$

4. The cost price of an article is 40% of the selling price. What percent of the cost price is the selling price?
   - (a) 140%
   - (b) 200%
   - (c) 220%
   - (d) 250%

5. A sum of ₹210 was taken as a loan. This is to be paid back in two equal installments. If the rate of interest be 10% compounded annually, then the value of each installment is
   - (a) ₹127
   - (b) ₹121
   - (c) ₹210
   - (d) ₹225

6. A train, 240 m long crosses a man walking along the line in opposite direction at the rate of 3 kmph in 10 seconds. The speed of the train is
   - (a) 63 kmph
   - (b) 75 kmph
   - (c) 83.4 kmph
   - (d) 86.4 kmph

7. 14 men can complete a piece of work in 24 days. How many additional men will be required to complete double the work in 16 days?
   - (a) 28
   - (b) 21
   - (c) 14
   - (d) 7

8. A, B, C subscribe together ₹50,000 for a business. A subscribes ₹4,000 more than B and B ₹5,000 more than C. Out of a total profit of ₹35,000, A receives
   - (a) ₹8,500
   - (b) ₹11,998
   - (c) ₹12,600
   - (d) ₹14,700

9. A copper wire of length 36 m and diameter 2 mm is melted to form a sphere. The radius of the sphere (in cm) is
   - (a) 2.5
   - (b) 3
   - (c) 3.5
   - (d) 4

10. If the square of the sum of two numbers is equal to 4 times of their product. then the ratio of these numbers is :
    - (a) 2 : 1
    - (b) 1 : 3
    - (c) 1 : 1
    - (d) 1 : 2

11. The number of seats in an auditorium is increased by 35%. The price of a ticket is also increased by 20%. Then the increase in revenue collection will be
    - (a) 62%
    - (b) 45%
    - (c) 65%
    - (d) 68%

12. If the ratio of areas of two similar triangles is 16 : 25, then the ratio of their corresponding sides is
    - (a) 3 : 5
    - (b) 3 : 4
    - (c) 4 : 5
    - (d) 4 : 3

13. With a two digit prime number, if 18 is added, we get another prime number with digits reversed. How many such numbers are possible?
    - (a) 2
    - (b) 3
    - (c) 0
    - (d) 1

14. X and Y can do a piece of work in 30 days. They work together for 6 days and then X quits and Y finishes the work in 32 more days. In how many days can Y do the piece of work alone?
    - (a) 30 days
    - (b) 32 days
    - (c) 34 days
    - (d) 40 days

15. A metal pipe of negligible thickness has radius 21 cm and length 90 cm. The outer curved surface area of the pipe in square cm is
    (a) 11880   (b) 11680
    (c) 11480   (d) 10080

16. A businessman allows a discount of 10% on the written price. How much above the cost price must he mark his goods to make a profit of 17%?
    (a) 30%   (b) 20%
    (c) 27%   (d) 18%

17. 930 coins consists of 1 rupee, 50 paise and 25 paise coins. Their values are in the ratio 5 : 6 : 4. The number of each type of coins respectively is
    (a) 310, 372, 248   (b) 454, 387, 124
    (c) 354, 285, 326   (d) 350, 440, 175

18. A batsman makes a score of 58 runs in the 15th innings and thus increases his average by 3 runs. What is the average after 15th inning?
    (a) 12   (b) 14
    (c) 16   (d) 18

19. The average of 5 consecutive numbers is n. If the next two numbers are also included, the average of the 7 numbers will
    (a) increase by 2   (b) increase by 1
    (c) decrease by 2   (d) decrease by 1

20. A trader has a weighting balance that shows 1,200 gm for a kilogram. He further marks up his cost price by 10%. Then the net profit percentage is
    (a) 32%   (b) 23%
    (c) 31.75%   (d) 23.5%

21. A car covers four successive 6 km stretches at speeds of 25 kmph, 50 kmph, 75 kmph and 150 kmph respectively. Its average speed over this distance is
    (a) 25 kmph   (b) 50 kmph
    (c) 75 kmph   (d) 150 kmph

22. The difference between C. I. (Compound Interest) and S.I. (Simple Interest) on a sum of ₹ 4,000 for 2 years at 5% p.a. payable yearly is
    (a) ₹ 20   (b) ₹ 10
    (c) ₹ 50   (d) ₹ 60

23. If $x = 997, y = 998, z = 999$, then the value of $x^2 + y^2 + z^2 - xy - yz - zx$ will be
    (a) 3   (b) 9
    (c) 16   (d) 4

24. A shopkeeper marks the price of an article at ₹ 80. What will be the selling price, if he allows two successive discounts at 5% each ?
    (a) ₹ 7.2   (b) ₹ 72.2
    (c) ₹ 72   (d) ₹ 85

25. The marked price of a mixie is ₹ 1600. The shopkeeper gives successive discount of 10% and x% to the customer. If the customer pays ₹1224 for the mixie, find the value of x :
    (a) 8%   (b) 10%
    (c) 12%   (d) 15%

GENERAL INTELLIGENCE AND REASONING

DIRECTIONS (Qs. 26-28) : In each of the following questions, select the related word/letters/ number/ figure from the given alternatives.

26. QIOK : MMKO : : YAWC : ?
    (a) USGA   (b) UESG
    (c) VUES   (d) SUEG

27. 987 : IHG : : 654 : ?
    (a) FDE   (b) FED
    (c) EFD   (d) DEF

28. Writer : Pen : : ?
    (a) Needle : Tailor   (b) Artist : Brush
    (c) Painter : Canvas   (d) Teacher : Class

DIRECTIONS (Qs. 29-30) : In the following questions a series is given, with one term missing. Choose the correct alternative from the given ones that will complete the series.

29. BCFG, JKNO, RSVW, ?
    (a) ZADE   (b) HIKL
    (c) STUX   (d) MNPQ

30. 5, 21, 69, 213, 645, __ ? __
    (a) 1670   (b) 1941
    (c) 720   (d) 1320

31. Rajiv is the brother of Arun. Sonia is the sister of Sunil. Arun is the son of Sonia. How is Rajiv related to Sunil?
    (a) son   (b) brother
    (c) father   (d) nephew

32. A boy's age is one fourth of his father's age. The sum of the boy's age and his father's age is 35. What will be father's age after 8 years?
    (a) 15   (b) 28
    (c) 35   (d) 36

33. In a certain code, "CERTAIN" is coded as "XVIGZRM", "SEQUENCE" is coded as "HVJFVMXV". How would "REQUIRED" be coded?
   (a) FJIVWVIR   (b) VJIFWTRV
   (c) WVJRIFVI   (d) IVJFRIVW

34. If + means ÷, − means ×, × means +, ÷ means −, then
   90 + 18 − 6 × 30 ÷ 4 = ?
   (a) 64   (b) 65
   (c) 56   (d) 48

35. If 16 − 2 = 2, 9 − 3 = 0, 81 − 1 = 8, then what is 64 − 4 = ?
   (a) 4   (b) 2
   (c) 6   (d) 8

DIRECTION (Q. 36): In the following question, select the missing number from the given responses.

36.
7	8	6
4	9	5
3	2	?
25	70	29

   (a) 9   (b) 8
   (c) 1   (d) 5

DIRECTION (Q. 37): In the question below, two statements are followed by two conclusions numbered I and II. Which one of the four alternatives is correct?

37. **Statement:**
   I.   All teachers are aged.
   II. Some women are teachers.
   Conclusion:
   I.   All aged are women
   II. Some women are aged.
   (a) Both conclusion I and II follow
   (b) Only conclusion I follows
   (c) Only conclusion II follows
   (d) Neither conclusion I nor II follows

38. How many triangles are there in the given figure?

   (a) 10   (b) 12
   (c) 14   (d) 11

39. Which one of the following diagrams represents the relationship among Delhi, Lucknow, Uttar Pradesh?

DIRECTION (Q. 40): In the following questions, which answer figure will complete the question figure?

40. **Question Figure:**

   Answer Figures:

41. Select the correct option that will be the mirror reflection of the problem figure.
   Question Figure :

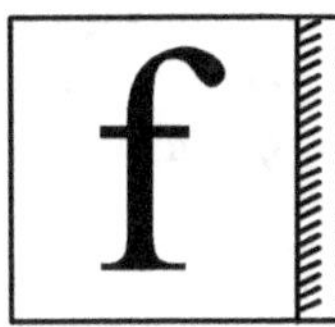

   Answer Figures :

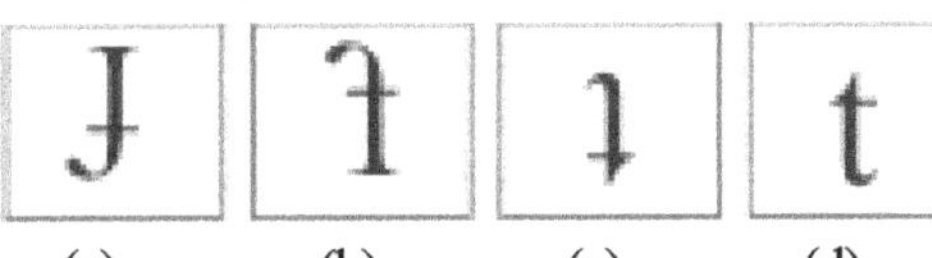

   (a)   (b)   (c)   (d)

42. If PARK is coded as 5394, SHIRT is coded as 17698 and PANDIT is coded as 532068, how would you code NISHAR in that code language?
   (a) 201739   (b) 261739
   (c) 266734   (d) 231954

43. If A is the mother of B and K, D is the husband of A. E is the son of D's brother. What is the relation of A with E
    (a) Mother in law   (b) Sister in law
    (c) Aunt   (d) Sister

44. A boy running towards South, turns to his right and runs. Then he turns to his right and finally turns to his left. Towards which direction is he running now?
    (a) East   (b) West
    (c) South   (d) North

45. Select the correct combination of mathematical signs to replace * signs and to balance the given equation.
    15 * 24 * 3 * 6 * 17
    (a) $+ \times = \div$ (b) $- \times = +$
    (c) $- \div + =$ (d) $+ \div - =$

46. Study the diagram given below and answer question.
    The Qualified and experienced doctors working in villages are represented by :

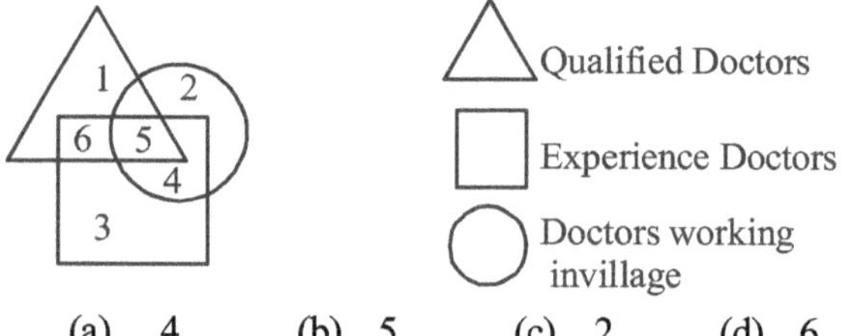

    (a) 4   (b) 5   (c) 2   (d) 6

DIRECTIONS (Qs. 47-48): In each question below are two statements followed by two conclusions numbered I and II. You have to take the two given statements to be true even if they seem to be at variance from commonly known facts and then decide which of the given conclusions logically follows from the given statements disregarding commonly known facts.

Give answer (a) if **only** conclusion I follows.
Give answer (b) if **only** conclusion II follows.
Give answer (c) if **either** conclusion I or conclusion II follows.
Give answer (d) if **neither** conclusion I nor conclusion II follows.

47. **Statements :**
    Some windows are grills.
    All glasses are grills.
    Conclusions :
    I.   All grills are windows.
    II. At least some grills are glasses.

48. **Statements :**
    Some painters are artists. Some dancers are painters.
    Conclusions :
    I.   All artists are dancers.
    II. All painters are dancers.

DIRECTIONS (Qs. 49-50): In each question below is given a statement followed by two conclusions numbered I and II. You have to assume everything in the statement to be true, then consider the two conclusions together and decide which of them logically follows beyond a reasonable doubt from the information given in the statement.

49. **Statements:** In a one day cricket match, the total runs made by a team were 200. Out of these 160 runs were made by spinners.
    Conclusions:
    I. 80% of the team consists of spinners.
    II. The opening batsmen were spinners.
    (a) Only conclusion I follows
    (b) Only conclusion II follows
    (c) Either I or II follows
    (d) Neither I nor II follows

50. **Statements:** The old order changed yielding place to new.
    Conclusions:
    I. Change is the law of nature.
    II. Discard old ideas because they are old.
    (a) Only conclusion I follows
    (b) Only conclusion II follows
    (c) Either I or II follows
    (d) Neither I nor II follows

BASIC SCIENCE AND ENGINEERING

51. In first angle projection method, object is assumed to be placed in
    (a) First quadrant   (b) Second quadrant
    (c) Third Quadrant   (d) Fourth quadrant

52. The dimensions of electric potential are :
    (a) $[ML^2T^{-2}Q^{-1}]$ (b) $[MLT^{-2}Q^{-1}]$
    (c) $[ML^2T^{-1}Q]$ (d) $[ML^2T^{-2}Q]$

53. The density of wood is 0.65 gcm^{-3} in CGS system. Its density in SI system is
    (a) 65 kgm^{-3} (b) 6.5 kgm^{-3}
    (c) 650 kgm^{-3} (d) 0.65 kgm^{-3}

54. Which of the following controls can change a car's velocity?
    (a) The gas pedal (b) The brake pedal
    (c) The steering wheel (d) All of the above
55. The work done on an object does not depend upon the
    (a) Displacement
    (b) Force applied
    (c) Angle between force and displacement
    (d) Initial velocity of the object
56. Newton's law of cooling is also applicable to
    (a) convection losses.
    (b) natural convection losses.
    (c) forced convection losses.
    (d) conduction losses.
57. Power factor of direct current is
    (a) Zero   (b) Lagging
    (c) Unity   (d) Leading
58. Which of the following is an example of a wheel and axle?
    (a) a pulley   (b) a screwdriver
    (c) a block and tackle (d) a nutcracker
59. Under the Health and Safety at Work Act 1974, an employer must:
    (a) Provide a bright, cheerful place to work
    (b) Safeguard the safety and health of all employees
    (c) Give everyone their very own copy of company safety policy
    (d) Provide personalized hard hats in a variety of colors
60. Good example of renew able energy resource is
    (a) Oil
    (b) Coal
    (c) Hydropower
    (d) All the above
61. What is a backup?
    (a) Restoring the information backup
    (b) An exact copy of a system's information
    (c) The ability to get a system up and running in the event of a system crash or failure
    (d) All of these
62. What is the numerical ratio of velocity to speed of an object ?
    (a) Always equal to one
    (b) Always less than one
    (c) Always greater than one
    (d) Either less than or equal to one.

63. A right regular hexagonal prism in resting on HP on its base, its top view is a
    (a) Square   (b) Rectangle
    (c) Hexagon   (d) Pentagon
64. Precision of vernier calipers is
    (a) 1 mm   (b) 1 cm
    (c) 0.1 mm   (d) 0.1 cm
65. Volume of glass is 5 m^3 and its density is about 3500 kg m^{-3}, its mass would be
    (a) 1750 kg   (b) 17500 kg
    (c) 4×10^{-4} (d) 175 kg
66. Negative acceleration is also known as
    (a) Retardation
    (c) Relaxation
    (c) Escalation
    (d) All of the above
67. Name the physical quantity that is defined as the rate of change of displacement.
    (a) velocity
    (b) acceleration
    (c) distance
    (d) speed
68. The gravitational potential energy of an object is due to
    (a) Its mass
    (b) Its acceleration due to gravity
    (c) Its height above the earth surface
    (d) all of the above.
69. Which of the following has highest heat capacity?
    (a) Water
    (b) Air
    (c) Soil
    (d) None of the above
70. International ohm is defined in terms of the resistance of
    (a) a column of mercury
    (b) a cube of carbon
    (c) a cube of copper
    (d) the unit lenght of wire
71. A hand truck is used in stores to move boxes. Which simple machines are part of a hand truck?
    (a) pulley and inclined plane
    (b) pulley and lever
    (c) lever and wheel and axle
    (d) inclined plane and wheel

72. When was OSHA enacted?
    (a) 1980
    (b) 1930
    (c) 1945
    (d) 1970
73. The best method of disposal of garbage is
    (a) Burning
    (b) Land filling
    (c) Incineration
    (d) Vermiculture
74. What is the Full Form of INTERNET?
    (a) INTER-national-NET-work
    (b) INTER-nodal-NET-work
    (c) INTER-nation-NET-work
    (d) None of these.
75. An electric filament bulb can be worked from
    (a) D.C. supply only
    (b) A.C. supply only
    (c) Battery supply only
    (d) All above

GENERAL AWARENESS AND CURRENT AFFAIR

76. Harshvardhana was defeated by
    (a) Prabhakaravardhana
    (b) Pulakesin II
    (c) Narasimhasvarma Pallava
    (d) Sasanka
77. Which is an extra-constitutional body ?
    (a) Language Commission
    (b) Planning Commission
    (c) Election Commission
    (d) Finance Commission
78. The judges of the Supreme Court retire at the age of:
    (a) 60 years   (b) 65 years
    (c) 62 years   (d) 58 years
79. 'Lumen' is the unit of
    (a) Illuminance
    (b) Brightness
    (c) Luminous flux
    (d) Luminous intensity
80. Silver halides are used in photographic plates because they are
    (a) oxidised in air
    (b) soluble in hyposolution
    (c) reduced by light
    (d) totally colourless

81. Which part becomes modified as the tusk of elephant?
    (a) Canine   (b) Premolar
    (c) Second incisor   (d) Molar
82. The food chain of the ecosystem is maintained by the activities of
    (a) Decomposers   (b) Predators
    (c) Producers   (d) Consumers
83. Blood is a :
    (a) reproductive tissue (b) connective tissue
    (c) epithelial tissue   (d) muscular tissue
84. Which of the following is the smallest bird?
    (a) Pigeon   (b) Parrot
    (c) Humming bird   (d) House sparrow
85. Greenpark Stadium is in
    (a) Bengaluru   (b) Dehradun
    (c) Chandigarh   (d) Kanpur
86. Satyadev Narayan Arya is the newly appointed governor of ____________.
    (a) Meghalaya
    (b) Haryana
    (c) Sikkim
    (d) Bihar
87. What is the theme for `National Technology Day' 2018?
    (a) Technology for inclusive and sustainable growth
    (b) Science for inclusive and sustainable growth
    (c) None of the given options is true
    (d) Science and Technology for a Sustainable Future
88. Name the state that has recently inaugurated its biggest solar power plant, with a capacity of 1 MW at Energy Awareness Park.
    (a) Sikkim
    (b) Arunachal Pradesh
    (c) Assam
    (d) Tripura
89. The velocity of sound in air (under normal conditions) is-
    (a) 30 m / sec
    (b) 320 m / sec
    (c) 332 m / sec
    (d) 3,320 m / sec

90. The largest artery in human body is
    (a) Aorta   (b) Capillary
    (c) Vena cava   (d) Pulmonary vein
91. The beach sands of Kerala are rich in
    (a) Calcium
    (b) Radium
    (c) Thorium
    (d) Manganese
92. The Himalayas is the example of ____
    (a) Fold mountains
    (b) Block mountains
    (c) Ancient mountains
    (d) Residual mountains
93. The largest irrigation canal in India is

    ____
    (a) Yamuna canal
    (b) Indira Gandhi canal
    (c) Sirhand canal
    (d) Upper Bari Doab canal
94. Nitrification is the biological process of converting
    (a) N_2 into nitrate
    (b) N_2 into nitrite
    (c) Ammonia into nitrite
    (d) Ammonia into N_2
95. Blood is red in colour due to the presence of
    ______________ .
    (a) Cytochrome
    (b) Chlorophyll
    (c) Hemocyanin
    (d) Haemoglobin
96. Which one of the following events in a botanical garden is never directly influenced by light?
    (a) Flowering
    (b) Photosynthesis
    (c) Transpiration
    (d) Fertilization
97. A group of interconnected islands is known as
    ______________.
    (a) Strait
    (b) Peninsula
    (c) Archipelago
    (d) Lagoon
98. Which of the following is usually not an airpollutant?
    (a) Hydrocarbons
    (b) Sulphur dioxide
    (c) Carbon dioxide
    (d) Nitrous oxide
99. Which of the following is the treatment of water pollution?
    (a) Bag house filter
    (b) Windrow composting
    (c) Venturi scrubber
    (d) Reverse Osmosis
100. Which cells in pancreas produce Insulin ?
    (a) Thymus
    (b) Estrogen
    (c) Corpus epididymis
    (d) Islets of Langerhans

HINTS & EXPLANATIONS

1. **(c)** Let the numbers be 3x and 4x.

   $\therefore$ Their LCM = 12x

   $\therefore$ 12x = 84

   $$\Rightarrow x = \frac{84}{12} = 7$$

   $\therefore$ Larger number

   $= 4x = 4 \times 7 = 28$

2. **(c)** Let 3 consecutive odd no. be x, x + 2 and x + 4 ATQ

   $$\frac{x + x + 2 + x + 4}{3} = 12 + \frac{1}{3}x$$

   $$\frac{3x + 6}{3} - \frac{x}{3} = 12$$

   $$= 2x + 6 = 36, \quad x = \frac{36 - 6}{2} = 15$$

   $\therefore$ last no. = 15 + 4 = 19

3. **(d)** If the S.P. of article be ₹x,

   then its CP $= x - \dfrac{x}{4} = ₹\dfrac{3x}{4}$

   $$\therefore \text{Gain\%} = \frac{\dfrac{x}{4}}{\dfrac{3x}{4}} \times 100 = \frac{100}{3} = 33\frac{1}{3}\%$$

4. **(d)** Let the S.P. of the article = ₹ 100

   $\therefore$ C.P. = ₹ 40

   $\therefore$ Required percentage $= \dfrac{100}{40} \times 100 =$ 250%

5. **(b)** Principal (P) = 210

   Rate (R) = 10%

   Let equal installment = x

   then,

   $$P = \frac{x}{\left(1 + \dfrac{r}{100}\right)^2} + \frac{x}{\left(1 + \dfrac{r}{100}\right)}$$

   $$210 = \frac{x}{\left(1 + \dfrac{10}{100}\right)^2} + \frac{x}{\left(1 + \dfrac{10}{100}\right)}$$

   $\therefore$ x = 121

6. **(c)** Let train speed be x

   relative speed = (x + 3) kmph

   $\therefore$ Time $= \dfrac{\text{Length of the train}}{\text{Relative speed}}$

   $$\Rightarrow \frac{10}{3600} = \frac{\dfrac{240}{1000}}{(x + 3)} = \frac{240}{1000(x + 3)}$$

   $\Rightarrow x + 3 = 86.4$

   $\Rightarrow x = 83.4 \text{ kmph}$

7. **(a)** $M_1 D_1 W_2 = M_2 D_2 W_1$

   $\Rightarrow 14 \times 24 \times 2 = M_2 \times 16 \times 1$

   $$\Rightarrow M_2 = \frac{14 \times 24 \times 2}{16} = 42$$

   $\therefore$ No. of additional men = 42 – 14 = 28

8. **(d)** A = B + 4000

   B = C + 5000

   A + B + C = 50000

   A + A – 4000 + A – 9000 = 50000

   So, A = 21000

   B = 17000

   C = 12000

   $\therefore$ A : B : C = 21000 : 17000 : 12000 = 21 : 17 : 12

   A's Profit $= \dfrac{21}{50} \times 35000 = ₹14700$

9. **(b)** Volume of the wire = $\pi r^2 h$

   $\therefore \pi \times 0.1 \times 0.1 \times 3600 \text{ cm}^3$

   $\Rightarrow 36\pi \text{ cm}^3$

   Volume cylinder = vol. sphere

   Volume of the sphere $= \dfrac{4}{3}\pi R^3$

   $= 36\pi$

$$\Rightarrow R^3 = \frac{36 \times 3}{4} = 27$$

$$\therefore R = \sqrt[3]{27} = 3 \text{ cm}$$

10. (c) Let the number be x and y.
According to question,
$$(x+y)^2 = 4xy$$
$$\Rightarrow x^2 + y^2 + 2xy - 4xy = 0$$
$$\Rightarrow (x-y)^2 = 0$$
$$\Rightarrow x = y$$

11. (a) Required increase
$$= \left(35 + 20 + \frac{35 \times 20}{100}\right)\%$$
$$= 62\%$$

12. (c) Ratio of corresponding sides
$$= \sqrt{\frac{16}{26}} = \frac{4}{5}$$

13. (a) Let the number be $10x + y$.
According to condition
$$10x + y + 18 = 10y + x$$
$$y - x = 2$$
So those numbers are 02, 13, 24, 35, 46, 57, 68, 79, 80
But 13 and 79 are prime numbers.

14. (d) $(X + Y)$'s 6 days' work $= \left(\frac{1}{30} \times 6\right) = \frac{1}{5}$.

Remaining work $= \left(1 - \frac{1}{5}\right) = \frac{4}{5}$

Now, $\frac{4}{5}$ work is done by Y in 32 days.

Whole work will be done by Y in $\left(32 \times \frac{5}{4}\right)$
$= 40$ days.

15. (a) Curved surface area of cylinder $= 2\pi rh$
$$= 2 \times \frac{22}{7} \times 21 \times 90 = 11880 \text{ sq.cm}$$

16. (a) Let CP $= ₹100$
Then, S.P $= ₹117$
Let marked price be Rs x.
Then, 90% of $x = 117$

$$\Rightarrow x = \left(\frac{117 \times 100}{90}\right) = 130$$

$\therefore$ Marked price $= 30\%$ above C.P.

17. (a) The ratio of number of coins $= 5 : 6 : 4$
$\therefore$ The number of one rupee coins
$$= \frac{930}{5 + 6 + 4} \times 5 = 310$$
The number of 50 paise coins
$$= \frac{930}{5 + 6 + 4} \times 6 = 372$$
The number of 25 paise coins
$$= \frac{930}{5 + 6 + 4} \times 4 = 248$$

18. (c) Let average for 14 innings be x. Then,

$$\frac{14x + 58}{15} = x + 3 \Rightarrow 15x + 45 = 14x + 58 \Rightarrow x = 13$$

$\therefore$ New average $= (x + 3) = 13 + 3 = 16$ runs

19. (b) Let the numbers be $n - 2, n - 1, n, n + 1$ and $n + 2$. Their average $= n$.
Next two consecutive numbers are $n + 3$ and $n + 4$.
Therefore the average of 7 consecutive numbers

$$= \frac{\begin{array}{l}(n-2) + (n-1) + n + (n+1) + (n+2) + \\ (n+3) + (n+4)\end{array}}{7}$$

$$= \frac{5n + 2n + 7}{7} = n + 1$$

20. (a) The trader professes to sell 1200 kg but sells only 1000 kg.
So profit $= 20\%$
Markup $= 10\%$

Total profit $= 10 + 20 + \frac{10 \times 20}{100} = 32\%$

21. (b)

$$\text{Average Speed} = \frac{\text{Total Distance Covered}}{\text{Total Time Taken}}$$

$$= \frac{6+6+6+6}{\frac{6}{25}+\frac{6}{50}+\frac{6}{75}+\frac{6}{150}} \Rightarrow \frac{24}{6\left[\frac{1}{25}+\frac{1}{50}+\frac{1}{75}+\frac{1}{150}\right]}$$

$$= \frac{24 \times 300}{6 \times 24} \Rightarrow 50 \text{ km/hr}$$

22. (b) Required difference $= \dfrac{PR^2}{(100)^2}$

$$\Rightarrow \frac{4000 \times 5 \times 5}{100 \times 100} = ₹10$$

23. (a) $x^2 + y^2 + z^2 - xy - yz - zx$

$$= \frac{2}{2}(x^2 + y^2 + z^2 - xy - yz - zx)$$

$$= \frac{1}{2}(2x^2 + 2y^2 + 2z^2 - 2xy - 2yz - 2zx)$$

$$= \frac{1}{2}(x^2 + y^2 - 2xy + y^2 + z^2 - 2yz + x^2 + z^2 - 2zx)$$

$$= \frac{1}{2}[(x-y)^2 + (y-z)^2 + (z-x)^2]$$

$$= \frac{1}{2}[(997-998)^2 + (998-999)^2 + (999-997)^2]$$

$$= \frac{1}{2}[1^2 + 1^2 + 2^2] = \frac{1}{2} \times 6 = 3$$

24. (b) Net discount $= \left(5 + 5 - \dfrac{25}{100}\right)\%$

$$= 9\frac{3}{4} = \frac{39}{4}\%$$

$$\therefore \text{S.P.} = 80 \times \frac{361}{400} = ₹72.2$$

25. (d) First discount

$$= \frac{1600 \times 10}{100} = ₹160$$

Price after it $= 1600 - 160$

$= ₹1440$

$$\therefore \frac{1440 \times x}{100} = 1440 - 1224 = 216$$

$$\therefore x = \frac{216 \times 100}{1440} = 15\%$$

26. (b) As,

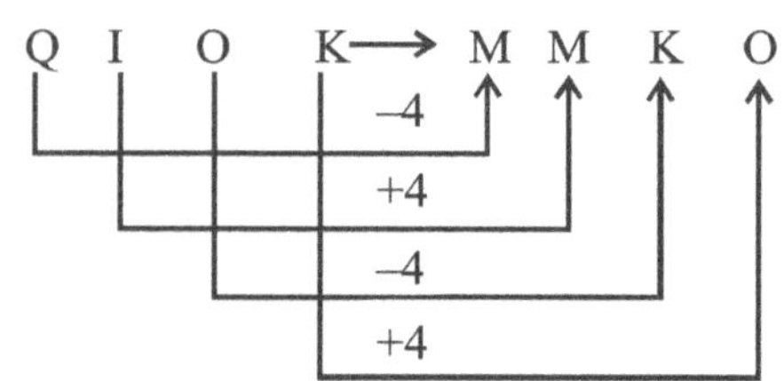

Similarly,

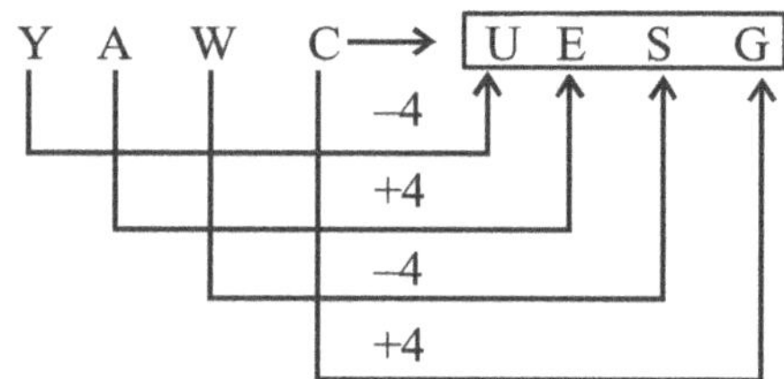

27. (b) As, 9   8   7

$\downarrow$ $\downarrow$ $\downarrow$

I   H   G

Similarly,

6   5   4

$\downarrow$ $\downarrow$ $\downarrow$

F   E   D

28. (c) Here, Writer uses pen for writting. Similarly, painter works on canvas.

29. (a) B C F G $\longrightarrow$ 2, 3, 6, 7

J K N O $\longrightarrow$ 10, 11, 14, 15

R S V W $\longrightarrow$ 18, 19, 22, 23

Next sequence $= 26, 27, 30, 31 = 26, 1, 4, 5$
$= $ Z A D E (subtract the excess value by 26)

30. (b) The pattern is as follows :

$21 - 5 = 16 \Rightarrow 16 \times 3 = 48$

$69 - 21 = 48 \Rightarrow 48 \times 3 = 144$

$213 - 69 = 144 \Rightarrow 144 \times 3 \Rightarrow 432$

$645 - 213 \Rightarrow 432 \Rightarrow 432 \times 3 = 1296$

and

$\boxed{1941} - 645 = 1296$

31. (d)

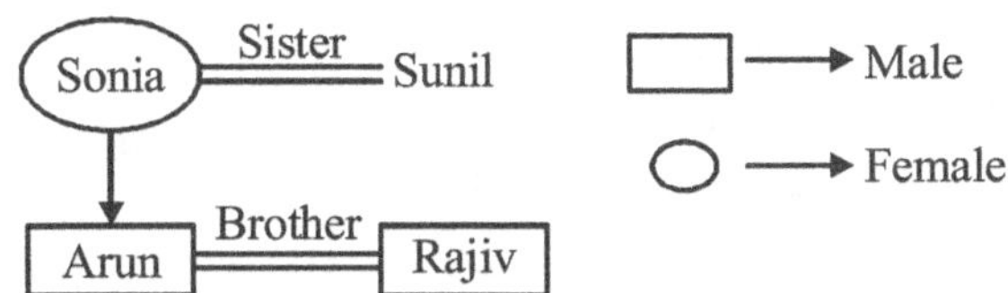

Therefore, Rajiv is nephew of Sunil.

32. (d) Let father's age is x yr.

Son's age is $\dfrac{x}{4}$ yr.

$$x + \dfrac{x}{4} = 35 \Rightarrow x = 28 \text{ yr.}$$

Father's age after 8 year is 36 years.

33. (d)
```
C   E   R   T   A   I   N
↕   ↕   ↕   ↕   ↕   ↕   ↕
X   V   I   G   Z   R   M
```

Pairs of Opposite Letters

```
S   E   Q   U   E   N   C   E
↕   ↕   ↕   ↕   ↕   ↕   ↕   ↕
H   V   J   F   V   M   X   V
```

Therefore,

```
R   E   Q   U   I   R   E   D
↕   ↕   ↕   ↕   ↕   ↕   ↕   ↕
I   V   J   F   R   I   V   W
```

34. (c) $90 \div 18 \times 6 + 30 - 4 = 56$

35. (a) $16 \Rightarrow (2+2)^2 = (4)^2$

$9 \Rightarrow (3+0)^2 = (3)^2$

$81 \Rightarrow (1+8)^2 = (9)^2$

Similarly, $64 \Rightarrow (4+4)^2 = (8)^2$

36. (c) First Column

$7 \times 4 - 3 = 28 - 3 = 25$

Second Column

$8 \times 9 - 2 = 72 - 2 = 70$

Third column

$6 \times 5 - ? = 29$

$\Rightarrow ? = 30 - 29 = \boxed{1}.$

37. (c) **38.** (c) **39.** (c) **40.** (a) **41.** (b)

42. (b) Letters have been coded as-

```
P   A   R   K   S   H   I   T   N   D
↓   ↓   ↓   ↓   ↓   ↓   ↓   ↓   ↓   ↓
5   3   9   4   1   7   6   8   2   0
```

```
        N   I   S   H   A   R
        ↓   ↓   ↓   ↓   ↓   ↓
Code for 2  6   1   7   3   9
```

43. (c)

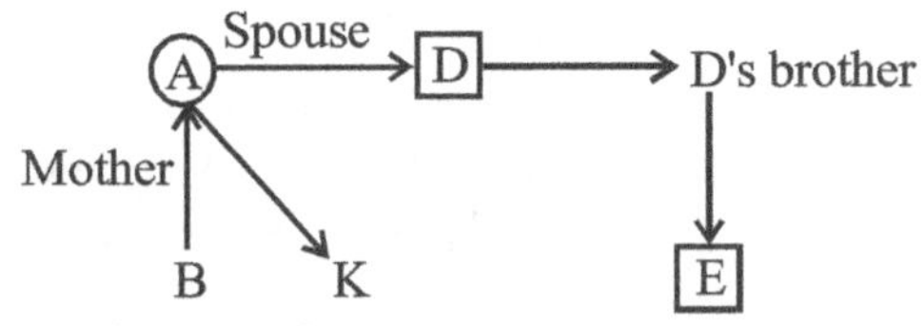

A is Aunt of E.

44. (b)

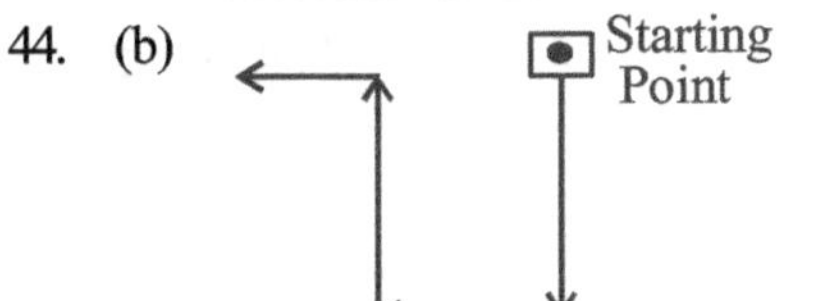

45. (d) $15 * 24 * 3 * 6 * 17$

$\Rightarrow 15 + 24 \div 3 - 6 = 17$

$\Rightarrow 15 + 8 - 6 = 17$

46. (b)

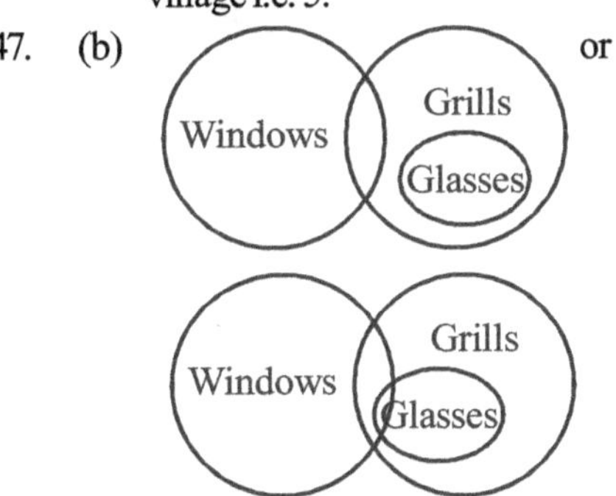

Hence, shaded portion in above diagram represents.
Qualified Experienced Doctors working in village i.e. 5.

47. (b)

Conclusion-I : False
II: True

48. (d)

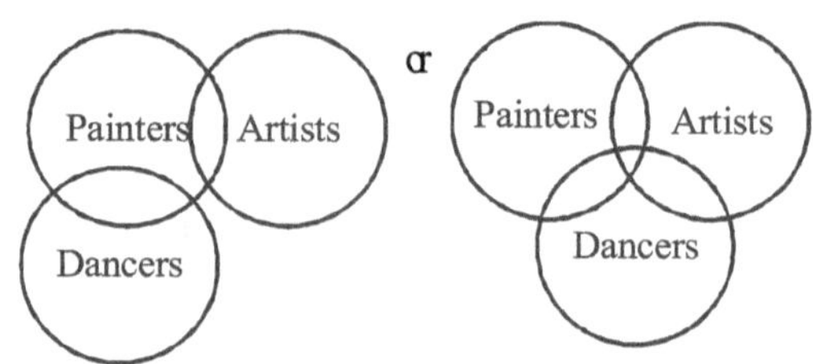

Conclusion-I : False

Conclusion-II: False

49. (d) According to the statement, 80% of the total runs were made by spinners. So, I does not follow. Nothing about the opening batsmen is mentioned in the statement. So, II also does not follow.

50. (a) Clearly, I directly follows from the given statement. Also, it is mentioned that old ideas are replaced by new ones, as thinking changes with the progressing time. So, II does not follow.

51.	(a)	52.	(a)	53.	(c)	54.	(d)	55.	(d)
56.	(c)	57.	(c)	58.	(b)	59.	(b)	60.	(c)
61.	(d)	62.	(d)	63.	(c)	64.	(c)	65.	(b)
66.	(a)	67.	(a)	68.	(d)	69.	(a)	70.	(a)
71.	(c)	72.	(d)	73.	(b)	74.	(a)	75.	(d)
76.	(b)	77.	(b)	78.	(b)	79.	(c)	80.	(c)
81.	(c)	82.	(a)	83.	(b)	84.	(c)	85.	(d)
86.	(b)	87.	(d)	88.	(b)	89.	(c)	90.	(a)
91.	(c)	92.	(a)	93.	(b)	94.	(c)	95.	(d)
96.	(d)	97.	(c)	98.	(d)	99.	(d)	100.	(d)